John Skalko

Disordered Actions

A Moral Analysis of Lying and Homosexual Activity

For my friends who live with same-sex attraction,

but desire to love purely.

You are the real heroes.

John Skalko

Disordered Actions

A Moral Analysis of Lying and Homosexual Activity

Bibliographic information published by Deutsche Nationalbibliothek
The Deutsche Nationalbibliothek lists this publication in the Deutsche Nationalbibliographie;
detailed bibliographic data is available in the Internet at http://dnb.ddb.de

©2019 editiones scholasticae
53819 Neunkirchen-Seelscheid
www.editiones-scholasticae.de

ISBN 978-3-86838-218-1

2019

Printed on acid-free paper

Printed in Germany
by CPI Buchbücher.de GmbH

Table of Contents

Introduction

Most people today would hold that lying is a bad action. When pressed, however, many would be tempted to allow for it in extreme circumstances. For instance, if one is hiding Jews and the Nazis come to the door, it seems morally permissible or even praiseworthy to lie, saying, "There are no Jews here in this house." But if extreme circumstances allow for what is normally bad to become good, does this not apply to other actions as well? Say you lied to the Nazis, but they decided to inspect your home anyway. As they ransack your belongings, they notice the Jews hiding in the cellar beneath the rug on the kitchen floor. Pulling the Jews out one by one, they line them up, ready to be summarily shot. The Nazi corporal draws his pistol, but before he is able to pull the trigger the commanding officer orders him to halt. The commander approaches you with a proposal. Remember that pig you've been raising in the backyard? Either you or one of the Jews must commit an act of bestiality with it, or you'll all be shot. What should you do? A consequentialist would conclude that there is no such thing as an action that should never be done regardless of consequences; in fact, all that counts are the consequences. Given that the consequences are extreme enough, one ought to commit the act of bestiality.

Most people who might be hesitant to justify the bestiality will freely admit that given dire enough circumstances lying can be justified. When pressed with what justification they have for their position frequently no further answer is given beyond that the consequences require it. But can consequences alone justify any action whatsoever?

Take the following example: there are seven people in a hospital who badly need organ donations. One person down the hallway is a perfect match for the seven and has all of the relevant organs. Let's presume even further that the medical personnel can get away with secretly killing the one person by a painless drug overdose. Nobody else is likely to copy their behavior, because it is done in secret. If the other seven are not given the organ donation, they will all die. According to consequentialism, since murdering the one for his organs would produce more good than bad consequences, it is good for him to be killed. If consequences alone justify an action, then murdering one person, even against his consent, so as to harvest his organs can be morally good.

Another famous example involves a sheriff in a small Southern town.[1] A black man has been falsely accused of raping a white woman at the local circus. The sheriff knows the black man is innocent and that the local racist mob has stirred up the populace against him. The mob threatens to riot, unless the sheriff personally lynches the black man. If the mob riots, they will burn local businesses and kill another twenty innocent people in the process. On a consequentialist account, since lynching the black man will save the lives of the innocent bystanders and prevent the riot, he ought to be lynched.

Consequentialist moral theory states that any action whatsoever is morally good if it produces more good consequences than bad. This moral theory has much prima facie plausibility; generally, we want to do good, and producing more good than bad seems all the better. What could be so wrong with that?

But imagine the following scenario: 60% of the world population could be extremely happy, but at the cost of the abject misery of enslaving the other 40%. Let us further envision that the sum total of happiness in the the 60% would be increased from 100 units of happiness to 1 trillion units. Prior to the slavery the 40% had only 500 units of happiness total; after the enslavement they decrease to 1 unit total. The total result in increased happiness would certainly be much greater after the slavery than before. So the enslavement of the 40% would produce more good consequences than bad. Thus, according to consequentialism, the other 40% ought to be enslaved.[2]

---

[1] For more on a variation of this example see H.J. McCloskey, "An Examination of Restricted Utilitarianism," *The Philosophical Review* 66, no. 4 (October 1957): 468-473. See also Patrick Lee, *Abortion & Unborn Human Life*, 2nd ed. (Washington, D.C.: Catholic University of America Press, 2010), 145-147.

[2] Cf. Lee, *Abortion & Unborn Human Life*, 144. Related to this enslavement difficulty is the utility monster objection, first attributed to Robert Nozick in *Anarchy, State, and Utopia* (Basic Books, 1974), 41-42. One version of the utility monster is as follows: if one person could immensely benefit from a ridiculous amount of happiness due to his special intellectual abilities to receive and enjoy such high levels of goodness, but at the expense of many others, utilitarian calculus would have to hold there is nothing wrong with this utility monster so long as the average or total

If consequences alone can justify lying, so too can just about anything else be justified. Consequentialism as a moral theory might be able to justify lying, but its acceptance entails certain unpalatable conclusions.[3] A hardened defender of consequentialism, however, might bite the bullet and argue that these seemingly heinous actions aren't so heinous after all.

What is the Good?

Consequentialism requires that one act so as to produce more *good* than bad consequences.[4] But *good* is said in many senses. Good is not predicated of things in the way in which numbers, size, or color are. A chair may be brown or white and compared to another chair that is more or less a shade of the same color, but the same cannot be said about the good. What makes a chair good is that it serves its purpose as a place for someone to sit upright. What makes a chair good is not what makes a fork good. A good fork is one that allows you to pick up food and place it in your mouth. A bad fork is one that is too dull, too sharp, etc. such that it either cannot pierce the food or it cuts your mouth. Yet what

---

level of happiness across the populace is greater than if there were no utility monster. Averages are upset and raised higher if the rate for one is exponentially higher than for the rest (e.g. if Trump's salary of over 400 million were calculated with the salaries of 100 middle-class wage earners, the average salary would raise significantly). See also Julia Driver, *Consequentialism* (New York: Routledge, 2012), 79.

[3] To get around the objections regarding the lynch mob case and the wholesale enslavement of a minority some consequentialists have proposed that one ought not to maximize the total good, but only the average good. But on this account, as Driver says, "it is wrong [then] to add to a population of fairly happy people additional people who are only slightly less happy" (Driver, *Consequentialism,* 3). Further, on the average good interpretation of consequentialism, it is better to have ten people with a high level of average happiness at say 50 units than a million people at an average level of say 30 units of happiness. Finally, enslavement of a minority might be justified if it raised the average happiness of the total population (Lee, *Abortion & Unborn Human Life*, 144).

[4] Various consequentialists may add further nuances to this proposoition. Some argue that you always ought to act so as to maximize good consequences; others argue that you ought to act so as to attain a certain minimal level of good (the average good), etc. My criticisms of consequentialism's account of the good apply to all the different variations of consequentialism.

makes a chair and fork the same silver color is the same: both have the same wavelength of light reflecting off the surface (or whatever makes silver to be the color silver). The color silver is predicated univocally of tables, knives, desks, chairs, paint, leaves, etc. but good is not, because what makes x good depends upon what x is. Since what makes x good depends upon what x is, this means *good* varies according to the natures of which it is predicated.[5] So to have *good* as the standard for determining the best course of action is like having a yardstick that changes depending upon the object you are measuring. If the yardstick changes length when you put it against a table and when you put it against a knife, what you have is a bad yardstick, a bad rule, a bad measure. This problem plagues all versions of consequentialism: they presuppose that the *good* can serve as an inflexible yardstick when it cannot. One needs a prior standard as to what counts as *good*, whether it be wealth, honor, pleasure, virtue, God, etc.

Some consequentialists attempt to identify the good, but run into even further problems. Jeremy Bentham and John Stuart Mill argued that pleasure was the standard. But their view failed to account for the fact that pleasure is only a consequent good.[6] Pleasure is not something that exists on its own; rather, it is dependent upon and follows upon some sort of activity such as working-out, reading, eating, or having sex. As a result, the types of pleasure differ radically, depending upon the type of activity one is engaging in. Such is why Mill concluded that it is only the

---

[5] Cf. P.T. Geach, "Good and Evil," *Analysis* 17, no. 2 (December 1956): 33-42. Also see Philippa Foot's *Natural Goodness* (New York: Oxford University Press, 2001) and Judith Jarvis Thomson's *Normativity* (Peru, Illinois, Open Court Publishing Company/Carus Publishing Company, 2008), especially Chapter 1.

[6] Cf. Aristotle, *Nicomachean Ethics* X.4.8 1174b31-33. "Pleasure completes the activity—not, however, as the state [a habit] does, by being present [in the activity], but as a sort of consequent end, like the bloom on youths" (*Nicomachean Ethics*, 2nd ed., trans. Terrence Irwin (Indianapolis/Cambridge: Hackett Publishing Company, Inc.), 159). The Greek text is as follows: τελειοῖ δὲ τὴν ἐνέργειαν ἡ ἡδονὴ οὐχ ὡς ἡ ἕξις ἐνυπάρχουσα, ἀλλ' ὡς ἐπιγινόμενόν τι τέλος, οἷον τοῖς ἀκμαίοις ἡ ὥρα ((I. Bywater, ed., *Aristotelis ethica Nicomachea* (Oxford: Clarendon Press, 1894 [repr. 1962]): accessed via *Thesaurus Linguae Graecae*, February 23, 2017, http://stephanus.tlg.uci.edu.proxy.bc.edu/Iris/Cite?0086:010:381339.

higher pleasures that we ought to maximize.[7] But even so, merely maximizing the higher pleasures poses particular difficulties for those who wish to justify lying or bestiality in difficult cases. Does telling the lie to the Nazi at the door really maximize higher pleasures? Would committing the bestiality really maximize pleasure for all involved? Perhaps, but it is difficult to see just how one would go about arguing it maximizes the higher pleasures, especially if it is very physically and psychologically painful for the agent to commit the act of bestiality due to intense emotional revulsion (plus any emotional revulsion experienced by other witnesses to the scene).

The pleasure view of the good also fails to account for bad pleasures. A hedonist might take pleasure in all sorts of bad activities like serial killing, masochism, catamites, bestiality, or necrophilia.[8] One may object that these involve harm to others. But some of these acts, such as bestiality or necrophilia, need not involve harm to others. Peter Singer records the story of a woman at Camp Leakey in Borneo, who was "suddenly seized by a large male orangutan, his intentions made obvious by his erect penis."[9] If the woman consented, took pleasure in the act, and no harm was done to either party, the bestiality would be morally justified on the hedonistic account.[10] The orangutan evidently wanted to engage in sexual activity with her. Similarly, necrophilia need not physically harm anyone (imagine it done hygienically with a condom), and so in some cases the hedonist would have to say it is morally good. A consequentialist account of pleasure, then, fails to account for bad pleasures. As a result, such actions count as morally good (at least in some or many cases) when they are in fact wrong and quite seriously wrong.

The pleasure account of the good also suffers from the pleasure-machine objection. Imagine you could plug yourself into a pleasure-inducing machine for the rest of your life. Once plugged into the ma-

---

[7] Mill's view develops in reply to the objection that if pleasure were the standard for happiness then men ought to act like pigs; cf. *Utilitarianism,* Chapter 2.

[8] Cf. Plato, *Gorgias* 494a-495a for a refutation of the view that all pleasure is good.

[9] Peter Singer, "Heavy Petting," *Utilitarian.net (originally Published in Nerve Magazine),* 2001, accessed December 7, 2018,
 http://www.utilitarian.net/singer/by/2001----.htm.

[10] Although Singer isn't a hedonist, he seems to think bestiality is okay in some cases.

chine the supercomputer feeds you countless intensely pleasing sensations and stimulates your brain into thinking you are a super-successful, multi-billionaire who is president of the world and can obtain any pleasure he wants.[11] Inside this fake world nothing goes wrong and you always get what you want. Would you plug yourself in? Most people would say no, because reality is better even if perhaps less pleasurable. Being plugged into the the supercomputer for the rest of one's life seems to entail a less than fully flourishing human life, even granted the immense pleasure that would result.[12]

On Mill's account of pleasure, it is difficult to see how the machine is really possible given that one cannot simulate the higher pleasures of intellectual activity (like philosophizing or cracking a difficult math problem), unless one is really doing such intellectual activity. Even in a video game or when plugged into the machine, if one is presented with a math problem, one is still actually doing a math problem. So on this account it seems difficult to see how the experience machine really would apply as a solid objection to a consequentialism based upon the higher pleasures alone.

But presumably it is possible that standing courageously against the temptation to lie or to commit the bestiality produces higher pleasures both for yourselves and for those you are hiding (even knowing they will die) inasmuch as such acts cause rejoicing in the deeds of a hero who stood by his principles unto death. So based upon this interpretation of *the good* as identical with higher intellectual pleasures one ought not to commit the bestiality or tell the lie.

Due to such difficulties concerning identifying the good with pleasure, other consequentialists have tried to specify the good as health, wealth, friendship, autonomy, and/or love.[13] As Julia Driver says, the difficulty with this approach is it seems ad hoc and arbitrary as to just

---

[11] A similar, but much less pleasing scenario, can be seen in the 1999 hit movie *The Matrix.* With the rise of virtual reality machines, this possiblity looks more real than ever before.

[12] Cf. Robert Nozick who first mentioned this example in *Anarchy, State, and Utopia* (Basic Books, 1974), 42-45.

[13] Cf. Driver, *Consequentialism*, 36-37.

what to put on the list as the objective standard for the good.[14] As she says,

> The worry about this general approach [of merely listing what the objective good is] is that…one loses prescriptive force. Apparent counter-examples are dealt with simply by adding one more thing to the intrinsic value list. A moral theory should do more than just list what is good. That's the difference between cataloguing and theorizing. A theory should systematize an area in such a way that a deeper understanding is achieved.[15]

Driver proposes that we can find some basic types of goods that all the others are reducible to, as a way of shortening the list.[16] But then the problem is how do we decide non-arbitrarily what counts as these basic goods?

With an arbitrary list of objective goods, you can justify just about any conclusion, depending upon what goods you wish to put on the list. For instance, if honesty were the only objective good on the list that ought to be maximized, then it would seem that lying is always wrong. But if maximizing the good of human life is all that counts, then lying is not wrong in cases where it could save lives. Consequentialism won't do as an adequate justification for lying, because consequentialism is a false moral theory. Is there, perhaps, another good reason we can give as to why lying is sometimes permissible?

Intrinsically Evil Actions

Thomas Aquinas held that no such reason exists. Both bestiality and lying are always wrong.[17] They fall within the category of actions that can

---

[14] Cf. Ibid., 36.

[15] Ibid., 38.

[16] Ibid.

[17] ST II-II, Q110, A3, ad 4: "Et ideo non est licitum mendacium dicere ad hoc quod aliquis alium a quocumque periculo liberet." ST II-II, Q154, A12, ad 1: "In sins contrary to nature, whereby the very order of nature is violated, an injury is done to God, the Author of nature. Hence Augustine says (Confess. iii, 8): "Those foul offenses that are against nature should be *everywhere and at all times detested and*

14

never be morally permissible. In later philosophical terminology such actions became known as intrinsically evil actions, actions that are always bad regardless of circumstances.[18] Intrinsically evil actions are not necessarily actions that are heinously evil, or instantiations of pure evil. Pure evil doesn't exist. Evil is the absence of a due good and so every evil is always associated with some good. Nor do all intrinsically evil actions necessarily mean the person who performs them becomes horribly corrupt. Not all intrinsically bad actions[19] are seriously bad, or seri-

---

punished" (emphasis added; Et ideo in peccatis contra naturam, in quibus ipse ordo naturae violatur, fit iniuria ipsi Deo, Ordinatori naturae. Unde Augustinus dicit, III *Confess. : Flagitia quae sunt contra naturam, ubique ac semper detestanda atqua punienda sunt* (Sancti Thomae de Aquino, *Summa Theologiae* [Rome: Editiones Paulinae, 1962])). In ST II-II, Q154, A11 Aquinas lists bestiality as one of the sins against nature. All further citations from the Summa are from the Pauline edition unless otherwise indicated.

[18] Aquinas himself never uses the phrase *intrinsece malum.* However, he clearly adhered to the view that some actions are always wrong regardless of consequences; see, for example, his commentary on the following passage in Aristotle's *Nicomachean Ethics*: "But presumably there are some things we cannot be compelled to do. Rather than do them we should suffer the most terrible consequences and accept death" (*Nicomachean Ethics* III.1.8 1110a26, trans. Terence Irwin). In his commentary on the passage, Aquinas agrees with Aristotle: "Et dicit quod quaedam operationes sunt adeo malae quod ad eas faciendas nulla sufficiens coactio adhiberi potest, sed magis debet homo sustinere mortem patiendo durissima tormenta quam talia operari, sicut beatus Laurentius sustinuit adustionem craticulae ne idolis immolaret" (Sancti Thomae De Aquino. *Sententiae Tertii Libri Ethicorum, Lectio* 2, p.122, Tomus XLVII, Volumen I, *Opera Omnia Iussu Leonis XIII P.M. Edita* (Roma, 1969). Lest one be tempted to say that Aquinas is merely expounding upon the meaning of Aristotle and not necessarily agreeing with him, I point out that he mentions the example of Saint Lawrence. Thomas would have held up the martyrdom of Saint Lawrence as an example of someone who suffers death rather than do something that ought never to be done.

Thomas also on various occasions strictly adheres to the Pauline principle in Romans 3:8 that one may never do evil so that good may come: *Super Sent. IV,* Q1, A1, qc1, ad 4; D17, Q2, A4, qc1, ad 4; D19, Q2, A3, qc2, ad 3; ST I-II, Q79, A4, s.c.; Q84, A4, ad5; ST II-II, Q64, A5, ad 3; ST III, Q68, A11, ad 3; *Super Psalmo 5, n. 3; Super Rom., cap. 3 l. 2; De Decem praeceptis, a. 1 co.*

[19] In contemporary English *evil* frequently connotes egregious badness, but that is not what is meant by the term *evil* in the phrase *intrinsically evil.* In order to avoid such confusion, I will be using the English term *bad* throughout much of what follows. If at times later in this book the term *evil* is used, I do not necessarily mean to

ously grave. Some are merely slighty bad actions, such as lying to save the Jews.

Bestiality and lying are not the only actions that Aquinas held are always bad. Murder, theft, robbery,[20] adultery, and homosexual activity[21] are also always bad. But that certain actions are always wrong doesn't entail that such actions are morally equal in the order of gravity. Clearly murder isn't morally equal to theft or robbery, let alone to lying. All that is meant by saying an action is always bad is simply that it can never be morally right.

Not all actions that are always wrong are wrong for the same reasons. The reason why murder is always wrong is going to be very different from the reason why lying is always wrong. But some of these actions might be wrong for similar reasons. Interestingly, Aquinas held that lying, bestiality, and homosexual activity were wrong for similar reasons. This isn't to say he thought these acts were equally bad, let alone morally equivalent. They clearly are not. Aquinas held that the syllogism showing why such actions are wrong involves a shared premise.[22] Lying is wrong because it violates the purpose of speech.[23] Homosexual acts are wrong because these acts oppose the purpose of the generative

---

imply that such evil is a heinous evil. All evils are bad, but not all evils are seriously bad or heinous.

[20] Aquinas held theft is intrinsically evil: ST II-II, Q66, A5; he held the same about robbery: ST II-II, Q66, A8.

[21] By *homosexual acts* I mean sexual activity between two members of the same-sex, as in males with males or females with females. Not all persons with homosexual desires engage in homosexual activity. Nor is it true that no heterosexuals engage in homosexual acts. Heterosexuals can and historically have engaged in homosexual activity, although typically less frequently and for different reasons than homosexuals would.

[22] Fr. Lawrence Dewan comes to a similar conclusion: "These sorts of abuses of nature [viz. lying] are analogous to what one finds in the criticism (ibid., q. 154, a. 12) of those sins of lust which are against nature, but in that latter case the matter is intrinsically grave" (Lawrence Dewan, "St. Thomas, Lying and Venial Sin," *Thomist: A Speculative Quarterly Review* 61, no. 2 (April 1, 1997): footnote 28). Janet Smith also sees the similarity in Aquinas's argumentation against lying and homosexual activity: Janet E. Smith, "Fig Leaves and Falsehoods, Pace Thomas Aquinas, Sometimes We Need to Deceive," *First Things*, June 2011, accessed October 7, 2014, http://www.firstthings.com/article/2011/06/fig-leaves-and-falsehoods.

[23] ST II-II, Q110, A3; *Super Sent. III,* D38, Q1, A3; *Quodlibet VIII,* Q6, A4.

power.[24] Although all sins in some way violate the *telos* of man, in both lying and homosexual activity the violation of natural teleology is more up front and evident. Speech is for truth, not for lying. The use of the generative power is for generation, not for sexual activity with another man (if you are a man) or with another woman (if you are a woman).

Why Aquinas?

For much of the rest of this book, we will be focusing on Aquinas's argument as to why lying and homosexual acts are always wrong. We will be neglecting Aquinas's account of bestiality largely because what he said on it is minimal, and because his arguments against homosexual activity entail his condemnation of bestiality. In other words, if homosexual acts are morally wrong as a misuse of the generative power, even more so are acts of bestiality morally wrong as a misuse of the generative power.

Further, we have not chosen to focus on Aquinas out of mere historical interest, nor do we appeal to him as a mere argument from authority. We have chosen to focus on Aquinas's argument for two reasons. First, he is the first philosopher in history to have given a robust philosophical argument against homosexual activity; that is, he gave an argument with a clear set of premises and a conclusion. While other philosophers shared his conclusion, most philosophers prior to him had at least one hidden premise, leaving it unclear how they arrived at their conclusion. Second, Aquinas's account speaks to us today. Whether we like him or not, his philosophy has had an enduring legacy across the West. No other philosopher has had as many schools or universities named after him. It is in part due to this enduring influence that various contemporary philosophers and scholars have brought Aquinas's argument to the fore in the debate over homosexuality. This book endeavors to do the same, but by placing his argument in its context and putting Aquinas in dialogue with contemporary thought. At times then when I will be commenting on Aquinas I do not do so with the mere intent of elucidating what he thought, but rather to see whether what he thought is

---

[24] SCG III, 122; *De Malo* Q15, A1.

true or consistent with what he says elsewhere. To that purpose, we now begin with an examination of the status of contemporary scholarship relevant to Aquinas's thought on these issues.

The State of the Question

Issues pertaining to Aquinas's view on lying and homosexual acts are of three general kinds: (1) some object to Aquinas's conclusions, (2) some object to Aquinas's arguments or premises for his conclusions, and (3) even those who agree with Aquinas cannot agree as to what his argument is, or they give alternate accounts, which they think better reach Aquinas's conclusions. I will discuss each of these issues in turn.

(1) Those who disagree with Aquinas's conclusions

The views of those who object to Aquinas's conclusion that lying and homosexual acts are bad can be subdivided into two kinds: (a) those who hold that Aquinas is just wrong to condemn such acts as bad, and (b) those who hold that even if such acts are bad, Aquinas cannot possibly be right that such acts are intrinsically evil.

On homosexual acts most authors who disagree with Aquinas, simply argue in favor of option (a): Aquinas was wrong to condemn such acts as morally wrong.[25] The arguments such authors advance in

---

[25] John Corvino, John McNeill, S.J., Gareth Moore, O.P., Andrew Sullivan, Burton Leiser, Peter Singer, Georges Lenferna, Michael Perry, and Thomas Nagel all argue that homosexual acts are morally good. Although not all of these authors directly engage with Aquinas, their arguments for the opposite conclusion entail a rejection of Aquinas on this issue. See John Corvino, *What's Wrong with Homosexuality?* (New York: Oxford University Press, 2013), 126; "Why Shouldn't Tommy and Jim Have Sex?," in *Same Sex Debating the Ethics, Science, and Culture of Homosexuality*, ed. John Corvino (Lanham, MD: Rowman & Littlefield, 1997), 3-4; John J. McNeill, S.J., *The Church and the Homosexual* (New York: Pocket Books, 1976), 106-107, 113-114; Gareth Moore, *A Question of Truth: Christianity and Homosexuality* (London: Continuum, 2003), 245-246; Andrew Sullivan, "Unnatural Law," *The New Republic*, March 24, 2003, 23; Burton M. Leiser, "Homosexuality, Morals, and the Laws of Nature," accessed October 21, 2014, http://faculty.mc3.edu/barmstro/leiser.html; Peter Singer, "Homosexuality Is Not Immoral," Project Syndicate, 2006, accessed October 21, 2014,

favor of their position can be categorized as (i) arguments from moral experience, (ii) from love, (iii) from good consequences, (iv) from lack of harm, and (v) from natural law. Gareth Moore and Michael Perry argue that (i) the moral experience of practicing homosexuals shows that homosexual activity must be a good action in at least some cases.[26] John McNeill and Burton Leiser argue (ii) that homosexual acts must be good if they proceed from love.[27] John Corvino argues (iii) from the good consequences that flow from homosexual acts:

> The basic case in favor of it is straight-forward: For some people, same-sex relationships are an important source of genuine human goods, including emotional and physical intimacy, mutual pleasure, and so on. That positive case must be balanced against any negatives— although, as we have seen, the standard objections fall apart under scrutiny.[28]

Peter Singer argues (iv) that if both individuals consent and the act harms no one, then it must be moral: "If a form of sexual activity brings satisfaction to those who take part in it, and harms no one, what can be immoral about it?"[29] Georges Lenferna goes so far as to argue that (v) it follows from the natural law. The natural law is about human flourishing. Homosexual activity, at times, is conducive to human flourishing. Ergo, it is good.[30]

---

http://www.utilitarian.net/singer/by/200610--.htm; Georges A. Lenferna, "Natural Law Ethics, Homosexuality and Morality," 2010, MS, Presented at the Postgraduate Philosophical Association Conference, accessed September 18, 2014, https://washington.academia.edu/AlexLenferna/Papers; Michael J. Perry, "The Morality of Homosexual Conduct: A Response to John Finnis," *Notre Dame Journal of Law, Ethics & Public Policy* 9, no. 1 (1995): 64; Thomas Nagel, "Sexual Perversion," in *The Philosophy of Sex: Contemporary Readings*, by Nicholas Power, Alan Soble, and Raja Halwani (Lanham: Rowman & Littlefield, 2012), 41.

[26] Moore, *A Question of Truth*, 245-246; Perry, "The Morality of Homosexual Conduct: A Response to John Finnis": 41.

[27] McNeill, *The Church and the Homosexual*, 106-107, 113-114; Leiser, "Homosexuality, Morals, and the Laws of Nature."

[28] Corvino, *What's Wrong with Homosexuality?*, 126.

[29] Singer, "Homosexuality Is Not Immoral."

[30] Lenferna, "Natural Law Ethics, Homosexuality and Morality."

When it comes to lying, nobody seems seriously to disagree with Aquinas that lying is wrong (that is that it is wrong in most or many cases), rather they disagree with Aquinas's conclusion in a different way. They claim that even if he is right that such acts are bad, it does not follow that they are intrinsically evil (so they affirm option (b)). In other words, there is nearly unanimous agreement that Aquinas correctly identifies lying as wrong, but there is much disagreement over whether lying is always wrong.

Many authors have argued that lying is sometimes morally permissible. Their justifications, however, vary. David Decosimo and Sissela Bok, for example, argue from an analogy with violence: If violence is generally condemned, yet at times permissible, cannot the same be said for lying?[31]

Others object to Aquinas's definition of a lie so as to get out of difficult scenarios (such as the one mentioned earlier with the Nazi at the door). These authors hold Aquinas is right that all lies are wrong, but argue that he is overly restrictive in his account as to what counts as a lie in particular situations.[32] Such authors typically argue that telling the Nazi at the door "There are no Jews here in this house" isn't a lie.

(2) Those who disagree with Aquinas's premises

Besides those who disagree with Aquinas's conclusions, there are those who disagree with Aquinas's premises for his conclusion. Aquinas's ar-

---

[31] Decosimo, "JUST LIES: Finding Augustine's Ethics of Public Lying in His Treatments of Lying and Killing;" Bok, *Lying*, 41, 45-46, 109, 115, 126, 130, 144, 213.

[32] See for example: Hugo Grotius, *On the Law of War and Peace*, trans. A.C. Campbell (London, 1814), accessed November 7, 2014, http://www.constitution.org/gro/djbp.htm; Kenneth W. Kemp and Thomas Sullivan, "Speaking Falsely and Telling Lies," *Proceedings of the American Catholic Philosophical Association* 67 (February 1, 1993); Benedict Guevin, "When a Lie Is Not a Lie: The Importance of Ethical Context," *Thomist: A Speculative Quarterly Review* 66, no. 2 (April 1, 2002).

20

gument against lying and homosexual acts are similar insofar as both arguments have similar premises:[33]

1. Violating a natural human function is always bad.
2. The function of speech is for conveying what is on one's mind and the function of the sexual organs is for the generation and education of offspring.
3. Thus, violating the natural function of speech by using it for lying or of the sexual organs by using them for ungenerative ends is always bad.

The objections to Aquinas's premises are of two general kinds, corresponding to each premise: (a) objections to Aquinas's normative teleology, and (b) objections to what Aquinas takes to be the teleology of speech and of the sexual organs or powers. Aquinas's normative teleology is simply his premise that violating the natural function of something or of a power is always bad. For centuries Aquinas's normative teleology went largely unchallenged. But with the demise of teleological philosophical systems and traditional natural law among modern philosophers, it was only a matter of time before the first premise became questionable. Recently, many philosophers have directly challenged the veracity of Aquinas's first premise.[34] Christopher Tollefsen, for example, challenges it along the following lines:

> [Aquinas's argument] looks very much like a variant of a perverted faculty argument, an argument that holds that the 'natural function' of something should not be thwarted deliberately. Such arguments are hardly compelling in their most common setting, which concerns the

---

[33] The argument given below may not be strictly valid, but it can be made so. I have simply presented it as written for the sake of simplicity and analysis of the core of Aquinas's argument. I will not comment at this time whether this argument accurately represents Aquinas; I only assert that many have taken it, or something like it, to be the core of his argument.

[34] Christopher Tollefsen, "Augustine, Aquinas, and the Absolute Norm Against Lying," *American Catholic Philosophical Quarterly* 86, no. 1 (2012): 123; Robert P. George, *In Defense of Natural Law* (Oxford: Clarendon Press, 1999), 161, 181, 293; Corvino, *What's Wrong with Homosexuality?*, 83-87.

use of bodily organs, such as sex organs. That the natural function of an organ *is* such and such does not provide a *reason* for agents to respect that function, at least, not absent some account of the relation of the function to a good that is preserved or promoted by that function. Thus, on their own, natural function arguments are empty of motivational significance.[35]

Some philosophers in addition to challenging the first premise, also challenge Aquinas's second premise.[36] The sexual organs don't merely have the education and generation of new life as their natural end. The sexual organs have other purposes, if any at all. Likewise, Aquinas's account of the purposes of speech seems overly restrictive. Speech has other purposes besides the communication of truth.

(3) Varying interpretations of Aquinas and competing accounts

Finally, there are those who are sympathetic to Aquinas's argument and to his conclusions, but reinterpret what Aquinas is saying and/or provide different arguments for the same conclusion. In short, these scholars offer competing accounts as to why lying and homosexual acts are bad.

Christopher Tollefsen and Joseph Boyle are sympathetic with Aquinas's views on lying, but they reinterpret his argument. They hold that his argument against lying is based upon a notion of basic goods.[37]

---

[35] Tollefsen, "Augustine, Aquinas, and the Absolute Norm Against Lying," *American Catholic Philosophical Quarterly* 86: 123.

[36] Corvino, *What's Wrong with Homosexuality?*, 85-87; Moore, *A Question of Truth*, 223; Burton Leiser, "Homosexuality and the 'Unnaturalness Argument'" Leiser, accessed October 17, 2013, http://faculty.cbu.ca/sstewart/sexlove/leiser.htm. See also Mark D. Jordan, *The Invention of Sodomy in Christian Theology* (Chicago: University of Chicago Press, 1997), 156.

[37] Christopher O. Tollefsen, *Lying and Christian Ethics* (New York, NY: Cambridge University Press, 2014), 50, 53-56; J. Boyle, "The Absolute Prohibition of Lying and the Origins of the Casuistry of Mental Reservation: Augustinian Arguments and Thomistic Developments," *The American Journal of Jurisprudence* 44, no. 1 (1999): 58.

John Finnis, Robert George, and Gerard Bradley argue homosexual activity is wrong because it violates personal integrity by making the body into an instrument for the conscious self.[38] Finnis says,

> [Extra-marital and thus homosexual activity] can <u>do</u> no more than provide each partner with an individual gratification. For want of a *common good* that could be actualised and experienced *by and in this bodily union*, that conduct involves the partners in treating their bodies as instruments to be used in the service of their consciously experiencing selves; their choice to engage in such conduct thus disintegrates each of them precisely as acting persons.[39]

Pruss argues from the impossibility of a one-body union, that is, a union of the reproductive type. With homosexual activity, he argues, one is desiring such a union and acting as if such a union were possible, when it is in fact not. This is tragic and morally inappropriate.[40]

Janet Smith argues that homosexual acts are wrong because they violate the good to which the sexual organs are ordered, namely, new human life.[41] All other organs are ordered to the good of the individual, but the sexual organs are ordered to the good of the species. So though one may use other organs for purposes other than their proximate end so

---

[38] John M. Finnis, "Law, Morality, and 'Sexual Orientation'" *Notre Dame Law Review* 69, no. 5 (1994). He also argues from an analogy with anonymous sex, prostitution, and masturbation. He further argues there that homosexual acts cannot be self-giving. In the newer version of his article in Corvino's anthology, *Same Sex: Debating the Ethics, Science, and Culture of Homosexuality,* he also argues that those advocating for homosexual acts in principle have no good arguments against promiscuity (21).
See also Robert P. George and Gerard V. Bradley, "Marriage and the Liberal Imagination," *The Georgetown Law Journal* 84: 302, 313-318. They argue there that homosexual acts violate the basic good of integrity since in them one treats one's body as a mere means/instrument for the conscious self. The body is not merely a pleasure-inducing machine.

[39] John Finnis, "Law, Morality, and 'Sexual Orientation,'" *Notre Dame Law Review* 69:5 (1994): 1066-1067.

[40] Alexander R. Pruss, *One Body: An Essay in Christian Sexual Ethics* (Notre Dame: University of Notre Dame Press, 2013), 367-373.

[41] Janet E. Smith, "Thomas Aquinas On Homosexuality," in *Homosexuality and American Public Life,* by Christopher Wolfe (Dallas: Spence Publishing Company, 1999), 129-140.

long as they fulfill their remote end of the good of the individual this does not hold with the sexual organs, because they are not ordered to the good of the individual. They are ordered to the good of new life.

At this point one thing is clear: there is much disagreement not only over the morality of lying and homosexual acts, but also over Aquinas's treatment of these topics. This book will attempt to resolve these difficulties and come to a clearer understanding of Aquinas's position. We will engage with the texts of Aquinas in order to see whether he was consistent and whether his philosophy can adequately ground a reply to contemporary objections on these issues. At times then we will go beyond Aquinas in order to arrive at the truth of the matter.

Chapter I: An Examination of Our Predecessors & Arguments in Favor of Homosexual Acts

According to Aquinas, an argument from authority is the weakest of all arguments. Nevertheless, it is still an argument.[42] We accept most of our beliefs on the basis of authority because we do not have the time to become experts in every field of study, and because when such knowledge is beyond our natural capacities we leave it to the more gifted to investigate.

Most of what we learn as a child is on the basis of the authority of our parents and our teachers, but even as adults many of our beliefs are still held on the basis of authority. Only a select few astronauts have perceived the roundnesss of the earth. We can see images of the earth taken by those in space or read the stories of those who have flown around the world, yet to appeal to these stories or photos is to trust their authors.[43] So unless one holds that most of our beliefs are unjustified most of the time, one cannot reasonably reject arguments from authority. Who counts as an authority is not always clear, but if the authorities are pretty universally agreed upon then there can be little reason for rejecting such appeals, barring good arguments to the contrary. This is why today many uncritically accept the conclusions of science on a host of issues—because they accept the authority of scientists to make scientific judgments on scientific questions.

---

[42] The argument from authority has been defended by C.F.J. Martin in *Thomas Aquinas: God and Explanations* (Edinburgh: Edinburgh University Press, 1997), 7-13. It is also the subject of book-length defenses by Douglas Walton in *Appeal to Expert Opinion: Arguments from Authority* (1997) and Linda Zagzebski in *Epistemic Authority: A Theory of Trust, Authority, and Autonomy in Belief* (2012).

[43] There are, of course, other ways of knowing the roundness of the earth, such as by observing the curved shadow of the earth on the moon during a partial lunar eclipse. Many people, however, haven't thought through the causes of the shadow on the moon and so it is reasonable to assume that most people take it on authority that the earth is round.

Yet scientists are not the only authorities. If you wish to know what happened during the sack of Rome by the Muslims in 846 AD, it is reasonable to appeal to what the historians have written on this event. In the area of ethics, however, the experts are not the historians, nor the scientists, but rather the philosophers, for the study of ethics properly speaking falls under the subject matter of philosophy (at least on a natural level; we will abstract from accounts of supernatural revelation). If the majority of scientists today hold a certain scientific position, such as the roundness of the earth, then we have good reason to hold such a view, unless there are compelling reasons to the contrary. The authorities, of course, could be wrong, but we cannot merely dismiss their position without argument. If the majority of scientists since the beginning of recorded history held to a certain position, this would be an even more compelling argument from authority. The more authorities who hold a given position increases the likelihood that such a position is true. Universal error is possible, but extremely improbable for an extended continuous period of time, particularly among those who are experts in the given field of study. Thus, a nearly unanimous consensus among philosophers throughout history on certain moral issues provides a strong argument from authority. With this background in mind, we will embark to show the philosophical record concerning the thoughts of the major philosophers on the morality or immorality of homosexual activity. Some philosophers, of course, never wrote on homosexual activity or never wrote very clearly on it, as such they have been excluded from the list that follows.

Homosexual Acts and the Witness
of the Philosophers

Plato (429-347 BC)
Anyone who was initiated long ago or who has been corrupted is not given to moving rapidly from here to there, towards beauty as it really is. Instead, he gazes on its namesake here on earth, and the upshot is that the sight does not arouse reverence in him. No, he surrenders to pleasure and tries like an animal to mount his partner and to father offspring, and having becoming habituated

to excess he is not afraid or ashamed to pursue *unnatural pleasures* [emphasis added].[44]

Phaedrus 250e-251a.[45]

And whether one makes the observation in earnest or in jest, one certainly should not fail to observe that *when male unites with female for procreation the pleasure experienced is held to be due to nature, but contrary to nature when male mates with male or female with female*, and that those first guilty of such enormities were impelled by their slavery to pleasure [emphasis added].[46]

Laws 636b-d.[47]

That was precisely the reason why I stated that in reference to this law I know of a device for making a natural use of reproductive intercourse,—on the one hand, by abstaining from the male and not slaying of set purpose the human stock,[48] nor sowing seed on rocks and stones[49] where it can never take root

---

[44] The Greek text is as follows: "ὁ μὲν οὖν μὴ νεοτελὴς ἢ διεφθαρμένος οὐκ ὀξέως ἐνθένδε ἐκεῖσε φέρεται πρὸς αὐτὸ τὸ κάλλος, θεώμενος αὐτοῦ τὴν τῇδε ἐπωνυμίαν, ὥστ᾽ οὐ σέβεται προσορῶν, ἀλλ᾽ ἡδονῇ παραδοὺς τετράποδος νόμον βαίνειν ἐπιχειρεῖ καὶ παιδοσπορεῖν, καὶ ὕβρει προσομιλῶν οὐ δέδοικεν [251α] οὐδ᾽ αἰσχύνεται παρὰ φύσιν ἡδονὴν διώκων:" (Plato, *Phaedrus* 250e-251a, in *Platonis Opera,* ed. John Burnet (Oxford University Press, 1903), http://data.perseus.org/texts/urn:cts:greekLit:tlg0059.tlg012.perseus-grc1, and http://data.perseus.org/texts/urn:cts:greekLit:tlg0059.tlg012.perseus-grc1.

[45] Plato, *Phaedrus* 250e-251a, trans. Robin Waterfield (New York: Oxford University Press Inc., 2002), 34.

[46] Greek text from Perseus is as follows: "[636ξ] ὅσαι τῶν ἄλλων μάλιστα ἅπτονται τῶν γυμνασίων: καὶ εἴτε παίζοντα εἴτε σπουδάζοντα ἐννοεῖν δεῖ τὰ τοιαῦτα, ἐννοητέον ὅτι τῇ θηλείᾳ καὶ τῇ τῶν ἀρρένων φύσει εἰς κοινωνίαν ἰούσῃ τῆς γεννήσεως ἡ περὶ ταῦτα ἡδονὴ κατὰ φύσιν ἀποδεδόσθαι δοκεῖ, **ἀρρένων δὲ πρὸς ἄρρενας ἢ θηλειῶν πρὸς θηλείας παρὰ φύσιν** καὶ τῶν πρώτων τὸ τόλμημ᾽ εἶναι δι᾽ ἀκράτειαν ἡδονῆς" (Plato, *Laws* 8.838e, in *Platonis Opera,* ed. John Burnet (Oxford University Press, 1903), http://data.perseus.org/citations/urn:cts:greekLit:tlg0059.tlg034.perseus-grc1:636c; emphasis added.

[47] Plato, *Laws* I.636b-d, vol. I, trans. R.G. Bury, Litt. D. (London: William Heinemann; New York: G. P. Putnam's Sons, 1961), 41.

[48] Other translation: "It's fine of you to take me up this way. For this was the very thing I said, that in regard to this law I had an art that would promote the natural use of sexual intercourse for the production of children—by abstaining on the one hand from intercourse with males, the deliberate killing of the human race..." (Plato, *The*

and have fruitful increase...This law...follows the dictates of nature, and it serves to keep men from sexual rage and frenzy and all kinds of fornication, and from all excess in meats and drinks, and it ensures in husbands fondness for their own wives : other blessings also would ensue, in infinite number, if one could make sure use of this law. Possibly, however, some young bystander, rash and of superabundant virility, on hearing of passing this law, would denounce us for making foolish and impossible rules, and fill all the place with his outcries [emphasis added].

Laws VIII.838e-c.[50]

Possibly, should God so grant, we might forcibly effect one of two things in this matter of sex-relations,—*either that no one should venture to touch any of the noble and freeborn save his own wedded wife, nor sow any unholy and bastard seed in fornication, nor any unnatural and barren seed in sodomy,— or else we should entirely abolish love for males...*[emphasis added].[51] [52]

Laws of Plato VIII.838e, trans. Thomas L. Pangle (New York: Basic Books, Inc., Publishers, 1980), 230.

[49] The Greek of the italicized text is as follows: "Ἀθηναῖος: καλῶς ὑπέλαβες: αὐτὸ γὰρ τοῦτο ἦν τὸ παρ' ἐμοῦ λεχθέν, ὅτι τέχνην ἐγὼ πρὸς τοῦτον τὸν νόμον ἔχοιμι τοῦ κατὰ φύσιν χρῆσθαι τῇ τῆς παιδογονίας συνουσίᾳ, **τοῦ μὲν ἄρρενος ἀπεχομένους,** μὴ κτείνοντάς τε ἐκ προνοίας τὸ τῶν ἀνθρώπων γένος, μηδ' εἰς πέτρας τε καὶ λίθους σπείροντας" (Plato, *Laws* 8.838e, in *Platonis Opera,* ed. John Burnet (Oxford University Press, 1903), http://data.perseus.org/citations/urn:cts:greekLit:tlg0059.tlg034.perseus-grc1:8.838e; emphasis added in bold to indicate the Greek for "abstaining from the male").

[50] Plato, *Laws* VIII.838e-c, vol. II, trans. R.G. Bury, Litt. D. (London: William Heinemann; New York: G.P. Putnam's Sons, 1926), 159-161.

[51] The Greek text of 841d is as follows: "[841δ] κἂν δυοῖν θάτερα βιασαίμεθα περὶ ἐρωτικῶν, ἢ μηδένα τολμᾶν μηδενὸς ἅπτεσθαι τῶν γενναίων ἅμα καὶ ἐλευθέρων πλὴν γαμετῆς ἑαυτοῦ γυναικός, ἄθυτα δὲ παλλακῶν σπέρματα καὶ νόθα μὴ σπείρειν, **μηδὲ ἄγονα ἀρρένων παρὰ φύσιν**: ἢ τὸ μὲν τῶν ἀρρένων πάμπαν ἀφελοίμεθ' ἄν"(Plato, *Laws* 8.841d, in *Platonis Opera,* ed. John Burnet (Oxford University Press, 1903), http://data.perseus.org/citations/urn:cts:greekLit:tlg0059.tlg034.perseus-grc1:8.841d; emphasis added in bold for "sow sterile seed in males against nature").

[52] Other translation: "*Either* no one is to dare touch any well-born and free person except the woman who is his wife, and no one is to sow unhallowed, bastard sperm in concubines or go against nature and sow sterile seed in males; *or* we should abolish erotic activity between males altogether..." (Plato, *The Laws of Plato,* VIII.841d, trans. Thomas L. Pangle (New York: Basic Books, Inc., Publishers, 1980), 233.

Laws VIII.841c-d.[53]

Aristotle (384-322 BC)

These states are bestial. Other states result from attacks of disease and in some cases from fits of madness—for instance, the person who sacrificed her mother and ate her, and the one who ate the liver of his fellow slave. Others result from diseased conditions or from habit—for instance, plucking hairs, chewing nails, even coal and earth, and *besides these sexual intercourse between males.*[54] For in some people these result from [a diseased] nature, in others from habit, as for instance, in those who have suffered wanton [sexual] assault since their childhood…Each of these states, then, is outside the limits of vice, just as bestiality is [emphasis added].

Nicomachean Ethics. VII.5.1148b25-32, 1149a-2.[55]

First Exception—Approving Homosexual Activity: Bion of Borysthenes (325?-255? BC[56])

A second-hand account of his thoughts are recorded in Diogenes Laertius:

He [Bion] denounced even Socrates, saying that if he had need of Alcibiades and held him off, he was foolish; if he didn't have need, he did nothing exceptional.

Frr. 57, 59.[57]

---

[53] Plato, *Laws* VIII.841c-d, vol. II, trans. R. G. Bury, Litt. D. (London: William Heinemann; New York: G. P. Putnam's Sons, 1926), 167.

[54] The Greek text of this sentence is as follows: "αἲ δὲ νοσηματώδεις ἢ ἐξ ἔθους, οἶον τριχῶν τίλσεις καὶ ὀνύχων τρώξεις, ἔτι δ᾽ ἀνθράκων καὶ γῆς, πρὸς δὲ τούτοις ἡ **τῶν ἀφροδισίων τοῖς ἄρρεσιν**" (Aristotle, *Nicomachean Ethics* VII.1148b.25, in *Aristotle's Ethica Nicomachea,* ed. J. Bywater (Oxford: Clarendon Press, 1894), http://data.perseus.org/citations/urn:cts:greekLit:tlg0086.tlg010.perseus-grc1:1148b.25; emphasis added for "sexual intercourse between males").

[55] Aristotle, *Nicomachean Ethics* VII.5.3.1148b25-32, 2nd ed., trans. Terrence Irwin (Indianapolis/Cambridge: Hackett Publishing Company, Inc.), 106-107.

[56] The Editors of Encyclopædia Britannica, *Encyclopaedia Britannica,* s.v. "Bion of Borysthenes," accessed August 21, 2015, http://www.britannica.com/biography/Bion-of-Borysthenes.

[57] Cf. Thomas K. Hubbard, ed., *Homosexuality in Greece and Rome: A Sourcebook of Basic Documents* (Berkeley, Los Angeles, London: University of California Press, 2003), 264-265.

Against Homosexual Activity:

Cicero (106-43 BC)[58]

But, in fact, how absurd the way their [Sparta's] young men exercise in the gymnasia! How lax the military training for their young cadets! How free and unrestricted their amorous fondling! There is no need to even mention the Eleans and the Thebans, for whom lust is granted unrestrained license in amorous relations with their free young men of free birth. The Spartans themselves permit it all when it comes to amorous relations with their young men, the one exception being the filthy act itself. An exceedingly thin wall is the only barrier to this excepted act; for they allow lovers to sleep with each other and embrace, just so long as there is covering between them.[59]

On the Republic 4.4.[60] [61]

---

[58] While the following quotes from Cicero do not explicitly indicate his moral disapproval, it is clearly implied. I have, thus, included Cicero, because it is highly probable that he disapproved of homosexual activity.

[59] The Latin is as follows: Ita sunt alte repetita quasi fundamenta quaedam verecundiae. Iuventutis vero exercitatio quam absurda in gymnasiis! quam levis epheborum illa militia! quam contrectationes et amores soluti et liberi! mitto apud Eleos et Thebanos, apud quos in amore ingenuorum libido etiam permissam habet et solutam licentiam; Lacedaemonii ipsi, cum omnia concedunt in amore iuvenum praeter stuprum, tenui sane muro dissaepiunt id, quod excipiunt; conplexus enim concubitusque permittunt palliis interiectis (M. Tullius Cicero, *Librorum de Re Publica Sex* 4.4, ed. C.F.W. Mueller (Leipzig, Teubner: 1889), 356, http://data.perseus.org/citations/urn:cts:latinLit:phi0474.phi043.perseus-lat1:4.4.
Note that according to *Lewis and Short* the Latin term *ephebus* refers to a youth from 18 to 20 years of age, that is, one who has just come to the age of manhood.

[60] Cf. Thomas K. Hubbard, ed., *Homosexuality in Greece and Rome: A Sourcebook of Basic Documents* (Berkeley, Los Angeles, London: University of California Press, 2003), 337. The quote is from Scipio, who takes the part of the wise man in the dialogue.

[61] Another text is as follows: "[During his prosecution of Verres, the governor of Sicily, for corruption, Cicero made the following remarks:] One could not produce a lazier and weaker man, someone who is more masculine among women and more unchaste a little lady among men" (*Against Verres* 2.2.192, in Thomas K. Hubbard, ed., *Homosexuality in Greece and Rome: A Sourcebook of Basic Documents* (Berkeley, Los Angeles, London: University of California Press, 2003), 339). The Latin is as follows: at homo inertior, ignavior, magis vir inter mulieres, impura inter viros muliercula proferri non potest (M. Tullius Cicero, *Against Verres*, eds. Albert Clark, William Peterson (Scriptorum Classicorum Bibliotheca Oxoniensis, 1917),

[In his speech against Catiline:] What enticements did any man ever hold out to the young that were so great as his? He himself loved some young men most shamefully, but was a slave most scandalously to the love of others, and promised to some the free enjoyment of their lusts, to others the death of their parents. He not only goaded them, but helped them to accomplish such deeds.[62]

Against Catiline 2.4.8.[63]

[Attacking Clodius:] After the death of his father, he devoted his earliest youth to satisfying the lusts of rich dandies, and when their intemperance had been fulfilled, he turned to domestic and even incestuous sexual acts. *Then, after he grew big and strong*, he went to the provinces for military service, and after patiently enduring the abuse of pirates, *he even satiated the lusts of the Cilicians and barbarians* [emphasis added].[64]

On the Response of the Diviners 42.[65]

192,   http://data.perseus.org/citations/urn:cts:latinLit:phi0474.phi005.perseus-lat1:2.2.192).

[62] [8] iam vero quae tanta umquam in ullo[5] iuventutis inlecebra fuit quanta in illo? qui alios ipse amabat turpissime, aliorum amori flagitiosissime serviebat, aliis fructum libidinum, aliis mortem parentum non modo impellendo verum etiam adiuvando pollicebatur (M. Tullius Cicero, *Against Catiline,* eds. Albert Clark, Albert Curtis Clark (Scriptorum Classicorum Bibliotheca Oxoniensis, 1908), http://data.perseus.org/citations/urn:cts:latinLit:phi0474.phi013.perseus-lat1:2.4).
The Latin term *iuventutis,* according to *Lewis and Short,* is the age of youth, which is from the 20th to the 40th year of age. The term thus appears to be referring to adults.
[63] Cf. Thomas K. Hubbard, ed., *Homosexuality in Greece and Rome: A Sourcebook of Basic Documents* (Berkeley, Los Angeles, London: University of California Press, 2003), 339.
[64] Qui post patris mortem primam illam aetatulam suam ad scurrarum locupletium libidines detulit, quorum intemperantia expleta in domesticis est germanitatis stupris volutatus : deinde iam robusts provinciae se ac rei militari dedit atque ibi piratarum contumelias perpessus, etiam Cilicum libidines barbarorumque satiavit (Cicero, *De Haruspicum Responsis* 42, in *Cicero: The Speeches with an English Translation* (Cambridge/London: Harvard University Press, William Heinemann Ltd., 1961), 370.
[65] Cf. Thomas K. Hubbard, ed., *Homosexuality in Greece and Rome: A Sourcebook of Basic Documents* (Berkeley, Los Angeles, London: University of California Press, 2003), 340.

32

Seneca the Younger (4 BC–65 AD)

There was this fellow, Hostius Quadra, whose behavior was so indecent it has
even been produced upon stage. When this rich, greedy man, a slave himself
to his 100,000,000 sesterces, was killed by his slaves, the emperor Augustus
considered his murder not worthy of punishment, and all but declared it a justifiable homicide. His depravity was not restricted to only one sex, but he was
voracious for men and women alike....Quadra actually used to cruise the
baths checking peckers, recruiting from the ranks of those who measured up
most impressively...But for Quadra, the beast, unsightly perversion was show
time, and no moonless night was dark enough to blot out his stage-strutting. "I
take on a man and a woman at the same time," he says.... "Where's the victim in a crime against nature?"...Revolting behavior![66]
Natural Questions 1.16.[67]

Dio Chrysostom (40–115 AD)

Is it possible that this intemperate race would hold off from abuse and corruption of males and impose upon themselves the clear and sufficient limit de-
creed by Nature? Wouldn't they rather seek another greater and more illicit
form of outrage once they had become in every way sated and full of their
unrestrained pleasure with women? Female conquests—especially of freeborn
maidens—appeared too easy and effortless for one hunting this game with
money...Instead he will cross over to the male side, desiring to commit
shameful acts with those who in the near future will be rulers, judges, and
generals, finding here a difficult and seldom acquired species of pleasure.[68]

---

[66] Hostius fuit Quadra obscenitatis in scaenam usque productae. Hunc divitem ava-
rum, sestertii milies servum, divus Augustus indignum vindicta iudicavit, cum a
servis occisus esset, et tantum non pronuntiavit iure caesum videri. Non erat ille ab
uno tantummodo sexu impurus, sed tam virorum quam feminarum avidus fuit....In
omnibus quidem balneis agebat ille dilectum et aperta mensura legebat viros...At
illud monstrum obscenitatem suam spectaculum fecerat et ea sibi ostentabat quibus
abscondendis nulla satis alta nox est. "Simul," inquit, "et virum et feminam pa-
tior....Quo nequitiam meam, si ad naturae modum pecco?" Facinus indignum!
(Seneca, *Naturales Quaestiones,* Book I, 16, in *Seneca in Ten Volumes,* vol. VII,
Naturales Quaestiones, vol. I (Cambridge: Harvard University Press; London: William Heinemann Ltd, 1971), 82-88.

[67] Cf. Hubbard, ed., *Homosexuality in Greece and Rome: A Sourcebook of Basic
Documents,* 392-393.

[68] The Greek text is as follows:

[149] εἶεν δή, παρ᾽ οἷς ἂν καὶ τὰ περὶ τὰς κόρας οὕτως ἁπλῶς ἔχῃ, τί χρὴ
προσδοκᾶν τοὺς κόρους, ποίας τινὸς παιδείας καὶ ἀγωγῆς τυγχάνειν; ἔσθ᾽ ὅπως ἂν

Orationes 7.149-150.[69]

Musonius Rufus (ca. 30-101 AD)

Not the least significant part of the life of luxury and selfindulgence [sic.] lies also in sexual excess; for example those who lead such a life crave a variety of loves not only lawful but unlawful ones as well, not women alone but also men; sometimes they pursue one love and sometimes another, and not being satisfied with those which are available, pursue those which are rare and inaccessible, and invent shameful intimacies, all of which constitute a grave indictment of manhood. Men who are not wantons or immoral are bound to consider sexual intercourse justified only when it occurs in marriage and is indulged in for the purpose of begetting children, since that is lawful, but unjust and unlawful when it is mere pleasure-seeking, even in marriage. *But of all sexual relations those involving adultery are most unlawful, and no more tolerable are those of men with men, because it is a monstrous thing and contrary to nature* [emphasis added].[70]

ἀπόσχοιτο τῆς τῶν *ἀρρένων* λώβης καὶ φθορᾶς τό γε ἀκόλαστον γένος, τοῦτον ἱκανὸν καὶ σαφῆ ποιησάμενον ὅρον τὸν τῆς φύσεως, ἀλλ' οὐκ ἂν ἐμπιμπλάμενον πάντα τρόπον τῆς περὶ γυναῖκας ἀκρασίας διακορὲς γενόμενον τῆς ἡδονῆς ταύτης ζητοίη ἑτέραν μείζω καὶ παρανομωτέραν ὕβριν; [150] ὡς τά γε γυναικῶν, αὐτῶν σχεδόν τι τῶν ἐλευθέρων καὶ παρθένων, ἐφάνη ῥᾴδια καὶ οὐδεὶς πόνος θηρῶντι μετὰ πλούτου τὴν τοιάνδε θήραν:...[151] καὶ τῷ ὄντι *θῆλυν* παντελῶς ἐπὶ *τὴν ἀνδρωνῖτιν* μεταβήσεται, τοὺς ἄρχοντας αὐτίκα μάλα καὶ δικάσοντας καὶ στρατηγήσοντας ἐπιθυμῶν καταισχύνειν, [152] ὡς ἐνθάδε που τὸ χαλεπὸν καὶ δυσπόριστον εὑρήσων τῶν ἡδονῶν εἶδος,
(Dio Chrysostom, *Orationes,* ed. J. de Arnim (Berlin: Weidmann, 1893), http://data.perseus.org/citations/urn:cts:greekLit:tlg0612.tlg001.perseus-grc1.7.149, http://data.perseus.org/citations/urn:cts:greekLit:tlg0612.tlg001.perseus-grc1:7.150, http://data.perseus.org/citations/urn:cts:greekLit:tlg0612.tlg001.perseus-grc1:7.151, http://data.perseus.org/citations/urn:cts:greekLit:tlg0612.tlg001.perseus-grc1:7.152). The Greek term *ἀρρένων* refers to males. The Greek *θῆλυν* refers to females, and *ἀνδρωνῖτιν* refers to males or male living quarters. Despite the technicalities of the terms, the passage is still clearly referring to male homosexual activity.

[69] Translation is from Thomas K. Hubbard, ed., *Homosexuality in Greece and Rome: A Sourcebook of Basic Documents*, 448.

[70] The Greek text is as follows: Μέρος μέντοι τρυφῆς οὐ μεξρότατον χἀν τοῖς ἀφροδισίοις ἐστιν, ὅτι ποχίλων δέονται παιδιχῶν οἱ τρυφῶντες οὐ νομίμων μόνον ἀλλὰ καὶ παρανόμων, οὐδὲ *θηλειῶν μόνον ἀλλὰ καὶ ἀρρένων*, ἄλλοτε ἄλλους θηρῶντες ἐρωμένους, καί τοῖς μὲν ἐν ἑτοίμῳ οὖσιν οὐχ ἀρκούμενοι, τῶν δὲ σπανίων ἐφιέμενοι, συμπλοκὰς δ'ἀσχήμονας ζητοῦντες, ἅπερ ἅπαντα μεγάλα

Lecture XII, On Sexual Indulgence.[71]

Athenagoras of Athens (133-190 AD):

But though such is our character (Oh! Why should I speak of things unfit to be uttered?), the things said of us are an example of the proverb, *"The harlot reproves the chaste."* For those who have set up a market for fornication and established infamous resorts for the young for every kind of vile pleasure— *who do not abstain even from males, males with males committing shocking abominations, outraging all the noblest and comeliest bodies in all sorts of ways, so dishonouring the fair workmanship of God* (for beauty on earth is not self-made, but sent hither by the hand and will of God)—*these men, I say, revile us for the very things which they are conscious of themselves,* and ascribe to their own gods, boasting of them as noble deeds, and worthy of the gods [emphasis added].[72]

A Plea for Christians.[73]

ἐγκλήματα ἀνθρώπου ἐστιν. χρὴ δὲ τοὺς μὴ τρυφῶντας ἤ μὴ κακοὺς μόνα μὲν ἀφροδίσια νομίζειν δίκαια τὰ ἐν γάμῳ καὶ ἐπὶ γενέσει παίδων συντελούμενα, ὅτι καὶ νόμιμά ἐστιν. τα δέ γε ἡδονὴν θηρώμενα ψιλὴν ἄδικα καὶ παράνομα, χᾶν ἐν γάμῳ ᾖ. συμπλοκαὶ δ' ἄλλαι αἱ μὲν κατὰ μοικείαν παρανομώταται, καὶ μετριώτεραι τούτων οὐδὲν αἱ *πρὸς ἄρρενας τοῖς ἄρρεσιν, ὅτι παρα φύσιν τὸ τόλμημα* (Gaius Musonius Rufus, *C. Musonii Rufi Reliquiae,* ed. O. Hense (Lipsiae: In Aedibus B.G. Teubneri, 1905), XII, lines 10-7, p.63-64, emphasis added).

[71] Musonius Rufus, *Musonius Rufus: The Roman Socrates,* trans. Cora E. Lutz (Yale University Press, 1947),
 https://sites.google.com/site/thestoiclife/the_teachers/musonius-rufus/lectures/12.

[72] The Greek text is as follows:
Ἀλλ' οἱ τοιοῦτοι (ὤ τί ἄν εἴποιμι τὰ ἀπὸρρητα ;) ἀκούμεν τὰ τῆς παροιμίας, Ἡ πόρνη τὴν σώφηονα. Οι γὰρ ἀγορὰν στήσαντες πορνείας, καὶ καταγωγὰς ἀθέσμους πεποιημένοι τοῖς νέοις πάσης αἰσχρᾶς τοονῆς, καὶ μηδὲ τῶν ἀρσένων φειδόμενοι, ἄρσενες ἐν ἄρσεσι τὰ δεινὰ κατεργαζόμενοι. δσων σεμνότερα καὶ εὐειδέστερα σώματα, παντοίως αὐθά ὑδρίζοντες. ἀτιμοῦντες καὶ τὸ ποιητὸν τοῦ Θεοῦ καλόν (οὐ γὰρ αὐτοποίητον ἐπὶ γῆς τὸ κάλλος, ἀλλὰ ἀπὸ χειρὸς καὶ γνώμης πευμόμενον τοῦ Θεοῦ), οὗτοι δὲ δὲ ἃ συνίσασιν αὐτοῖς καὶ τοὺς σφετέρους λέγουσι θεοὺς (4), ἐπ' αὐτῶν, ὡς σεμνὰ, καὶ τῶν θεῶν αὐτὰ αὐχοῦντες, ταῦτα ἡμᾶς λοιδοροῦνται. (ΑΘΗΝΓΟΡΟΥ ΑΘΗΝΑΙΟΥ ΦΙΛΟΣΟΦΟΥ ΧΡΙΣΤΙΑΝΟΥ (Athenagorae Atheniensis Philosophi Christiani), *ΠΡΕΣΒΕΙΑ ΠΕΡΙ ΧΡΙΣΤΙΑΝΩΝ (Legatio pro Christianis),* Latin trans. Gesnero, vol. 6 of *Patrologiae Graecae,* ed. J.P. Migne (In via dicta *d'amboise,* prope portam lutetiae parisiorum vulgo *d'enfer* nominatam seu petit-montrouge, 1856), p. 968, chapter 34).

[73] Athenagoras of Athens, *A Plea for Christians,* trans. B.P. Pratten, in *Ante-Nicene Fathers,* vol. 2, eds. Alexander Roberts, James Donaldson, and A. Cleveland Coxe

Plotinus (204/5-270 AD) & Porphyry (234-305 AD)

The rhetorician Diophanes read a defence of Alcibiades in Plato's 'Banquet' in which he asserted that a pupil for the sake of advancing in the study of virtue should submit himself to carnal intercourse with his master if the master desired it. Plotinus repeatedly started up to leave the meeting, but restrained himself, and after the end of the lecture gave me, Porphyry, the task of writing a refutation. Diophanes refused to lend me his manuscript, and I depended in writing my refutation on my memory of his arguments. When I read it before the same assembled hearers I pleased Plotinus so much that he kept on quoting during the meeting. "So strike and be a light to men."[74]
Porphyry On the Life of Plotinus and the Order of His Books, 15.1-17.[75]

Augustine (354-430 AD)

Shameful acts which are contrary to nature, such as the acts of the Sodomites (Gen. 19: 5ff), are everywhere and always to be detested and punished. Even if all peoples should do them, they would be liable to the same condemnation by divine law; for it has not made men to use one another in this way. Indeed the social bond which should exist between God and us is violated when the nature of which he is the author is polluted by a perversion of sexual desire.[76]

(Buffalo: Christian Literature Publishing, 1885), revised and edited for New Advent by Kevin Knight, http://www.newadvent.org/fathers/0205.htm.

[74] Ὅτε δὲ ὁ ῥήτωρ Διοφάνης ἀνέγνω ὑπὲρ Ἀλκιβιάδου τοῦ ἐν τῷ "Συμποσίῳ" τοῦ Πλάτωνος ἀπολογίαν δογματίζων χρῆναι ἀρετῆς ἕνεκα μαθήσεως εἰς συνουσίαν αὐτὸν παρέχειν ἐρῶντι ἀφροδισίου μίξεως τῷ καθηγεμόνι, ἤιξε μὲν πολλάκις ἀναστὰς ἀπαλλαγῆναι τῆς συνόδου, ἐπισχὼν δ' ἑαυτὸν μετὰ τὴν διάλυσιν τοῦ ἀκουστηρίου ἐμοὶ Πορφυρίῳ ἀντιγράψαι προσέταξε. Μὴ θέλοντος δὲ τοῦ Διοφάνους τὸ βιβλίον δοῦναι διὰ τῆς μνήμης ἀναληφθέντων τῶν ἐπιχειρημάτων ἀντιγράψας
ἐγὼ καὶ ἐπὶ τῶν αὐτῶν ἀκροατῶν συνηγμένων ἀναγνοὺς τοσοῦτον τὸν Πλωτῖνον ηὔφρανα, ὡς κἂν ταῖς συνουσίαις συνεχῶς ἐπιλέγειν· (Porphyry, *Porphyry On the Life of Plotinus and the Order of His Books,* 15, trans. A.H. Armstrong (Cambridge, MA: Harvard University Press; London: William Heinemann Ltd., 1966), 42.

[75] Porphyry, *Porphyry On the Life of Plotinus and the Order of His Books,* 15, trans. A.H. Armstrong (Cambridge, MA: Harvard University Press; London: William Heinemann Ltd., 1966), 43.

[76] itaque flagitia, quae sunt contra naturam, ubique ac semper detestanda atque punienda sunt, qualia sodomitarum fuerunt. quae si omnes gentes facerent, eodem criminis reatu diuina lege tenerentur, quae non sic fecit homines, ut se illo uterentur modo. uiolatur quippe ipsa societas, quae cum deo nobis esse debet, cum eadem

Confessions III.viii.15.[77]

After this promise Lot was delivered out of Sodom, and a fiery rain from heaven turned into ashes that whole region of the impious city, where custom had made sodomy as prevalent as laws have elsewhere made other kinds of wickedness. But this punishment of theirs was a specimen of the divine judgment to come.[78]

City of God XVI.30.[79]

Unless perchance we have forgotten that this did come to pass in Sodom, where males burning towards males with hideous lust could not so much as find the door of the house in which were the men they sought; when that just man, in a case altogether most similar, would not tell a lie for his guests, whom he knew not to be Angels, and feared lest they should suffer a violence worse than death.[80]

---

natura, cuius ille auctor est, libidinis peruersitate polluitur (Augustine Hipponensis, *Confessionum libri tredecim,* III.8.1-7, CC SL, 27 (L. Verheijen, 1981), *Notitia Clavis Patrum Latinorum,* 251, in *Library of Latin Texts – Series A,* http://clt.brepolis.net/LLTA/pages/TextSearch.aspx?key=PAUG_0251_).

[77] Augustine, *Confessions,* trans. Henry Chadwick (Oxford, New York: Oxford University Press, 1992), 45-46.

[78] post hanc promissionem liberato de sodomis loth et ueniente igneo imbre de caelo tota illa regio impiae ciuitatis in cinerem uersa est, ubi *stupra in masculos* in tantam consuetudinem conualuerant, quantam leges solent aliorum factorum praebere licentiam.
uerum et hoc eorum supplicium specimen futuri iudicii diuini fuit [emphasis added] (Augustinus Hipponensis, *De Ciuitate Dei,* CC SL, 47; 48 (B. Dombart / A. Kalb, 1955), in *Library of Latin Texts – Series A,*
http://clt.brepolis.net/LLTA/pages/TextSearch.aspx?key=PAUG_0313_).

[79] Augustine, *The City of God,* trans. Marcus Dods, in *Nicene and Post-Nicene Fathers, First Series,* vol. 2, ed. Philip Schaff (Buffalo, NY: Christian Publishing Co., 1887), rev. and ed. Kevin Knight, http://www.newadvent.org/fathers/120116.htm.

[80] nisi forte obliti sumus hoc fuisse in sodomis factum, ubi masculi in masculos nefanda libidine accensi nec ostium domus, in qua erant quos quaerebant, inuenire potuerunt, quando uir iustus in causa omnino simillima pro suis hospitibus mentiri noluit, quos esse angelos nesciebat et uim morte peiorem ne paterentur timebat (Augustinus Hipponensis, *Contra mendacium,* s. 5 p.C, CPL 0304, CSEL, 41 (J. Zycha, 1900), p. 469-528, in *Library of Latin Texts –Series A,*
http://clt.brepolis.net/LLTA/pages/TextSearch.aspx?key=PAUG_0304_).

Against Lying par. 34.[81]

Avicenna (980-1037 AD)

"Also, [those] acts must be prohibited which, even if permitted, would be detrimental to the city's growth—like fornication and sodomy, which dispense with the best foundation on which the city stands: that is, marriage."[82]
The Metaphysics of the Healing, Book X, Chapter 4.4

Anselm of Canterbury (1033-1109 AD)

Eadmer's description of an exchange between William Rufus and Anselm:

[The King asked,] mockingly, "But you, what would you speak about in such a Council?" To this Anselm replied: "That most shameful crime of sodomy, not to speak of illicit marriages between persons of kindred blood…that crime, I say, of sodomy, but lately spread abroad in this land, has already borne fruit all too abundantly and has with its abomination defiled many. If it be not speedily met with sentence of stern judgment coming from you and by rigorous discipline on the part of the Church, the whole land will, I declare, become little better than Sodom itself."[83]

Al-Ghazali (1056-1111 AD)

One of the companions (of the Prophet, *pbuh*) said: "I fear not the wild lion as much as I fear the companx [sic.] of a beardlesss asetic young man." Suhcan (*al-Thawri*) said: "if a man cajoles a young man with two of his toes out of lust, he is a Sodomite." One of the forefathers is quoted saying: "there will be three types of Sodomites in this community (Islamic *ummah*): one that gazes, one who embraces, and one who acts." Should the evil of looking for the beginner be great, however much he tries he will fail to lower his sight and con-

---

[81] Augustine, *To Consentius, Against Lying,* trans. H. Browne, in *Nicene and Post-Nicen Fathers, First Series,* vol. 3, ed. Philip Schaff (Buffalo, NY: Christian Literature Publishing Co., 1887), rev. and ed. Kevin Knight, http://www.newadvent.org/fathers/1313.htm.

[82] Avicenna, *The Metaphysics of the Healing,* Book X, Chapter 4, para. 4, trans. Michael E. Marmura (Provo, Utah: Brigham Young University Press, 2005), 371.

[83] Glenn W. Olsen, "St. Anselm and Homosexuality," *Anselm Studies, Proceedings of the Fifth International Saint Anselm Conference: St. Anselm and St. Augustine-Episcopi Ad Saecula,* vol. II (White Plains, New York: Kraus International Publications, 1988): 114.

trol his thoughts. It is more proper (under such circumstances) for him to curb such a lust with marriage. It is possible that the rage of a certain self cannot be quieted by hunger.[84]

"Curbing the Two Appetites," Chapter VII.

Peter Abelard (1079-1142)

From which it is clear that it implies that the sexual intercourse of the abominable sodomites goes away from the creation of God and the institution of nature, by which they only pollute themselves, not producing the fruit of offspring.[85]

Expositio in Hexameron par. 292.1730.

Exceedingly vile is a whore, but viler yet is a sodomite; worse than a female prostitute is a male one; female intercourse brings forth fruit in childbearing; a sodomite is only defiled when he has sex.[86]

Carmen at Astralabium 221-224.[87]

---

[84] Al-Ghazali, "*Kasr al Shahwatayn* (Curbing the Two Appetites)," in *Ihya"Ulum al-Din (Revivification of the Sciences of Religion)*, trans. Caesar E. Farah (Minneapolis: Bibliotheca Islamica, 1992), Chapter VII,
 http://www.ghazali.org/works/abstin.htm.

[85] Ex quo patenter insinuat quantum a creatione dei et institutione nature+ illa sodomitarum abhominabilis commixtio recedat, qua se ipsos tantum polluunt, nullum de prole fructum reportantes. Dampnantur et ex hoc loco precipue dampnatores nuptiarum, cum primis hominibus creatis ex auctoritate dominica coniugium statim sanctitum sit (Petrus Abaelardus, *Expositio in Hexameron,* par. 292, pag. 66, linea 1730-34, CC CM, 15 (M. Romig, D. Luscombe, 2004), in *Library of Latin Texts – Series   A,*
http://clt.brepolis.net.ezproxy.stthom.edu/LLTA/pages/TextSearch.aspx?key=MAB AEC15A_,
http://clt.brepolis.net.ezproxy.stthom.edu/LLTA/pages/TextSearch.aspx?key=MAB AEC15A_.

[86] Vile nimis scortum sed uilior est sodomita; peior quam meretrix femina uir meretrix. femineus coitus fructum pariendo reportat; polluitur tantum dum sodomita coit (Peter Abelard, *Carmen Ad Astralabium* (Groningen, 1987), p. 119).

[87] Peter Abelard, *Carmen ad Astralabium,* 221-224, trans. Juanita Feros Ruys, in *The Repentant Abelard: Family, Gender, and Ethics in Peter Abelard's Carmen ad Astralabium and Planctus,* (New York: Palgrave MacMillan, 2014), 148.

Averroes (1126-1198 AD)

Therefore all these deeds are deadly and wolf-like: and some of them are done on account of disease and madness which either is because of a disease, as what happens with a man who insanely ate his mother, and of how another ate the liver of his companion. But on account of sicknesses and habits they are so, as the delight of pulling out hair and of biting nails, and of eating charcoal and mud. And concerning the sexual activity of males, indeed this happens in some on account of an evil of birth, but in some on account of habit, as those who have been imprisoned since childhood.[88]

Middle Commentary on the Nicomachean Ethics VII.5.B-C.p.101v.[89]

Moses Maimonides (1135-1204 AD)[90]

Mishneh Torah (Repetition of the Torah), Sefer Kedushah (Holiness) Issurei Biah (forbidden sexual relations):

---

[88] D. Oia igitur hec facta feralia sunt et lupina: et quedam eoru fiunt propter egritudinem et amentiam que aut propter amentiam, ut qd narrat de viro, qui amens factus comedit matrem suam: et de altero, qui comedit hepar socii sui. que vero pp egritudines et assuetudines sunt, ut delectatio ex depilatione capilloru, et precisione unguium, et comestioe carbonu et luti. D. et de istis est concubitus masculoru. etenim hoc accidit quibusda horum ex parte naturae malae, quibusda vero ex parte consuetudinis: ut illis qui consueuerunt incarceratione statim a pueritia (Averrois Cordubensis, *In Moralia Nicomachia Expositione,* in *Tertium Volumen Aristotelis Stagiritae Libri Moralem totam Philosophiam complectentes cum Averrois Cordubensis in Moralia Nicomachia Expositione, Et in Platonis Libros de Republica Paraphrasi* (Venetiis Apud Iunctas, 1562), 101v.). The translation is my own.

[89] As evidence that Averroes agrees with Aristotle, unless he explicitly says otherwise, I cite the following passages: "Avicenna, who followed Aristotle only in dialectics, but in other things he erred and chiefly in the case of metaphysics. This is because he began, as it were, from his own perspective" (Averroes ((Ibn Rushd) of Cordoba, *Long Commentary on the De Anima of Aristotle,* trans. Richard C. Taylor (New Haven & London: Yale University Press, 2009), Book III, n.30, p.374-375). "For I believe this man [Aristotle] was a model in nature and the exemplar which nature found for showing the final human perfection in the material realm" (Averroes ((Ibn Rushd) of Cordoba, *Long Commentary on the De Anima of Aristotle,* Book III, n.14, p. 345). Both passages make it reasonable to assume that Averroes respected and loved Aristotle so much that his commentaries always indicate agreement with him, unless he explicitly says otherwise. Many thanks to Brandon K. White for pointing out these passages.

[90] While the following texts are from a religious context, Maimonides was also a philosopher; I include them insofar as they still indicate his thoughts on the morality of the acts in question.

40

Chapter One, Halacha 4:
The following transgressions are punishable by stoning: one who has relations with his mother, with his father's wife, his son's wife; she is called his daughter-in-law, one who sodomizes a male, a male who has relations with an animal, and a woman who has relations with an animal.[91]

Chapter One, Halacha 14
When a man enters into relations with a male or has a male enter into relations with him, once the corona is inserted [into the anus] they should both be stoned if they are both adults. As [Leviticus 18:22] states: "Do not lie with a man," [holding one liable for the act, whether] he is the active or passive partner.[92]

Chapter Fourteen, Halacha 10
The only sexual relations forbidden to a gentile are: his mother, his father's wife, his maternal sister, a married woman, a male, and an animal, as will be explained in *Hilchot Melachim UMilchomoteihem*. Other relations forbidden the Jews are permitted to them.[93]

Chapter Twenty One, Halacha 8
Lesbian relations are forbidden. This is "the conduct of Egypt" which we were warned against, as [Leviticus 18:3] states: "Do not follow the conduct of Egypt." Our Sages said: What would they do? A man would

---

[91] Moses Maimonides, *Mishneh Torah, Sefer Kedushah, Issurei Biah, Chapter One, Halacha 1*, trans. Eliyahu Touger (Moznaim Publications), accessed September 6, 2015, http://www.chabad.org/library/article_cdo/aid/960647/jewish/Issurei-Biah-Chapter-One.htm.

[92] Moses Maimonides, *Mishneh Torah, Sefer Kedushah, Issurei Biah, Chapter One, Halacha 14*, http://www.chabad.org/library/article_cdo/aid/960647/jewish/Issurei-Biah-Chapter-One.htm.

[93] Moses Maimonides, *Mishneh Torah, Sefer Kedushah, Issurei Biah, Chapter Fourteen, Halacha 10*, trans. Eliyahu Touger (Moznaim Publications), accessed September 6, 2015, http://www.chabad.org/library/article_cdo/aid/960662/jewish/Issurei-Biah-Chapter-Fourteen.htm.

marry a man, a woman would marry a woman, and a woman would marry two men.[94]

Chapter Twenty Two, Halacha 6
We do not entrust an animal, beast, or fowl to a gentile shepherd, not even a male animal to a male shepherd and a female animal to a female shepherd, because they are all suspect to sodomize animals. We have already explained that [gentiles] are forbidden to engage in homosexuality or sodomy. And [Leviticus 19:14] states: "Do not place a stumbling block before the blind."[95]

Albert the Great (ca. 1200-1280 AD)

Sodomy is a sin against nature, males with males, or females with females...If it is asked, which of these things is the worst sin? It must be said that the deformity of all sins is measured by three things, namely grace, reason, and nature. And that which is contrary to grace, reason and nature is the worst, as is the case with sodomy.[96]
Summae Theologiae, Secunda Pars, Q122, M1, A4.

---

[94] Moses Maimonides, *Mishneh Torah, Sefer Kedushah, Issurei Biah, Chapter Twenty One, Halacha 8,* trans. Eliyahu Touger (Moznaim Publications), accessed September 6, 2015, http://www.chabad.org/library/article_cdo/aid/960669/jewish/Issurei-Biah-Chapter-Twenty-One.htm.

[95] Moses Maimonides, *Mishneh Torah, Sefer Kedushah, Issurei Biah, Chapter Twenty Two, Halacha 6,* trans. Eliyahu Touger (Moznaim Publications), accessed September 6, 2015, http://www.chabad.org/library/article_cdo/aid/960670/jewish/Issurei-Biah-Chapter-Twenty-Two.htm.

[96] *Sodomia* est peccatum contra naturam, masculi cum masculo, vel foeminae cum foemina. De quo dicitur, ad Roman. 1, 26 et 27 : *Tradidit illos Deus in passionem ignominiae,* scilicet ut faciant quae non conveniunt. *Nam foeminae eorum mutaverunt naturalem usum, in eum usum qui est contra naturam. Similiter autem et masculi, relicto naturali usu foeminae, exarserunt in desideriis suis in invicem, masculi in masculos turpitudinem operantes, et mercedem quam oportuit erroris sui in semetipsis recipientes.* Si quaeratur, Quod istorum sit majus peccatum? Dicendum, quod deformitas omnium peccatorum mensuratur tribus, scilicet gratia, ratione, et natura. Et illud quod est contra gratiam, rationem et naturam, maximum est, sicut est sodomia (D. Alberti Magni, *Summae Theologiae, Secunda Pars,* Q122, M1, A4 (Parisiis: Ludovicum Vives, Bibliopolam Editorem, 1895), 400-401). The translation is my own.

Certain things are mortal sins; certain things are not mortal, as venial sins. Some of the mortal ones are against grace, as fornication; some of the mortal ones are against grace and reason, as perjury. Now, some of the mortal ones are against grace and against reason and against nature, as sodomy.[97]
Commentary on the Sentences, Lib. IV, dist. 14, *Expositio Textus.*

"Whether lust is against the natural law?"
Solution: We say that in us there is a twofold nature: one, which we share with the beasts, and this does not require determinate matter, except due sex. Hence, lust universally is not against this nature. But any species of lust is thus said to be against nature insofar as it is distinguished, that a certain sin is against grace alone, such as infidelity; but a certain one against grace and reason, such as adultery; but a certain one against grace, reason and nature, such as sodomy.[98]
Quaestio de Luxuria, A3, *Solutio.*[99]

Roger Bacon (ca. 1214/20-1292 AD)

In the first place, the preservation of the human speices is considered in the line of propagation with a view to bind the people by laws in their increase. Therefore legislators give the laws of marriage and determine how they must be made and how obstacles may be removed; and especially do they decree

---

[97] Quaedam enim est culpa mortalis, quaedam non mortalis, ut veniale peccatum. Quaedam mortalis, contra gratiam, ut fornicatio : quaedam mortalis et contra gratiam et contra rationem, ut perjurium : quedam autem mortalis et contra gratiam et contra rationem et contra naturam, ut sodomia (D. Alberti Magni, *Commentarii in IV Sententiarum* (Dist. I-XXII), vol. 29, ed. Borgnet (Parisiis apud Ludovicum Vives, Bibliopolam Editorem, 1894), 453b. The English translation is my own.

[98] Solutio: Dicimus, quod in nobis est duplex natura: una, in qua communicamus cum brutis, et haec non requirit determinatam materiam nisi debitum sexum. Unde luxuria universaliter non est contra naturam istam. Sed aliqua species luxuriae sic dicitur contra naturam, sicut distinguitur, quod quoddam peccatum est contra gratiam solum, ut infidelitas; quoddam vero contra gratiam et rationem, ut adulterium; quoddam vero contra gratiam, rationem et naturam, ut sodomia (Sancti Doctoris Ecclesiae Alberti Magni Ordinis Fratrum Praedictorum Episcopi, *Quaestio de Luxuria,* in *Opera Omnia,* vol. XXV, part II, *Quaestiones* (Monasterii Westfalorum in Aedibus Aschendorff, 1993), 151).

[99] An additional text where Albert discusses the issue is in his *Commentary on Luke 17:29:* (D. Alberti Magni, Ratisbonensis Episcopi, Ordinis Praedicatorum, *Ennarationes in Secundam Partem Lucae (X-XXIV),* in *Opera Omnia,* vol. 23, ed. Borgnet, (Parisiis apud Ludovicum Vives, Biblipolam Editorem, 1895), p. 487-488).

that fornicators and sodomites be excluded from states, who are inimical to the fabric of the state, since they draw men away from that which is a better thing in states, namely, marriage, as Avicenna and others maintain.[100]

Opus Major, Moral Philosophy: Second Part, Chapter 1: Concerning the observance of the laws of marriage and of the state.[101]

Bonaventure (ca. 1217-1274 AD)[102]

And so the text continues: *He rained down fire and sulfur from heaven and destroyed them all,* that is the Lord, through the severity of avenging justice. Genesis 19:24-25 states: "Therefore, the Lord rained down upon Sodom and Gomorrah brimstone and fire from the Lord out of heaven."…For it is directly against the Incarnate Word and the nature that the Son of God made heavenly, angelic, and divine and makes that nature more vile than brute nature, subverting the laws of nature which the brute animals observe. And therefore, this sin is punished not only by *fire,* but also by *sulfur* because of the burning fire and stench of most inordinate lust. Romans 1:27 says this of *the burning fire:* "They burned in their lusts towards one another, men with men doing shameless things." Isaiah 34:3 speaks of *the stench*: "From their carcasses a stench will rise. The mountains will be melted with their blood."[103]

---

[100] Secunda pars descendit ad leges et statua hominum inter se. Et consideratur primo salus humane speciei secundum lineam generationis pro populo multiplicando legibus ligaturo. Et ideo dantur leges coniungii; et statuunt quomodo habet fieri et qualiter impedimenta amoveantur, et precipue quod a civitatibus excludantur fornicatores et sodomite, qui "inducunt contrarium constructioni civitatis", quoniam "retrahunt homines ab eo, quod melius est in civitatibus, scilicent coniugio", ut Avicenna et alii volunt (Roger Bacon, *Rogeri Baconis Moralis Philosophia,* ed. Ferdinand Delorme and Eugenio Massa (Turici, 1953), Pars Secunda, 1.1, p. 39).

[101] Roger Bacon, *The Upus Major of Roger Bacon,* vol. II, trans. Robert Belle Burke (Philadelphia: University of Pennsylvania Press, 1928), 660.

[102] While the following texts are from a religious context, Bonaventure was still a philosopher.

[103] Et ideo addit: *Pluit ignem et sulpur de caelo et omnes perdidit,* scilicet Dominus, per severitatem iustitiae ulciscentis; Genesis decimo nono : "Igiture pluit Dominus super Sodomam et Gomorrham sulphur et ignem de caelo a Domino…"…quia directre est contra Verbum incarnatum et naturam, quam Filius Dei fecit caelestem, angelicam et divinam, facit viliorem, quam sit natura brutalis, subvertendo naturae leges, quas bruta animalia servant. Et ideo non tantum *igne,* sed etiam *sulphure* punitur hoc vitium propter inordinatissimae libidinis incendium et foetorem. De *incendio,* ad Romanos primo : "Exarserunt in concupiscentiis suis in invicem, masculi in masculos turpitudinem operantes;" de *foetore,* Isaiae trigesimo quarto: "De cadaveribus eorum ascendet foetor, tabescent montes a sanguine eorum" etc. (Doctoris

Commentary on the Gospel of St. Luke 17:29.[104]

Thomas Aquinas (ca. 1225-1274 AD)

To the second, it must be said that by human nature one may mean either that which is proper to man and in this way all sins inasmuch as they are contrary to reason are contrary to nature, as Damascene makes clear in Book II. Or we may mean that which is common to man and the other animals, and in this way certain special sins are said to be against nature, as against the sexual union of male and female, which is natural to all animals, is the copulation of males, which specifically is called a vice against nature.[105]
ST I-II, Q94, A3, ad 2

Now, something can be considered to be contrary to human nature in two ways. In one way, "contrary to nature" of the difference constitutive of man, which is rational; and thus every sin is said to be contrary to the nature of man inasmuch as it is contrary to right reason…In another way something is said to be contrary to the nature of man by notion of his genus, which is animal. Now, it is manifest that according to the intention of nature, the sexual union of the sexes in animals is ordered to the act of generation. Hence, the mode of every sexual union from which generation cannot follow, is contrary to the nature of man inasmuch as he is an animal.[106]

Seraphici S. Bonaventurae S.R.E. Episcopi Cardinalis, *Commentarius In Evangelium S. Lucae,* Chapter 17, v.29, in *Opera Omnia,* vol. VII, ed. Collegii A S. Bonaventura (Ad Claras Aquas (Quaracchi) Prope Florentiam, Ex Typographia Collegii S. Bonaventurae, 1895), p. 442-443.)

[104] English translation is taken from: St. Bonaventure, *St. Bonaventure's Commentary on the Gospel of Luke Chapters 17-24,* Chapter Seventeen, n.50 (verse 29), trans. Robert J. Karris, O.F.M., Th.D. (Saint Bonaventure, NY: Franciscan Institute Publications, 2004), p.1681-1682.

[105] Ad secundum dicendum quod natura hominis potest dici vel illa quae est propria homini: et secundum hoc, omnia peccata, inquantum sunt contra rationem, sunt etiam contra naturam, ut patet per Damascenum in II Libro. Vel illa quae est communis homini et aliis animalibus: et secundum hoc, quaedam specialia peccata dicuntur esse contra naturam; sicut contra commixtionem maris et feminae, quae est naturalis omnibus animalibus, est concubitus masculorum, quod specialiter dicitur vitium contra naturam. The English translation is my own.

[106] Est autem considerandum quod dupliciter est aliquid contra naturam hominis. Uno modo contra naturam differentiae constitutivae hominis, quae est rationale; et sic omne peccatum dicitur esse contra naturam hominis, inquantum est contra rationem rectam. Unde et Damascenus dicit in II lib. quod angelus peccans versus est ex

Commentary on Romans 1:26-27, Lecture 8, n.149.

Meister Eckhart (1260-1328 AD)
Chapter Nineteen
Now, the sin, which is, mentioned here, namely sodomy, lacks a twofold order, namely by which activity is ordered to generation and pleasure ordered to work, according to the nature of this it is the worst. How even more so it recedes from and is opposed to generation, which is the very "work of nature," according to Damascene, and whose terminus is being, so much that it even more recedes from the good, which is convertible with being, and consequently it is worse.[107]

Book on the Stories of Genesis, Chapter 19.

Walter Burley (ca. 1275-1344 AD)
In the first part [Aristotle] posits a division of pleasures, which are pleasures according to nature and those that are contrary to nature, and he subdivides each of the members...

[Where Aristotle says,] "or from custom," he gives examples of those pleasurable things which happen contrary to nature from custom; he says some from custom pleasure in plucking out hairs or in chewing fingernails or eating coals or earth, *or pleasure in coitus with males.*[108] Concerning these it must be understood that the bestial may be taken in two ways: in a broad sense...thus

---

eo quod est secundum naturam in id quod est praeter naturam. Alio modo dicitur esse aliquid contra naturam hominis ratione generis, quod est animal. Manifestum est autem quod, secundum naturae intentionem, commixtio sexuum in animalibus ordinatur ad actum generationis, unde omnis commixtionis modus, ex quo generatio sequi non potest, est contra naturam hominis inquantum est animal (S. Thomae Aquinatis, Super Epistolas S. Pauli Lectura, Super Rom. Cap. 1, Lectio 8, n.149, ed. P. Raphaelis Cai, O.P., VIII Revisa ed., vol. I (Taurini, Romae: Marietti, 1953), p. 28).

[107] Capitulum Undevicesimum. Peccatum autem, de quo hic mentio, sodomiae scilicet, caret duplici ordine, quo scilicet operatio ordinatur ad generationem et delectatio ordinatur ad opus, propter quod secundum ipsius naturam pessimum est. Quanto enim magis recedit et opponitur generationi, quae est ipsum 'opus naturae,' secundum Damascenum, et cuius terminus est esse, tanto magis recedit bono, quod cum ente convertitur, et consequentur peius est. (Meister Eckhart, *Liber parabolarum Genesis, Capitulum Undevicesimum,* in *Die Deutschen und lateinischen Werke,* vol. 1, (Stuttgart-Berlin: Verlag von W. Kohlhammer, Juli 1938), 655-656.) The English translation is my own.

[108] Emphasis added.

the bestial may be taken in the first chapter of this book where it is said that all the bestial is contrary to heroic virtue. In another way, it may be taken strictly, thus it only extends to an inclining habit to something pleasurable contrary to nature from a perverse complexion or thus it is distinguished against other inclining delightful habits to something contrary to nature on account of sicknesses or customs.[109]
Exposition on the Ten Books of Aristotle's Ethics, Book VII, Chapter 5.

Nicholas of Cusa (1401-1464 AD)

Ruminate over your mortal sins, inasmuch as they displease God: inasmuch as pride so expelled Lucifer from heaven, inasmuch as gluttony and disobedience Adam from paradise, inasmuch as lust destroyed Sodom and Gomorrah![110]
Sermon V: "Do Not Fear," On the Feast Day of John the Baptist, 29.16-21.

Francisco de Vitoria (ca. 1480-1546 AD)

In the following texts, Francisco de Vitoria argues against the Spanish treatment of the natives; he argues that even if the natives had commit-

---

[109] In prima point unam divisionem delectationis que est in delectationem secundum naturam, vel in delectationem contra naturam, vel subdividit utrumquae membrum…[vel ex consuetudine.] exemplificat de his que contra naturam fiunt delectabilia ex consuetudine dicens omnia quidam ex consuetudine delectant evuellere sibi pilos vel corrodere ungues vel comedere carbones vel terram, vel quidam delectantur in coitu masculorum. C intelligendum est h. omnia bestialitas accipitur dupliciter: uno modo large?pto? omni habitu faciente delectationem contra naturam, sive ille habitus insit ex perversitate nature fine ex egritudine sive ex consuetudine: vel sic accipitur bestialitas primo capitulo huius libri ubi dicitur omnia bestialitas contrariat virtuti heroice. Alio modo acciptur stricte vel sic solum se extendit ad habitum inclinantes ad aliquod delectabile contra naturas ex perversitate complexioinis vel sic distinguitur contra alios habitus inclinantes delectabiliter ad aliquod contra naturam propter egritudines aut consuetudines (Burlaeus, Gualterus, *Expositio Gualteri Burlei super decem Libros Ethicorum Aristotelis,* bk. VII, ch. 5 (Venetiis: Arte Simonis de Luere, 1500), p.111rb-112va, http://hdl.handle.net/2027/uc1.31158010821410).

[110] Rumina in te peccata mortalia, quantum Deo displiceant: quantum superbia, ut luciferum e caelo expelleret, quantum gula et inoboedientia, ut Adam de paradiso, quantum luxuria, ut Sodomam et Gomorrham subverteret! (Sermo V, 29, lines 16-21, p.89, http://www.cusanus-portal.de/content/werke.php?id=Sermo_V_29). The English translation is my own. Although this text is a religious text, insofar as Nicholas of Cusa was a philosopher it still indicates his views on the morality of homosexual activity.

ted sins against nature (such as homosexual acts), such actions still wouldn't justify making war upon them. Although de Vitoria isn't commenting directly on the morality of homosexual actions, he adopts the traditional language of calling them "sins against nature," indicating his moral disapproval.

Another, and a fifth, title is seriously put forward, namely, the sins of these Indian aborigines. For it is alleged that, though their unbelief or their rejection of the Christian faith is not a good reason for making war on them, yet they may be attacked for other mortal sins which (so it is said) they have in numbers, and those very heinous. A distinction is here drawn with regard to mortal sins, it being asserted that there are some sins, which are not against the law of nature, but only against positive divine law, and for these the aborigines can not be attacked in war, while *there are other sins against nature, such as* cannibalism, and promiscuous intercourse with mother or sisters and *with males*, and for these they can be attacked in war and so compelled to desist therefrom. The principle in each case is that, in the case of sins which are against positive law, it can not be clearly shown to the Indians that they are doing wrong, whereas *in the case of the sins which are against the law of nature, it can be shown to them that they are offending God*, and they may consequently be prevented from continuing to offend Him. Further they can be compelled to keep the law which they themselves profess. Now, this law is the law of nature....16. *I, however, assert the following proposition: Christian princes can not, even by the authorization of the Pope, restrain the Indians from sins against the law of nature or punish them because of those sins*....Let this suffice about false and inadequate titles to seize the lands of the Indians.[111]

---

[111] Alius titulus praetenditur serio, et est Titulus Quintus, scilicet, *peccata ipsorum barbarorum.* Dicunt enim quod licet non possint bello infestari ratione infidelitatis suae aut quia non recipient fidem Christianam, possunt tamen bello peti propter alia peccata mortalia, quae multa habent et ipsa gravissima, ut ajunt.

Circa peccata autem mortalia distingunt. Dicunt enim quod sunt aliqua peccata, quae non sunt contra legem naturae, sed solum contra legem divinam positivam ; et pro his barbari non possunt infestari bello.

Alia autem sunt contra naturam, ut esus carnis humanae, concubitus indifferens cum matre, sororibus et cum masculis ; et pro his possunt infestari bello et cogi ut ab his desistant. Et ratio utriusque est ; quia circa alia peccata quae sunt contra legem positivam, non potest eis ostendi evidenter, quod male faciant ; circa alia autem quae sunt contra legem naturae, potest eis ostendi quod offendunt Deum ; et per consequens possunt coerceri ne offendant eum amplius.

De Indis Relectio Prior, The First Relectio, On the Indians Lately Discovered, Second section, n.16.[112]

Fourth Conclusion: "Christian princes cannot wage war on the infidels by reason of their crimes against nature any more than on account of other crimes which are not contrary to nature, namely on account of sodomy more than on account of fornication."

The first is proven above, since just as fornication and theft are contrary to natural right, neither is it held that whence the princes are more defenders of the natural law than of the divine positive law. Further, they are equally obligated not to steal as not to sleep with the male. Further, some crimes are graver than any sin against nature, such as homicide. Why then on account of sin against nature can they vanquish the infidel, and not on account of other sins? And nevertheless, it is evident that homicide is evil.[113]

Praeterea possunt cogi ut servent legem, quam ipsi profitentur ; ea autem est lex naturae ; ergo. Haec est opinio Archiepis. Florent. (33. part. tit. 22. cap. 5. S. 8.) port August. de Anch. Idem Svlvest. in verb. *Papa. S. Septimo ;* et est opinion Innocene. in cap. *Quod super his* (De Voto) ubi expresse dicit : *Credo quod si Gentiles, qui non habent nisi legem naturae, contra legem naturae faciant, poterunt per Papam puniri. Et arguitur* Genes. 19, *ubi Sodomitas puniti sunt a Deo. Cum autem Dei judicia sint nobis exemplaria, non video quare Papa, qui est Vicarius Christi, hoc non possit.* Haec Innocen. Et eadem ratione poterunt authoritate Papae puniri a Principibus Christianis.

16. Sed pono conclusionem: *Principes Christiani, etiam authoritate Papae, non possunt coercere barbaros a peccatis contra legem naturae, nec ratione illorum eos punier.*...Haec de falsis et non idoneis titulis occupandi provincias barbarorum sufficiant (Maestro Fray Francisco de Vitoria, *Primera Relección De Los Indios, De los títulos ilegítimos de conquista,* in *Relecciones Teológicas,* vol. II, ed. Luis G. Getino (Madrid: Imprenta La Rafa, 1934), 15.30-16.30, p. 346-353).

[112] English translation is from: Franciscus de Victoria, *De Indis et de Iure Belli Relectiones Being Parts of Relectiones Theologicae XII,* trans. John Pawley Bate, ed. Ernest Nys (Oceana Publications),
 http://www.constitution.org/victoria/victoria_4.htm. Emphasis added.

[113] Quarta Conclusio: *Principes christiani non possunt inferre bellum infidelibus ratione delictorum contra naturam plus quam propter alia delicta quae non sunt contra naturam, puta propter peccatum sodomiae plus quam propter peccatum fornicationis.* Probatur primo ut supra, quia ita fornicatio et furtum est contra ius naturale, nec habetur unde principes magis sint defensores iuris naturalis quam divini positivi. Item illi aequaliter obligantur non furari et non cubare cum masculo. Item aliqua delicta sunt graviora quam aliquod peccatum contra naturam, ut homicidium. Quare ergo propter peccatum contra naturam possunt infideles debellari, et non propter alia peccata? Et tamen est evidens quod est malum homicidium (Francisco

On Temperance.

Giordano Bruno (1548-1600 AD)

During his interrogation before the inquisition, philosopher Giordano Bruno indirectly revealed his thoughts about same-sex sexual activity by alluding to them in the phrase "sin against nature."

[Inquisitor:] What in your opinion constitutes the sin of the flesh outside of the sacrament of marriage?

[Bruno:] As for that, I have sometimes spoken of it, saying that the sin of the flesh, speaking in general, is the lesser sin than the others, and in species the sin of adultery is the greater sin of those of the flesh, except[114] the sin against nature; and I made it that the sin of simple fornication is so slight that it was close to a venial sin. This, yes, I have sometimes said; and I know and recognize this error, because I remember what Paul says, that fornicators cannot possess the kingdom of God.[115]

[And later on in the same round of questioning, Bruno added:]

…I have said the truth about all the matters that were asked of me and that I remembered…And likewise I maintain that I have said what is just and true, and that I shall say it in the future; and I confess that I shall never be convinced by another belief.[116]

---

de Vitoria, *Relectio de temperantia, Quarta Conclusio,* in *Obras de Francisco de Vitoria* (Madrid: Biblioteca de Autores Cristianos, 1960), p. 1050).

[114] The Italian word here is *levato.* Arthur D. Imerti also translates it as *except* given the context: cf. Giordano Bruno, *The Expulsion of the Triumphant Beast,* trans. & ed. Arthur D. Imerti (New Brunswick, NJ: Rutgers University Press, 1964), 57.

[115] "In^tus che opinione ha esso constituto del peccato della carne fuori del sacramento del matrimonio?

R^dit: Quanto a questo io ne ho parlato qualche volta, dicendo che il peccato della carne, parlando in genere, era il minor peccato delli altri, ed in spezie il peccato dell'adulterio era il maggior peccato delli altri della carne, levato il peccato contra natura ; ed ho fatto che il peccato della semplice fornicazione sia tanto leggiero che fosse vicino al peccato veniale. Questo sí che ho detto qualche volta ; e so e conosco de aver detto errore, perché mi riccordo che san Paulo dice, quod fornicarii non possidebunt regnum Dei. Tueday, June 2nd, 1592." (Vincenzo Spampanato, ed., *Vita di Giordano Bruno: con documenti editi e inediti,* vol. 2, *Documenti veneti, XII* (Messina: G. Principato, 1921), Tueday, June 2nd, 1592, p. 725.) The English translation is my own.

[116] Ho detto la verità in tutte le cose mi sono state dimandate e che mi sono riccordato…e cosí protesto de aver detto il giusto e vero, e de dirlo per l'avenir, e confido di non esser mai convinto in altro (Vincenzo Spampanato, ed., *Vita di*

Questioning before the Inquisition, Tuesday, June 2nd, 1592.[117]

Francisco Suarez (1548-1617 AD)[118]
6. *First the conclusion of faith. –It is handed on by the Council of Trent. — First it is proved. —Second. —Third.*—Therefore, I say first: any mortal sin, that is, is so grave that from it man turns away from God as from his ultimate end, it cuts off grace from any man…This is asserted of the faith; the Council of Trent hands it on, in session 6, chapter 15, saying…and likewise defines it in canon 27, and for the proof of this truth, it brings in first that 1 Corinthians 6: "Do you not know that the wicked will not possess the kingdom of God? Be not willing to go astray: neither fornicators, nor servants of idols, nor adulterers, nor the effeminate, nor those sleeping with males, nor those-speaking-evil, nor the greedy, will possess the kingdom of God."[119]
On the Permanence of Grace, or its Loss, Chapter III, n. 6.

Giordano Bruno, Documenti veneti, XII, p. 728). The translation for this passage is from *The Expulsion of the Triumphant Beast,* trans. & ed. Arthur D. Imerti, 59.
[117] As further evidence that Giordano Bruno was telling the truth here it must be noted that he was later burned at the stake for refusing to recant some of his beliefs (cf. *The Expulsion of the Triumphant Beast,* trans. & ed. Arthur D. Imerti, p. 63-65). If Bruno spoke his mind even to the point of death, then we should take Bruno at his word here: he held that sins against nature were evil and worse than adultery.
[118] Although the following quote is from a religious text, I have included it insofar as Suarez was a philosopher and it indicates his thoughts on the matter in question.
[119] Caput III. Utrum Gratia, Et Virtutes Ac Dona, Quae Illam Comitantur, Per Quodlibet Peccatum Mortale, Et Per Solum Illud Amittantur? 6. *Conclusio prima de fide. -Traditur a Concilio Tridentino. —Probatur primo. — Secundo.—Tertio.—* Dico ergo primo : quodlibet peccatum mortale, id est, ita grave ut ex se hominem a Deo ut ultimo fine avertat, excludit gratiam a quocumque homine, qui toto tempore, priusquam tale peccatum committeret, vel (ut aiunt) immediate ante instans in quo peccat, erat justus, sive ille homo sit praedestinatus, sive non sit, et sive sit baptizatus baptismo aquae, sive tantum flaminis. Haece assertio est de fide ; tradit illam Concilium Tridentium, sess. 6, cap. 15, dicens…Idemque definit canon. 27, et ad probandum veritatem hanc, inducit primo illud, 1 Corinth. 6 : *Nescitis quia iniqui regnum Dei non possidebunt? Nolite errare : neque fornicarii, neque idolis servientes, neque adulteri, neque molles, neque masculorum concubitores, neque maledici, neque rapaces, regnum Dei possidebunt* (R.P. Francisci Suarez, *Tractatus de Gratia Dei, Lib. XI De Perpetuitate Gratiae, Vel Amissione, Caput III,* in *Opera Omnia,* vol. 9 (Parisiis: Ludovicum Vivès, 1858), 644-645).

Francis Bacon[120] (1561-1626 AD)

In his book The New Atlantis, Bacon discusses his vision of the ideal commonwealth. It is told through a fictional account of his travels in the south Pacific. The expedition he is with runs out of food and supplies, but luckily happens upon an island. The island is the civilization of Bensalem. It is a paradise symbolizing Bacon's ideal commonwealth. Bacon asks about the island's customs concerning marriage. In the process the governor of the island makes some comments about the islanders' (and thus Bacon's) views on homosexual practices:

And because propagation of families proceedeth from the nuptial copulation, I [Bacon] desired to know of him what laws and customs they had concerning marriage…

To this he [the governor of the House of Strangers] said, "You have reason for to commend that excellent institution of the Feast of the Family. And indeed we have experience that those families that are partakers of the blessing of that feast do flourish and prosper ever after in an extraordinary manner. But hear me now, and I will tell you what I know. You shall understand that there is not under the heavens so chaste a nation as this of Bensalem; nor so free from all pollution or foulness….For there is nothing amongst mortal men more fair and admirable, than the chaste minds of this people. Know therefore, that with them there are no stews, no dissolute houses, no courtesans, nor anything of that kind. Nay they wonder (with detestation) at you in Europe, which permit such things. They say ye have put marriage out of office: for marriage is ordained a remedy for unlawful concupiscence; and natural concupiscence seemeth as a spar to marriage. But when men have at hand a remedy more agreeable to their corrupt will, marriage is almost expulsed. And therefore there are with you seen infinite men that marry not, but chose rather a libertine and impure single life, than to be yoked in marriage; and many that do marry, marry late, when the prime and strength of their years is past. And when they do marry, what is marriage to them but a

---

[120] Though Bacon was in his liftetime accused of sodomy (cf. Lisa Jardine and Alan Stewart, *Hostage to Fortune: The Troubled Life of Francis Bacon* (New York: Hill and Wang, 1999), 464-466), it is disputed among scholars whether or not these charges are true. Charges of sodomy were a way to discredit high-ranking officials at the time. Even if these charges were true in Bacon's case, the quoted text from *The New Atlantis* makes his position clear on the matter. It is possible though that in his personal life Bacon was just inconsistent or incontinent with his beliefs on the matter.

very bargain….The haunting of those dissolute places, or resort to courtesans, are no more punished in married men than in bachelors. And the depraved custom of change, and the delight in meretricious embracements, (where sin is turned into art,) maketh marriage a dull thing, and a kind of imposition or tax. They hear you defend these things, as done to avoid greater evils; as advoutries, deflowering of virgins, *unnatural lust*, and the like. But they say this is a preposterous wisdom; and they call it Lot's offer, who to save his guests from abusing, offered his daughters: nay they say farther that there is little gained in this; for that the same vices and appetites do still remain and abound; unlawful lust being like a furnace, that if you stop the flames altogether, it will quench; but if you give it any vent, it will rage" [emphasis added].
The New Atlantis.[121]

Thomas Hobbes (1588-1679 AD)

Concerning multitude, it is the duty of them that are in sovereign authority, to increase the people, in as much as they are governors of mankind under God Almighty, who having created but one man, and one woman, declared that it was his will they should be multiplied and increased afterwards. And seeing this is to be done by ordinances concerning copulation: they are by the law of nature bound to make such ordinances concerning the same, as may tend to the increase of mankind. And hence it cometh, that in them who have sovereign authority: *not to forbid such copulations as are against the use of nature*; not to forbid the promiscuous use of women; not to forbid one woman to have many husbands; not to forbid marriages within certain degrees of kindred and affinity: *are against the law of nature.* For though it be not evident, that a private man living under the law of natural reason only, doth break the same, by doing any of these things aforesaid; *yet it is manifestly apparent, that being so prejudicial as they are to the improvement of mankind, that not to forbid the same, is against the law of natural reason,* in him that hath taken into his hands any portion of mankind to improve.
The Elements of Law Natural and Politic, Part II, *De Corpore Politico,* Chapter 28, Of the Duty of Them that have Sovereign Power, n. 1-3.[122]

---

[121] Sir Francis Bacon, *The New Atlantis,* ed. Michael and William Fishburne (1627), http://www.gutenberg.org/files/2434/2434-h/2434-h.htm.

[122] Thomas Hobbes, *The Elements of Law, Human Nature and De Corpore Politico,* ed. Gaskin (Oxford/New York: Oxford University Press, 2008), 172-173; emphasis added.

[The Gentiles have] made holy; as Caverns, Groves, Woods, Mountains, and whole Lands; and have attributed to them, not onely the shapes, some of Men, some of Beasts, some of Monsters; but also…besides, Anger, Revenge, and other passions of living creatures, and the actions proceeding from them, as Fraud, Theft, Adultery, Sodomie, and any vice that may be taken for an effect of Power, or a cause of Pleasure; and all such Vices, as amongst men are taken to be against Law, rather than against Honour.
Leviathan, Part I, Of Man, Chapter XII, Of Religion [55-56], l. 12-23.[123]

John Locke (1632-1704 AD)

59. Be it then as Sir R*obert* says, that *Anciently,* it was *usual* for Men to *sell and Castrate their Children,* O. 155 [231]. Let it be, that they exposed them; Add to it, if you please, for this is still greater Power, that they begat them for their Tables to fat and eat them: If this proves a right to do so, we may, by the same Argument, justifie Adultery, Incest and Sodomy, for there are examples of these too, both Ancient and Modern; Sins, which I suppose, have their Principal Aggravation from this, that they cross the main intention of Nature, which willeth the increase of Mankind, and the continuation of the Species in the highest perfection, and the distinction of Families, with the Security of the Marriage Bed, as necessary thereunto.
First Treatise on Government, Ch. VI Of Adam's Title to Sovereignty by Fatherhood, section 59.[124]

Gottfried Wilhelm Leibniz (1646-1716 AD)

From here, the nefarious crime of sodomy and in public polygamy is contempt for the womanly sex.[125]
Consilium Aegyptiacum, 13.[126]

---

[123] Thomas Hobbes, *Leviathan,* ed. Noel Malcolm, vol. 2 The English and Latin Texts (Oxford: Clarendon Press, 2012), 174. The Leviathan was originally a work in English. It later had a Latin printing. In this regard, it is interesting to note that in the later Latin edition the words "Sodomie," "or a cause of Pleasure" are omitted.

[124] John Locke, *Two Treatises of Government: In the Former, The False Principles and Foundation of Sir Robert Filmer, and His Followers are Detected and Overthrown. The Latter is an Essay concerning the True Original, Extent, and End of Civil-Government,* in *Two Treatises of Government,* ed. Peter Laslett (New York: Cambridge University Press, 2013), 183.

[125] Hinc nefandum sodomiae crimen et in media polygamia contemptus sexus muliebris. The translation is my own.

54

Montesquieu (1689-1755 AD)

Please god that I may not diminish the horror that one has for a crime that religion, morality, and policy condemn in turn…It is singular that among ourselves three crimes, magic, heresy, and the crime against nature, of which it can be proved that the first does not exist, that the second is susceptible to infinite distinctions, interpretations and limitations, and that the third is often hidden, were all three punished by the penalty of burning.

I shall assert that the crime against nature will not make much progress in society unless the people are also inclined to it by some custom, as among the Greeks, where the young people performed all their exercises naked, as among ourselves where education at home is no longer the usage, as among the Asians where some individuals have a large number of wives whom they scorn while others can have none. Do not clear the way for this crime, let it be proscribed by an exact police.[127]

The Spirit of Laws, Book XII, Chapter 6, "On the crime against nature."[128]

---

[126] Leibniz, *Consilium Aegyptiacum,* in *Leibnitii De Expeditione Aegyptiaca Ludovico XIV Franciae Regi Proponenda Scripta Quae Supersunt Omnia Adjecta Praefatione Historico-Critica,* ed. Onno Klopp (Hanoverae, 1864), 190.

[127] A Dieu ne plaise que je veuille diminuer l'horreur que l'on a pour un crime que la religion, la morale et la politique condamnent tour à tour…Il est singulier que, parmi nous, trois crimes: la magie, l'hérésie et le crime contre nature, dont on pourrait prouver, du premier, qu'il n'existe pas; du second, qu'il est susceptible d'une infinité de distinctions, interprétations, limitations; du troisième, qu'il est très souvent obscur, aient été tous trois punis de la peine du feu.

Je dirai bien que le crime contre nature ne fera jamais dans une société de grands progrès, si le people ne s'y trouve porté d'ailleurs par quelque coutume, comme chez les Grecs, où les jeunes gens faisaient tous leurs exercices nus; comme chez nous, où l'éducation domestique est hors d'usage; comme chez les Asiatiques, où des particuliers ont un grand nombre de femmes qu'ils méprisent, tandis que les autres n'en peuvent avoir. Que l'on ne prépare point ce crime, qu'on le proscrive par une police exacte (Montesquieu, *De l'Esprit des lois,* vol. I, Livre XII, Chaptire VI "Du Crime Contre Nature," (Rue des Saints-Pères, Paris: Éditions Garnier Frères 6, 1961), 202-203).

[128] Montesquieu, *The Spirit of the Laws* trans. and eds. Anne M. Cohler, Basia Carolyn Miller, and Harold Samuel Stone (Cambridge: Cambridge University Press, 1989), 193-194.

Voltaire (1694-1778 AD)

How did it come about that a vice which would destroy mankind if it were general, that a sordid outrage against nature, is still so natural?...When the young males of our species, brought together, feel the force which nature begins to unfold in them, and fail to find the natural object of their instinct, they fall back on what resembles it. Often, for two or three years, a young man resembles a beautiful girl, with the freshness of his complexion, the brilliance of his coloring, and the sweetness of his eyes; if he is loved, it's because nature makes a mistake; homage is paid to the fair sex by attachment to one who owns its beauties, and when the years have made this resemblance disappear, the mistake ends...It is well known that this mistake of nature is much more common in mild climates than in the icy north, because the blood is more inflame there and opportunity more frequent: also, what seems only a weakness in young Alcibiades is a disgusting abomination in a Dutch sailor or a Muscovite sutler.[129]

Philosophical Dictionary, s.v. "So-Called Socratic Love."[130]

The emperors Constantin II & Constance his brother, are the first ones who brought the death penalty against this depravity, which dishonors human nature (code, liv. 9, tit. 9.). The new [constitution] 141 of Justinian is the first imperial rescript in which we have the use of the word *sodomie.* This expression was only known long after the Greek and Latin translations of Jewish

---

[129] Comment s'est-il pu faire qu'un vice, destructeur du genre humain, s'il était général, qu'un attentat infâme contre la nature, soit pourtant si naturel?...Les jeunes mâles de notre espèce, élevés ensemble, sentant cette force que la nature commence à déployer en eux, et ne trouvant point l'objet naturel de leur instinct, se rejettent sur ce qui lui ressemble. Souvent un jeune garçon, par la fraicheur de son teint, par l'éclat de ses couleurs et par la douceur de ses yeux, ressemble pendant deux ou trois ans à une belle fille ; si on l'aime, c'est parce que la nature se méprend : on rend hommage au sexe, en s'attachant à ce qui en a les beautés, et, quand l'âge a fait évanouir cette resemblance, la méprise cesse...On sait assez que cette méprise de la nature est beaucoup plus commune dans les climats doux que dans les glaces du septentrion, parce que le sang y est plus allumé, et l'occasion plus fréquente : aussi, ce qui ne paraît qu'une faiblesse dans le jeune Alcibiade est une abomination dégoûtante dans un matelot hollandaise et dans un vivandier moscovite (Voltaire, *Dictionnaire philosophique,* s.v. "Amour Nommé Socratique" (Garnier Press, 1967), 18-19).

[130] Voltaire, *Philosophical Dictionary,* trans. Peter Gay, s.v. *"Amour Nommé Socratique/So-Called Socratic Love,"* (New York: Harcourt, Brace & World, Inc., 1962), 76-77.

books. The depravity was previously designated specifically by the term *pedixatio* taken from Greek…This despicable vice of man is not known to us in the harsh climates. There was not at all a law in France for its investigation and for its punishment. One can imagine finding one in the institutions of Saint Louis. "If anyone is suspected of *bulgarie*, secular justice must take him, and send him to the bishop; and if it is proven, he must be burned, and all his personal property goes over to the baron."[131] The word *bulgarie*, which only signifies heresy was taken as the sin against nature. And it is on this text that the burning alive of the few wretches convicted of this filth was established, more made to be buried in the darkness of oblivion than to be illuminated by the flames of the pyres in the eyes of the multitude.

The miserable ex-Jesuit also as vile by his doorstep against so many honest people as by the public crime of his debauchery…was, however, only condemned to secret flogging in the prison from the beggars of Bissetre. One has already noticed that the punishments are often arbitrary and that they should not be; that it is the law and not the man who ought to punish.

The punishment imposed to this man was sufficient, but it could not be the usefulness that we desire, since not being public it was not exemplary.[132]

---

[131] This passage from the law is very difficult old French, but luckily a translation of the full law can be found in *The Etablissements de Saint Louis: Thirteententh-Century Law Texts from Tours, Orléans, and Pairs,* trans. F.R.P. Akehurst, The Laws of St. Louis, The Customs of Touraine and Anjou (University of Pennsylvania Press, 1996), p. 59: "90. On punishing heretics and unbelievers. If someone is suspected of heresy [*bougrerie*], the judge should arrest him and send him to the bishop; and if he is convicted, he should be burned; and all his personal property goes to the baron. And this is how heretics [*herite*] should be dealt with, provided their case is proved; and all their personal property goes to the baron <or to the prince. And it is written in the *Decretals,* as the title 'On the meaning of words,' in the chapter Super quibusdam. And customary law is in agreement."
This passage can be found on Google Books:
https://books.google.com/books?id=209BCgAAQBAJ&pg=PR21&dq=The+Etablis sments+de+Saint+Louis&hl=en&sa=X&ved=0ahUKEwiL4_KchbLMAhVrv4MK HWnbBvIQ6AEIIDAA#v=snippet&q=unbelievers&f=false.
[132] Article XIX, *De la Sodomie:* "Les empereurs Constantin II & Constance son frère, sont les premiers qui aient porté peine de mort contre cetter turpitude qui deshonore la nature humaine (code, liv. 9. tit. 9.) La novelle 141. De Justinien est le premiere rescript impérial dans lequel on ait employé le mot *sodomie.* Cette expression ne fut connu que longtems après les traductions grecques, & latines des livres juifs. La turpitude quelled ésigne était auparavant spécifiée par le terme *pedixatio* tiré du grec.

The Price of Justice and Humanity, Article XIX *On Sodomy.*[133]

David Hume (1711-1776 AD)

A very small variation of the object, even where the same qualities are preserved, will destroy a sentiment. Thus, the same beauty, transferred to a dif-

---

L'empereur Justinien dans sa novelle ne decerne aucune peine. Il se borne à inspirer l'horreur que mérite une telle infamie. Il ne faut pas croire que ce vice devenu trop commun dans la ville des Fabricius, des Catons & des Scipions, n'eut pas été réprimé par les loix. Il le fut par la loi Scantinia qui chassait les coupables de Rome, & leur sefait payer une amende. Mais cette loi fut bientôt oubilée, surtout quand César vainqueur de Rome corrompue plaça la débauche sur la chaire du dictateur, & quand Adrien la divinisa.

Constantin second & Constance étant consuls ensemble, furent donc les premiers qui s'armèrent contre le vice trop honoré par César. Leur loi *Si vir nubit,* ne spécifie pas la peine ; mais elle dit, que la justice doit s'armer de glaive ; *Jubemus armari jure gladio ultore* ; & qu'il faut des suplices recherchés : *exquisitis poenis.* Il paraît qu'on fut toujours plus sévère contre les corrupteurs des enfants, que contre les enfants mêmes ; & on devait l'être.

Loríque ces délits aussi secrets que l'adultère, & aussi difficiles à prouver, sont portés aux tribunaux qu'ils scandalisent, loríque ces tribunaux sont obliges d'en connaître, ne doivent-ils pas soigneusement distinguer entre l'homme fait, & l'âge innocent qui est entre l'enfance & la jeunesse?

Ce vice indigne de l'homme n'est pas connu dans nos rudes climats. Il n'y eut point de loi en France pour sa recherche & pour son châtiment. On s'imagina en trouver une dans les établissements de Saint Louis. *Si aucan est soupçonneux de bulgarie, justice laïc li doit prendre, & l'enveyer à l'évêque; & se il en est prouvé, l'en doit ardoir, & tui li meuble sont au baron.* Le mot *bulgarie,* qui ne signifie qu'heresie fut pris pour le péché contre nature. Et c'est sur ce texte qu'on s'est fondé pour brûler vifs le peu de malheureux convaincus de cette ordure, plus faite pour être ensevelie dans les ténèbres de l'oubli, que pour être éclairée par les flammes des buchers aux yeux de la multitude.

Le miserable ex-jésuite aussi infâme par ses seuilles contre tant d'honnêtes gens, que par le crime public d'avoir débauché dans Paris jusqu'à des ramoneurs de cheminée, ne fut pourtant condamné qu'à la sustigation secrete dans la prison des gueux de Bissetre. On a déja remarqué que les peines sont souvent arbitraires, & qu'elles ne devraient pas l'être; que c'est la loi, & non pas l'homme qui doit punir.

La peine impose à cet homme était suffisante; mais elle ne pouvait être de l'utilité que nous désirons, parce que n'étant pas publique elle n'était pas exemplaire."

[133] Voltaire, *Prix de la Justice et de L'humanité,* Article XIX, *De la Sodomie* (*A Géneve*: 1778), 76-79. The translation is largely my own. Many thanks to Brandon K. White for his assistance in understanding the word *bulgarie,* and especially to Dr. Oliva for assistance with the more difficult translations in this passage.

ferent sex, excites no amorous passion, where nature is not extremely perverted.[134]

An Enquiry Concerning the Principles of Morals, Section 5 Why Utililty Pleases, Part I, footnote 17.

Immanuel Kant (1724-1804 AD)

Sexual union (commercium sexuale) is the reciprocal use that one human being makes of the sexual organs and capacities of another (*usus membrorum et facultatum sexualium alterius*). This is either a *natural* use (by which procreation of a being of the same kind is possible) or an *unnatural* use, and unnatural use takes place either with a person of the same sex or with an animal of a nonhuman species. Since such transgressions of laws, called unnatural (*crimina carnis contra naturam*) or also unmentionable vices, do wrong to humanity in our own person, there are no limitations or exceptions whatsoever that can save them from being repudiated completely.[135]

The Metaphysics of Morals, The Doctrine of Right, Part I: Private Right, Section III: On Rights to Persons Akin to Rights to Things, On the Right of Domestic Society, Title 1: Marriage Right.[136]

Just as love of life is destined by nature to preserve the person, so sexual love is destined by it to preserve the species; in other words, each of these is a *natural end,* by which is understood that connection of a cause with an effect in which, although no understanding is ascribed to the cause, it is still thought by

---

[134] David Hume, *An Enquiry Concerning the Principles of Morals, A Critical Edition* ed. Tom L. Beauchamp (Oxford: Clarendon Press/Oxford University Press, 2010), Section 5, Part I, footnote 17, p. 34.

[135] Geschlechtsgemeinschaft (commercium sexuale) ist der wechselseitige Gebrauch, den ein Mensch von eines anderen Geschlechtsorganen und Bermögen macht (usus membrorum et facultatum sexualium alterius), und entweder ein natürlicher (modurch seines Gleichen erzeugt werden kann), oder unnatürlicher Gebrauch und dieser entweder an einer Person ebendesselben Geschlechts, oder einem Thiere von einer anderen als der Menschen-Gattung; welche Übertretungen der Geseße, unnatürliche Laster (crimina carnis contra naturam), die auch unnennbar heißen, als Lästion der Menschheit in unferer eigenen Person durch gar seine Ginschränfungen und Ausnahmen wider die gänzliche Berwersung gerettet werden können (Immanuel Kant, *Die Metaphysik der Sitten,* in *Kant's Werke,* Band VI (Berlin: Königlich Preukishen Akademie der Wissenschaften, Druck und Verlag von Georg Reimer, 1907), 277).

[136] Immanuel Kant, *The Metaphysics of Morals*, trans. Mary Gregor (Cambridge, New York, Melbourne: Cambridge University Press, 1996), 61-62.

analogy with an intelligent cause, and so as if it produced human beings on purpose. What is now in question is whether a person's use of his sexual capacity is subject to a limiting law of duty with regard to the person himself or whether he is authorized to direct the use of his sexual attributes to mere animal pleasure, without having in view the preservation of the species...

But it is not so easy to produce a rational proof that unnatural, and even merely unpurposive, use of one's sexual attribute is inadmissible as being a violation of duty to oneself (and indeed, as far as its unnatural use is concerned, a violation in the highest degree). – The *ground of proof* is, indeed, that by it man surrenders his personality (throwing it away), since he uses himself merely as a means to satisfy an animal impulse.[137]
The Metaphysics of Morals, The Doctrine of Virtue, Doctrine of the Elements of Ethics, Part I: On Duties to Oneself as Such, Book I: Perfect Duties to Oneself, Chapter 1: A Human Being's Duty to Himself as an Animal Being, Article II: On Defiling Oneself by Lust.[138]

The *crimina carnis* are contrary to self-regarding duty, because they run counter to the ends of humanity. A *crimen carnis* is a misuse of the sexual impulse. Every use of it outside the state of wedlock is a misuse of it, or *crimen carnis.* All *crimina carnis* are either *secundum,* or *contra, naturam.* The former are contrary to sound reason; the latter, to our animal na-

---

[137] So wie die Liebe zum Leben von der Natur zur Erhaltung der Person, so ist die Liebe zum Geschlecht von ihr zur Erhaltung der Art bestimmt; d. i. eine jede von beiden ist Naturzwed, unter welchem man diejenige Berfnüpfung der Urfache mit einer Mirfung versteht, in welcher jene, auch ohne ihr dazu einen Berstand beizulegen, diese doch nach der Analogie mit einem solchen, also gleichsam absichtlich Menschen hervorbringend gedacht wird. Es trägt sich nun, ob der Gebrauch des leßteren Bermögens in Anfehung der Person selbst, die es ausübt, unter einem einschränfenden Pflichtgeseß stehe, oder ob diese, auch ohne jenen Zwed zu beabsichtigen, den Gebrauch ihrer Geschlechtseigenshaften der bloßen thierischen Lust zu widmen befugt sei, ohne damit einer Pflicht gegen sich selbst zuwider zu handeln...Der Bernunstbeweis aber der Unzulässigseit jenes unnatürlich und selbst auch des blos unzwectmäßigen Gebrauchs seiner Geschlechtseigenschaften als Berleßung (und zwar, was den ersteren betrifft, im höchsten Grade) der Pflicht gegen sich selbst ist nicht so leicht geführt. - Der Beweisgrund liegt freilich darin, daß der Mensch seine Persönlichseit dadurch (wegwerfend) aufgiebt, indem er sich blos zum Mittel der Befriedigung thierischer Triebe braucht (Immanuel Kant, *Die Metaphysik der Sitten,* in *Kant's Werke,* Band VI (Berlin: Königlich Preukishen Akademie der Wissenschaften, Druck und Verlag von Georg Reimer, 1907), 424-425).
[138] Immanuel Kant, *The Metaphysics of Morals*, trans. Mary Gregor (Cambridge, New York, Melbourne: Cambridge University Press, 1996), 178-179.

ture....*Crimina carnis contra naturam* involve a use of the sexual impulse that is contrary to natural instinct and to animal nature...

Second among the *crimina carnis contra naturam* is intercourse *sexus homogenii,* where the object of sexual inclination continues, indeed, to be human, but is changed since the sexual congress is not heterogeneous but homogeneous, i.e., when a woman satisfies her impulse on a woman, or a man on a man. This also runs counter to the ends of humanity, for the end of humanity in regard to this impulse is to preserve the species without forfeiture of the person; but by this practice I by no means preserve the species, which can still be done through a *crimen carnis contra naturam,* only that there I again forfeit my person, and so degrade myself below the beasts, and dishonor humanity.

The third *crimen carnis contra naturam* is when the object of sexual inclination continues to be of the opposite sex, indeed, but is other than human. This includes sodomy, for example, the intercourse with animals. It also runs counter to the ends of humanity, and is contrary to natural instinct; by this I degrade humanity below the animal level, for no animal turns away from its own species. All *crimina carnis contra naturam* debase the human condition below that of an animal, and make man unworthy of his humanity; he then no longer deserves to be a person, and such conduct is the most ignoble and degraded that a man can engage in, with regard to the duties he has towards himself. Suicide is certainly the most dreadful thing that a man can do to himself, but is not so base and ignoble as these *crimina carnis contra naturam* which are the most contemptible acts a man can commit.
Georg Ludwig Collins, *From the Lectures of Professor Kant Königsberg, Winter Semester, 1784-5, On Morality,* 1. Of Duties to Oneself, Of *Crimina Carnis.*[139]

Possibly Neutral on Homosexual Activity:
Adam Smith (1723-1790 AD)
The following words from Adam Smith are hearsay, from what Alexander Dalrymple records of a private conversation he had with Smith. Adam Smith never wrote anything on the topic of sodomy and the thoughts of Dalrymple on Smith have not been corroborated by anyone else. Dalrymple was an opponent of Smith on the deregulation of the corn

---

[139] Immanuel Kant, *Lectures on Ethics,* ed. Peter Heath and J.B. Schneewind, trans. Peter Heath (Cambridge: Cambridge University Press, 1997), 160-162.

trade.[140] *So whether what is recorded below about Smith is true depends upon how honest Dalrymple was on this matter.*

A man of much more respectable talents, *Adam Smith,* had treated *Forestalling* as an imaginary evil! Adam Smith, whom I knew well,[141] was a man of much investigation, knowledge, and sagacity; with a heart overflowing with benevolence and sociability; but he was strongly influenced with *French Philosophy* and *sysitme!* To mention two circumstances, in which I cannot be *mistaken,* because spoken to myself, and, although contradictory to the sentiments I had expressed not spoken in publick, where men often sport opinions for argument, but in the familiarity of individual conversation, where the unreserved sentiments are spoken. There were, "That the Christian Religion *debased* the *human mind;*" and that "*Sodomy* was a thing in itself *indifferent.*" The considerate part of mankind will think that the opinions of such a man, or of any man, are not to be admitted as *infallible dogmas*; but to be fairly weighed, before they are adopted.
Alexander Dalrymple, *Thoughts of an Old Man, of Independent Mind, Though Dependent Fortune, on the Present High Price of Corn.*[142]

Against Homosexual Activity:
Edmund Burke (1729-1797 AD)
Dear Sir,

In consequence, I suppose, of what I said in the house a few days ago, I received the Letter which I have the honour of enclosing to you. These Wretches [who attempted to commit homosexual acts and were condemned to

---

[140] E.P. Thompson, *Customs in Common: Studies in Traditional Popular Culture* (New York: New Press, 1993), 201; see also John Gascoigne, *Science in the Service of Empire: Joseph Banks, the British State and the Uses of Science in the Age of Revolution* (Cambridge, UK: Cambridge University Press, 1998), 89.

[141] Dalrymple did indeed know Adam Smith well. Smith thought Dalrymple was a good man, and Ian Ross's biography of Smith describes Dalrymple in laudatory terms. So there is good reason to believe Dalyrmple is being honest here. This is also the opinion of Samuel Fleischacker (personal email dated November 12, 2015), author of the Stanford entry on Adam Smith's moral and political philosophy.

[142] Alexander Dalrymple, *Thoughts of an Old Man, of Independent Mind, Though Dependent Fortune, on the Present High Price of Corn* (London: Bunney and Gold, Shoe-lane, 1800), 4.

the pillory][143] desire in my opinion a thing which, I will not say in humanity; but I really think in Justice, cannot be denied to them; that their punishment should be nothing more than it is the intention of the Law to measure out to them…But as one part of the <Sen>tence seems enough in conscience for the Offence, might it not be as well that the other should be remitted.
"*To* Alexander Wedderburn-[16 *April* 1780]."[144]

Approving Homosexual Activity:
Marquis de Sade (1740-1814 AD)

[Dolmancé:] In a word, I personally go by the following principle: If nature actually prohibited the bliss of sodomy, incest, masturbation, etcetera, would nature make them all so pleasurable? Nature cannot possibly tolerate things that truly outrage it.[145]
Philosophy in the Boudoir, Third Dialogue.[146]

Approving Homosexual Activity:
Jeremy Bentham (1748-1832 AD)

---

[143] The note by the editor indicates that the context is that two persons were condemned to the pillory for attempting to commit homosexual acts. One of them died as a result of the brutality of the mob. Burke thought the pillory was excessive punishment and so sought to have this sort of punishment abolished (cf. *The Correspondence of Edmund Burke,* vol. IV, 230). Also, Richard Norton does well in documenting the case of these two men accused of attempting homosexual acts as published in the newspapers of early April 1780: Rictor Norton (Ed.), Burke Proposes Abolition of the Pillory, 1780, *Homosexuality in Eighteenth-Century England: A Sourcebook,* 23 February 2007, updated 25 November 2014 <http://rictornorton.co.uk/eighteen/1780burk.htm>.

[144] Burke, "*To* Alexander Wedderburn-[16 *April* 1780]", in *The Correspondence of Edmund Burke,* vol. IV, ed. John A. Woods (Cambridge/Chicago: Cambridge University Press/The University of Chicago Press, 1963), 230-231.

[145] En un mot, sur toutes ces choses, je pars, moi, toujours d'un principe : si la nature défendait les jouissances sodomites, les jouissances incestueuses, les pollutions, etc., permettrait-elle que nous y trouvassions autant de plaisir? Il est impossible qu'elle puisse tolérer ce qui l'outrage véritablement (Marquis de Sade, *La Philosophie dans le boudoir,* vol. I (London: 1795), https://fr.wikisource.org/wiki/La_Philosophie_dans_le_boudoir/Tome_I/Troisième_Dialogue).

[146] Marquis de Sade, *Philosophy in the Boudoir,* trans. Joachim Neugroschel (New York: Penguin, 2006), 50.

Note: the following texts are from the first systematic treatise in the history of philosophy arguing in favor of homosexual practices and their decriminalization. The length of the treatise prevents my quoting it in full, but the full-text can be found online here:

> *http://www.columbia.edu/cu/lweb/eresources/exhibitions/sw25/bentham/index.html#36*

I have selected key passages from it indicating Bentham's thoughts about the morality of homosexual practices, as well his thoughts on bestiality:

To what class of offences shall we refer these irregularities of the venereal appetite which are stiled unnatural? When hidden from the public eye there could be no colour for placing them any where else: could they find a place any where it would be here. I have been tormenting myself for years to find if possible a sufficient ground for treating them with the severity with which they are treated at this time of day by all European nations: but upon the principle [of] utility I can find none.

Offences of impurity--their varietys

The abominations that come under this heading have this property in common, in this respect, that they consist in procuring certain sensations by means of an improper object. The impropriety then may consist either in making use of an object

1. Of the proper species but at an improper time: for instance, after death.
2. Of an object of the proper species and sex, and at a proper time, but in an improper part.
3. Of an object of the proper species but the wrong sex. This is distinguished from the rest by the name of paederasty. p.390
4. Of a wrong species.
5. In procuring this sensation by one's self without the help of any other sensitive object.

Paederasty makes the greatest figure

The third being that which makes the most figure in the world it will be proper to give that the principal share of our attention. In settling the nature and tendency of this offence we shall for the most part have settled the nature and tendency of all the other offences that come under this disgusting catalogue.

...Among the antients--whether it excluded not the regular taste[147]

A circumstance that contributes considerably to the alarms entertained by some people on this score is the common prejudice which supposes that the one propensity is exclusive of the other. This notion is for the most part founded on prejudice as may be seen in the works of a multitude of antient authors in which we continually see the same person at one time stepping aside in pursuit of this eccentric kind of pleasure but at other times diverting his inclination to the proper object....Let us be unjust to no man: not even to a paederast. In all antiquity there is not a single instance of an author nor scarce an explicit account of any other man who was addicted exclusively to this taste. Even in modern times the real womenhaters are to be found not so much among paederasts, as among monks and catholic priests, such of them, be they more or fewer, who think and act in consistency with their profession.

...Whether worse between men and women than between men

Thus far his business goes on smoothly: he may hang or burn the parties according as he fancies without difficulty. But he will probably be a little at a loss when he comes to enquire with the Jesuit Sanchez (De Matrimonio) how the case stands when the man for example, having to do with a woman, begins in one part and consummates in another; thinks of one person or of one part while he is employing himself with another; begins with a woman and leaves her in the lurch. Without calling in the principle of utility such questions may be multiplied and remain undecided for evermore; consult the principle of utility, and such questions never will be started.

Bestiality

An abomination which meets with as little quarter as any of the preceding is that where a human creature makes use in this way of a beast or other sensitive creature of a different species. A legislator who should take Sanchez for his guide might here repeat the same string of distinctions about the vas proprium and improprium, the imaginations and the simultaneity and so forth. Accidents of this sort will sometimes happen; for distress will force a man upon strange expedients. But one might venture to affirm that if all the sovereigns in Europe were to join in issuing proclamations inviting their subjects to this exercise in the warmest terms, it would never get to such a heighth as to be productive of the smallest degree of political mischief. The more of these sorts of prosecutions are permitted the more scope there is given for malice or extortion to make use of them to effect its purpose upon the innocent, and the

---

[147] Original spelling of *antients* has been retained.

more public they are the more of that mischief is incurred which consists in shocking the imaginations of persons of delicacy with a very painful sentiment.

Burning the animal

Some persons have been for burning the poor animal with great ceremony under the notion of burning the remembrance of the affair. (See Puffendorf, Bks. 2, Ch. 3, 5. 3. Bacon's Abridg. Title Sodomy. J.B.) A more simple and as it should seem a more effectual course to take would be not to meddle or make smoke [?] about the matter.
Offences Against One's Self: Paederasty [Unpublished].[148]

The following is from the notes Bentham wrote related to this essay; these quotes below were not incorporated into the actual text of the essay:

How came scratching not to be held abominable?
It is wonderful that nobody has ever yet fancied it to be sinful to scratch where it itches, and that it has never been determined that the only natural way of scratching is with such or such a finger and that it is unnatural to scratch with any other. (As in Russia the only way of making the sign of the cross is with two fingers and it is heterodox to make it with three. J.B.) in antient Persia it was infamous to have a cold and to take those measures which nature dictates for relieving oneself from the inconvenience of such an indisposition. (Xenophon, cyropaedia. J.B.)
Notes Relative to Bentham's Essay on Paederasty.[149]

The mode being by supposition the sexual, but without so much as potential prolifickness, parties between whom the gratification is shared may be either male and male or female and female.

---

[148] Jeremy Bentham, *Offences Against One's Self: Paederasty*, Unpublished MS, accessed November 13, 2015,
http://www.columbia.edu/cu/lweb/eresources/exhibitions/sw25/bentham/index.html
.

[149] Jeremy Bentham, *Offences Against One's Self: Paederasty, Notes Relative to Bentham's Essay on Paederasty*, Unpublished MS, accessed November 13, 2015, http://www.columbia.edu/cu/lweb/eresources/exhibitions/sw25/bentham/index.html.

For the sake of clearness, first suppose it between male and male: it finds, then, in the language a word by which it is distinguished: it is termed *paederasty*...In the respect of any ulterior effects with relation to the parties or party concerned, paederasty and bestiality seem to stand upon the same ground. Mischief to health from excess being supposed absent, both seem equally innoxious.

...Sexual intercourse between the opposite sexes without the sanction of marriage is productive of mischief and danger in a variety of shapes from which the like intercourse between two persons of the same sex, be it male or female, is free.

1. On the part of the female, loss of reputation, loss of the place she occupied in society—a mischief, when not actual, always probable.
2. For prevention of this loss, in case of pregnancy, measures taken for procuring abortion, and on failure of those measures, infanticide.

Of any of the known measures that can be employed to procure abortion, danger more or less considerable to health is an attendant consequence: and lest this danger should not be sufficiently severe, legislators, with their usual barbarity, have stept in and converted this measure of security into a crime.

The same barbarity has stept in to aggravate the still heavier sufferings of the female in the case of infanticide. For the being which is endued with afflictive sensibility, and that in the most exquisite degree, they have no sympathy: of their stock of that article, the whole is carefully reserved for the being which itself has none. The physical image being in both cases the same, and they blind to the pathological effects, they confound this case with that of murder committed on an adult.

Sextus, Chapter 12: Beneficial tendencies of certain of these modes.[150]

Against Homosexual Activity:
Johann Gottlieb Fichte (1762-1814 AD)

When a woman surrenders herself to a man from love, the morally necessary result is marriage.

Firstly, on the part of the woman. By giving herself, she gives herself *wholly,* with all that is hers, with her strength, her will, and, in short, with her whole empirical Ego ; moreover, she gives herself *for ever....* Secondly, on the

---

[150] Jeremy Bentham, *Sextus, Chapter 12,* in *Of Sexual Irregularities, and Other Writings on Sexual Morality*, ed. Philip Schofield, Catherine Pease-Watkin, and Michael Quinn (Oxford, UK: Clarendon Press, 2014), 97-99.

part of the man. The whole moral character of woman rests upon the above conditions. Now no man has a right to demand the sacrifice of a human character. The man can therefore accept the submission of the woman only on these conditions, on which alone woman can make the surrender; for otherwise man would treat woman not as a moral being, but as a mere thing...

From these premises it appears that *the satisfaction of the sexual impulse is permitted only in marriage, in the stated significance of the word.*[151] *The Science of Ethics as Based on the Science of Knowledge,* Part II, Book V, Concerning Particular Duties.[152]

Such a union as we have described is called a *marriage.* Marriage is a *complete union* of two persons of both sexes, based upon the sexual impulse, and having its end in itself.[153] *The Science of Rights,* First Appendix to the Science of Rights: Fundamental Principles of the Rights of Family, Corollaria, n. 2.[154]

Karl Wilhelm Friedrich Schleiermacher (1768-1834 AD)

Satisfaction of the sexual function within the same sex is unnatural from the physical point of view alone and so cannot be enobled by the addition of any ethical element.[155]

---

[151] Ergiebt sich das Weib aus Liebe einem Manne, so entsteht dadurch moralisch nothwendig eine *Ehe.*

Zuvörderst von des Weibes Seite. Dadurch, dass sie sich giebt, giebt sie sich ganz, mit allem ihrem Vermögen, ihren Kräften, ihrem Willen, kurz, ihrem empirischen Ich; und sie giebt sich auf *ewig*....Es geht diesen Sätzen hervor, dass die Befriedigung des Geschlechtstriebes nur in der Ehe (in dem angezeigten Sinne des Wortes) erlaubt... (Johann Gottlieb Fichte, *System der Sittenlehre nach den Principien der Wissenschaftslehre, 1798,* in *sämmtliche Werke,* vol. IV (Berlin: Verlag von Veit und Comp., 1845), 330-331).

[152] Johann Gottlieb Fichte, *The Science of Ethics as Based on the Science of Knowledge,* trans. A.E. Kroeger, ed. W.T. Harris (London: Kegan Paul, Trench, Trübner & Co., Ltd., 1897), 344-345. Emphasis added.

[153] Eine Verbindung, wie die beschriebene, heisst heisst *eine Ehe.* Die Ehe ist eine durch den Geschlechtstrieb begründete *vollkommene Vereinigung* zweier Personen beiderlei Geschlechts, die ihr eigener Zweck ist (Johann Gottlieb Fichte, *Grundlage des Naturrechts nach Principien der Wissenschaftslehre, 1796,* in *sämmtliche Werke,* vol. III (Berlin: Verlag von Veit und Comp., 1845), 315).

[154] J.G. Fichte, *The Science of Rights,* trans. A.E. Kroeger (Philadelphia: J.B. Lippincott & Col, 1869), 405-406.

Lectures on Philosophical Ethics, Ethics 1812/13: Introduction and doctrine of goods, The highest good, Part III On perfect ethical forms, On the sexes, and the family, n.25.[156]

Arthur Schopenhauer (1788-1860 AD)

Note: In the third edition to The World as Will and Representation, Schopenhauer added a section on pederasty. Although in the passage quoted below he clearly condemns man-boy sexual relations, his comments throughout also indicate that he also includes in his condemnations of pederasty any sort of man-man sexual activity. Schopenhauer wrote the following text because a problem troubled him: how is it that this vice appears so universally (albeit hidden) across history and cultures and yet it is so unnatural? How can the unnatural be so universal? The solution, he says, is that nature permits this vice so as to avoid the greater evil of deformed offspring. If such people were to procreate they would produce deformed offspring and so nature allows them to fall into this horrific monstrous vice:

Considered in itself, pederasty[157] appears to be a monstrosity, not merely contrary to nature, but in the highest degree repulsive and abominable; it seems an act to which only a thoroughly perverse, distorted, and degenerate nature could at any time descend, and which would be repeated in quite isolated cases at most. But if we turn to experience, we find the opposite; we see this vice fully in vogue and frequently practiced at all times and in all countries of the

---

[155] Die Befriedigung der Geschlechtsfunction innerhalb deselben Geschlechts ist unnatürlich schon innerhalb der physischen Seite selbst und kann also durch nichts dazukommendes Ethisches veredelt werden (Friedrich Daniel Ernst Schleiermacher, *Ethik (1812/13),* ed. Hans-Joachim Birkner (Hamburg: Felix Meiner Verlag, 1981), 84).

[156] Friedrich Schleiermacher, *Schleiermacher: Lectures on Philosophical Ethics,* trans. Louise Adey Huish, ed. Robert B. Louden (Cambridge, U.K.: Cambridge University Press, 2002), 64.

[157] It must be noted that Schopenhauer here is using the term *pederasty* to encompass not just man-boy sexual relations, but also man-man sexual relations. This should be evident from the example he gives of Alcibiades who was a man when he tried to seduce Socrates, and also that the proscriptions Schopenhauer seems to be alluding to in the Old and New Testament refer to homosexual activity more generically. Thus, though his sense of the term *pederasty* certainly encompasses man-on-boy-relations it also certainly encompasses man-on-man.

world, in spite of its detestable nature.…All the authors of antiquity give more than abundant proof of this.…In the *Symposium,* Plato even mentions to the credit of Socrates, as an unexampled act of heroism, that he scorned Alcibiades who offered himself to him for this purpose.…Now that something so thoroughly contrary to nature, indeed going against nature in a matter of greatest importance and concern to her, should arise from nature herself is such an unheard-of paradox, that its explanation confronts us as a difficult problem. However, I shall now solve it…

The result of this discussion is that, whereas the vice we are considering appears to work directly against the aims and ends of nature, and that in a matter directly against the aims and ends of nature, and that in a matter that is all-important and of the greatest concern to her, it must in fact serve these very aims, although only indirectly, as a means for preventing greater evils.…Thus she has in view the important object of preventing miserable and wretched offspring which might gradually deprave the whole species; and, as we have seen, she has no scruples in the choice of means. The spirit in which she goes to work here is the same as that in which she urges wasps to sting their young to death, as mentioned above in chapter 27. For in both cases she resorts to what is bad in order to avoid what is worse.[158]

---

[158] Un sich selbst betrachtet nämlich stellt die Päderastie sich dar als eine nicht bloß widernatürliche, sondern auch im höchsten Grade widerwärtige und Abicheu erregende Monstrosität, eine Handlung, auf welche allein eine völlig perverse, veridyrobene und entartete Menichennatur irgend ein Mal hätte gerathen fönnen, und die sich höchstens in ganz vereinzelten Fällen wiederholt hätte. Wenden wir nun aber uns an die Erfahrung; sofinden wir das Gegentheil hievon: wir sehen nämlich dieses Laster, troß seiner Abicheulichfeit, zu allen Zeiten und in allen Ländern der Welt, völlig Gdwange und in häufiger Ausübung…Hievon zeugen alle alten Gchriftsteller, mehr als zur Genüge. Zumal sind die Dichter sammt und sonders voll dadon: nicht ein Mal der seurche ßirgil ist auszunehmen (Ecl. 2). Gogar den Dichtern der Urzeit, dem Orpheus (den deshalb die Mänaden zerrissen) und dem Thamnris, ja, den Göttern selbst, wird es angedichtet. Ebenfalls reden die ßhilosophen viel mehr von dieser, als von der Weiberliebe: besonders scheint ßlato fast seine andere zu sennen, und eben so die Gtoifer, welche sie als des Weisen würdig erwähnen (Stob. ecl. eth., L. II, c. 7). Gogar dem Gofrates rühmt ßlato, im Gnmposion, es als eine beispiellose heldenthat nach, daß er den, sich ihm dazu anbierenden Alsibiades verichmäht habe… Auch den Hebräern war dies Laster nicht unbesannt; da Altes und Neues Testament desselben als strasbar erwähnen. Im Christlichen Europa endlich hat Religion, Gefesgebung und offentliche Meinung ihm mit aller Macht entgegenarbeiten müssen: im Mittelalter stand überall Lodestrafe darauf, in Franfreich noch im 16. Jahrhundert der Feuertod, und in England wurde noch während des ers-

The World as Will and Representation, 3rd edition, Appendix to the Preceding Chapter [Ch. XLIV, The Metaphysics of Sexual Love].[159]

Auguste Comte (1798-1857 AD)

It would suffice, if necessary, to recall on this matter, *those vile loves*, so justly condemned by Catholicism, and which have always been the moral shame of all of antiquity, even among its more eminent personages, because one cannot conceive a more pronounced sign of little consideration granted to women than this monstrous partiality that otherwise sought the development of the more pure friendly emotions, in essentially reserving the sexual union for its indispensable physical purpose, as it has been systematically exposed with such revolting naivety in Greece and Rome, that so many illustrious philosophers and men of the State, in all other respects very commendable. *The*

---

ten Drittels dieses Jahrhunderts die Lodestrafe dafür unnachläßlich vollzogen; jeßt ist es Deportation auf Lebenszeit…

Das nun aber etwas so von Grund aus Naturwidriges, ja, der Natur gerade in ihrem wichtigsten und angelegensten Zwed Entgegentretendes aus der Natur selbst hervorgehen sollte, ist ein so unerhörtes Paradoxon, daß dessen Erflarung sich als ein schweres Problem darstellt, welches ich jedoch jest…

Aus dieser Darstellung ergiebt sich, daß, wahren das in Betracht genommene Laster den Zweden der Natur, und zwar im Allerwichtigsten und ihr Angelegensten, gerade entgegenzuarbeiten scheint, es in Wahrheit eben diesen Zweden, wiewohl nur mittelbar, dienen muß, als Abwendungsmittel größeret Uebel. Es ist nämlich ein Bhänomen der absterbenden und dann wieder der unveifen Zeugungstraft, welche der Species Gefahr proben: und wiewohl sie alle Beide aus moralischen Grunden pauūren sollten; so war hierauf doch nicht zu rechnen; da überhaupt die Natur das eigentlich Moralische bei ihrem Treibeu nicht tu Anfchlag bringt. Demnach griff die, in Folge ihrer eigenen Gefeße, in die Enge getriebene Natur, mittelst Bertehrung des Instinsts, zu einem Nothbehelf, einem Stratagem, ja, man möchte sagen, ste bauete sich eine Gfelsbrüde, um, wie, oben dargelegt, von zweien Uebeln dem größsern zu entgehen. Sie hat nämlich den wichtigen Zwed im Auge, unglücflichen Zeugungen vorzubeugen, welche allmälig die ganze Species depraviren sönnten, und da ist sie, wie wir gesehen haben, nicht strupulös in der Wahl der Mittel. Der Geist, in welchem sie hier verfährt, ist der selbe, in welchem sie, wie oben, Kapitel 27, angeführt, die Wespen antreibt, ihre Jungen zu erstechen: denn in beiden Fällen greist fte zum Schlimmen, um Schlimmerem zu entgehen: ste führt den Geschlechtstrieb irre, um seine verderblichsten Folgen zu vereiteln (Arthur Schopenhauer, *Die Welt als Wille und Vorstellung, Dritte, verbesserte und beträchtlich vermehrte Auflage, Zweiter Band* (Leipzig: Brodhaus, 1859), 642-644, 647-648).

[159] Arthur Schopenhauer, *The World as Will and Representation*, 3rd ed., vol. II (Indian Hills, CO: Falcon's Wing Press, 1958), 561-562, 566.

close correlation of this great primitive aberration with the habitually too iso-lated life of the male sex among hunters or even pastoral peoples, and then, despite the agricultural state, among nations constantly at war, is also so ob-vious as to require no explanation, when one thinks about the happy influence the almost continual company of both sexes has in this regard in our modern life [emphasis added].[160]
Physique sociale, Cinquante-Troisième Leçon, 300-301.[161]

William James (1842-1910 AD)

The fondness of the ancients and of modern Orientals for forms of unnatural vice, of which the notion affects us with horror, is probably a mere case of the way in which this instinct may be inhibited by habit. We can hardly suppose that the ancients had by gift of Nature a propensity of which we are devoid, and were all victims of what is now a pathological aberration limited to indi-viduals. It is more probable that with them the instinct of physical aversion toward a certain class of objects was inhibited early in life by *habits,* formed under the influence of *example;* and that then a kind of sexual appetite, of which very likely most men possess the germinal possibility, developed itself in an unrestricted way.
The Principles of Psychology, vol. II, Chapter XXIV: Instinct, Love.[162]

---

[160] Il suffirait, au besoin, de rappeler à ce sujet, ces amours infâmes, si justement réprouvées par le catholicisme, et qui ont toujours fait la honte morale de l'antiquité tout entière, même chez ses plus éminents personnages: car on ne saurait concevoir un symptôme plus prononcé du peu de considération alors accordée aux femmes que cette monstrueuse prédilection qui faisait chercher ailleurs le développement des plus pures émotions sympathiques, en réservant essentiellement l'union sexuelle pour son indispensable destination physique, comme l'ont systématiquement expo-sé, avec une si révoltante naïvete, dans Grèce et à Rome, tant d'illustres philosophes et hommes d'Etat, à tous autres égards très recommandables. L'intime corrélation de cette grande aberration primitive avec la vie habituellement trop isolée du sexe mâle chez les peuples chasseurs ou même pasteurs, et ensuite, malgré l'état agricole, chez les nations constamment en guerre, est d'ailleurs trop évidente pour exiger aucune explication, quand on pense à l'heureuse influence qu'exerce, à cet égard, dans notre vie moderne, la société presque continuelle des deux sexes. The translation is my own.
[161] *Physique sociale (Cours De Philosophia Positive, Leçons 46 à 60),* vol. II, ed. Jean-Paul Enthoven (Paris: Hermann, 1975), *Cinquante-Troisième Leçon,* 300-301.
[162] William James, *The Principles of Psychology,* vol. II (New York: Henry Holt and Company, 1913), 438-439.

George Santayana (1863-1952 AD)

Americanism allows that laissez-faire in moral life which it denies in commerce and industry. Not, of course, that it officially tolerates burglars, murderers, forgers, or adulterers. Legal morality still adheres to the general code of Christendom: but all religions, and therefore all theoretical codes of morals, were to be equally tolerated. The question at once arises, how long, if all moral codes are tolerated, those who hold those views can be restrained from putting them in practice. And what authority can the dominant morality retain? Evidently none: yet it is wonderful how long it has taken the liberal world to discover that it has deliberately abandoned mankind to moral anarchy. It has been only in recent years that the Russian revolution, Madam Caillaux, D. H. Lawrence, and André Gide have openly and conscientiously written down robbery, murder, adultery, and sodomy among the inalienable rights of man.

"Americanism," in *The Idler and His Works and Other Essays.*[163]

Bertrand Russell (1872-1970 AD)

Lawrence has the same feeling against sodomy as I have; you had nearly made me believe there is no great harm in it, but I have reverted; and all the examples I know confirm me in thinking it is sterilizing.

Letter to Ottoline Morrell, 8 March 1915, Monday Morning.[164]

The 20ᵗʰ Century

It is not always easy to pinpoint who will go down in history as the major philosophers of the 20th century. While it is easy to note that those such as Jean-Paul Sartre will long be remembered, once one gets past the mid-twentieth century it becomes increasingly difficult to see whom posterity will honor as the eminent philosophers. What must be noted, however, is that a shift happened in thought on homosexual activity in the 20th century. After Jean-Paul Sartre more philosophers began to approve of homosexual activity. Some still opposed homosexuality, such

---

[163] George Santayana "Americanism," in *The Idler and His Works and Other Essays,* ed. Daniel Cory (New York: George Braziller, Inc., 1957), 40. This essay originally appeared in English in the *Virginia Quarterly Review* in 1955.

[164] Bertrand Russell, Letter 255, To Ottoline Morrell, 8 March 1915, in *The Selected Letters of Bertrand Russell, The Public Years, 1914-1970,* ed. Nicholas Griffin (London and New York: Routledge, 2002), 35.

as Theodor Adorno[165] and Ernest Gellner.[166] Others, such as Peter Geach[167] and Elizabeth Anscombe,[168] while not commenting on the condition of homosexuality as such, held that engaging in homosexual acts is morally wrong. Yet, Jean-Paul Sartre,[169] Simone de Beauvoir,[170] A.J. Ayer,[171] Michel Foucault,[172] Richard Rorty,[173] Thomas Nagel,[174] and Pe-

---

[165] Max Horkheimer and Theodor W. Adorno, *Dialektik der Aufklärung: Philosophische Fragmente* (Surkamp: 1981), 217-218; Max Horkheimer and Theodor W. Adorno, *Dialectic of Enlightenment: Philosophical Fragments,* trans. Edmund Jephcott, ed. Gunzelin Schmid Noerr (Stanford, CA: Stanford University Press, 2002), 158-159; Max Horkheimer and Theodor W. Adorno, *Dialektik der Aufklärung: Philosophische Fragmente* (Surkamp: 1981), 290; Theodor W. Adorno, *Minima Moralia: Reflexionen aus dem beschädigten Leben* (Frankfurt: Suhrkamp, 1951), 51.

[166] Sarah Gellner, Letter to the Editor, "Memories of Ernest Gellner," *London Review of Books*, August 25, 2011, accessed February 2, 2016, http://www.lrb.co.uk/v33/n16/letters.

[167] Peter Geach, *The Virtues: The Stanton Lectures 1973-4* (Cambridge: Cambridge University Press, 1977), 148-149.

[168] Anscombe, Elizabeth. "Contraception and Chastity," 1972. Accessed February 03, 2016. http://www.orthodoxytoday.org/articles/AnscombeChastity.php.

[169] Jean-Paul Sartre, *Being and Nothingness: An Essay on Phenomological Ontology,* trans. Hazel E. Barnes (New York: Philosophical Library, 1956), 63; Hilary Robinson, ed., *Feminist-Art-Theory: An Anthology 1968-2014,* 2nd ed. (West Sussex, UK: Wiley Blackwell, 2015), 396; Heberto Padilla, *Self-Portrait of the Other: A Memoir,* trans. Alexander Coleman (New York: Farrar, Straus, and Giroux, Inc., 1990), 92.

[170] Simone De Beauvoir, *The Second Sex*, trans. H.M. Parshley (New York: Alfred A. Knopf, 1957), 407, Simone De Beauvoir, *The Second Sex*, trans. H.M. Parshley (New York: Alfred A. Knopf, 1957), 424.

[171] A.J. Ayer, C.H. Rolph, and Anthony Grey, "Debate on Homosexuality," *Sunday Times* (London), December 12, 1965; Ayer became president of the Homosexual Law Reform Society in September 1963; cf. Ben Rogers, *A.J. Ayer: A Life* (New York: Grove Press, 1999), 284.

[172] Michel Foucault, *The History of Sexuality,* vol. I: An Introduction, trans. Robert Hurley (New York: Vintage Books, 1978), 101; Michel Foucault, "Friendship as a Way of Life," in *Ethics: Subjectivity and Truth,* ed. Paul Rabinow, trans. Robert Hurley and others (New York: The New Press, 1997), 135-137.

[173] Richard Rorty, "Religion in the Public Square: A Reconsideration," *Journal of Religious Ethics* 31(1) (Spring 2003), 143, 146; Richard Rorty, *An Ethics for Today: Finding Common Ground between Philosophy and Religion* (New York and Chichester, West Sussex: Columbia University Press, 2011), 7-8.

[174] Nagel, "Sexual Perversion," 41.

ter Singer[175] all either clearly or at least implicitly approved of homosexual activity. The reasons for this shift in thought can largely be traced to Sartre's denial of nature; if nature is what you create, only meaningful insofar as you give it meaning, then the traditional condemnations of homosexual activity as unnatural make little sense.

Analysis

From the above survey of the major philosophers throughout history, it is clear that the overwhelming majority of them held that homosexual acts are morally wrong. Moral philosophy or ethics falls under the purview of the study of philosophy. Ergo, philosophers are natural authorities on moral issues. Since the overwhelming majority of philosophers condemn homosexual activity, there is good reason to accept their conclusion (unless of course there are good reasons to the contrary). Further, the consensus of experts on this issue is very strong. Indeed, there are few, if any, cases of greater consensus of authorities. Perhaps, the only other issue where there is as much consensus among experts throughout the ages is on the existence of God and the soul. Ergo, there is good reason, based on authority, to accept the proposition that homosexual acts are wrong.

The experts, of course, are not infallible. The tradition could be wrong. Sometimes experts are mistaken. The probability that they are wrong decreases when an overwhelming number of them are in agreement, yet the possibility still remains that they could be wrong. The only way we can know they are wrong (on a natural level) is by examining the arguments. Are there good arguments to the contrary? Are there compelling arguments to the contrary regarding homosexual activity? We will examine these questions in the next section.

---

[175] Singer, "Homosexuality Is Not Immoral."

Arguments that Homosexual Acts are Morally Good

In more recent years, many have argued that homosexual acts are good. I will examine their arguments in this section and treat like arguments together. The arguments in favor of homosexual activity are of six general kinds: (a) from moral experience, (b) from love, (c) from good consequences, (d) from consent and lack of harm, (e) from justice, and (f) from the natural law.

Gareth Moore and Michael Perry make argument (a) - from moral experience in favor of homosexual activity. Moore claims that if all homosexual activity were bad, then no practicing homosexual would be happy. But there are happy homosexuals who engage in sexual activity with each other. Therefore, homosexual activity cannot always be morally bad.[176] Likewise, Perry argues as follows, quoting from Sr. Margaret A. Farley, R.S.M.:

> The final source for Christian ethical insight is [contemporary experience]….I am referring primarily to the testimony of women and men whose sexual preference is for others of the same sex. Here, too, we have as yet no univocal voice putting to rest all of our questions regarding the status of same-sex relations. We do, however, have some clear and profound testimonies to the life-enhancing possibilities of same-sex relations and the integrating possibilities of sexual activity within these relations. We have the witness that homosexuality can be a way of embodying responsible human love and sustaining Christian friendship.[177]

In short, Moore's and Perry's argument is this: some homosexuals experience homosexual acts as morally good and fulfilling, and so such acts cannot possibly be morally evil.

It is possible, however, for one to be mistaken in moral judgments and in the emotions by perceiving what is evil as if it were good and vice-versa. This is simply the phenomena that Aristotle, Aquinas, and others refer to as moral vice. Both the intellect and the emotions have

---

[176] Cf. Gareth Moore, *A Question of Truth*, 245-246.
[177] Perry, "The Morality of Homosexual Conduct: A Response to John Finnis," 41.

gone awry such that one truly believes what is evil is good and fulfilling for the person; as such, one emotionally desires it. Aquinas mentions, for example, certain instances of theft that were considered morally good among the Germans.[178] In our country, many considered the slavery of the black population to be morally good. Many of the slave-owners truly believed what they were doing was morally good (even for their slaves) and perhaps even experienced it as such. Likewise, some drug users experience smoking heroin or snorting cocaine as morally good. But just because one experiences something as morally good does not make it so. Morality is not solely about our intuitions or our experiences, which are as varied as people, and which are often wrong. Moral goodness or badness do not depend upon whether or not some people experience it as good or bad. Morality runs deeper than mere feelings.

John McNeill and Burton Leiser argue (b) from love. They both claim homosexual practices can be good if they proceed from genuine acts of love.[179] Their argument can be put into syllogistic form as follows:

1. Any human action that proceeds from love must be a good action.
2. Homosexual acts between consenting homosexual adults sometimes proceed from love.
3. Ergo, homosexual acts in such cases are morally good.

But what do McNeill and Leiser mean by love in premise one and premise two? By "love" they might mean one of three things: (1) willing the good to another or (2) the emotion of desiring, or (3) warm affection. If they mean willing the good to another, then their argument is either beg-

---

[178] ST I-II, Q94, A6. The other sin that Aquinas alludes to in this text that can be blotted out from the heart of man and actually experienced as if it were good is same-sex sexual activity, the unnatural vice.

[179] Cf. McNeill, *The Church and the Homosexual*, 106-107, 113-114; Leiser, "Homosexuality, Morals, and the Laws of Nature": "the burden is on those who advocate the ostracism of homosexuals to demonstrate that there are cogent reasons for so punishing human beings whose only crime, if it is one, is to engage in the only form of love-making that they feel capable of."

ging the question or has premises no more evident than its conclusion. For on this meaning of "love" their argument would be:

1. Any human action that proceeds from willing the good to another must be a good action.
2. Homosexual acts between consenting homosexual adults sometimes proceed from willing the good to another.
3. Ergo, homosexual acts in such cases are morally good.

Why should we accept the second premise? This premise is precisely the subject under debate: Is homosexual activity willing the good to another or is it in reality willing evil? Consequently, the second premise implicitly assumes what the argument tries to prove: that homosexual acts are morally good.

Another possibility is that McNeill and Leiser mean "love" as emotional desire. In this case, the first premise becomes problematic:

1. Any human action that proceeds from emotional desire must be a good action.
2. Homosexual acts between consenting homosexual adults sometimes proceed from emotional desire.
3. Ergo, homosexual acts in such cases are morally good.

But vengeance, bestiality, and rape all proceed from an emotional desire on the part of the agent. Yet none of these are morally good.

If by "love" they mean (3) "warm affection," then their argument would be as follows:

1. Any human action that proceeds from a warm affection must be a good action.
2. Homosexual acts between consenting homosexual adults sometimes proceed from a warm affection.
3. Ergo, homosexual acts in such cases are morally good.

The difficulty is that now the first premise justifies adultery, incest, and polygamy, all of which can result from a "warm affection." This second line of reasoning, then, is unsuccessful no matter the meaning of the word "love."

John Corvino argues (c) from the good consequences that follow from homosexual activity:

> We have spent the last five chapters examining the moral evidence surrounding homosexuality. The basic case in favor of it is straightforward: For some people, same-sex relationships are an important source of genuine human goods, including emotional and physical intimacy, mutual pleasure, and so on. That positive case must be balanced against any negatives—although, as we have seen, the standard objections fall apart under scrutiny.[180]

In an earlier work, Corvino argues in a similar vein:

> I assume that Tommy and Jim have sex with each other (although I've never bothered to ask). Furthermore, I contend that they probably *should* have sex with each other. For one thing, sex is pleasurable. But it is also much more than that: a sexual relationship can unite two people in a way that virtually nothing else can. It can be an avenue of growth, of communication, and of lasting interpersonal fulfillment. These are reasons why most heterosexual couples have sex even if they don't want children, don't want children yet, or don't want additional children. And if these reasons are good enough for most heterosexual couples, then they should be good enough for Tommy and Jim.[181]

Corvino concludes his essay by saying, "To put the argument simply, Tommy and Jim's relationship makes them better people. And that's not just good for Tommy and Jim: that's good for everyone."[182]

Corvino's argument in the first text seems to be as follows:

1. Any human action that is a source of genuine human goods, including emotional, physical intimacy, mutual pleasure, and so on, is in itself a morally good action.

---

[180] Corvino, *What's Wrong with Homosexuality?*, 126.
[181] Corvino, "Why Shouldn't Tommy and Jim Have Sex?", 3-4.
[182] Ibid., 16.

2. Sexual activity between homosexuals is sometimes a source of such goods.
3. Ergo, sexual activity between homosexuals is in itself morally good.

The first premise suggests that any human action that produces good consequences (or much more good consequences than bad) is morally good. This claim, however, is highly implausible. Lying may produce many more genuine human goods such as more money, or emotional intimacy, and mutual pleasure, but it is still morally wrong. Likewise, stealing in order to give alms to the poor may produce many genuine human goods, such as an increase in joy for the poor beggar, and perhaps the sparking of a new relationship between the giver and the beggar. Yet stealing is still wrong. Prostitution also can be a source of physical, emotional intimacy, mutual pleasure and genuine human goods like gainful employment, etc. But it is still morally wrong.

Further, Corvino's argument presupposes the truth of consequentialism; its veracity as an adequate moral theory has already been found to be lacking.

Corvino's argument in the second quote (mentioned earlier) is slightly different, and can be put in valid form as follows:

1. Any human action that is an avenue of growth, communication, lasting interpersonal fulfillment, and makes you a better person is a morally good action.
2. Sexual activity between homosexuals sometimes is such an avenue of growth, communication, and lasting interpersonal fulfillment, making them better persons.
3. Ergo, homosexual acts between homosexuals are sometimes morally good.

Why should we accept the second premise and its claim that homosexual acts can make someone a better person? Homosexual activity could do this only if it were a truly good action, but that is precisely the issue under dispute. Corvino's argument has a premise no more evident than his conclusion.

To argue that x is good because x makes you a better person, one must first give a persuasive account as to why x makes you a better person. To argue that occasional recreational drug use is good because it makes one a better person, one must first show that it in fact does make one a better person. Yet this is precisely what Corvino has failed to do with homosexual activity——failed to give any principled reason why sexual activity between two males or two females in itself makes them better persons.[183]

Perhaps, Corvino means to make an argument from moral experience, or the experience of certain practicing homosexual couples. Some homosexuals, Corvino seems to claim, experience homosexual activity as an action that results in making them better persons.

But such a claim suffers from the same problems surrounding the argument (a) from moral experience, which was critiqued earlier. Experience is generally a poor guide to morality, because experiences are so varied, and because they are often mistaken. People's moral judgments and emotions are often skewed due to vice, corrupt habits, or cultures. The fact that many in ancient Greece practiced man-boy relations and held it was good and experienced it as such does not make it good.[184]

Peter Singer makes the case for homosexual activity (d) from consent and lack of harm[185]:

The stronger objection to the prohibition of homosexuality is to deny the claim that lies at its core: that sexual acts between consenting people of the same sex are immoral....If a form of sexual activity brings

---

[183] I grant for the sake of argument that all sorts of other actions involved in a homosexual relationship might make them better persons, e.g. caring for the other when sick, helping the other person with a difficult homework problem, making breakfast, etc. What I object to, however, is Corvino's claim that homosexual acts, which I define as homosexual activity that is ordered towards orgasm (viz. anal sex, oral sex, genital rubbing, fisting, intercrural sex, etc.), makes one a better person.

[184] I refer my reader to many of the dialogues of Plato where these relations are frequently alluded to, i.e., *Phaedrus, Symposium*, etc.

[185] Chris Meyers also makes a nearly identical argument in *The Moral Defense of Homosexuality: Why Every Argument Against Gay Rights Fails* (Lanham, Boulder, New York, London: Rowman & Littlefield, 2015), 204-205. His argument there is based on the utilitarian principle of utility, which interestingly is at the end of the same section where he seems to deny it as being a good moral theory (206).

satisfaction to those who take part in it, and harms no one, what can be immoral about it?[186]

Singer's argument seems to be as follows:

1. Any sexual act between consenting adults that brings satisfaction and harms no one is not immoral.
2. Homosexual activity can be between consenting adults in a way that brings satisfaction and harms no one.
3. Ergo, homosexual activity is not immoral.

Presumably, what Singer means by "harms no one" is physical or psychological harm. As such, the first premise allows for incest. Incest can be between consenting adults and in a way that neither physically, nor psychologically harms anyone.[187] So it follows that on the first premise incest is morally good.

Singer could, of course, qualify his first premise to read, "any sexual act between *unrelated* consenting adults that neither physically nor psychologically harms anyone is not immoral."

It remains that adultery could be morally good. For it need not physically nor psychologically harm anyone and it can be between consenting adults (all parties—both husbands and both wives—could consent).

Perhaps, then, what Singer means by his first premise is something like this: "any sexual act between unrelated consenting adults *and that is not adultery* is not morally wrong so long as it does not physically or psychologically harm anyone."

Besides, being ad hoc and rather awkwardly worded, this adapted premise still suffers from other difficulties. On such an account there are no specifically sexual virtues or vices. Sexual morality is simply an extension of the virtue of justice: do not harm anyone. It fails to account

---

[186] Singer, "Homosexuality Is Not Immoral."

[187] If every act of incest involves psychological harm, then Adam and Eve's children psychologically harmed each other. But they did not. Further, there are contemporary cases of consensual incest that seem to involve no such harm, insofar as both parties enjoyed it and agreed to it as consenting adults.

for the specialness of sex. Rendering your wife the marriage debt is different in kind than merely repaying a loan or the $100 you owed your friend. But if sexual morality is simply an extension of the virtue of justice, as Singer seems to claim, then there really is not much difference (in regards to the kind of morality being applied) between repaying a debt and having sex with your wife. The same general rules of morality would apply in both cases: do no harm, repay your debts, render what is due, etc. Christopher Martin puts it best, which due to his British wit, I will quote in full:

> I have the impression that there is quite a widespread belief that there is no virtue that has to do with good dispositions towards sexuality as such: only an application in a particular field of other more general virtues such as justice, faithfulness, considerateness, etc. I don't want to deny that there are applications in this field of these other virtues. They are particularly important because this is a particularly important field. But I do want to deny that these applications of more general virtues and vices are the only moral considerations to be raised with regard to sexuality.
>
> …So: what is your view on this question? Consider this: do you think that there is anything wrong in any kind of sexual behavior (between consenting adults, of course) which is not e.g. dishonest, cruel irresponsible, exploitative, bad-mannered etc.? If you don't, then you share the modern view which I am disputing. I agree, let me stress, that it's wrong to display any of these vices in your sexual life: I think that it may even be usually worse to show these vices in your sexual life than in other, less important fields. It's usually worse to show these vices in your sexual life than in your relations with the person at the supermarket check-out, of course, but that would be because your sexual life is more important to you than your relations with the person at the supermarket check-out, (presumably) your partners' sexual lives are more important to them than the supermarket employee's relation with you is to him or her. But the point is this: are ways of going wrong like this, which are ways of going wrong in other fields of life as well, the only ways of going wrong in your sexual life?
>
> If you answer "yes" to this question…then we are faced with a disagreement…For this is just the idea which I think is odd. It strikes me as being equivalent to saying that sex is no more special than are cut

flowers. Notice, I don't say: it's equivalent to thinking that sex is no more important than cut flowers. I don't suppose many people think that. It is the *specialness* of sex that I am interested in here, rather than its importance. Cut flowers aren't special: sex is. Cut flowers are certainly a thing about which you can go wrong. But you cannot go wrong about cut flowers in ways that are specific to cut flowers: there are no ways of going wrong about cut flowers that aren't ways of going wrong in other, probably more important, fields of life....You can be dishonest about cut flowers: you can steal them or pretend they grew in your garden when they didn't, or that you arranged them yourself when you didn't. You can be irresponsible about cut flowers: you can spend too much time or money on getting them or arranging them, to the manifest detriment of other people you have a responsibility to. You can be cruel with cut flowers: you can be callously indifferent to the sufferings of other people in your home who suffer from hay fever and are therefore allergic to them....So my idea is that in the case of cut flowers there's nothing you can do wrong which wouldn't be wrong in any other circumstances: and nothing you can do right, either. There is and probably can be no special virtue, no special vice, to do with cut flowers. Is sex in the same position? This strikes me as incredible.[188]

Acceptance of Singer's first premise, however, seems to entail precisely the position Martin is critiquing. On Singer's view sex is no more special than cut flowers. There is good reason then to doubt the veracity of Singer's first premise.

Many will agree with the premise that "any sexual act between consenting adults, who are not related to each other, and that is not adultery, is not morally wrong so long as it does not physically or psychologically harm anyone." But when asked for the basis of this premise, they have little to say beyond claiming it is the obvious truth. Less than two decades ago, however, the same would have been said about sexual activity between two males or two females, namely, that it is obviously wrong. Many would have held to the same shared proposition but with an added caveat: "any sexual act between consenting adults, who are not related to each other, and that is not adultery, is not morally wrong so

---

[188] C.F.J. Martin, "Are There Virtues and Vices That Belong Specifically to the Sexual Life?," *Acta Philosophica* IV, no. 2 (1995): 205-206.

long as it does not physically or psychologically harm anyone, *and is between a man and a woman.*" But why are all these items grouped together on this list? They are seemingly grouped together in order to rule out things like rape, incest, adultery, and masochism. Nothing prevents someone, however, from adding a prohibition on homosexual acts to the list. Singer's first premise (as modified) is really an ad hoc list. Saying any action that is not rape, incest, adultery, etc. and that falls in the category of sexuality is in itself not morally wrong is much like saying any action that is not gluttony, drunkenness, and that falls in the category of eating is in itself not morally wrong. This may be true, but fails to provide an account as to why it is true. Similarly, Singer fails to provide any rationale for his key premise. Any weight it carries is due only to our existing cultural milieu. But many other cultures throughout history would have found this premise just as evidently inadequate on the grounds that fornication is wrong.

Chris Meyers argues homosexual activity is morally good (e) from justice. In his book, *A Moral Defense of Homosexuality,* Meyers gives what he calls the "Simple Argument" in favor of homosexual acts:

1. "For an action or practice to be morally wrong, it must have some wrong-making feature.
2. Wrong-making features include the following: the action or practice i) causes harm or ii) violates some competent person's autonomy or iii) is unfair or iv) violates someone's individual rights or v) etc.
3. Homosexual relations between two consenting adults do not have any of these features. In other words, i) it is not harmful, ii) it does not violate anyone's autonomy, iii) it is not unfair, iv) it does not violate anyone's individual rights, v) etc.
4. Therefore, homosexual relations between mutually consenting adults are not morally wrong."[189]

The difficulty is with Meyers's second premise. On such an account there are plenty of actions that do not count as morally wrong, but that

---

[189] Meyers, *The Moral Defense of Homosexuality,* 197-198.

many would admit are morally wrong or problematic.[190] Necrophilia, for example, as sexual activity with a corpse need not cause physical harm to the person (imagine it being done hygienically, or say with a condom), nor to anyone else, because the corpse is not a human being, so it cannot be harmed in the relevant sense. It also does not ii) violate anyone's autonomy, nor is it iii) unfair; it also does not iv) violate anyone's rights, because corpse's have no rights. You may say it violated the previous wishes of the person who died, but there could be a man's wife who died granting him explicit permission to perform the act in question. As for v) and what Meyers's means by "etc." is not very clear. Ergo, based on the second premise necrophilia is not morally wrong.

Also, on the second premise gluttony, hatred, unforgiveness, impatience, pride, and excessive anger (that harms nobody) are not morally wrong. On his account, the sin of the devil (pride) is actually no sin at all (until it leads to harming others).

Further, neglecting your natural talents i) need not harm anyone, ii), nor violate anyone's autonomy, nor iii) be unfair, nor iv) violate anyone's rights. You can be a lazy person on a tropical island for the rest of your life and fail to cultivate your natural talents and be a perfectly moral person based off of Meyers's second premise.

Meyers's second premise also seems to allow for certain acts of bestiality. Sexual acts with an animal need not ii) violate anyone's autonomy, nor need they be iii) unfair (if one can be "unfair" to animals at all), nor iv) do they violate someone's individual rights. Bestiality also need not i) cause harm to the person or the animal. As John Corvino says, "While bestiality is often harmful to animals, it need not be: there's an urban legend that comes to mind involving a woman, a dog, peanut butter, and a surprise party."[191] Thus, Meyers' second premise miscategorizes many immoral actions as morally acceptable.

One may object and say the animals cannot consent. But consent is, at best, a weak argument. As Corvino says, "Of course, there's the

---

[190] Much of what follows is developed from my earlier criticisms in the online journal *Public Discourse:* John Skalko, "Homosexuality and Bad Arguments," *Public Discourse* (August 5th, 2016), http://www.thepublicdiscourse.com/2016/08/16808/. Any repetition here has been used with permission.

[191] Corvino, *What's Wrong with Homosexuality?*, 128.

issue of consent. On the other hand, we do plenty to animals without their consent, including many uncontroversial interactions."[192] If we can kill them without their consent, then why not other things? Ergo, based on Meyers's second premise some acts of bestiality are morally permissible.

Finally, the problem with Meyers's account of the wrongness of actions is that all sins boil down to sins against justice. There are no sins against prudence, temperance, fortitude, etc. Actions are wrong only because they are against justice. Consequently, there are no specifically sexual sins. Sexual acts are wrong not because they are sexual deviations, but because they violate one of the norms of justice. On this account, it is hard to see why contraceptive rape would be a morally distinctive sin against justice than mere assault and battery; such rape would presumably be even a less serious sin than battery since contraceptive rape might cause less physical harm. A rapist, on Meyers's view, presumably should not be charged with rape, but rather with assault and battery. On his account, rape is not wrong qua disordered use of sexuality, but only qua physical assault. Meyers's view thus becomes subject to all the criticisms raised earlier by Christopher Martin: the moral norms governing sex are no more special than the moral norms governing cut flowers.

Georges Lenferna argues homosexual acts are morally good (f) from the natural law. He says that since the natural law is based upon human flourishing, any action that contributes to human flourishing must be in accordance with the natural law.[193] Homosexual acts can contribute to human flourishing. Ergo, they must be in accordance with the natural law and so be morally good. His argument in valid form would thus be as follows:

---

[192] Ibid., 128.

[193] "As natural law ethicists hold that what is moral is the use of reason to direct oneself towards what is one's flourishing life, which as we have shown may be different for different individuals, then for the homosexual man or woman, for whom the sex of 'Bradshaw's Ideal Couple' is not an option, who is engaged in the ideal type of homosexual relationship, sex may indeed be not only not an immoral choice but even a moral one, which contributes to their overall flourishing" (Lenferna, "Natural Law Ethics, Homosexuality and Morality").

1. Whatever contributes to human flourishing is in accordance with the natural law.
2. Homosexual activity contributes (at times) to human flourishing.
3. Ergo, it is in accordance with the natural law.

Unfortunately, Lenferna gives no evidence for his second premise, and it is not clear what exactly he means by "flourishing." Perhaps, he means that engaging in homosexual activity makes some people better persons (echoing Corvino). But why should we believe that? Such a claim is no more evident than the claim that homosexual activity is morally good. Whatever is morally wrong degrades the person precisely as a flourishing human being. If homosexual activity is morally wrong, it cannot possibly be in accord with human flourishing.

Second, the same argument Lenferna gives could be turned on its head:

1. Whatever is contrary to human flourishing is against the natural law.
2. Homosexual activity is contrary to human flourishing.
3. Ergo, homosexual activity is not in accordance with the natural law.

Many today, and even a majority of peoples throughout history particularly among the moral experts (the philosophers) held to the second premise. Lenferna denies it, and gives no evidence for his claim, so without better evidence that the tradition is wrong, the weight of the consensus of the great philosophers should stand.

Perhaps, what Lenferna really means by the second premise, or the support he would invoke for its veracity, is that many homosexuals experience same-sex sexual activity as if it were morally good and they believe they have grown closer together in love because of it. This evidence, however, is just a rehashing of the argument from moral experience (cf. Gareth Moore and Michael Perry earlier), which we have already found to be wanting. It does not account for the reality of moral vice, that people can truly believe and experience evil as if it were good. Their experience does not change good into evil, but rather reflects the deep disordered nature of their intellect, will, and emotions. Likewise, it does not account for the fact that many homosexuals experience same-sex sexual activity as morally destructive.[194]

Finally, good statistical evidence calls into doubt the claim that homosexual activity leads to human flourishing or personal fulfillment:

- In 1999 a New Zealand study, "Is Sexual Orientation Related to Mental Health Problems and Suicidality in Young People?" was done on 1,007 people, of whom 2.8% were found to be gay, lesbian, or bisexual. Data was gathered from these groups on the occurrence of various psychiatric disorders. The results indicated that gays, lesbians, and bisexuals as a whole had an increased risk of major depression (400% times the normal rate), generalized anxiety disorder (280%xs), multiple disorders (590%xs), and suicidal ideation (540%xs).[195]

- In 1999 another study, "Sexual Orientation and Suicidality," was done comparing twins in which one had same-sex partners while the other did not. It found that "same-gender orientation is significantly associated with each of the [different] suicidality measures" as the twin who had same-sex partners was more likely to commit suicide. This difference was also adjusted for substance abuse and depressive symptoms (other than suicidality) and it still found that the homosexual was a much greater risk for suicide. Thus, they concluded, "the

---

[194] Cf. Daniel Mattson and Rilene in the *Desire of the Everlasting Hills*, both of whom I met in person and have every reason to believe their story is true (the movie can be found for free here: https://everlastinghills.org/movie/). These people had nothing to gain from telling their stories, particularly in today's culture where much hatred is expressed toward those who view homosexual acts as morally problematic. There is every reason to believe their stories are true. Numerous other homosexuals relate that after engaging in homosexual activity they felt a deep emptiness, heartache, and disappointment. See Joseph Prever (cf. the movie *The Third Way*, *http://www.blackstonefilms.co/thethirdway/*); Andrew Comiskey, and Doug Mainwaring (Doug Mainwaring, "Hearts, Parts, and Minds: The Truth Comes Out," Public Discourse, March 09, 2015, accessed March 12, 2016, http://www.thepublicdiscourse.com/2015/03/14510/). The movie *The Third Way* also has numerous other testimonies from homosexuals about deep loneliness, emptiness, and pain. All these real persons experienced homosexual acts either at the time or years later as inherently unfulfilling, robbing them of their life and joy.

[195] Fergusson, D.M., et al., *Archives of General Psychiatry* 56, 10(1999): 876.

substantially increased lifetime risk of suicidal behaviors in homosexual men is unlikely to be due solely to substance abuse or psychiatric comorbidity."[196]

- In 2001 a study in the Netherlands, "Same-Sex Behavior and Psychiatric Disorders, Findings from the Netherlands Mental Health Survey and Incidence Study," was done on a representative sample of the Dutch population. They found that over the course of 12 months homosexual men had a higher rate of mood disorders (293%xs) and anxiety disorders (261%xs) than heterosexual men. Also, homosexuals in general were more than twice as likely as heterosexuals to have had two or more disorders during their lifetime.[197]

- In 2003 a study in the Netherlands, "Same-Sex Sexuality and Quality of Life: Findings from the Netherlands Mental Health Survey and Incidence Study," found that homosexual men suffered from a lack of self-esteem compared to heterosexual men.[198]

- In a 2006 a study in the Netherlands, "Sexual Orientation and Mental and Physical Health Status: Findings from a Dutch Population Survey," found that "gay[s]/lesbian[s]…reported more acute mental health problems than heterosexual people and their general mental health was poorer."[199]

- In "A General Review of Recent Reports on Homosexuality and Lesbianism" John R. Hughes lists some other stunning connections between homosexuality and other disorders: "'Fisting' refers to placing the fist into the anal canal and was reported done to 13% of gays within the previous 12 months. In another study the prevalence was similar at 1/6 (17%). In two unbelievable instances the hand and arm were actually inserted for 15 cm in one victim and the other victim a dildo was placed into the sigmoid colon. In both instances the colon was perforated.…27% of gay males were considered to have a mental disorder and 43% were reported in another study. In a study comparing lesbian and heterosexual women using various multivariate anal-

---

[196] Herrell, R., et al., *Archives of General Psychiatry* 56 (1999): 867-874.

[197] Sandfort, T.G., *Archives of General Psychiatry* 58, 1(2001): 85-91.

[198] Sandfort, T.G., et al., *Archives of Sexual Behavior* 32, 1 (2003): 15-22.

[199] Sandfort, T.G., et al., *American Public Health Association* 96, no. 6 (June 2006): 1119-1125.

yses, the lesbians were reported as generally having poorer mental health."[200]

- According to a study in the *Journal of Family Violence,* 44% of male homosexual relationships reported physical abuse, while 55% of lesbians reported physical abuse.[201] But, for heterosexual couples only 25% reported physical abuse.[202]

- A study of 2,881 homosexuals found that "approximately 2 of 5 MSM [men who have sex with men] (39%) reported experiencing at least 1 type of battering [by their male partner] during the previous 5 years, with almost 1 of 5 (18%) experiencing multiple forms of battering (34% reported psychological/symbolic violence, 22% physical violence, and 5% sexual violence). In a nationally representative sample of heterosexual men (defined in the study as men who reported cohabitation with women), 7.7% reported lifetime physical or sexual partner violence, compared with 23% (95% CI=21.5%, 25.4%) of our urban MSM who reported such battering during the previous 5 years....Similarly, Zierler and colleagues found that among a nationally representative sample of HIV-infected individuals, 7.5% of heterosexual men had experienced some type of battering (since HIV diagnosis), compared with 39% of our sample (within the past 5 years)....In general, the 5-year prevalence of physical battering among urban MSM (22.0%) was significantly higher than either the annual prevalence of severe violence (3.4%) or the annual prevalence of total violence (11.6%) among a representative sample of women who were married or cohabiting with men....This study demonstrates that intimate partner abuse among urban MSM is a very serious health problem."[203]

---

[200] John R. Hughes, "A General Review of Recent Reports on Homosexuality and Lesbianism," *Sexuality and Disability* 24, no. 4 (December 2006): 199-200.

[201] Susan C. Turell, "A Descriptive Analysis of Same-Sex Relationship Violence for a Diverse Sample," *Journal of Family Violence* 13, no. 3 (2000): 281-293.

[202] Ibid., 287.

[203] Gregory L. Greenwood, et al,, "Battering Victimization among a Probability-based Sample of Men Who Have Sex with Men," *American Journal of Public Health* 92 (December 2002): 1966-67.

- The Gay and Lesbian Medical Association itself admits "lesbians are more likely to have risk factors for breast cancer," "lesbians have higher risks for certain types of gynecological (GYN) cancers compared to straight woman," "lesbians are more likely to be overweight or obese compared to heterosexual women," "lesbians use tobacco more often than heterosexual women do," "heavy drinking and binge drinking are more common among lesbians compared to other women," and "lesbians may use drugs more often than heterosexual women."[204]

- A 2018 study found that "LGBQ youth were more than 3 times more likely (odds ratio [*OR*] = 3.08) than non-LGBQ peers to have attempted suicide…"[205]

- In a 2012 literature review the authors noted, "Researchers and clinicians have proposed that affiliation with gay culture is related to elevated substance use in LGB communities. Although Bux (1996) concluded, based on empirical evidence available at the time, that there was little support for the LGB lifestyle contributing to elevated substance use and substance-related problems, more recent research suggests otherwise.…It is interesting to note that Stall et al. (2001) found that both low and high affiliation with gay culture was associated with heavy drinking and frequent illicit drug use; MSM [men who have sex with men] who reported moderate levels of gay culture affiliation (measure by gay bar attendance and/or use of gay media sources) reported the lowest levels of heavy drinking and illicit drug use, whereas more frequent attendance at gay bars and less frequent use of gay-oriented media were associated with heavier drinking and more alcohol-related problems."[206]

---

[204] Tonia Poteat, "Top Ten Things Lesbians Should Discuss with their Health Care Providers," *Gay and Lesbian Medical Association* May 2012, http://www.glma.org/index.cfm?fuseaction=Page.viewPage&pageID=691.

[205] Christopher R. De Cou and Shannon M. Lynch, "Sexual Orientation, Gender, and Attempted Suicide Among Adolescent Psychiatric Inpatients," *Psychological Services* 15, no. 3 (2018): 363.

[206] Kelley E. Green and Brian A. Feinstein, "Substance Use in Lesbian, Gay, and Bisexual Populations: An Update on Empirical Research and Implications for Treatment," *Psychology of Addictive Behaviors* 26, no. 2 (2012): 272.

- A 2015 study found that "Among YMSM [young men who have sex with men], 39% reported IPV [intimate partner violence] victimization, 31% reported perpetration, and 25% reported mutual IPV."[207]
- A 2017 study indicated that "mounting evidence suggests IPV [intimate partner violence] may be more common among LGBT individuals than heterosexuals."[208]

One may object to these findings by saying that these disorders in homosexuals are caused by anti-homosexual bias, not by the homosexual condition itself. Thus, oppression leads them to depression, suicidal behavior, which in turn leads to intimate partner violence. This possibility cannot be ruled out in all cases, but it seems unlikely that it is the full explanation. Many of these studies were conducted in countries where homosexuality is well accepted. The Netherlands, where many of the studies cited were conducted, is notorious for its promotion of homosexuality. As for the study done in New Zealand: "Young adults in New Zealand are far more accepting of same-sex relationships than are their American counterparts."[209] Finally, if societal oppression and "discrimination" really fully account for all of these additional disorders, then we would expect that as societies became more accepting of homosexuality and homosexual activity there would be a corresponding significant decrease in the correlative disorders and that such disorders should eventually die out. But we do not find such decrease. In fact, more recent studies indicate reasons to believe that higher levels of disorders continue to exist among persons with same-sex attraction even after rates of societal approval have significantly increased.[210] And conversely, higher rates of

---

[207] Christopher B. Stults, et al., "Intimate Partner Violence Perpetration and Victimization Among YMSM: The P18 Cohort Study," *Psychology of Sexual Orientation and Gender Diversity* 2, no. 2 (2015); 152.

[208] Tyson R. Reuter, Michael E. Newcomb, and Sarah W. Whitton, "Intimate Partner Violence Victimization in LBGT Young Adults: Demographic Differences and Associations With Health Behaviors," *Psychology of Violence,* 7, no. 1 (2017): 101.

[209] Skegg, K., et al. "Sexual Orientation and Self-harm in Men and Women." *American Journal of Psychiatry* 160, no. 3 (2003): 545.

[210] According to Gallup public support for considering same-sex unions as valid marriages under the law increased by 37% between 2012 and 2018 (Gallup, "Gay and Lesbian Rights," https://news.gallup.com/poll/1651/gay-lesbian-rights.aspx,

societal acceptance and legalization of same-sex unions haven't led to decreased rates of minority distress.[211]

Moreover, oppression of homosexuals would not likely lead to intimate partner violence. Although discrimination may lead to increased depression and suicidal behavior, suicidal thoughts do not typically lead to beating and abuse of another.[212] As the philosopher Michael Levin has pointed out, if the disorders associated with homosexuality were merely due to societal oppression, then we would expect to find these disorders also in other oppressed population like the European Jews. But we do not.[213] Consequently, their cause is not due to societal oppression; rather,

---

accessed November 16, 2018). If social pressure and "discrimination" were really the deciding factor causing higher levels of disorders among homosexuals, then we should expect an inverse relationship between higher societal acceptance and the level of corresponding disorders. But do we see a corresponding 37% drop in the levels of disorder among homosexuals after increased societal acceptance? The more recent studies mentioned earlier (among others) indicate grounds for doubt.

[211] Cf. Mark Regnerus, "Scientists Have Unwittingly Revealed that the *Obergefell* Decision Did Nothing to Diminish Sexual Minority Distress," *Public Discourse* June 9th, 2018, https://www.thepublicdiscourse.com/2018/06/21866/.

[212] If anything the evidence indicates the converse, namely that being subjected to domestic violence leads to suicidal behavior: Rebecca Clay, "Suicide and Intimate Partner Violence," *Monitor on Psychology* 45, no. 10 (2014), accessed January 5, 2018: http://www.apa.org/monitor/2014/11/suicide-violence.aspx; World Health Organization, *Understanding and Addressing Violence against Women,* WHO/RHR/12.36, 2012, p. 5, accessed December 15, 2016, http://apps.who.int/iris/bitstream/10665/77432/1/WHO_RHR_12.36_eng.pdf.

[213] Michael Levin, "Why Homosexuality Is Abnormal," *Monist* 67, no. 2 (April 1984): 251-283. Chris Meyers replies to Levin by saying that the reason why homosexuals had an increase in promiscuity is because they were not given an appropriate sexual outlet in which to express themselves (viz. in a societally sanctioned marriage). This lack of proper outlet can also lead to increased loneliness, irresponsibility, and superficiality (178-179). Meyers further claims that if homosexuals were allowed to marry, they would become more responsible (179). In reply to Meyers, it must be noted that nothing of what he says explains the increase in partner violence among homosexual couples. If being oppressed increased intimate partner violence, then we should expect to find the same thing in the European Jews, especially during the time of the holocaust. But we do not. Further, suffering together for the same cause should lead to greater love and intimacy. So we should expect there to be less partner violence in societies where same-sex couples are treated with contempt. Further, Meyers's points can be assessed by looking at the data in countries that have already legalized and largely accept same-sex unions. Is there any decrease in suicide, mood disorders, substance abuse, and other mental health prob-

it is due to a homosexuality that, when acted upon, tends to lead to such things. If a man can never find true satisfaction in another man, then one might expect to find an increase in intimate partner violence. The man is expecting what cannot be got from his partner. Seeking happiness in what leads to emptines is bound to lead to an increased risk of suicide and depression.

Some may claim that correlation does not imply causation and so you cannot infer that homosexual activity or the homosexual condition itself is *the cause* of the corresponding increase in disorders among homosexuals. The same argument, however, can be used against those who claim that societal disapproval is *the cause* of the corresponding disorders. If you want to undercut our argument for the cause of the corresponding disorders by claiming you can *in no way ever* know cause and effect[214], then you can't go on claiming you have knowledge of cause in effect in other cases.

For all the reasons just mentioned, the second premise of Lenferna's argument is highly questionable. Homosexual activity seems to be linked with an increase in all sorts of mental disorders and problems. As such, it does not contribute to true human flourishing.

A final counterargument I wish to address is the "born that way" argument. It claims that since certain people are born with a sexual orientation towards those of the same-sex, they cannot possibly be morally responsible for it. Further, it must be good, because nature has implanted such desires within them.

This argument has some truth in it. If such a person is born with a homosexual orientation, then they are not morally responsible for it. No

---

lems in these countries? It seems not; a 2010 report from the Netherlands on lesbian partner violence indicates that the levels are comparable to the 55% indicated in the study done in the United States (Susanne Kers, *Empirical Analysis I: L(G)BT Communities Handling Domestic Violence in Women-to-women Relationships,* report, June 2010, p. 6, p. 21, accessed March 17, 2016, http://www.lars-europe.eu/en/material/1rst_national_report_nl.pdf).

[214] Psychologists are making a philosophical not a psychological point in claiming we cannot know cause and effect. The view that we cannot know causes can be traced back to the philosopher David Hume. His view suffers from numerous difficulties, including the fact that Hume himself inconsistently smuggles in causal language in the very work where he denies knowledge of causes.

one can be blamed for what is beyond his control. But human actions—as opposed to dispositions—are by definition within a person's control. Any individual can be blamed for voluntarily acting on a disposition; for it is possible to refrain from such acts.

Further, being born with a certain condition does not automatically make it good. Someone may be born with a cleft palate, or with a deformed artery, but that does not make such conditions good. Likewise, some are born with certain genetic predispositions to alcoholism, but this does not mean such disordered desires for alcohol are morally good.

Objections

One may have remaining doubts about the argument from authority. Would not the same argumentation justify slavery or the oppression of women? It would seem not. Many of the philosophers on the list would condemn slavery, in the sense of owning another as property and having unlimited power over them.[215] Seneca in his *Moral Letters to Lucilius,* Letter 47, writes that slaves must not be treated as if they were beasts of burden, that slaves should be treated with kindness, and that slaves be inspired to serve not out of fear, but out of respect. Further, Augustine,[216] Moses Maimonides,[217] Thomas Aquinas,[218] Duns Scotus,[219] Francisco de Vitoria, Francisco Suarez,[220] John Locke,[221] Immanuel

---

[215] I grant that for some of the philosophers mentioned their views on slavery are more complicated and nuanced than I am able to discuss here. All I wish to point out is that they would condemn slavery in the strict sense as I have defined it here as having unlimited power over another. Whether one is able to enslave prisoners of war or criminals is another issue, which even my objector might grant can be morally licit.

[216] For more on Augustine's views on slavery see: http://www.augnet.org/en/works-of-augustine/his-impact/2437-slavery/. As with other authors mentioned here, Augustine's views are a bit more complicated, but he definitely would have opposed chattel slavery as practiced in the antebellum South.

[217] *Mishneh Torah, Sefer Kinyan, Avadim,* Chapter Nine, http://www.chabad.org/library/article_cdo/aid/1363819/jewish/Chapter-Nine.htm.

[218] ST Supplement, Q52, A2, co., ad 1, and ad 2; cf. also ST II-II, Q104, A5.

[219] *Ordinatio* IV, D36, Q1.

[220] John P. Doyle, *Collected Studies on Francisco Suarez, S.J.* (Leuven University Press, 2011), 350-352.

Kant,[222] Edmund Burke,[223] and George Santayana[224] opposed chattel slavery. The argument from authority thus would not lend moral support to chattel slavery.

As for the oppression of women, no philosopher, or very few, would have asserted, "women ought to be oppressed." Various philosophers have made sexist statements about woman, but there are also numerous statements to the contrary among various philosophers. For example, Plato in Book V of *The Republic* famously held that men and women should receive the same education, and that both can participate equally in the civic life of the city, etc. Thomas Aquinas held that women are not to be subject to men as slaves,[225] nor are husbands allowed to kill their wives on their own authority, even if the wife be caught in the very act of adultery.[226] Aquinas also held that the wife is not bound to pay the marriage debt to her husband if he does not ask for it, whereas the husband is bound to pay the marriage debt to his wife even if she does not ask for it.[227] The husband must also be sensitive to the needs of his wife, as he is bound to offer it to her if he notices she desires it, and even if she does not ask for it.[228] Further, all the Christian Medieval philosophers would have been aware of St. Paul's letter in Ephesians 5:25 where he admonishes husbands to love your wives, as Christ loved the Church, and gave himself up [even unto death] for her.

---

[221] *Second Treatise of Government,* Chapter IV: Of Slavery.

[222] *The Science of Right,* Division of the Science of Right, First Part, Private Right, Of the Mode of Having Anything External as One's Own, Constitutional and Juridical Consequences arising from the Nature of the Civil Union, D. The Right of Assigning Offices and Dignities in the State.

[223] *Sketch of the Negro Code,* http://www.econlib.org/library/LFBooks/Burke/brkSWv4c7.html.

[224] Santayana, *Reason in Art* Chapter II: "Some arts, but no men, are slaves by nature" (In *The Life of Reason,* vol. IV. New York: Dover Publications, 1982. Accessed January 5, 2018, https://www.gutenberg.org/files/15000/15000-h/vol4.html).

[225] ST I, Q92, A3.

[226] ST Supplement, Q60, A1.

[227] ST Supplement, Q64, A5, ad 2.

[228] Ibid. Q64, A2. None of these quotes are meant to excuse other statements from Aquinas on woman, but rather to point out that he does have positive things to say about the relations between the sexes and the dignity of woman.

Even granted that a single proposition can be found that most philosophers held throughout history about women (e.g. "women are generally intellectually inferior"), the point is that we have good reasons to believe the contrary. As we have examined, we do not have good reasons to the contrary with regards to homosexual activity.

Conclusion

Since there are no good arguments to the contrary, and since most of the moral experts (the philosophers) throughout history have condemned homosexual activity, as morally bad, it is highly probable that it is a bad action. Prior to the 20th century and Sartre, about 92% of all the major philosophers throughout history (who wrote on the topic) condemned it; about 2% neither condemned nor approved of it; and only about 6% approved of it. After Sartre through the last few decades, those condemning it dropped to about 80%. Still, imagine if we had the same consensus among experts on just about any other issue. We would surely be justified in saying they are probably right. Few similar consensuses can be found among the experts.

Chapter II: What is a Lie?

In the last we chapter, we examined arguments in favor of homosexual acts and found them to be lacking. We have also found the consensus of the philosophers against homosexual acts to be quite strong. We have yet to treat directly Aquinas's thought on the matter. Before doing so, however, we digress to engage his thought on the morality of lying. Aquinas held that lying and homosexual acts are both wrong for similar reasons. He also held that both actions are always wrong regardless of circumstances. We will begin first with his account of lying and then see how or whether it applies to the morality of homosexual conduct. Before addressing Aquinas's account of the immorality of lying, however, we must first start with an account of what constitutes a lie. This is important in order for one to see which speech acts fall under the condemnation of lying and which do not. Just as an incorrect definition of murder may free the guilty (or unjustly condemn the innocent), so too an incorrect definition of lying has moral implications.

There has been much discussion in the literature in the last few decades concerning what constitutes a lie. Many different definitions have been proposed. We will be assessing these different definitions here in order to see where Aquinas's account falls and because we are not merely commenting on Aquinas's definition of lying for its own sake. We want to know whether what he said is true, particularly in relation to the most recent research on this issue.

For the sake of greater clarity, I begin with a broad division of definitions of lying into what I call the moral and non-moral definitions of lying (each of which has further subdivisions). The moral definitions of lying include moral terms such as *right, undue, unreasonable*, or *wrong* within the definition. Non-moral definitions, by contrast, include no moral terms either explicitly or implicitly. Non-moral definitions are overwhelmingly the more widely accepted view, both among philosophers and the common man. Nevertheless, it is important to treat the moral definitions, which would, if correct, have a significant impact on the debate over the morality of lying.

Part One: Moral Definitions of Lying

By far the most famous moral definition of lying is that proposed by Janet Smith, Charles Curran, and the first printing of the *Catechism of the Catholic Church,* no. 2483.[229] Smith proposes that the correct definition of lying is to speak or act against the truth in order to lead into error *someone who has the right to know the truth.*[230] This definition of lying has its origins in the Protestant lawyer Hugo Grotius,[231] although it was not adopted in Catholic circles until the late 18th century.[232] This view will be called the "right to know" view or the "Grotian definition" of lying.

Other moral definitions of lying are not as popular, but have been proposed. P. Seraphinus a Loiano defines a lie as "the denial of communicable truth." He defines "communicable truth" as "truth which is not part of a secret that ought to be preserved or that could licitly be preserved."[233] Aemilio Berardi and Brouillard define lying as an untruth

---

[229] Smith, "Fig Leaves and Falsehoods." Charles E. Curran, "Absolute Norms and Medical Ethics," in *Absolutes in Moral Theology?* (Washington, D.C.: Corpus Books, 1968), 124.
The qualifier "who has the right to know the truth" was later dropped in the second and final edition of the Catechism. As late as 2008 the Vatican website still retained the "right to know" qualifier in the English and German editions, although not in the Latin, Italian, or French (cf. Lawrence Dewan, "St. Thomas, Rhonheimer, and the Object of the Human Act," *Nova et Vetera,* English Edition 6, no. 1 (2008): 95). They later dropped the qualifier in the English; as of my writing this (March 21st, 2018) the qualifier still remains in the German on the Vatican website.
[230] Smith, "Fig Leaves and Falsehoods."
[231] Tollefsen, *Lying and Christian Ethics,* 27. Julius A. Dorszynski, *Catholic Teaching About the Morality of Falsehood*, PhD diss., The Catholic University of America, 1948 (Washington, D.C.: Catholic University of America Press, 1948), 30. Technically Dorszynski does not say this view was first invented by Grotius, but Grotius is the first one that Dorszynski mentions as holding this view. Apparently, he is not aware of anyone before Grotius who held such a view.
[232] Gregor Müller, OSB, *Die Wahrhaftigkeitspflicht Und Die Problematik Der Lüge* (Freiburg, Basel, Wien: Herder, 1962), 212; also footnote 9.
[233] Loiano, *Institutiones,* 2, 510, 512, cited in Julius A. Dorszynski, *Catholic Teaching About the Morality of Falsehood*, 14.

that harms society.[234] Hilary of Poitiers defines it as an untruth that injures our neighbor.[235] Arthurus Vermeersch and others define lying as *formal* speech contrary to the mind.[236] By formal speech they mean "speech which one is not morally forced to utter."[237] Jean-Jacques Rousseau defines a lie as "to conceal a truth we ought to make manifest."[238] Hadley Arkes defines lying as "an unjustified act of speaking falsely."[239] Don Fallis says that lying occurs when "(a) you say something that you believe to be false and (b) you believe that you are in a situation where the following [Gricean] norm of conversation is in effect: *'Do not say what you believe to be false.'*"[240]

---

[234] Berardi, *Praxis confessariorum,* 409, Brouillard, "Le mensonge," *Etudes,* 205 (1930), 190 ff, cited in Dorszynski, *Catholic Teaching About the Morality of Falsehood,* 49.

[235] St. Hilary of Poitiers, *Tractatus in Ps. 14,* v. 2, 3 (*CSEL,* 22, 91), as cited in Dorszynski, 50.

[236] Vermeersch, *Theologie moralis principia,* 2, 661, as cited in Julius A. Dorszynski, 67.

[237] Ibid., 67.

[238] Mary Gennuso, "What's in a Lie? Rousseau's 'Reveries' and Ribbon Incident," *International Studies In Philosophy* 38, no. 1 (January 1, 2006): 48.

[239] Arkes, "When Speaking Falsely Is Right."

[240] Don Fallis, "What Is Lying?," *Journal of Philosophy* 106, no. 1 (January 1, 2009): 56. Paul Grice first introduced the Gricean norms in his 1989 work, "Logic and Conversation" (*Studies in the Way of Words,* 22-40). The topic of lying is only treated tangentially in Grice's original work. Grice's main point is to explicate different senses of conversational implicature, and in doing so which conversational moves should be ruled out (e.g. when should you say little and just leave unsaid what is merely implied?). According to Grice, the overarching condition for conversation is what he calls the "Cooperative Principle". "Make your conversational contribution such as is required, at the stage at which it occurs, by the accepted purpose or direction of the talk exchange in which you are engaged" (26). Under this general condition are four submaxims or norms of conversation related to quantity, quality, relation, and manner. Under quantity fall the following maxims: "Make your contribution as informative as is required (for the current purposes of the exchange)" and "Do not make your contribution more informative than is required." Under quality falls the supermaxim "Try to make your contribution one that is true," and the submaxims of "Do not say what you believe to be false" and "Do not say that for which you lack adequate evidence." Under relation falls the one maxim of "Be relevant." Under manner falls the supermaxim of "Be perspicuous" and various submaxims like "Avoid obscurity of expression," etc. Fallis, in his definition of lying, is referring to Grice's maxim of quality. It is unclear whether or why it is important that Fallis borrows this norm from Grice's work. Fallis' definition seems

Problems

These moral definitions, however, all encounter serious objections. I will begin with objections to the Grotian definition and then treat the other moral definitions.[241]

The first set of objections to the Grotian definition is that it claims certain statements are not lies, although most people would consider them to be lies. For example, nobody in the grocery store has any right to know I have $5 in my pocket. Yet if I walk around the grocery store and randomly go up to strangers telling them "I have no money in my pocket" I would surely be lying. But it follows on the "right to know" view that this is no lie, which is counterintuitive. As Edward Feser says,

> In this connection, it is not the Scholastic, but rather those who propose redefinitions of lying like "A lie is a falsehood told to someone who has a right to the truth," who are at odds with common sense, at least where the definition of *what a lie is* is concerned.[242]

A second objection may be raised against the "right to know" view. Nobody in the waiting room of the doctor's office has any right to know my life story. If I went around telling them untrue fanciful stories about my childhood, I would be lying. However, on the "right to know" view not only is this not a lie, but if I acted in this manner at the doctor's office every day I would not be telling lies; furthermore, I would not rightly be called a pathological liar.

One may object that in the grocery store and in the doctor's office people do have a right to know the truth. I am violating their rights by

---

easily analyzable on its own terms apart from any specification that his norm is borrowed from Grice.

[241] For further details see: John Skalko, "Catholics and Hugo Grotius' Definition of Lying: A Critique," *Proceedings of the American Catholic Philosophical Association* (89) (2015): 159-179. Much of my criticisms in the following section repeat, at least in part, what I have stated earlier in my 2015 article (see above). They are reprinted here with permission.

[242] Edward Feser, "What Counts as a Lie?," *Edwardfeser.blogspot.com* November 15, 2010, accessed December 12, 2018,
  http://edwardfeser.blogspot.com/2010/11/what-counts-as-lie.html.

knowingly uttering falsehoods to them. Ergo, I am lying. To this objection, I reply as follows: if these random people really have a right to know, then it follows that you owe the truth to them. Whatever one has a right to is due to that person. Since that person has a right to the truth, it follows that he is due the truth. But denying another what is his due is wrong. Ergo, it follows that not telling him the truth is wrong. Silence is not telling him the truth. Thus, it follows that being silent to random people about these random facts is morally wrong. On this interpretation of the "right to know" view, it logically follows that one is morally obligated to go around telling random people random truths that you know.

This leads to a third objection. If the Nazi at the door has no right to know whether I am hiding Jews in my home, then not only could I tell him, without lying, that "I am hiding no Jews;" I would also be an honest man in so doing. On the "right to know" definition, the honest man can fabricate false stories in doctors' offices, tell random customers falsehoods about how much money is in his pocket, and tell people falsehoods about what he had for breakfast.[243] Further, consider someone who truthfully told the Nazi at the door that he is hiding Jews. Though this would be stupid, such a man is surely honest. On the "right to know" definition, however, the one who speaks falsely is just as honest. If he did not lie, but still spoke propositionally, then he must have been speaking honestly. It surely seems strange to call the one who utters a falsehood honest.

Further, if one wishes to redefine lying in terms of the "right to know", then so too must one redefine perjury. As Aquinas says, quoting from Hugh of Saint Victor, in ST II-II, Q98, A1, perjury is "a lie confirmed by an oath."[244] An oath is to call upon God as witness that what one says is true.[245] On the Thomistic definition of a lie, a lie is asserting as true what one believes to be false.[246] So perjury is asserting as true

---

[243] Tollefsen, *Lying and Christian Ethics,* 29.

[244] Sed contra est quod periurium definitur esse *mendacium iuramento firmatum.* All Latin citations from the Summa are from the Pauline edition unless otherwise indicated.

[245] ST II-II, Q89, A1.

[246] More on this definition in Aquinas will be given later, but for now I offer the following texts as an indication of its veracity: *Super Sent. III,* D38, Q1, A3: quandocumque aliquis loquitur quod in corde non habet...Hoc autem contingit in

what one believes to be false by calling upon God as a witness. On the Grotian definition of lying, it follows then, not only that saying an untruth to someone who has no right to know is not lying, but also that saying such an untruth cannot constitute perjury. Thus, if a Nazi came to your door and you said, "I swear by God, I am hiding no Jews" when in fact you are, then you are not perjuring yourself.

Hugo Grotius claims his definition of lying does not pertain to the taking of oaths. This claim, however, is ad hoc. The existing or permanent rights of the Nazi are in no sense violated if you call upon God as a witness to your statement.

A sixth difficulty for the Grotian definition is as follows: people generally do not have a right to know the truth about what your religion is. It is not a "a violation of the existing and permanent rights of the person" to tell them you are Catholic when you are really Lutheran. On what basis do they have any right to know this? It is true that Our Lord says we must not deny our faith before others,[247] but on the Grotian definition it would follow only that our speaking falsely is wrong due to disobedience to his command, not because it is a lie. If one accepts the Grotian (or Smith's) definition, however, telling someone "I am a Catholic" when one is Lutheran would not be a lie.

On the Grotian definition too it would follow that if the martyrs had not borne witness to Christ, but in order to save their own lives, they had instead denied that they were followers of Jesus Christ, they would not have been liars. Telling their persecutors that they were not followers of Christ would have been no violation of the "existing and permanent rights" of the persecutors. Ergo, the martyrs would not have lied if they

---

omni mendacio. Latin is from Moos. *Quaestiones de Quolibets VIII*, Q6, A4: et ideo quando aliquis voce enuntiat quod non habet in mente, quod importatur in nomine mendacii. Latin is from the Leonine, vol. 12. ST II-II, Q110, A1: Sed tamen ratio mendacii sumitur a formali falsitate, ex hoc scilicet quod aliquis habet voluntatem falsum enuntiandi. Unde et mendacium nominatur ex eo quod contra mentem dicitur.

[247] Cf. Matthew 10:32-33: "Everyone who acknowledges me before others I will acknowledge before my heavenly Father. But whoever denies me before others, I will deny before my heavenly Father" (NAB); Luke 12:8-9: "I tell you, everyone who acknowledges me before others the Son of Man will acknowledge before the angels of God. But whoever denies me before others will be denied before the angels of God" (NAB).

had denied their faith.

Further, on the Grotian definition it follows that lying under duress is a contradiction in terms.[248] If one's life is in danger and someone points a gun at you and says, "Tell me a lie or I'll kill you" it is literally impossible for you to tell him a lie. Why? Because such a person has no right to anything that you know. Consequently, the implications are that whatever you tell him is not a lie. If the murderer is smart enough and knows that it is impossible for you to lie to him, then he will have to kill you in any event, if he wishes to carry through on his threat.

Further, on the "right to know" definition, it follows not only that telling the Nazi at the door "I am hiding no Jews" is not lying, but also that anything one says to the Nazi about the Jews' whereabouts is not a lie. In other words, imagine the following scenario. You are hiding a family of Jews at your home. The Nazi comes to the door and asks, "Are you hiding any Jews?" The Nazi has no right to know you are hiding them. On the "right to know" definition it is absolutely impossible for you to lie to the Nazi about the whereabouts of those Jews. You can tell him any wild manner of stories about those Jews, but whatever you say about their whereabouts is no lie. This is a bit strange. As James Mahon says, "surely…it is *possible* to lie to a would-be murderer, whether it is impermissible…or permissible."[249]

Further, if one accepts Grotius's or Smith's definition, then since lying violates the rights of another, this means that all lies are contrary to justice. Injustice is thus included in the very definition of lying. Ergo, to say "lying is unjust" would be a tautology.[250] It would thus be impossible for one to give a demonstration that lying is unjust and nearly pointless to argue with someone whether lying is unjust. One who does not see that lying is unjust would not understand the meaning of the terms. That "lying is unjust" is a tautology becomes particularly clear on

---

[248] This view is expressed as an objection to a similar definition of lying in Mahon, *Stanford Encyclopedia of Philosophy,* s.v. "The Definition of Lying and Deception," Section 2.3, accessed December 12, 2018,
http://plato.stanford.edu/entries/lying-definition/.
[249] Cf. Mahon, *Stanford Encyclopedia of Philosophy,* s.v. "The Definition of Lying and Deception," Section 2.3, accessed December 12, 2018.
[250] Cf. Mahon, *Stanford,* s.v. "The Definition of Lying and Deception," Section 2.3.

Arkes' definition of lying as "an unjustified act of speaking falsely." This poses a problem for the "right to know" view. Whatever one may hold about the morality of lying surely it is possible for one to understand what a lie is and yet hold, without contradiction, that lying is not always unjust.

The last major set of objections to the "right to know" view is that it makes all acts of lying seriously bad acts. A major motivation for accepting the Grotian definition is that the traditional absolute view that all lying is wrong seems overly harsh. Ironically, however, the Grotian view is overly harsh in its own way. Let us begin with Augustine's eightfold division of lying:[251]

1. Lies in matters of religious doctrine (a mischievous lie[252]),
2. Lies against man that profit nobody, but injure someone (a mischievous lie),
3. Lies against man that injure someone but profit another (a mischievous lie),
4. Lies for the mere sake of lying and deceiving,
5. Lies for the sake of pleasing (jocose lies),
6. Lies for the sake of profiting someone in saving money (an officious lie),
7. Lies for the sake of saving a man from death (an officious lie),
8. Lies for the sake of saving one from unlawful defilement of the body (an officious lie).

The Grotian definition of lying states that a lie must be "a violation of the existing and permanent rights of the person, to whom a discourse or particular signs, are directed." It follows that merely officious lies, to which Augustine refers in his three last kinds of lies, cannot possibly be lies, for they benefit someone but harm no one. Further, Augustine's fifth kind of lying is for the sake of humor (jocose lies), which harms

---

[251] Augustine, *De Mendacio (On Lying)*, n. 25, trans. H. Brown, ed. Kevin Knight, vol. 3, Nicene and Post-Nicene Fathers, First Series (Buffalo: Christian Literature Publishing Co, 1887), accessed December 12, 2018, http://www.newadvent.org/fathers/1312.htm.
[252] Augustine's eightfold taxonomy is organized by Aquinas in ST II-II, Q110, A2 into mischievous, jocose, officious, and pathological lies.

nobody. Consequently, on the Grotian definition such lies do not exist. This means that the only actual cases of lying belong to the first four kinds of lies. Because the first three of these injure another, Aquinas groups them together as mischievous lies. All mischievous lies are seriously bad actions.[253] The fourth kind of lie is that which is told out of the mere enjoyment of lying, by one who is a pathological vicious liar. Such lies are also gravely evil. Thus, it follows that the only kind of lies that exist on the Grotian definition are grievously evil and seriously flawed actions. The paradox here is that on the "right to know" view there is no such thing as a "little white lie," and "it is also not possible to tell an intentionally benevolent lie."[254]

In sum, the Grotian or "right to know" definition of lying suffers from a host of difficulties and ought to be abandoned.[255]

Likewise, the definitions of Berardi, Brouillard, Vermeersch, and Rousseau suffer from difficulties. On Berardi and Brouillard's definition a lie is an untruth that harms society. A first problem with their definition is that it is unclear what exactly constitutes harming society. What type of harm? How grievous? Does doing any action that only slightly harms myself constitute enough harm that it also harms society? Or is it only harm that affects society as a whole? If only harm that affects all of society, then can I utter an untruth, without thereby lying, that harms my

---

[253] Cf. ST II-II, Q110, A4, s.c., ad 1; ST II-II, Q112, A2, ad 3. Further, intending to injure another unjustly is a flawed action against justice and according to Thomas all flawed actions against justice are gravely bad in their kind (cf. ST II-II, Q59, A4: "Omne autem nocumentum alteri illatum ex se caritati repugnat"; see also obj. 2 and ad 2).

[254] Mahon, *Stanford Encyclopedia of Philosophy,* Summer 2009 Edition, s.v. "The Definition of Lying and Deception," Section 1.6, accessed December 12, 2018, https://stanford.library.sydney.edu.au/archives/sum2009/entries/lying-definition/.

[255] The difficulty with the moral definitions of lying is that one can presumably keep modifying them to try to get out of these counterexamples. Alan Vincelette, for example, attempts to save the Grotian definition by replying to many of my earlier criticisms (see "On the Warranted Falsehood, or in Defense of the Grotian Qualifier: A Response to Tollefsen and Skalko," *Bogoslovni vestnik* 77, no. 3/4 (2017): 637-653). While Vincelette does avoid many of my earlier criticisms, his new account has not answered all of my criticisms, and his own definition suffers from further problems. For a full reply see my article: "Why the Revised Grotian Definition of Lying Still Fails: A Reply to Vincelette," *Bogoslovni vestnik* 78, no. 1 (2018): 67-77.

neighbor monetarily if it does not affect society as a whole? Further, on their definition, does it follow that I could tell all manners of untruths to prisoners on death row since these untruths are not harming society? If any of these cases counts as lying on their definition, then what non-arbitrary line can be drawn, such that telling the Nazi at the door, "There are no Jews in my house," does not constitute lying?

Further, under Berardi and Brouillard's definition little white lies do not exist. White lies, by definition, are lies that are small and harm nobody.

Rousseau's definition of lying as "conceal[ing] a truth we ought to make manifest" is also problematic. It confuses unjustified deception, silence, and mental reservation with lying. Staying silent when one ought to speak is wrong, but surely it is not the same thing as lying. Likewise, making a mental reservation when one ought to speak clearly is wrong, but surely this is not the same thing as telling a lie.[256]

Fallis defines a lie as, when "(a) you say something that you believe to be false and (b) you believe that you are in a situation where the following [Gricean] norm of conversation is in effect: *'Do not say what you believe to be false*;'" his definition has been criticized in the literature so much that Fallis himself later abandons his earlier position.[257] Fallis offers the following critique of his earlier position:

> Suppose that Sheldon…someone who is socially clueless—is aware that people do not usually say what they do not believe, but is not

---

[256] In fairness to Rousseau, he later qualifies his definition of lying as "everything, which contrary to the truth, hurts justice in any way whatsoever is a lie" (Gennuso, 50). If this is indeed Rousseau's later definition, and he is not confused in changing his account, then many of my earlier criticisms of Smith's and Grotius's accounts would apply to Rousseau's definition.

[257] For the criticisms see: Mahon, *Stanford Encyclopedia of Philosophy*, s.v. "The Definition of Lying and Deception," Summer 2009 Edition, Section 1.6; James Edwin Mahon, "Two Definitions of Lying," *International Journal of Applied Philosophy* 22, no. 2 (2008): 226-227; Andreas Stokke, "Lying and Asserting," *Journal of Philosophy* 110, no. 1 (January 1, 2013): 2-6. Don Fallis later abandons his earlier position in "Davidson Was Almost Right about Lying," *Australasian Journal of Philosophy* 91, no. 2 (2013): 349-350, 352. As pointed out earlier, to understand Fallis's definition of a lie, it is not necessary to delve into much detail regarding Paul Grice's conversational norms.

aware that people think that people *ought not* to say what they do not believe. Because he knows that people regularly tell the truth, it might occur to him to say something that he does not believe to Penny—such as 'On Friday night, we're going to participate in my cousin Leopold's drug intervention'—in order to deceive her. While he knows that there is such a *regularity*, he is not aware that there is a *norm* against saying what you do not believe. Even so, he seems to be lying.[258]

I have three final criticisms that apply to all of these moral definitions of lying. First, on all these accounts it is not possible to lie to the Nazi at the door about the whereabouts of the Jews they are seeking to kill. One can tell any manner of wild stories about their whereabouts, but no matter what one says on such definitions of lying, it follows that one is not lying.

Second, since lying is opposed to the virtue of truthfulness, it follows that if one is not telling a lie, one is not acting against the virtue of truthfulness. On all these accounts, telling the Nazi at the door that you are not hiding any Jews is not a lie. Thus, on all these accounts telling such an untruth is not acting against the virtue of truthfulness. In short, these accounts claim that the honest man can speak untruths that he knows to be false without in any way taking away from his honesty. But how can asserting what you know to be false not be contrary to honesty?

Finally, it appears that the primary motivation for accepting these moral definitions of lying is that one wishes to uphold the absolute view that all lies are wrong but still allow for more leeway in particular cases than is normally allowed. The same redefinition, however, may be applied to other types of actions. If lying can be redefined in moral terms, then why cannot abortion be redefined as the "undue taking of a fetus's life," or murder as "unnecessary killing," or homosexual acts as "unloving sexual activity between two persons of the same sex"? The result here is to make moral absolutes empty of any significant content. This consequence is not a mere theoretical slippery slope, but has already been embraced by the Proportionalists.[259]

---

[258] Ibid., 349.

[259] Charles E. Curran, "Veritatis Splendor: A Revisionist Perspective," in *Veritatis Splendor: American Responses*, ed. Michael E. Allsopp and John J. O'Keefe (Kan-

Part Two: Non-moral Definitions of Lying

Besides all the definitions that define lying with moral terms, there are also a host of definitions of lying that do not add any such moral qualifiers to the definition. Aquinas is among those who had a non-moral definition of lying. Since this book is primarily on Aquinas, I will begin with an analysis of his definition and then proceed to treat other non-moral definitions.

In ST II-II, Q110, A3, Aquinas describes a lie as *voce significet id quod non habet in mente.*[260] This description, however, is not the full picture. The phrase "signify by voice what one has not in the mind" is merely a shorthand definition of his more complete account given earlier in Q110, A1, where he says that in order for a manifestation or enunciation to be a lie, it must be a voluntary act that is intended. This manifestation or enunciation must further be of what is false, though not of any falsity. Falsity must be distinguished into material and formal falsity. Material falsity is simply the fact that what is said is false. Say for example Bob's car is blue. Someone who says, "Bob's car is green," would thus be asserting a material falsity. Formal falsity is the intention to say what one believes to be false.[261] Formal falsity is essential to a lie, whereas material falsity is not. One who *intends to* speak falsely but accidentally tells the truth really is telling a lie. Thus, if Bob says his car is blue when he really thinks it is red, then he is telling a lie, even if inci-

---

sas City, MO: Sheed & Ward, 1995), 232: "All would agree that murder is always wrong because by definition murder is *unjustified* killing" (emphasis added). Ibid., 238: "Likewise, revisionist moral theologians are willing to accept some intrinsically evil acts when the object of the act is described in formal terms..." Interestingly, Charles Curran specifically adopts a moral definition of lying in order to deny the perverted faculty argument, cf. Curran, "Absolute Norms and Medical Ethics," 124.

[260] In his *Commentary on the Nicomachean Ethics* Book IV.7, Lecture 15, he describes it as *repraesentat rem aliter quam sit mentiendo;* in his *Quaestiones de Quolibets* VIII, Q6, A4, he describes lying as *quando aliquis voce enuntiat quod non habet in mente;* and in his *Super Sent.* III, D38, A3, he describes lying as *quandocumque aliquis loquitur quod in corde non habet.*

[261] This definition of formal falsity may require further nuancing, but it will work for our purposes here.

dentally minutes before he spoke a mass mob ran out into the parking lot and painted it blue. Conversely, one who intends to speak the truth, but accidentally tells something false is not lying. Thus, if Bob says his car keys are on his dresser, and truly believes it, then he is not lying, even if minutes before he spoke the cat swallowed his keys and ran off with them. Formal falsity, or the intention to say what one believes to be false, is essential to a lie; material falsity is not. Thus, what Aquinas means in ST II-II, Q110, A3 by "signify[ing] what one has not in the mind" is that one says what one believes to be false.

In A1, Aquinas uses the words *manifestatio sive enuntiatio* to describe the type of speech used in telling a lie. This is a significant point. It is not speech *per se* or words or mere signs or voice themselves that are being abused in telling a lie. It is *manifestatio sive enuntiatio.* Words in themselves as mere signs are neither true nor false.[262] Further, not all sentences are true or false. A prayerful request, for example, is neither true nor false.[263] Questions are neither true nor false, nor are commands. Only propositions or assertions are true or false.[264]

---

[262] Cf. Aristotle, *De Interpretatione,* trans. E.M. Edghill, in *The Basic Works of Aristotle,* ed. Richard McKeon (New York: Modern Library, 2001), Chapters 1 & 4. Cf. Aquinas, *Expositio libri Peryermeneias*, Book I, Lesson 3.

[263] Aristotle, *De Interpretatione,* Chapter 4.

[264] Cf. Aristotle, *De Interpretatione,* Chapter 4. The Greek term Aristotle uses for propositions is ἀπόφανσις. Liddell and Scott define it as a declaration or a statement (Cf. Henry George Liddell and Robert Scott, comps., *A Greek-English Lexicon*, s.v. "ἀπόφαν-σισ, εωσ, ή"). Aquinas's translation of this Greek term is *enunciatio.* Edghill translates the term as a proposition. The Latin meaning of Aquinas's use of the term, *enunciatio,* is practically synonymous with that of assertion: "Next he shows that this definition differentiates the enunciation from other speech, when he says, *Truth or falsity is not present in all speech however*, etc. In the case of imperfect or incomplete speech it is clear that it does not signify the true or false, since it does not make complete sense to the mind of the hearer and therefore does not completely express a judgment of reason in which the true or false consists. Having made this point, however, it must be noted that there are five species of perfect speech that are complete in meaning: enunciative, deprecative, imperative, interrogative, and vocative....Of these species of speech the enunciative is the only one in which there is truth or falsity, for it alone signifies the conception of the intellect absolutely and it is in this that there is truth or falsity....These four species of speech do not signify the conception of the intellect in which there is truth or falsity, but a certain order following upon this. Consequently, truth or falsity is not found in any of them, but only in enunciative speech, which signifies what the mind con-

Assertions are crucial to Aquinas's account of lying.[265] As evidence of this point, I cite ST II-II, Q110, A3, ad 1, where Aquinas clarifies his notion of lying even further:

---

ceives from things. It follows that all the modes of speech in which the true or false is found are contained under the enunciation, which some call *indicative* or *suppositive*" (Cf. Thomas Aquinas, *Expositio Libri Peryermeneias*, trans. Jean T. Oesterle (Milwaukee: Marquette University Press, 1962), Book I, Lesson 7.4-5, accessed January 16, 2019, http://dhspriory.org/thomas/PeriHermeneias.htm#1). The point here is that regardless of how one translates the Greek term, there is only one mood of speech that involves truth or falsity. For much of this paper I will refer to this mood as that of assertion instead of a proposition or the indicative, etc. The reason for this is that actors make what appear to be propositions, but do not really assert what they are saying. Both Aquinas and Aristotle, it seems, would categorize the speeches of the actor of Hamlet (as opposed to the character) as something other than assertions or *enunciatio.* The person playing the part of a character is not asserting what he says to be true or false. Thus, when Romeo tells Juliet "I love you" he is only speaking this as Romeo and not from his own person, unless of course he really does love her in real life. This type of speech in playacting is not involved in the meaning of Aristotle's ἀπόφανσις nor Aquinas's *enunciatio.* Thus, I will translate Aquinas's Latin and Aristotle's Greek as *assertion.*

[265] Rockcastle's research on this matter has been a great asset for bringing to light various passages on the importance of assertions in Aquinas's account. What follows is largely inspired by the texts cited in S. Austen Rockcastle, "St. Thomas Aquinas On The Nature And Morality Of Lying" (PhD diss., University of St. Thomas - Houston, 1993), Chapter 9. Joseph Boyle also holds that assertions are fundamental to a proper understanding of Aquinas's account of lying; see "The Absolute Prohibition of Lying and the Origins of the Casuistry of Mental Reservation: Augustinian Arguments and Thomistic Developments": 59. Aquinas uses *enuntiatio* or *enuntiat,* which I take to be practically the same as an assertion, many times during his discussion of lying: Cf. ST II-II, Q110, A1, "Whether lying is always opposed truth?", s.c.: Sed contra est quod Augustinus dicit, in libro *contra Mendacium*: *Nemo dubitet mentiri eum qui falsum* **enuntiat** *causa fallendi. Quapropter* **enuntiationem** *falsi cum voluntate ad fallendum prolatam, manifestum est esse mendacium;* ST II-II, Q110, A1, co: "Respondeo dicendum quod actus moralis ex duobus speciem sortitur: scilicet ex obiecto, et ex fine. Nam finis est obiectum voluntatis, quae est primum movens in moralibus actibus....Quae quidem manifestatio, sive **enuntiatio,** est rationis actus conferentis signum ad signatum....Inquantum tamen huiusmodi manifestatio sive **enuntiatio** est actus moralis, oportet quod sit voluntarius ex intentione voluntatis dependens. Obiectum autem proprium manifestationis sive **enuntiationis** est verum vel falsum. Intentio vero voluntatis inordinatae potest ad duo ferri: quorum unum est ut falsum **enuntietur;** aliud quidem est effectus proprius falsae **enuntiationis,** ut scilicet aliquis fallatur. Si ergo ista tria concurrant, scilicet quod falsum sit id quod **enuntiatur,** et quod adsit voluntas falsum **enuntiandi,** et iterum intentio fallendi, tunc est falsitas materialiter, quia fal-

It is unlawful to hold that something false is asserted (*aliquod falsum asseri*) either in the Gospel or in any canonical Scriptures, or that the writers thereof have told lies....Hence Augustine says (De Consens. Evang. ii): "He that has the wit to understand that in order to know the truth it is necessary to get at the sense, will conclude that he must not be the least troubled, no matter by what words that sense is expressed."[266]

Note that in the reply to the first objection Aquinas does not use the phrase "signify what one has not in the mind" to describe the nature of a lie. Rather he uses the phrase *aliquod falsum asseri*. This is a good indication that one should not take his description of lying as "signify[ing] what one has not in the mind" in the *responsio* of Q110, A3 as his final word on the nature of lying.

Further evidence that assertions are crucial to Aquinas's account of lying can be found in his *Commentary on the Sentences* III, D38, A5, ad 1:

---

sum dicitur; et formaliter, propter voluntatem falsum dicendi; et effective, propter voluntatem falsitatem imprimendi. Sed tamen ratio mendacii sumitur a formali falsitate: ex hoc scilicet quod aliquis habet voluntatem falsum **enuntiandi.** Unde et mendacium nominatur ex eo quod *contra mentem* dicitur. Et ideo si quis falsum **enuntiet** credens illud verum esse, est quidem falsum materialiter, sed non formaliter....Sic ergo patet quod mendacium directe et formaliter opponitur virtuti veritatis;" ST II-II, Q110, A3, ad 6: "sicut Augustinus dicit, in libro *contra Mendacium, quidquid figurate fit aut dicitur, non est mendacium. Omnis enim* **enuntiatio** *ad id quod* **enuntiat** *referenda est: omne autem figurate aut factum aut dictum hoc* **enuntiat** *quod significat eis quibus intelligendum prolatum est.*" Emphasis added. Sorensen, who I do not think is a Thomist, also agrees that "Thomas Aquinas condemned lies as a perversion of the practice of **assertion**" (Roy Sorensen, "Bald-Faced Lies! Lying Without The Intent To Deceive," *Pacific Philosophical Quarterly* 88, no. 2 (2007): 254; emphasis added).

[266] Translation is adapted from the Fathers of the English Dominican Province: (Thomas Aquinas, *Summa Theologica*, trans. Fathers of the English Dominican Province, 2nd and Revised ed., vol. II-II (1920), accessed June 3, 2015, http://www.newadvent.org/summa/3.htm). Ad primum ergo dicendum quod nec in Evangelio, nec in aliqua Scriptura canonica fas est opinari aliquod falsum **asseri,** nec quod scriptores earum mendacium dixerunt....Unde Augustinus dicit, in libro *de Consensus Evangelist.: Nullo modo laborandum esse iudicat qui prudenter intelligit ipsas sententias esse necessarias cognoscendae veritati, quibuslibet verbis fuerint explicatae.* Emphasis added.

114

> It must be said that he who speaks falsely in disputations, although knowingly, does not lie, unless he speaks assertively (*nisi asserendo dicat*): since he does not speak falsely from his own person, but by playing the part (*gerens personam*) of the person who denies the truth.[267]

In other words, when one poses hypothetically in a disputation a position that one does not hold, this does not count as a lie. One may say in the midst of a debate: "God does not exist. If this is true, then it follows that there is no necessary being." The first sentence, though spoken, would not constitute a lie even if believed to be false so long as the one who says it is not speaking assertively.

From this *Sentences* text, it also follows that actors are not telling lies when they say things they do not believe. As Rockcastle says, "though Laurence Olivier, in the role of Hamlet, may utter a **contra mentem** proposition such as, for example, 'I am the prince of Denmark,' he does not lie unless he fully commits himself to it, because he does not assert the proposition as Laurence Olivier, but speaks it as Hamlet."[268] The whole context of a play indicates that assertions are being suspended. Olivier isn't making an assertion when he takes on the role of Hamlet. Actors aren't asserting insofar as the person who is the actor isn't really asserting what the character is saying. But within the context of the play it could be said that Hamlet asserts he is the prince of Denmark. The character of a play qua character can be said to be making an assertion. But the character of a play qua the real person behind the character isn't asserting. In other words, Olivier might be an actor playing the part of Hamlet. When Hamlet says he is the prince of Denmark, Hamlet is making an assertion, but Olivier isn't. Assertions don't occur in plays qua the person behind the role, but assertions do occur insofar as the

---

[267] Ad primum ergo dicendum quod ille qui disputando falsum loquitur, quamvis scienter, non mentitur, nisi **asserendo** dicat: quia non ex sua persona falsum illud **enuntiat**, sed gerens personem veritatem negantis.
The translation is my own with the aid of Rockcastle, p. 272. The Latin is from the Moos, p. 1275.
[268] Rockcastle, "St. Thomas Aquinas On The Nature And Morality Of Lying," 274. Emphasis included in the original.

characters qua characters may assert. Hamlet qua Hamlet may be telling a lie, but since Hamlet is a fictional character it is only this fictional character who is lying, not Olivier. Olivier the person can't lie when in the persona of Hamlet, because he qua himself is using speech in a non-assertive way. Actors then are not liars.

Nor do figures of speech count as lies. In ST II-II, Q111 A1, ad 1, Aquinas cites Augustine in support of his view that figures of speech do not count as lies:

> And he cites the example of figures of speech, in which one poses something not as thus asserting it to be (*ut asseratur ita esse*), but we propose it as a figure of another thing which we wish to assert (*assere-re*).[269]

Thus, when Christ pretended he would go farther (Lk. 24:28), he did not lie, as he was merely signifying that he would be going farther by ascending into heaven. Christ was not literally asserting he would go farther. He was signifying something deeper. Similarly, when Abraham told Pharaoh that Sarah was his sister he did not lie. He spoke truly, for she was related to him on his father's side.[270] If one uses words to signify something true, even if in a different sense than their literal meaning, one is not lying. Assertions are necessary for a lie, but even assertions must take into account the nuances of language. In order to assert something as true without lying, one need not fully state everything. One may leave out some details or allow the speaker reasonably to fill in the gaps of the statement. Thus, if there is some reasonable sense in which the assertion is true, which is intended by the speaker and can be understood by a prudent listener, then there is no lie.

Assertions differ from other speech acts. To assert is to put oneself behind the truth of what one says.[271] In asserting one is claiming or pre-

---

[269] Et subiungit exemplum de figurativis locutionibus, in quibus fingitur quaedam res non ut *asseratur* ita esse, sed eam proponimus ut figuram alterius quod *assere* volumus. Emphasis added. The translation is my own.

[270] Cf. ST II-II, Q110, A3, ad 3 and Genesis 20:12.

[271] The etymology of the word assertion is from the Latin *asserere,* which is *ad* (to) + *serere* (to join) (OED). This indicates that in making an assertion one is joining

senting something as if it were true.[272] Tollefsen explains the nature of assertion as follows: "an assertion *that P* involves a communication of judgment *that P.*"[273] The asserter communicates to another that he judges that P is, in fact, true.

Let me explain the terms of Tollefsen's definition of assertion. Communication is "always addressed to someone, whether that someone is a particular person or a more general audience."[274] This can be either an audience that is physically present or removed, as in the case of speaking via radio or on the TV or in writing. The audience can also be a future audience, as in the case of writing a book, for which the audience may not yet exist. "In a *judgment,* a knower affirms the predicate to be true of the subject."[275] Although Tollefsen does not explicitly mention it, not all propositions need be propositional in surface form; some things are propositional in terms of the deep grammar, such as "Yes" or "No."[276] "Yes" and "no," though appearing to be simple words, actually

---

oneself or committing oneself to the claim that one makes. One is putting one's person behind the truth of what one speaks.

[272] Rickaby also seems to grasp well the nature of an assertion as used within a lie when he says that speech as used in a lie indicates an "outward affirmation, the appearance of a serious will to apply predicate to subject" (Rickaby, *Moral Philosophy*, 226, quoted in Dorszynski, *Catholic Teaching About the Morality of Falsehood*, 69-70).

[273] Tollefsen, *Lying and Christian Ethics*, 20.

[274] Ibid., 19.

[275] Ibid., 18.

[276] Cf. Etienne Gilson, *Linguistics and Philosophy: An Essay on the Philosophical Constants of Language* (Notre Dame, IN: University of Notre Dame Press, 1988), 71-72. Cf. also Thomas Aquinas, *Expositio Libri Peryermeneias*, trans. Jean T. Oesterle (Milwaukee: Marquette University Press, 1962), Book I, Lesson 3.11-12, accessed June 1, 2015, http://dhspriory.org/thomas/PeriHermeneias.htm#1: "Here he concludes from what has been said that since there is truth and falsity in the intellect only when there is composition or division, it follows that names and verbs, taken separately, are like thought which is without composition and division; as when we say 'man' or 'white,' and nothing else is added. For these are neither true nor false at this point, but when 'to be' or 'not to be' is added they be come [to be] true or false…Although one might think so, the case of someone giving a,, [sic.] single name as a true response to a question is not an instance that can be raised against this position; for example, suppose someone asks, 'What swims in the sea?' and the answer is 'Fish'; this is not opposed to the position Aristotle is taking here, for the verb that was posited in the question is understood." As further evidence of this

express whole propositions and are assertions. In reply to a question from person A, "Did you eat breakfast?", person B asserts, "Yes," meaning "I ate already." So in judgment one affirms a proposition as true or false.

From this definition of assertion as *a communication* of judgment that P, it follows that if there is no person to whom one is intending *to communicate* then it does not count as an assertion. Thus, it is not possible to tell lies while in a closed room or while speaking to the wall with nobody else around. It is also not possible to tell a lie to oneself, as properly speaking there is no such thing as communicating with oneself. One already knows one's own thoughts. Communication necessarily involves the intention to convey the concepts of the mind to another. If there is no other that is present or intended, then it does not count as communication. Thus, neither assertion nor lying are possible in scenarios where there is no intended audience for a speech.

Aquinas also adds that the intention to deceive is not essential to telling a lie.[277] Thus, in situations where there is no possibility of deception and so no intention to deceive, it is still possible to lie.[278] As we will see in further detail in the next section, the intention to deceive is not essential to a lie. Bald-faced lies are possible. Intention to deceive isn't necessary, but it doesn't follow that an audience isn't necessary. Assertions by definition are acts of communication. Every act of genuine communication requires an intended audience. Where there is no audience there is no communicative action and so no assertion is possible. Just as a glass eye that looks like a real eye and shares many features in common with a real eye doesn't make it a real eye, so too a man who utters "Santa Claus is real" in an empty soundproof room might look like he is asserting, but he is not.

---

point one can find that among the Irish there was traditionally no such thing as the words *yes* or *no* (Stenson, *Basic Irish: A Grammar and Workbook,* 2008, 101). This lack of such words is why today many of them will simply repeat what the speaker said or say, "It is," in order to indicate approval rather than saying *yes.* Many thanks to Dr. Christopher Martin for pointing out this unique fact about the Irish language.

[277] Cf. also ST II-II, Q110, A1, ad 3.

[278] More will be said on this later when we get to rival accounts of the definition of lying towards the end of this chapter.

Thus, for Aquinas, the definition of a lie is "asserting something that one believes to be false."[279] Assertion by its very nature is proposing to another something as if it were true.[280]

Other non-moral definitions of lying

Aquinas's definition, however, is not the only non-moral definition of lying. Many other such definitions have been presented, especially within the past few decades. An easy way to understand why so many different definitions have been proposed is to start with the standard definition of lying as "uttering a falsehood with the intention to deceive."[281] A first problem with this definition is that there seem to be cases where it is possible to lie, even though no intentional deception is involved. This is called the phenomena of the bald-faced lie.[282] Take the following scenario given by Carson:

> Suppose that a college Dean is cowed whenever he fears that someone *might* threaten a law suit and has a firm, but unofficial policy of never upholding a professor's charge that a student cheated on an exam unless the student confesses in writing to have cheated. The Dean is very cynical about this and believes that students are guilty *whenever* they are charged. A student is caught in the act of cheating on an exam by copying from a crib sheet. The professor fails the student for the course and the student appeals the professor's decision to the Dean who has the ultimate authority to assign the grade. The student is privy to information about the Dean's *de facto* policy and, when called before the Dean, he (the student) affirms that he didn't cheat on the exam. He

---

[279] We will see later whether this definition of Aquinas requires a slight nuancing; it may not quite be the full picture of Aquinas's account.

[280] Tollefsen gives a similar formulation: "in asserting, one puts forth a proposition and endorses that proposition as genuinely reflecting the way things are" (Christopher Tollefsen, "Lying: The Integrity Approach," *The American Journal of Jurisprudence* 52, no. 1 (2007): 276).

[281] Merriam Webster adopts a similar definition: "to make an untrue statement with intent to deceive" (Merriam-Webster.com, s.v. "lie," accessed December 12, 2018, http://www.merriam-webster.com/dictionary/lie).

[282] Sorensen, "Bald-Faced Lies! Lying Without The Intent To Deceive," 251.

claims that he was not copying from the crib sheet. He claims that he inadvertently forgot to put his "review sheet" away when the exam began and that he never looked at it during the exam. The student says this on the record in an official proceeding and thereby warrants the truth of statements he knows to be false. He intends to avoid punishment by doing this. He may have no intention of deceiving the Dean that he didn't cheat. (If he is really hard-boiled, he may take pleasure in thinking that the Dean knows that he is guilty.) An objector might continue and say that the student intends to deceive *someone*—his parents or future employers. However, this isn't necessarily the case. The student may not care whether or not others know that he cheated (he might freely and cynically tell others about his cheating), but simply want to have his grade changed. (If it helps, suppose that the will of a deceased relative calls for the student to inherit a great deal of money if he graduates from the college in question with a certain grade-point average.)[283]

Let us add further here that the professor brings in the security camera from the classroom as evidence that the student cheated, so it is very clear that the Dean, the professor, and the student all know that he cheated. Though there is no intention to deceive on the part of the college student, he still lied.[284] Ergo, the intention to deceive cannot be part of the definition of lying.

In response to similar scenarios, many try (albeit unsuccessfully) to nuance what is meant by "intention to deceive."[285] But even if this nu-

---

[283] Thomas L. Carson, "The Definition of Lying*," *Nous* 40, no. 2 (2006): 290.

[284] As further evidence of this point, it must be noted that a study of 216 participants found that 93.98% of them were definitely sure that such examples of bald-faced falsehood still count as lies (Cf. Adam J. Arico and Don Fallis, "Lies, Damned Lies, and Statistics: An Empirical Investigation of the Concept of Lying," *Philosophical Psychology* 26, no. 6 (2013): 799).

[285] Nobody has been able to refute all of Carson's counterexamples. Some scholars have, however, tried to nuance the meaning of the intention to deceive condition. Mahon, for example, discusses such nuancings (e.g. by Frankfurt, Chisholm and Feehan, Simpson) of the intention to deceive condition: see Mahon, "Two Definitions of Lying," 219-223. He ultimately accepts a nuanced version of Kupfer's understanding of intention to deceive as the best definition of lying (Mahon, "Two Definitions," 227-228). Jennifer Lackey also tries to nuance her account of deception, albeit I think unsuccessfully, in light of the examples of bald-faced lies; cf. J.

120

ancing would save the definitions from the counterexample of the college Dean, the new (what I would call gerrymandered) definitions would still suffer from other difficulties.

Another such difficulty is explicating what is meant by *falsehood*. Is it that the speaker says what is literally false or merely what the speaker believes to be false?[286] What if the speaker does not believe it to be false, but merely has no idea whether it is true or false? Did he lie?

Further, what does *uttering* mean in the standard definition of lying? In playacting or telling jokes one is making a speech act, but do these count as utterances in the relevant sense? What if a drunken or an insane man blurts out something he believes is false? Does this count as an utterance? Is it possible to make an utterance to eavesdroppers or if nobody is in the room? Does that mean you can lie to eavesdroppers or when nobody is within earshot?

The definition of lying has turned out to be much more complicated than one may have presupposed. In order to make sense of the multitude of rival non-moral definitions of lying, I will categorize them based upon four types of differences:

1. Those that differ based upon the addressee requirements. In other words, can you lie to children, the insane, an animal, or a computer? Can you lie to eavesdroppers or yourself?
2. Those that differ based upon the intent to deceive requirements.
3. Those that differ based upon truthfulness requirements.
4. Those that differ based upon the communicative act requirement. Thus, some say the type of speech act required is a warrant, or an endorsement, or an assertion, but there are differing views as to what counts as an assertion.

Lackey, "Lies and Deception: An Unhappy Divorce," *Analysis* 73, no. 2 (2013): 241-242.

[286] Coleman and Kay hold that it must be literally false; Mahon also criticizes them on this point. Cf. Mahon, "Two Definitions of Lying," 218-219. Carson also holds that literal falsehood is necessary: Carson, "The Definition of Lying*," 285.

Some of the definitions differ from others in more ways than one, but I have organized the definitions according to the above list in order to make some sense out of the rival accounts.

i) The addressee condition

Aquinas's definition of lying is asserting what one believes to be false. Since Aquinas's account is also situated within the context of the virtue of truthfulness, and truthfulness is always in relation to another human being,[287] it follows that on his account it is not possible to lie to oneself or to an animal or a computer. Some alternative definitions of lying, however, allow for lying to oneself,[288] or to an animal,[289] or to no one,[290] etc. These scenarios are borderline cases though, so I will not attempt to settle the debates over whether these cases count as lies.

Alan Donagan offers an interesting variant of the addressee condition. He defines lying as *freely* making a statement believed to be false to another fully responsible and rational person with the intention that that other person believe that statement to be true.[291] The difficulty with his definition is that it is not possible to lie under duress, as such an utterance would not be free. Thomas More refused to swear the oath of succession, but according to Donagan if More had instead taken the oath, although believing its contents to be false, he would not have lied. On Donagan's definition both affirming and denying that one is hiding

---

[287] ST II-II, Q109, A3.

[288] Chisholm and Feehan hold that it is possible to lie to one's future self. Cf. Roderick M. Chisholm and Thomas D. Feehan, "The Intent to Deceive," *The Journal of Philosophy* 74, no. 3 (March 01, 1977): 158. Sorensen also discusses this possibility, cf. Roy Sorensen, "Bald-Faced Lies! Lying Without The Intent To Deceive," 259.

[289] Chisholm and Feehan mention this case of lying to an animal and seem to indicate that it is possible to lie to an animal, but they do not firmly take a position on this issue. Cf. Chisholm and Feehan, "The Intent to Deceive," 158.

[290] Warren Shibles's definition seems to allow for lying to an empty room, which is precisely the point on which Mahon critiques him; cf. Mahon, "Two Definitions of Lying," 215-216.

[291] As cited in James Edwin Mahon, *Stanford Encyclopedia of Philosophy,* s.v. "The Definition of Lying and Deception," section 2.3. On Donagan's definition lying under duress is a contradiction in terms, and it is not possible to lie to children or the insane.

Jews to the Nazi at the door is equally an act of truthfulness; neither statements are lies.

ii) The intent to deceive condition

As mentioned earlier, Aquinas explicitly denies that the intent to deceive is essential to lying.[292] I think he is right for the reasons mentioned earlier by Carson. There are just too many counterexamples that show it is possible to lie without intending to deceive.[293]

iii) Differing accounts of the truthfulness condition

Carson proposes that if something is in fact materially true, but formally false, then it is not a lie. Carson's account, if true, would contradict Aquinas's claim that lying depends upon intention and that it is possible to lie even if one's words happen to be materially true (ST II-II, Q110,

---

[292] ST II-II, Q110, A1.

[293] Other examples of bald-faced lies mentioned by Sorensen include the following: (1) "After the [Iraq] war starts, Asne Seierstad sneaks into a civilian hospital. She is surprised to see a ward of wounded soldiers. This suggests that Iraqi military hospitals are overcrowded. 'How many soldiers have you admitted today?' I ask a doctor. 'There are no soldiers here,' the doctor says. 'But they are wearing uniforms?' 'I see no uniforms,' he says, and pushes me out…the doctor's secondary lie, 'I see no uniforms' is effortless" (Sorensen, "Bald-Faced Lies! Lying Without The Intent To Deceive," 253). (2) "Once when the pianist Anton Rubinstein was practicing, the telephone rang inconveniently. His servant François picked up the phone and reported to the female caller that the maestro was not home. She objected 'But I hear him playing.' 'You are mistaken, Madame' insisted François 'I'm dusting the piano keys.'…François loyally sustains the pretext.…However, he is not being deceptive because he does not intend the caller to be taken in by such a preposterous lie" (Ibid., 253). (3) "Consider a blond-haired, blue-eyed Swedish immigrant to Canada who obtains a subsidy for Eskimos by simply swearing he is an Eskimo. He is exploiting a loophole. For administrative simplicity, government bureaucrats do not use any further test. The bureaucrat may tell the Swede that he is telling a bald-faced lie. The Swede can stand on his rights and prevail" (Ibid., 261). (4) "For instance, the shopkeeper in the Monty Python 'Parrot' sketch wrongly refuses to accept the customer's complaint that he was sold [a] dead parrot. The shopkeeper wastes the customer's time by asserting that the parrot is just resting. He exasperates the customer with a string of further lies: the parrot is stunned; the parrot is a 'Norwegian Blue' and is pining for the fiords; this species prefers to be on its back (and so had to be nailed to its perch).…Bald-faced lying is comical – from a safe distance. Those enmeshed in the absurdity are generally annoyed by it" (Ibid., 263).

A1). Carson's claim, however, is so counterintuitive that it should not be taken seriously. For on Carson's account it would follow that if Ibietta is taken prisoner and tortured to reveal the whereabouts of his friend, and Ibietta tells his torturers that his friend is at the cemetery believing him to really be hiding in the library, then Ibietta is not lying if unknown to him his friend really is hiding in the cemetery. Aquinas holds that Ibietta lied. But if he is wrong, then no one lies who intends to lie but by accident speaks the truth. But making the definition of lying depend upon chance seems mistaken.[294]

Aquinas's definition of lying seems to require that the speaker assert something he believes to be false.[295] Other accounts of lying, however, hold that the speaker need not believe what he asserts to be false; rather only that the speaker asserts what he does not believe to be true.[296] The difference arises in a case like the following: at a cocktail party Bob, wishing to impress a pretty lady with his knowledge of British royal history, tells all kinds of truthful, intricate stories about various historical British monarchs. Unfortunately, the pretty lady also is an expert in British royal gossip and history. Bob is then hard-pressed to win her heart and so makes up a nice little anecdote about George III's favorite type of tea. Bob is unaware whether his statement is true or false. In fact, all the better if what he says were true, in case the pretty lady decides to look up this riveting anecdote afterwards.

Did Bob tell a lie? On the definition of lying as asserting what one believes to be false, he did not. Bob did not assert what he believes to be false, rather he asserted what he did not believe to be true. Bob neither believes nor disbelieves what he asserted. This mere lack of belief is why some would categorize his anecdote as bullshit and not lying.[297]

---

[294] Mahon makes a similar criticism of Coleman and Kay's definition of lying, so this example is inspired by him: Mahon, "Two Definitions of Lying," 219.

[295] ST II-II, Q110, A1, co. and ad 1; *Super Sent.* III, D38, Q1, A1, c. and ad 1.

[296] Carson proposes this distinction though his subsequent definition of lying allows for both possibilities. Cf. Thomas L. Carson, "Lying, Deception, and Related Concepts," in *The Philosophy of Deception*, by Clancy W. Martin (Oxford: Oxford University Press, 2009), 156.

[297] Cf. Harry G. Frankfurt, *On Bullshit* (Princeton, NJ: Princeton University Press, 2005), 33-34, 55-56, 61.

But on the definition of lying as asserting what one does not believe to be true, it follows that he did lie.

Whether Aquinas held to the former definition (asserting what you believe to be false) or the latter (asserting what you do not believe to be true) is difficult to tell, but prima facie it appears he may have held to the former definition of lying as asserting what you believe to be false.[298] In ST II-II, Q110, A1 Aquinas defines lying in terms of formal falsity. Unfortunately, from this definition, serious problems arise.

If lying is merely asserting what you believe to be false (as opposed to asserting what you do not believe to be true), then this means not only that Bob was not lying about George III's tea, but also that one could assert all sorts of ridiculous things in similar situations without lying. If your mother asked you where her favorite book is and you have no idea where it is, you could thus assert it is on the front lawn or on the bookcase or in the dog's stomach without lying (so long as you really do not actually believe it is false that it is in any of these locations). You are not asserting anything you believe to be false; you are merely asserting what you do not believe. Likewise, it seems that under oath in court one could assert all sorts of things about the whereabouts of Jim on the night of the murder without lying, that is, so long as one really has no idea whether or not Jim was at the specified location you assert. Surely, however, these statements would count as perjury under the law; likewise, it is a lie to tell your mother "your book is on the lawn" even if you have no idea whether it is there. It is counterintuitive to claim otherwise. Ergo, if Aquinas's definition of lying is merely asserting what you believe to be false, then it seems Aquinas gave an incorrect account of the nature of lying.[299]

---

[298] ST II-II, Q110, A1, co. and ad 1; *Super Sent.* III, D38, Q1, A1, c. and ad 1.

[299] Perhaps one may wish to say the cases I have mentioned are instances of bullshit and not lying. Bullshitting is merely asserting something that you do not believe to be true, but nor do you believe to be false (you have no idea one way or the other). Lying, on the other hand, (as opposed to this account of bullshit) is asserting what you believe to be false. Say for the sake of argument, I grant this distinction between bullshitting and lying. Still, on Aquinas's account, since both are contrary to the virtue of truthfulness, both bullshitting and lying would count as vices. Further, bullshitting might still be abusing assertions (by engaging in an act of assertion with a natural *telos* of truth, but ordering it away from truth to what you don't know to be

On the other hand, Aquinas also indicates that a lie is speaking what is not in the heart,[300] asserting what one has not in the mind,[301] and signifying by words what one has not in the mind;[302] that is why Aquinas says, *"mendacium* is named from what is said to be *contra mentem."*[303] Since Bob spoke contrary to what was in his heart, it follows on Aquinas's account that Bob told a lie. So the earlier passages where Aquinas defines a lie in terms of formal falsity does not mean Aquinas meant to define a lie as "asserting what one believes to be false," but rather more like "asserting *contra mentem,"* where *"contra mentem"* means "what one does not believe." This latter account seems more like what Aquinas meant by formal falsity.

In light of the counterexample of the cocktail party, it appears that the correct definition of lying is asserting what one does not believe to be true, as opposed to asserting what one believes to be false.[304]

---

true), though perhaps not as badly as in the case of lying. In bullshitting one is not acting directly contrary to the truth, whereas in lying (on this definition) one is acting directly contrary to what one believes to be true.

[300] In *Super Sent. III,* D38, Q1, A3: quandocumque aliquis loquitur quod in corde non habet (S. Thomas Aquinatis, *Scriptum Super Sententiis Magistri Petri Lombardi,* ed. R.P. Maria Fabianus Moos, *tomus* III, p. 1268).

[301] *Quaestiones de Quolibets* VIII, Q6, A4: quando aliquis uoce enuntiat quod non habet in mente, quod importatur in nomine mendacii (Sancti Thomae Aquinatis, *tomus* XXV, *volumen* 1 of *Quaestiones de Quolibet,* in *Opera Omnia Iussu Leonis XIII P.M. Edita* (Roma: Commissio Leonina, 1996), p. 75).

[302] ST II-II, Q110, A3: voce significet id quod non habet in mente.

[303] ST II-II, Q110, A1, co.: Unde et mendacium nominatur ex eo quod *contra mentem* dicitur. The translation is my own.

[304] I am not aware of anyone prior to Carson who has raised this seemingly subtle distinction between asserting (or as Carson says "making a statement") what you believe to be false and asserting what you do not believe to be true. Carson, however, leaves it open as to which definition is correct. It seems to me, however, that the account of asserting what you do not believe is the correct definition. Cf. Thomas L. Carson, "The Definition of Lying*," *Nous* 40, no. 2 (2006): 287; Thomas Carson, "Liar Liar," *International Journal of Applied Philosophy* 22, no. 2 (2008): 193; Thomas L. Carson, "Lying, Deception, and Related Concepts," 157.

iv) Differing accounts of the speech-act condition

Some hold that the speech-act requirement for lying is that of warrants, others that it is an endorsement, and others that it is an assertion, but they drastically differ in their accounts of what an assertion is.

Warrants

Carson holds that the type of speech act that is essential to lying is a warrant.[305] His most recent definition of lying is as follows:

> A person S tells a lie to another person S1 iff: 1. S makes a false statement x to S1, 2. S believes that x is false or probably false (or, alternatively, S doesn't believe that x is true), 3. S states x in context in which S thereby warrants the truth of x to S1, and 4. S does not take herself to be not warranting the truth of what she says to S1.[306]

A warrant is a kind of guarantee or promise that what one says is true.[307] This can be done either implicitly or explicitly, as happens in the case of taking an oath in court that all of one's testimony will be true.[308] Whether what one says is a warrant is partly dependent upon one's intention, but also partly dependent upon context.[309] The possible contextual factors that determine whether or not one is making a warrant are multifarious; it is impossible to list all that might either suspend warranting or put warranting into effect.[310] For example, saying things in the clear context of a joke or a story are cases of suspending a warrant.[311]

Caron's definition has much to be said for it, but it faces multiple difficulties. First, on Carson's definition one can intend to lie, but not be guilty of the moral act of lying if one's audience thinks one is not warranting. Take the following counterexample given by Arico and Fallis:

---

[305] Thomas Carson, "Second Thoughts about Bluffing," *Business Ethics Quarterly* 3, no. 4 (1993): 321; Thomas L. Carson, "The Definition of Lying*," *Nous* 40, no. 2 (2006): 298; Carson, "Liar Liar," 195; Carson, "Lying, Deception, and Related Concepts," 171.

[306] Carson, "Lying, Deception, and Related Concepts," 171.

[307] Ibid., 165, 167.

[308] Ibid., 167.

[309] Ibid., 168-169.

[310] Ibid., 168.

[311] Ibid., 168.

A politician intends to tell slanderous falsehoods about his opponent on the evening news. Unfortunately, on the same day he is also scheduled to appear on *Saturday Night Live.* Right before he goes on for what is really *Saturday Night Live,* the politician gets mixed up and thinks he is really going on the evening news. So he goes and gives his slanderously untruthful speech about his opponent, thinking he is on the evening news. His audience roars with laughter. The politician intended to tell a lie in this case, yet on Carson's definition he did not. The politician failed to meet the third necessary condition for lying: making a statement in a context in which he warrants the truth of x. *Saturday Night Live* is definitely not a context in which one warrants the truth of what one says. Thus, on Carson's definition it follows that the politician did not lie even though he intended to do so.[312] In fact, Carson himself holds that in this scenario the politician did not lie.[313]

Yet, surely the politician did lie. A moral action is given its species by intention, and not by whether or not the act happened to be successful.[314] A murderer is morally speaking still a murderer even if he happens to be a bad shot and accidentally misses. Likewise, the fact that one intends to lie and then commands the act of lying makes one a liar, even if some unknown contextual clue makes one not to be warranting the truth of one's statements to the audience.[315]

Further, Carson's claim that the politician did not lie is counterintuitive. An excellent empirical study by Fallis and Arico has also shown that most competent English language speakers take it that the politician did, in fact, tell a lie.[316]

---

[312] Arico and Fallis, "Lies, Damned Lies, and Statistics: An Empirical Investigation of the Concept of Lying," 793.

[313] Carson, "Lying, Deception, and Related Concepts," 169.

[314] ST II-II, Q64, A7, Q110, A1; ST I-II, Q18, A4. ST I-II, Q20, A4: "Now, the involuntary, just as it does not merit punishment or reward in doing good or evil, so too neither does it take someone away from reward or punishment, if a man involuntarily simply speaking fails to do good or evil." The translation is my own. The Latin is as follows: "Involuntarium autem, sicut non meretur poenam vel praemium in operando bonum aut malum, ita non tollit aliquid de praemio vel de poena, si homo involuntarie simpliciter deficiat ad faciendum bonum vel malum."

[315] I mean *command* in the Thomistic sense of the term.

[316] Arico and Fallis, "Lies, Damned Lies, and Statistics," 805.

An objection may be raised here against such an empirical study entering the debate.[317] Definitions within ethics are not up for popular vote. The correct definition of murder or stealing does not change based upon popular vote, nor does it depend upon often faulty intuitions.

In reply to this objection, it must be said that the definition of lying is not a debate about the moral good or evil of an action. Intuitions and statistical studies are not always good guides for determining whether an action is good or bad. Nevertheless, when it comes to debates over definitions, intuitions have a role to play, particularly within the realm of language and the meanings of certain words. As Arico and Fallis say,

> If we want to understand features of the social world, ordinary usage is a good place to start....And given that lying is a common and salient feature of the social world, it is entirely likely that studying ordinary language will be extremely useful in advancing our understanding of what it means to lie....While a competent speaker could be mistaken about the metallurgic reality [and thus the definition] of aluminum, it is less clear how one could be similarly confused about social reality. For instance, unlike with the term 'aluminum', there is no extra-social court of appeals for determining the meaning of the term 'lying.' Given its fundamentally social basis, lying does not seem to be the sort of thing about which people can be systematically mistaken.[318]

In other contexts, intuitions are generally not a good guide; when it comes to the definition of lying, however, intuitions might be the best guide available. Intuitions may not settle the matter, but they are a good place to start, particularly if the overwhelming majority of speakers of the language have the same intuitions about whether something is a lie. These general intuitions about lying can, of course, be sharpened or made more precise by later philosophical reflection.

---

[317] This objection and the following replies are inspired by Arico and Fallis, "Lies, Damned Lies, and Statistics," 795-796.

[318] Arico and Fallis, "Lies, Damned Lies, and Statistics," 796. Cf. Don Fallis, "Lying and Deception," *Philosophers' Imprint* 10, no. 11 (November 1, 2010): 5.

Thus, since Carson's account yields a counterintuitive conclusion about the politician, this counts against the plausibility of his definition being true.

Carson's definition faces a second major problem, for it seems (contrary to his position) that it is possible to lie, even when one makes an explicit proviso that one is not warranting.[319] A beggar confronts Jim on the street, asking him for money. Jim can tell the beggar "I am not making any promises nor guarantees here, but I will get you some money tomorrow," and yet still be lying, as when he has no intention to get the money. On Carson's account making a promise or a guarantee is necessary for lying, as guaranteeing is by definition part of a warrant for Carson, and warranting is by definition part of lying. Consequently, on Carson's definition Jim did not lie. But surely he did.[320]

Assertions

Roderick Chisholm and Thomas Feehan define a lie as asserting a proposition to another that the speaker believes is not true or that the speaker believes is false.[321] By an assertion they mean stating a proposition to another under conditions that justify the hearer in believing that he (the speaker) not only accepts that proposition, but also intends to contribute causally to the hearer's believing that he (the speaker) accepts that proposition.[322] More precisely, an assertion occurs when the one making the statement believes the conditions apply, whether or not they in fact do.

This definition of lying, at face value, seems to be the same as Aquinas's. In fact, it is not. For its account of assertion smuggles in the intent to deceive condition[323], something foreign to Aquinas's definition. Since intention to deceive is essential to Chisholm and Feehan's definition, it follows that Carson's criticism of the intention to deceive condition applies equally well here. Recall the earlier example of the cheater

---

[319] Arico and Fallis, "Lies, Damned Lies, and Statistics," 793.
Sorensen also criticizes Carson's account on the same grounds: Sorensen, "Bald-Faced Lies! Lying Without The Intent To Deceive," 254.
[320] Further, out of a study of 216 participants, at least 93.75% rated proviso lies as lies (Cf. Arico and Fallis, "Lies, Damned Lies, and Statistics," 798-799).
[321] Chisholm and Feehan, "The Intent to Deceive," 152.
[322] Ibid.
[323] Ibid., 153.

and the college Dean.[324] The student lied, even though there was no intent to deceive. Bald-faced lies are possible, but under Chisholm and Feehan's definition they are not. The cheating student does not intend to contribute causally to the Dean believing the proposition "I didn't cheat." Nor does the cheating student believe that the Dean is justified in believing that he (the student) accepts the proposition "I didn't cheat." Thus, under Chisholm and Feehan's definition bald-faced lies are impossible.

A second objection to their view is the following case raised in Augustine: a man knows that bandits besiege the road ahead. This man knows that his friend does not trust him, so he says that "There are no bandits on the road ahead" in order to get the friend to think there are bandits and so save his life.[325] Intuitively, the man lied to his friend, even though for a good end. Yet, on Chisholm and Feehan's account he did not; for the speaker did not intend to contribute causally to his friend believing that he (the speaker) accepts the proposition "There are no bandits on the road ahead." In fact, Chisholm and Feehan openly admit on their definition that the speaker did not lie.[326] Surely, however, the speaker did lie.[327]

Andreas Stokke defines lying as asserting something you believe to be false.[328] An assertion, according to Stokke, is proposing that a proposition become common ground.[329] "Conversations evolve against a background of mutually shared information called *common ground.* An assertion is a proposal to add to, or update, the common ground with new information."[330] The common ground is defined as:

---

[324] Carson, "The Definition of Lying*," 290.

[325] Chisholm and Feehan, "The Intent to Deceive," 153-154.

[326] Ibid., 154.

[327] For another criticism of their definition see Jonathan E. Adler, "Lying, Deceiving, or Falsely Implicating," *The Journal of Philosophy* 94, no. 9 (September 01, 1997): 443, footnote 25.

[328] Stokke, "Lying and Asserting," 1.

[329] Ibid., 1.

[330] Ibid., 12.

> It is common ground that *p* in a group if all members accept (for the purpose of conversation) that *p,* and all believe that all accept that *p,* and all believe that all accept that *p,* etc.[331]

Acceptance is something weaker than belief.[332] On this definition, says Stokke, cases of irony do not count as lying, since the speaker does not intend the ironic statement to "become part of what is commonly accepted for the purpose of conversation."[333] Bald-faced lies are also possible on this definition; according to Stokke: "The student is proposing to update the common ground…[and] wants herself and the Dean to mutually accept that she did not plagiarize."[334]

Stokke's understanding of common ground is unclear; his application of it to bald-faced lies is especially puzzling. All involved know that the student cheated and that the student is lying. The student has no intent that the Dean and others mutually accept that she cheated. The student intends only to pass the class; she does not care that others know she cheated or is lying. On Stokke's own account, then, the student is not proposing to update the common ground and ergo she is not lying. Stokke needs to be clearer how, on his account, bald-faced lies are possible.

Finally, Don Fallis provides a powerful counterexample to Stokke's account:

> In a deserted parking garage in our nation's capital, a devious Deep Throat attempts to mislead a journalist by saying, "I am saying this only to you. And I am going to say it only once. If you repeat it (or say anything that presupposes it), I will deny it. The Attorney-General himself was behind the cover-up." Deep Throat does not seem to be proposing that the claim that the Attorney-General was behind the cover-up be added to the common ground of the conversation. In fact…Deep Throat is pretty clearly proposing that this information *not* be added to the common ground. Even so, Deep Throat seems to be lying as he knows that the Attorney-General was *not* behind the cover-up. Moreo-

---

[331] Ibid., 14.
[332] Ibid., 13-14.
[333] Ibid., 16.
[334] Ibid., 18.

ver, he intends to represent himself as believing that the Attorney-General is behind the cover-up.[335]

Deep Throat is not proposing that his untruthful assertion be mutually accepted for the purposes of conversation, since in any further conversation he will deny it. Consequently, Stokke's account of assertion (and lying) ought to be rejected, unless he can further clarify what he means by common ground.

Sorensen also defines lying in terms of assertion,[336] but does not really define assertion. His definition of lying as "asserting what one does not believe"[337] also seems to be the same as Aquinas's insofar as his account does not seem to yield any counterintuitive cases.

I now turn to an account of lying that seems much closer to the truth. Donald Davidson defines lying as follows:

> A liar may not even intend to make his victim believe that he, the liar, believes what he says. The only intentions a liar must have, I think, are these: (1) he must intend to represent himself as believing what he does not (for example, and typically, by asserting what he does not believe), and (2) he must intend to keep this intention (though not necessarily what he actually believes) hidden from his hearer. So deceit of a very special kind is involved in lying, deceit with respect to the sincerity of the representation of one's beliefs.[338]

In other words, lying is (1) intending to represent yourself as believing what you do not (typically by asserting what you do not believe) and (2) intending to keep this intention (though not necessarily what you actually believe) hidden from your hearer.

Davidson's account is good in some respects, but ultimately it fails as a satisfactory definition. As Fallis points out, he is mistaken in thinking that assertion is not always necessary for lying (he indicates this by

---

[335] Fallis, "Davidson Was Almost Right about Lying," 351.

[336] Sorensen, "Bald-Faced Lies! Lying Without The Intent To Deceive," 251-264.

[337] Sorensen, "Bald-Faced Lies!," 256.

[338] Donald Davidson, "Deception and Division," in *The Multiple Self*, ed. Jon Elster (Cambridge: Cambridge University Press, 1987), 88.

the word "typically").[339] Second, "Davidson's second mistake is his claim...that a liar must intend to hide his intention to represent himself as believing what he does not."[340] In this respect, although Davidson inconsistently says the contrary, Davidson's account rules out certain cases of bald-faced lies. In certain bald-faced lies one does not intend to keep his intention hidden from the hearer, yet such examples seem to count as lies.[341] Davidson's account is close to the mark but still ought to be rejected.

Don Fallis, in a later article, offers a definition of lying as "assert[ing] something that you do not believe."[342] An assertion here means "representing yourself as believing what you say."[343] Fallis claims that "saying" is distinct from what is merely implied, thus allowing for the possibility of equivocations being distinct from lies.[344]

Fallis further explicates his conception of representation, which is based, at least in part, upon Davidson. He says,

> Representing yourself as believing something is a special case of *presenting yourself* to the world as having a certain property. This is suggested by the analogies that Davidson and others have used to elucidate the concept. For instance, Max Black (1952: 31) notes that "to write a cheque is to represent oneself as having money in the bank to honour the cheque". Similarly, people typically present themselves as wanting to win a game simply by virtue of playing it...."whether they want to win or not."...you can present yourself to the world as having properties you do not have as well as properties that you do have. For instance, you can present yourself as having money in the bank (e.g., by writing a cheque) even when your bank account is empty. Second, you can present yourself as having a property even if you do not intend anyone to believe that you have the property....For instance, if the person to whom you are writing a cheque is sure that you are destitute, you

---

[339] Fallis, "Davidson Was Almost Right about Lying," 342.
[340] Ibid., 343.
[341] Cf. Ibid., 342-343.
[342] Ibid., 345.
[343] Ibid.
[344] Ibid, 346.

might not expect or intend him to believe that you have sufficient funds in the bank.[345]

On Fallis's account, bald-faced lies are possible. The creditor can know your check really has no funds to back it up and yet you can still write the check, that is represent yourself as having a certain property of appropriate funds. Likewise, the college dean can know the student is not telling the truth and yet the student can still represent himself as if he did not cheat, that is, present himself as having a certain property of not having cheated.

Fallis also adds that representing is not the same thing as pretending. "First, you can certainly do the former without doing the latter. For instance, if [the shepherd boy in the famous story of the boy who cried wolf] shouts [that he saw a wolf] because he *did* see a wolf, the shepherd boy is still representing himself as believing that there is a wolf, but he is not pretending to believe it."[346] Second, playacting is also a pretending, but not a representing.[347]

Fallis seems correct in his general definition of asserting, although he seems to differ slightly from my definition of asserting (and what I hold would be Aquinas's). While Fallis focuses inward, on the mental state of the speaker himself, my Thomistic account focuses outward, on some reality presented as true. In other word, the Thomistic focus is on "presenting *something* as if it were true," instead of "representing *yourself* as believing what you say." Perhaps, this focus inward rather than outward makes a significant difference, but it seems to overlap enough with Aquinas's account that it will make little difference when treating the morality of lying in the next chapter.[348] As such, a lie is properly de-

---

[345] Ibid., 339-340.

[346] Ibid., 341.

[347] Ibid.

[348] Fallis's example of playing a game may be problematic. It is not clear that playing a game is always making an assertion of wanting to win; although it is presumed that you want to win (unless you indicate otherwise), one can still feasibly present oneself in the game by certain facial signs or words as not wanting to win. In spite of this bad example, Fallis seems to be on the mark in describing assertions as representing oneself as having a certain mental state. I prefer the language of "presenting" over "representing" but this is perhaps more a quibble than anything. I think the other example of writing a check is good. Writing a check and signing it

fined as "asserting what you do not believe," where assertion is taken to mean "presenting something as if it were true" or "representing yourself as believing what you say."[349] This is the correct definition of lying, though it does not fully answer all of our questions.

Opting out and contextual linguistics

A key aspect of assertion is that it has its natural purpose or *telos* even apart from the other intentions of the human agent making an assertion. Just as sex has its natural *telos* of procreation when the human agent uses the contraceptive pill, so too do assertions have their natural *telos* when the human agent is telling a lie. Likewise, heating still has its natural *telos* for heat, even if the human agent intended to use it to cool. The difference between asserting and heating, however, is that assertions, being a part of language, are more complicated. Language is a natural human creation, and so too are assertions; heating is not. The sun would still heat even if man never existed, but human language would not exist if no man ever existed. Further, language changes over time, even though its fundamental nature remains the same. Assertions have some variability in regards to certain things annexed to their nature, though their fundamental *telos* does not change. What counts as an assertion or the context that determines whether or not one is making (or can make) an assertion varies from culture to culture, and from place to place, whereas with heating there are no culturally-dependent contextual rules that determine whether an act of heating is heating. Heating is heating whether in India or America, or on the moon. For example, it is practi-

---

with your name on it is making an assertion that you have the money in the bank or will pay the amount you wrote in exchange for the goods or services provided. Writing a check for an amount you know you cannot and will not pay, and affixing your signature to it, thus counts as a lie.

[349] Fallis is not the only one who holds this account of assertion. He also cites Max Black ("Saying and Disbelieving," *Analysis* 13/2 (1952): 31), Unger (*Ignorance* (Oxford: Oxford University Press, 2002), 257), Rescorla ("Assertion and its Constitutive Norms," *Philosophy and Phenomenological Research* 79/1 (2009): 108-14), and Davidson (*Inquires into Truth and Interpretation* (New York: Oxford University Press, 2001), 268) as holding the same definition of assertion (Cf. Fallis, "Davidson Was Almost Right," 338-339).

cally impossible for anyone to take you as making an assertion (or telling a lie) if one says it on *Saturday Night Live* (SNL) or while laughing hysterically, but heating that occurs on SNL or on the street is still heating. Similarly, prefacing your statement with "once upon a time," indicates you are not making an assertion, but rather suspending assertions by telling a fairy tale. In fact, no matter how hard the agent tries or intends, he simply cannot possibly be making an assertion if he prefaces his statement with "once upon a time." So there is something about assertions that are beyond the control of the agent. The conventions of society regarding certain contextual clues as to whether an assertion is in effect are in most cases beyond our control. I do not think it possible, nor necessary, fully to list all the contextual clues governing assertions. But it is generally presumed that one is making an assertion, unless one is giving a command, asking a question, or there are good contextual clues to the contrary such as acting on stage, telling a joke, laughing, saying "once upon a time," writing a fiction book, etc.[350]

Kenneth Kemp and Thomas Sullivan have appropriately noted the special relation between assertions and contextual clues. As a result, they have proposed that assertion-making occurs when there is "a reasonable expectation that the speaker is using speech to communicate his thoughts to us."[351] Kemp and Sullivan then conclude that since the Nazi-at-the-door scenario includes no reasonable expectation that one will be speaking the truth, one is not making an assertion in telling the Nazis "we are hiding no Jews;" consequently, one is not lying.

What is strange about their position is that on such an account it is impossible to lie to the Nazis, *or even assert the truth,* about the whereabouts of the Jews one is hiding. Presumably, also on their account anyone caught in a difficult situation cannot either lie or make a true assertion. Thus, a witness put on the stand in a Mafia trial is not lying, nor perjuring himself, if he is being severely threatened with death if he tells the truth. There is no reasonable expectation that he would tell the truth in such a situation.

---

[350] Kenneth Kemp and Thomas Sullivan give some nice examples of other contextual clues. See "Speaking Falsely and Telling Lies," *Proceedings of the American Catholic Philosophical Association* 67 (February 1, 1993): 160-161.
[351] Kemp and Sullivan, "Speaking Falsely and Telling Lies," 161.

These difficulties point to a further problem: what or who determines what counts as *a reasonable expectation*? If it is merely the whims of the speaker, then anybody could get out of lying if they simply see it as a reasonable case in which to utter a formal falsehood. If *true morality* determines whatever counts as *a reasonable expectation*, then it seems we are back to the Grotian definition of lying, by incorporating moral terms into the definition of lying. The conventions of society seem to be the more reasonable position, in that the rules governing whether assertion is possible are determined by the society of language users and not merely the whims of the agent. But there is no societal rule governing assertions that suspends them from being assertions simply because the case is one of blackmail or the Nazi-at-the-door scenario.[352]

Assertions and Final Causality

Given our analysis of assertions, it remains to determine why there are assertions. In other words, we must see what is the natural purpose of asserting. Aquinas's argument against lying hinges upon what this natural purpose is. Here I will give a basic positive account as to the proximate natural end of all assertions. More complicated objections will be answered in the next chapter.

Assertions can be used for all sorts of ends such as fraternal correction, issuing a verdict, consoling a friend, or giving an argument, but all these further purposes can be subsumed under *the* natural purpose, the proximate purpose that assertions have (even to some extent independent of the further ends of the agent asserting), which is to convey the truth to another. There are many types of speech acts, but there must exist one whose purpose is to convey the truth to another. If no speech act had this purpose, the human race would perish. Nobody could order food or exchange any goods if assertions did not exist.

---

[352] I am not even sure whether it is possible for such a convention to exist. If it did, then nobody (not even the Nazis) could reasonably accuse the person of lying (or asserting something true). In writing a fiction novel or playacting, by contrast, nobody can reasonably accuse the author or the actors of telling lies, or of making true assertions.

138

Those wishing to justify lying may claim that the purpose of an assertion is to tell a lie. On such an account, however, anyone who told the truth would be violating the purpose of an assertion. The objector, however, may modify his account of assertions by claiming that their purpose is *either* to convey the truth *or* to tell a lie. But such an account is as ad hoc as saying the purpose of eating is *either* bulimia *or* nourishment. Further, the purpose of conveying the truth is what is presupposed in every lie; lies are successful because they are parasitic upon the fundamental *telos* of asserting, namely, formal truth. If the purpose of asserting were really both untruths and truths, then one would naturally not trust another's assertions and assertions would become impossible. Who could possibly rationally believe any stranger's assertions when 50% of the time they might be using assertions *qua untruthful purpose* or the other 50% of the time *qua truthful purpose*? Likewise, if the purpose of eating were to nourish and also not to nourish, then anytime one ate one would have to worry whether one was going to starve.[353]

Finally, if the natural proximate *telos* of asserting is lying, then a circularity problem arises. To say asserting is for the sake of lying is to say, "*asserting* is for the sake of '*asserting* what you do not believe;'" for every lie is by definition also an assertion. But to say, "*asserting* is for the sake of '*asserting* what you do not believe'" is circular; it is like saying asserting is for the sake of asserting, that x is the final cause of itself. Likewise, to say that eating is for the sake of gorging is to say eating is for the sake of eating excessively, which would make eating the final cause of itself. The point is not to deny that an agent can engage in eating for the sake of gorging, nor that an agent can engage in asserting for the sake of lying (as the *finis operantis*), but that it is incoherent to claim that the natural *telos*, the *finis operis*, of asserting is for the sake of lying and that the *finis operis* of eating is gorging.[354]

---

[353] I am indebted to Brandon K. White for much of this paragraph.

[354] The advocate of lying may raise the following ingenious objection: since assertions are integral parts to every lie and every integral part is for the sake of its whole, the purpose of asserting must be lying. This argument can be put into premise form as follows:

1. Every integral part is for the sake of its whole.
2. An assertion is an integral part of a lie.
3. Ergo, an assertion is for the sake a lie.

More objections dealing with the purpose of assertions will be discussed in the next chapter. Let this section suffice for now as a general sketch about the natural proximate purpose of asserting. Assertions exist in the first place for conveying formal truth to another.

Conclusion

Most of the definitions of lying we have examined in this chapter suffer from various difficulties.[355] What emerges as the correct definition of

---

The difficulty with the argument is that the conclusion does not follow. The argument is invalid due to an equivocation on "an." In the second premise, what is meant by "an assertion" is this particular assertion, or every assertion that is in a lie is an integral part of a lie. But in the conclusion what is meant by "an assertion" is assertions as such. Ergo, the argument is invalid; and it is just as invalid as saying since food is an integral part of food poisoning, food as such is for the sake of food poisoning (many thanks to Brandon K. White for this last example).

Kevin Gallagher proposes a definition of assertions as *holding out something for another to believe.* On his account this holding out is what the purposes of assertions are. The problem with his account, however, is that it becomes impossible to make an assertion to another when that other already knows what you intend to assert. It is not possible to intend another to gain what he already has, and so it is not possible to intend for Bob to believe x when he already in fact believes x. This impossibility is further strengthened by the fact that one cannot intend the impossible: since it is impossible to *hold out x for Bob to believe* (because he already believes it), it is impossible for one to assert to him. For example, if Bob already believes that a triangle is a three-sided plane figure, then it is impossible for me *to hold it out to him* that "a triangle is a three-sided plane figure," because on Gallagher's account it is not being *held out for him to believe.* Such a claim is, however, highly counterintuitive, as surely one can assert something to another even if the hearer already believes it to be true.

[355] Alexander Pruss has another definition that includes endorsements instead of assertions. Pruss holds that endorsements, not assertions *per se,* are necessary for lying. Assertions are mere instances of endorsements. In an assertion one expresses a proposition and endorses it (Alexander R. Pruss, "Lies and Dishonest Endorsements," *Proceedings of the American Catholic Philosophical Association* 84 (January 1, 2010): 216). In making an endorsement one solicits the trust of another (Pruss, "Lies and Dishonest Endorsements," 216, 219). Why lying is so wrong, Pruss argues, is because one is soliciting another's trust, while at the same time betraying that trust.

Pruss's account seems plausible, even though it is not entirely clear why he prefers the terminology of endorsements over assertions. It is also not entirely clear what the difference is for Pruss between assertions and endorsements, as he no-lying is "asserting what one does not believe to be true," where asserting is "presenting something to another as if it were true." By "presenting" is meant putting yourself behind it, that is, binding yourself to it; such

---

where strictly defines endorsements and his objections to assertion accounts arc not compelling.

Interestingly, Pruss's account of the wrongness of lying seems similar to Aquinas's in that the very nature of the act itself is disordered. Yet they differ. For Aquinas, assertions and their due order to the truth are being abused, whereas for Pruss it is endorsements and their order to soliciting trust that are being abused.

If Pruss's account were right and Aquinas's wrong, then it seems that the same conclusions would largely follow concerning the morality of lying (Pruss, like Aquinas, holds to the absolutist view on lying. Cf. Christopher Tollefsen and Alexander Pruss, "The Case Against False Assertions," *First Things*, September 22, 2011, accessed January 16, 2019, http://www.firstthings.com/web-exclusives/2011/09/the-case-against-false-assertions); the odd exception is that Pruss thinks that on his account one can tell the Nazi that one is hiding no Jews, even though one in truth is. This odd case has to do with Pruss's understanding of speaking your interlocutor's language and not with his account of endorsements (Cf. Alexander R. Pruss, "Lying and Speaking Your Interlocutor's Language," *Thomist: A Speculative Quarterly Review* 63 (July 1, 1999). Pruss says that for the Nazis *Jew* designates a subhuman class of trafficker's in vice; consequently, when one tells the Nazi at the door, "there are no Jews here," one really means, "there are no sub-human, cold-hearted, shameless, calculating traffickers in vices in my house" (445-446).

Tollefsen, however, shows that Pruss's account of lying in terms of speaking your interlocutor's language is wanting: "if S is what the Nazi means by 'Jew," then the sentence 'Jews are S' will be, for the Nazi, a tautology; yet in, for example, a passage of *Mein Kampf* to which Pruss refers, Hitler describes his 'realization' about the Jews as a discovery, a synthetic rather than an analytic truth; hence the description of Nazi ideology as a form of scientific racism" (Tollefsen, *Lying and Christian Ethics,* 171). Further, it is a historical fact that the Nazis legally identified certain people as Jews based upon genetic descent or religious belief (for a related point see Tollefsen, 171-172).

Apart from his mistaken views on speaking your interlocutor's language (which need not negatively affect this account of endorsements), I see no way reasonably to critique Pruss's account, given the paucity of Pruss's writing on the nature of endorsements. Pruss's view of endorsements, however, does not pose a problem for Aquinas, in that it does not provide a refutation of Aquinas's account, nor need it be fundamentally contrary to Aquinas's account. In fact, it is possible that Pruss has just given an added reason as to why lying is wrong independent of Aquinas's account. Lying can, by definition, both involve assertions and endorsements. It would thus be wrong for two different, though interestingly similar reasons: it is a disordered use of assertions and a disordered use of endorsements.

does not occur in jokes, playacting, or writing fiction. By "something" is meant a verbal or nonverbal proposition. By "to another," is meant to another rational being, as assertions are a part of language, which is inherently relational. Since language is conveying the conceptions of the mind to another, assertions must be in relation to another if they are to be a part of language.[356] Further, since the proper use of assertions falls under the virtue of truthfulness, and truthfulness shares in the notion of justice since it is in relation to another[357], it follows that assertions are only in relation to another. By "as if it were true" is meant that your speech (whether in verbal on nonverbal signs), by social convention of the signification of the words, represents what you believe to be true in reality. Assertions exist for the sake of truth. This definition of lying seems also to be Aquinas's.

Given this correct definition of lying, we will examine why lying is wrong in the next chapter and how Aquinas's argument against lying fares based upon this definition.

---

[356] ST I, Q107, A1: Nihil est enim aliud loqui ad alterum, quam conceptum mentis alteri manifestare.

[357] ST II-II, Q109, A3.

Chapter III: Why is Lying Wrong?

Most people hold that lying is wrong. A common explanation given for why it is wrong is that it violates the trust of another. Aquinas, however, gives an added, more sophisticated reason on why it is wrong. This added reason presupposes an account of the nature of language and assertions, which we have already touched upon in the previous chapter. Aquinas further famously argued that lying is always wrong; it is an intrinsically evil action. It is always wrong for reasons similar to why homosexual acts are always wrong. But was Aquinas right in condemning all lies? In order to answer that question, we must proceed first to see just what Aquinas's argument is. In other words, before seeing why Aquinas held lying is always wrong, we must first investigate why he held lying is wrong in the first place. This chapter then will not attempt to defend the view that lying is always wrong (the absolutist view); here we only wish to see whether Aquinas gave good reasons as to why lying is wrong, even if only defeasibly so.

Part One: Aquinas's Argument Against Lying

Aquinas directly treats the wrongness of lying in four main texts. His first treatment can be found in his early work, *Commentary on the Sentences of Peter Lombard,* Book III, D38, Q1 (written 1252-1256). His second treatment lies within his *Quaestiones de Quolibets* VIII, Q6, A4 (written 1256-1259). His third treatment is in his *Commentary on the Nicomachean Ethics*, Book IV.7, Lecture 15 (written 1271-1272). His fourth and final treatment can be found in the *Summa Theologiae, secunda secundae* Q109-113 (written 1271-1272). I will begin with his treatment in his early work of the *Commentary on the Sentences.* In *Super sent.* III, D38, Q1, A3 the question is asked, "Whether every lie is a flawed-action?" Aquinas answers as follows:

> It must be said that since evil follows from any single defect, corruption of any circumstance, even when other required circumstances are

present, renders a flawed-action in the area of morals. So that if one takes from where he should not, then flawed-action will not be avoided, no matter what good he intends, and even if other circumstances are well ordered. Now since speech (*locutio*) was contrived for expressing the conception of the heart (*conceptionem cordis*), whenever one speaks (*loquitur*) what one has not in the heart, one speaks what one ought not to speak (*loquitur quod non debet*). Now this happens in every lie. Whence, every lie is a flawed-action, however much one lies on account of the good.[358]

Here Aquinas's argument is centered upon the purposes of speech, *locutio*. Aquinas says, "Speech was contrived for expressing the conception of the heart," so that "whenever one speaks what one has not in the heart, one speaks what one ought not to speak." An evil circumstance, especially that of an undue circumstance, renders an act morally evil. Speaking contrary to the conceptions of the heart is a bad circumstance. Ergo, lying is bad. If one were to put Aquinas's argument into formal logic, his argument would be as follows:

1. The purpose of speech is to express the conceptions of the heart.
2. If the purpose of speech is to express the conceptions of the heart, then using speech to express what is not on the heart is bad.
3. Thus, using speech to express what is not in the heart is bad (from 1 & 2).
4. Lying is using speech to express what is not in the heart.
5. Thus, lying is bad (from 3 & 4).

---

[358] Responsio. Dicendum quod cum malum omnifariam contingat, cujuslibet circumstantiae perversitas, etiam aliis circumstantiis debitis existentibus, peccatum in moribus facit; ut si aliquis accipiat unde non debet, quantumcumque bonum intendat, vel aliae circumstantiae ordinatae videantur, peccatum non evitabitur. Cum autem locutio inventa sit ad exprimendam conceptionem cordis, quandocumque aliquis loquitur quod in corde non habet, loquitur quod non debet. Hoc autem contingit in omni mendacio. Unde omne mendacium est peccatum, quantumcumque aliquis propter bonum mentiatur (S. Thomae Aquinatis, *Scriptum Super Sententiis,* vol. III, ed. Maria Fabianus Moos, O.P. (Pariis: P. Lethielleux), p. 1268-1269).

The difficulty centers on the second premise. Let us keep it in mind as we proceed to Aquinas's second treatment of lying in his *Quaestiones de Quolibets,* VIII, Q6, A4:

> Whenever one act has any disorder inseparably annexed to it, it never can be done well. Since disorder itself is some excess or deficiency, it cannot be taken in such acts as the mean, in which virtue consists, as is clear from the Philosopher in *II Ethic.* Now an act of such a kind is a lie. Written words (*verba*) or spoken words (*voces*)[359] were invented in order to be signs of understanding, as it is said in *I Periher.* Therefore, when one asserts with a word (*voce enuntiat*) what one has not in the mind, which is what is meant by the word "lie," there is a disorder through the abuse of word (*per abusum vocis*). Therefore, we conclude that a lie is always a flawed-action.[360]

---

[359] In the text of the *De Interpretatione* used by Aquinas, I have struggled to understand whether there is any significant difference in the Latin between *verba* and *voces*. It would be rather strange if Aquinas were merely repeating himself, so the best I can make out of the difference Aquinas is trying to convey here is the difference between written and spoken words. So, I have taken the liberty of translating the terms differently as "written or spoken words." Aristotle's Greek is translated with the Latin word *voces* when he says that "*spoken words* are the symbols of mental experience and written words are the symbols of spoken words. Just as all men have not the same writing, so all men have not the same speech sounds, but the mental experiences, which these directly symbolize, are the same for all, as also are those things of which our experience are the images" (*De Interpretatione* 1.16a, translation from E.M. Edghill). The Latin is much terser than the English translation: "Sunt ergo ea que sunt in *voce* earum que sunt in anima passionem note. – Et ea que scribuntur eorum que sunt in *voce*. Et quemadmodum nec littere omnibus eedem, sic nec eedem *voces* – Quorum autem hee primorum note sunt, eedem omnibus passiones anime sunt, et quorum hee similitudines, res etiam eedem" (emphasis added; Sancti Thomae De Aquino, *Opera Omnia Iussu Leonis XIII P. M. Edita, Tomus I* 1, Expositio Libri Peryermenias, Editio altera retractata* (Roma: Commissio Leonina, 1989), Book I, *lectio* 2, p. 9).

[360] Quandocunque aliquis actus habet aliquam inordinationem inseparabiliter annexam, nunquam potest bene fieri, quia ipsa inordinatio est aliquid superfluum vel diminutum, et ita non potest in tali actu medium accipi, in quo virtus consistit, ut etiam patet per Philosophum in II Ethicorum. Huiusmodi autem actus est mendacium : ad hoc enim inventa sunt verba vel voces ut sint signa intellectuum, ut dicitur in principio Peryermenias, et ideo quando aliquis voce enunciat quod non habet in mente, quod importatur in nomine mendacii, est ibi inordinatio per abusum vocis. Et ideo concedimus quod mendacium semper est peccatum. (Sancti Thomae de

Note here some differences from the early text of Aquinas's *Commentary on the Sentences.* Aquinas has dropped his discussion of circumstances and his mention of the example of theft ("if one takes from where he should not").[361] His argument is more clearly influenced by Aristotle, as Aquinas quotes from him twice. Aquinas's argument is more closely connected with the notion of vice as in itself incapable of being the mean of virtue than is his earlier argument in the *Sentences.*

Despite these differences, in other respects the essential core of his argument is the same, although expressed in different terminology. In the *Sentences*'s commentary Aquinas says the purpose of *locutio* is to express the *conceptionem cordis,* whereas in the *Quodlibet* he says the purpose of *verba* or *voces* is to be *signa intellectuum.* In the *Sentences,* lying is wrong because one *loquitur* what one has not in the heart, whereas in the *Quodlibet* lying is wrong because one *enuntiat* what one has not in the mind (*mente*). Though different terminology is used, Aquinas's fundamental point here is that in lying one is violating the teleology of *locutio, verba,* or *voces.*

In his *Commentary on the Nicomachean Ethics,* Book IV.7, Lecture 15, Aquinas writes:

Next when [Aristotle] says, "a lie is per se, etc." he shows what in the aforementioned conditions are praiseworthy and blameworthy. He says that a lie is according to itself depraved and ought to be avoided, the truth is good and praiseworthy. Signs were instituted in order that they might represent things as they are and therefore if one represents some-

---

Aquino, *Opera Omnia Iussu Leonis XIII P.M. Edita, Tomus XXV, Quaestiones De QuoLibet,* Volumen 1 (Roma: Commissio Leonina, 1996), *QuoLibet VIII,* Q6, A4, p. 75-76).

[361] Aquinas uses *circumstances* in different senses. In the Sentences text he is using *circumstances* in the sense of *due circumstances*, which are circumstances that give moral species (e.g. place is a circumstance, but it renders an act in the moral species of sacrilege if it occurs in a church or holy place). Other circumstances do not give moral species, but merely increase or decrease the goodness of the existing moral act (e.g. theft is wrong, but more wrong if one steals from a poor person than a rich man). For a more complete discussion of this issue in Aquinas see: Joseph Pilsner, *The Specification of Human Actions in St Thomas Aquinas* (Oxford: Oxford University Press, 2006), 180-198.

thing other than it is by lying, he acts disorderly and viciously. He who speaks the truth acts ordinately and virtuously.[362]

Notice that the argument is shortened. Of further interest is that Aquinas's argument against lying does not actually appear in the text of Aristotle cited. Furthermore, Aquinas still seems to leave it unanswered why *signa* are so special that using them contrary to their end is bad.

In ST II-II, Q110, A3, Aquinas also argues that lying is always wrong. This work was written simultaneously with his commentary on Aristotle's Nicomachean Ethics.[363] Thomas's argument in Article 3 is as follows:

> What is according to itself bad from its genus, in no way can be good and licit, since for anything to be good, it is required that all things rightly concur. For the good is from a complete cause, bad from a singular defect, as Dionysius says in Chapter IV of *De Div. Nom.* Now lying is bad from its genus. For it is an act bearing upon undue matter, since words (*voces*) are naturally signs of what is understood (*signa naturaliter intellectuum*), it is unnatural and undue that one signify with words (*voce significet*) that which one has not in the mind (*mente*). Whence the Philosopher says in *IV Ethic.* that "lying is *per se* perverse and ought to be avoided, but truthfulness is good and praiseworthy." Whence every lie is a flawed-action, as Augustine asserts in the book *Against Lying.*[364]

---

[362] Deinde cum dicit: *Per se autem mendacium* etc., ostendit quid in praedictis habitibus sit laudabile et vituperabile. Et dicit quod mendacium secundum se est pravum et fugiendum, verum autem est bonum et laudabile. Ad hoc enim signa sunt instituta quod repraesentent res secundum quod sunt et ideo, si aliquis repraesentat rem aliter quam sit mentiendo, inordinate agit et vitiose, qui autem verum dicit, ordinate agit et virtuose (Sancti Thomae de Aquino, *Opera Omnia Iussu Leonis XIII P.M. Edita, Tomus XLVII, Volumen II, Sententia Libri Ethicorum,* IV, *lectio* 15, 81-99, (Romae: Sanctae Sabinae, 1969), p. 252). The translation is my own.

[363] Jean-Pierre Torrell, O.P., *Saint Thomas Aquinas,* 343.

[364] Respondeo dicendum quod illud quod est secundum se malum ex genere, nullo modo potest esse bonum et licitum, quia ad hoc quod aliquid sit bonum, requiritur quod omnia recte concurrant; *bonum* enim est *ex integra causa, malum autem est ex singularibus defectibus,* ut Dionysius dicit, IV cap. *de Div. Nom.* Mendacium autem est malum ex genere. Est enim actus cadens super indebitam materiam, cum enim voces sint signa naturaliter intellectuum, innaturale est et indebitum quod aliquis

Despite some slight differences, the core of Aquinas's argument has remained the same. Aquinas uses somewhat different terminology to express the same basic idea. In the *Sentences*'s *locutio* is to express the *conceptionem cordis*, in the *Quodlibet voces* and *verba* are *signa intellectuum*, in the Ethics commentary *signa* are instituted to represent *res* as they are, and finally in the *Summa voces* are *signa naturaliter intellectuum*. In the *Sentences* lying is described as *loquitur* what one has not in *cordis*, in the *Quodlibet* lying is described as *enuntiat* what one has not in *mente*, in the *Nicomachean Ethics* commentary lying is described as *repraesentat rem aliter quam sit*, and in the *Summa* lying is described as *significet* what one has not in *mente*. Aquinas seems somewhat loose with his terminology here although the core idea is the same: the purpose of speech is to convey what is in one's mind. Violating this end by using speech for any contrary purpose is always wrong.

Part Two: A Rival Interpretation of Aquinas

Various ethicists of the New Natural Law School (NNL) agree that lying is wrong, but they reinterpret Aquinas's argument, claiming that Aquinas's case against lying is different from the one I have presented.

a) The rival interpretation & its problems

Christopher Tollefsen and Joseph Boyle both hold that Aquinas's argument against lying is based upon a notion of basic goods.[365] Boyle says that Aquinas's argument in Q110, A3 against lying is rather an extension of his earlier argument in Q110, A1 that lying is opposed to truthful-

---

voce significet id quod non habet in mente. Unde Philosophus dicit, in IV Ethic., quod *mendacium est per se pravum et fugiendum, verum autem et bonum et laudabile*. Unde omne mendacium est peccatum, sicut etiam Augustinus asserit, in libro *contra Mendacium*.

[365] Cf. Tollefsen, *Lying and Christian Ethics,* 50, 53-56; Boyle, "The Absolute Prohibition of Lying and the Origins of the Casuistry of Mental Reservation: Augustinian Arguments and Thomistic Developments": 58.

ness.[366] Aquinas's argument that lying abuses assertions merely points out the fact that lying contradicts the human good of truth.[367] But the human good of truthfulness is a basic good, "constitutive of human well-being."[368]

Tollefsen goes so far as to say that Aquinas's argument against lying is not a perverted faculty argument at all.[369] Aquinas's "dark statement" in Q110, A3 that "as words are naturally signs of intellectual acts, it is unnatural and undue for anyone to signify by words something that is not in his mind," is merely meant to point out the fact that lying violates the basic goods of personal integrity and community.[370] It is this twofold contrariety to the human good that is unnatural.[371] Tollefsen says that, for Aquinas, basic goods are intrinsically desirable, things that ought to be sought for their own sake and not for the sake of anything else.[372] They are also incommensurable.[373]

The New Natural Law interpretation faces serious difficulties. First, Aquinas in his treatment of lying does not hold to the theory of

---

[366] Boyle, "The Absolute Prohibition of Lying and the Origins of the Casuistry of Mental Reservation: Augustinian Arguments and Thomistic Developments": 61-62.

[367] Ibid.

[368] Ibid., 58.

[369] "The argument is not based on any idea of the thwarting or perverting of the natural function of something, whether speech or tongue. It is grounded in human good and a sound sense of what is chosen in this particular choice: to assert what is contrary to one's mind" (Tollefsen, *Lying and Christian Ethics*, 56). John Finnis also holds that Aquinas is not making a perverted faculty argument; cf. John Finnis, *Aquinas: Moral, Political, and Legal Theory* (New York: Oxford University Press, 1998), 155. Finnis in that chapter does not say directly that lying violates basic goods. His account there seems to be part of the inspiration for Tollefsen's treatment, but in seminal form. Finnis asserts that lying is an act of duplicity (158). This seems to foreshadow Tollefsen's later development that lying violates personal integrity.

[370] Tollefsen, "Augustine, Aquinas, and the Absolute Norm Against Lying": 128-129. Tollefsen claims that Aquinas holds that personal integrity is a basic good: *Lying and Christian Ethics*, 53-55. He also claims that society or community is a basic good for Aquinas: Ibid., 50.

[371] Ibid; *Lying and Christian Ethics*, 56.

[372] Tollefsen, "Augustine, Aquinas, and the Absolute Norm Against Lying," 125-126.

[373] For a good summary of the basic tenets of the New Natural Law Theory see Christopher Tollefsen, "The New Natural Law Theory," *Lyceum* X, no. 1.

basic goods, nor does he do so anywhere else. Aquinas nowhere asserts that truth or personal integrity or community is a basic good.[374] On the contrary, Aquinas says that God alone is the ultimate end of man and that all other human actions and goods ought to be ordered to him as to an ultimate end.[375] Nor does he anywhere hold that such goods of truth or personal integrity or community are incommensurable.

Further, if Aquinas's meaning of *unnatural* and *undue* in ST II-II, Q110, A3 is really that two basic goods are opposed, then why does he not say so explicitly? Throughout his career Aquinas reserves a special phrasing for the evil inherent in every lie as "a disorder *through the abuse of word*" in *Quodlibet* VIII,[376] "acting disorderly" in his *Commentary on the Nicomachean Ethics,*[377] and "unnatural and undue" in the *Summa.*[378] Aquinas is most reasonably interpreted as claiming that lying—as an inordinate abuse *of words*—is unnatural and undue not because it violates the basic goods of integrity and community; rather he is more reasonably interpreted as claiming that lying—as an inordinate

---

[374] Tollefsen cites ST I-II, Q94, A2 as evidence of his view, but nowhere in the text does Aquinas assert that any of the goods he lists there are the ultimate end of man nor that they are incommensurable. Tollefsen has a stronger case in claiming that they are underivable from other goods since Aquinas indicates in 94, 2 that their pursuit is *per se nota.* Even though I grant that these precepts are *per se nota* in a certain sense, Tollefsen's claim that they are underivable from other goods still does not follow. Some *per se nota* propositions are *derivable* from other propositions, and are dependent upon their terms, although not demonstratively dependent. That a whole is greater than its part depends upon the principle of noncontradiction, even though both propositions are *per se nota.* For more on this type of non-syllogistic epistemological dependence see Steven J. Jensen, *Knowing the Natural Law: From Precepts and Inclinations to Deriving Oughts* (Washington, D.C,: Catholic University of America Press, 2015), 33-35.

[375] In ST I-II, Q2, A8 Aquinas asserts that happiness consists in God alone. In Q3, A1, ad 3 he asserts that man's last end is happiness. In ST I-II, Q6, prologue, Aquinas says that it is through human acts that one orders oneself toward happiness or away from it. In Q18, A9 he says that every individual human act is good or evil. Every human act either is or is not ordered to God as an ultimate end. Further, in Q71, A6 Aquinas maintains that any action not ordered towards God as an ultimate end is a sin.

[376] *Quaestiones de Quolibets* VIII, Q6, A4: est ibi inordinatio per abusum vocis.

[377] *Commentary on NE* IV.7, *Lectio 15:* Et ideo si aliquis repraesentat rem aliter quam sit, mentiendo, *inordinate agit* et vitiose (emphasis added).

[378] ST II-II, Q110, A3: innaturale est et indebitum.

abuse of words—is unnatural and undue because of a disorder in the very act itself as violating a fundamental aspect of language.

A final problem for Tollefsen's interpretation regards his understanding of personal integrity. If by personal integrity he means something as restricted as presenting oneself as one is, then this is simply nothing other than the virtue of truthfulness. Thus, if his reading of Aquinas is right, what Aquinas is really saying in Q110, A3 is that lying contradicts the virtue of truthfulness. But then why did Aquinas not just repeat what he said earlier in Q110, A1? Contrary to Tollefsen, A3 is more reasonably interpreted as adding a further argument beyond pointing out that whatever contradicts the virtue of truthfulness is a flawed-action.

If by personal integrity Tollefsen means something broader than mere lying, then his argument fails. As Christopher Kaczor says, donating a kidney involves personal dis-integration of one's body.[379] Acting in theatre or putting on a costume involves "intentionally creating a division between the inner and outer self" even if this involves no act of assertion.[380] In short, if Aquinas is really saying that lying (or even acts that are not lying such as failing to keep a promise) is wrong because it violates personal integrity in the broad sense, then his argument fails to be a successful argument, as it would rule out playacting or kidney donation. The New Natural Law position on lying does not present a faithful interpretation of Aquinas.[381]

---

[379] Kaczor, "Can It Be Morally Permissible to Assert a Falsehood in Service of a Good Cause?," 108.

[380] Ibid.

[381] Besides myself, Dewan, Feser, Petri, and Wahl also hold (contrary to the New Natural Law Theorists) that Aquinas's argument against lying is indeed a perverted faculty argument. Cf. Dewan, "St. Thomas, Lying and Venial Sin," footnote 28; Edward Feser, "Smith, Tollefsen, and Pruss on Lying"; Petri and Wahl, "Live Action and Planned Parenthood: A New Test Case for Lying": 444, 449. Janet Smith also holds that it is a perverted faculty argument, but objects to Aquinas's account of the purposes of language. Cf. Smith, "Fig Leaves and Falsehoods"; Smith, "Why Tollefsen and Pruss Are Wrong about Lying."

b) Further NNL texts from Aquinas

But the New Natural Lawyers could marshal texts from Aquinas against my interpretation. In certain passages Aquinas seems to deny that natural ends, and thus the natural end of language, have any moral implications.[382] In one passage, for example, Aquinas indicates that natural species are irrelevant for moral species:

> [Text one:] It is possible that an act which is one with respect to the species of nature may be ordered to diverse acts of the will, as the act of killing a man, which is the same thing with respect to the nature of the species, can be ordered, as to an end, to the conservation of justice, or to the satisfaction of anger. And from this there will be diverse acts with respect to the species of moral habit, because in the one case there will be an act of virtue, in the other case there will be an act of vice. For a motion does not receive its species from that which is its term *per accidens,* but only from that which is its term *per se.* But moral ends are accidental to a natural thing, and *conversely the aspect of a natural end is accidental to something moral.* And so nothing prevents acts which are the same in the species of nature from being diverse with respect to the species of moral habit, and conversely.[383]

So it appears that the natural end (of language) cannot be the due end, because nature is irrelevant to morality.

---

[382] I am indebted to the following article for my discussion of the following three texts from Aquinas (although I have added some responses of my own): Michael Augros and Christopher Oleson, "St. Thomas and the Naturalistic Fallacy," *The National Catholic Bioethics Quarterly* 13, no. 4 (winter 2013): 645-661.

[383] ST I-II, Q1, A3, ad 3; the translation is from Augros and Oleson's article with emphasis added: Possibile tamen est quod unus actus secundum speciem naturae, ordinetur ad diversos fines voluntatis: sicut hoc ipsum quod est occidere hominem, quod est idem secundum speciem naturae, potest ordinari sicut in finem ad conservationem iustitiae, et ad satisfaciendum irae. Et ex hoc erunt diversi actus secundum speciem moris: quia uno modo erit actus virtutis, alio modo erit actus vitii. Non enim motus recipit speciem ab eo quod est terminus per accidens, sed solum ab eo quod est terminus per se. Fines autem morales accidunt rei naturali; et e converso ratio naturalis finis accidit morali. Et ideo nihil prohibet actus qui sunt iidem secundum speciem naturae, esse diversos secundum speciem moris, et e converso.

Other similar texts from Aquinas seem to indicate that one ought not to follow nature:

> [Text two:] For if some activities are found in man which are not subject to the will and to reason, they are not properly called human, *but natural*, as is clear in the case of the activities of the vegetative soul. *Such things in no way fall under the consideration of moral philosophy.* But just as the subject of natural philosophy is motion, or the mobile thing, so the subject of moral philosophy is human action ordered to an end, or else man insofar as he is voluntarily acting for an end [emphasis added].[384]

> [Text three:] But there are many people who follow natural impulses, and few, in fact only the wise, who do not follow natural impulses and occasions for acting badly.[385]

In reply to the first text, it must be said that Aquinas is saying that natural species alone do not give moral species. Natural species are by definition the species of actions abstracted from moral considerations. Nevertheless, the natural ends of human powers do play a role in giving moral species if one's willingly engages a natural power or action that involves some order to the human good. Such is why in ST II-II, Q154, A11 Aquinas gives a crucial role to natural ends in the specification of human acts as good or bad:

---

[384] *Commentary on the Ethics,* Book I, lectio 1, n. 3; translation is from Augros and Oleson, p. 646-647: Dico autem operationes humanas quae procedunt a voluntate hominis secundum ordinem rationis; nam, si quae operationes in homine inveniuntur quae non subiacent voluntati et rationi, non dicuntur proprie humanae sed naturales, sicut patet de operationibus animae vegetabilis, quae nullo modo cadunt sub consideratione moralis philosophiae. Sicut igitur subiectum philosophiae naturalis est motus vel res mobilis, ita etiam subiectum moralis philosophiae est operatio humana ordinata in finem vel etiam homo prout est voluntarie agens propter finem (Sancti Thomae de Aquino, *Sententiae Primi Libri Ethicorum* 1.1.43-54, in *Opera Omnia Iussu Leonis XIII P.M. Edita,* vol. XLVII, volume I (Romae, 1969), p.4).

[385] SCG III, 85: Sed plures sunt qui impetus naturales sequuntur, pauciores autem, scilicet soli sapientes, qui occasiones male agendi et naturales impetus non sequuntur (S. Thomae Aquinatis, *Liber de Veritate Catholicae Fidei contra errores Infidelium seu Summa Contra Gentiles,* vol. III, ch. 85, n.2616 (Taurini, Romae: Marietti, 1961), p. 124). The translation is from Augros and Oleson.

There is a determinate species of lust where a special aspect of deformity occurs, which happens in any unbecoming sexual act. It can occur in two ways. In one way, when it is repugnant to right reason, which is common in every vice of lust. In another way, even beyond this, when it is repugnant to the very order of the sexual act that is fitting to the human species, which is called the vice against nature.[386]

Notice that in the above text Aquinas implies that sexual acts contrary to nature are given a different moral species than sexual acts merely contrary to reason. Natural ends can play a role in moral specification of actions. Aquinas gives a similar emphasis to natural ends as morally relevant in other texts, such as ST II-II, Q110, A3, Q154, A12, and DM Q15, A1. The first text from Aquinas is thus no objection to Aquinas's argument against lying.

As for the second text, Aquinas merely means that such activities are irrelevant for moral philosophy insofar as they are not human acts; he is not saying there that they are irrelevant once human agency enters the picture. In fact, his discussion of disordered eating seems to indicate the opposite: the natural *telos* of actions are morally relevant provided they involve an act proceeding from reason and will.[387] Properly speaking the vegetative powers of nutrition, growth, and generation are not the subjects of moral virtue because the proper acts of such powers are completely involuntary. Nevertheless, insofar as the use of such powers pertains to the concupiscible power, the desires and pleasures of touch as

---

[386] Respondeo dicendum quod, sicut supra dictum est, ibi est determinata luxuriae species ubi specialis ratio deformitatis occurit quae facit indecentem actum venereum. Quod quidem potest esse dupliciter. Uno quidem modo, quia repugnat rationi rectae: quod est commune in omni vitio luxuriae. Alio modo, quia etiam, super hoc, repugnat ipsi ordini naturali venerei actus qui convenit humanae speciei: quod dicitur vitium contra naturam. The translation is my own.

[387] DM Q15, A1: "every human act is disordered which is not proportionate to its due end, as eating is disordered if it is not proportionate to the health of the body to which it is ordained as its end."
The Latin is as follows: Omnis actus humanus dicitur esse inordinatus qui non est proportionatus debito fini: sicut comestio est inordinate si non proportionetur corporis salubritati ad quam ordinatur sicut ad finem (Sancti Thomae de Aquino, *Opera Omnia Iussu Leonis XIII P.M. Edita,* Tomus XXIII, *Quaestiones Disputatae de Malo,* (Romae, Paris: Commissio Leonina, 1982).

found in eating, drinking, and sexual activity pertain to temperance.[388] Aquinas is also very clear that sexual activity involves many moral considerations, even though it makes use of the generative faculty (which he places among the vegetative powers).[389]

As for the third text, Aquinas is not saying that following nature or the natural end is bad *simpliciter*. Nature is a multifaceted term with many senses. The context of the text is SCG III, 85, where Aquinas argues that the celestial bodies are not the causes of our acts of the will or choice. So when he says that many follow *natural* impulses and act badly, he means that the action of the heavenly bodies causes certain sensible desires, which most follow even contrary to reason. These impulses are *natural* insofar as these impulses are natural qua our animal nature, but as abstracted from the rational. Both animals and man are emotionally affected by the movements of the heavenly bodies like the sun insofar as they share the same emotions (lower sensitive appetites) in common.

But following the lower sensitive appetites contrary to reason (as is the case in gluttony) is morally wrong, because the lower powers ought to be subordinated to the higher. The natural end still remains the due end, but for Aquinas the natural end of man is higher than merely each individual faculty acting for its end; the lower powers and their natural ends must be ordered to the higher powers, because the natural end of the lower powers is to be so subordinated. The lower powers, when not subordinated to reason, are unnatural, because all the powers exist for the good of man, which consists principally in an activity of reason; consequently, the lower powers are naturally for the sake of the higher. The third text thus does not negate the truth that the natural end is the due end, nor that the natural end of language is its due end.

Further, the natural end of the concupiscible power is simply sensible pleasures or pains.[390] In fact, it is impossible for any action of the concupiscible power not to be ordered to its natural end.[391] If it were not, it would cease to be an act of the concupiscible power. For human be-

---

[388] Cf. ST II-II, Q141, A5, A7; Q151, A3.

[389] ST II-II, Q153, A2, A3; Q154, A12; ST I-II, Q78, A2.

[390] ST I-II, Q23, A1; ST I, Q81, A2, ad 1.

[391] By *natural end* I mean the proximate natural end, which man shares in common with the animals.

ings, however, it is natural to desire these pleasures or pains only according to reason. The lower powers ought to be subordinated to the higher. It is *natural qua animal* that man pursue any pleasure or avoid any pain (so long as they are ordered to the hierarchy of bodily goods, especially animal life). But *it is not natural qua rational nature*; it is rather *natural qua rational* nature to avoid any pleasures contrary to reason.

No texts from Aquinas provide sound objections to Aquinas's argument that lying is wrong because it violates the natural end of language, which is simply to say that Aquinas is consistent. Aquinas clearly affirms the importance of nature (and so natural ends) for morality in multiple texts, such as ST I-II, Q71, A1, co.:

> Virtue is a certain goodness; *the goodness of anything whatsoever consists in this that it fittingly accords with the mode of its own nature.* Now that to which virtue is ordered is a good action, as is clear from what was stated above.
>
> According to this, therefore, three things are found to be opposed to virtue. One of these is flawed-action, which is opposed to it on the part of that to which virtue is ordered; for *flawed-action properly names a disordered (inordinatum) action, just as the act of virtue is an ordered and due action.* Insofar as the notion of virtue follows upon what is a certain goodness it is opposed to wickedness. But according to that which is directly of the notion of virtue, vice is opposed to virtue; *indeed the vice of anything whatsoever seems to be that it is not disposed according to what is fitting to its own nature.* Hence Augustine says in *De Libero Arbitrio III, "What you see to be lacking to the perfection of nature, may be called a vice."*[392]

---

[392] Virtus sit bonitas quaedam: in hoc enim consistit uniuscuiusque rei bonitas, quod convenienter se habeat secundum modum sua naturae. Id autem ad quod virtus ordinatur, est actus bonus, ut ex supradictis patet. Secundum hoc igitur tria inveniuntur opponi virtuti. Quorum unum est peccatum, quod opponitur sibi ex parte eius ad quod virtus ordinatur: nam peccatum proprie nominat actum inordinatum, sicut actus virtutis est actus ordinatus et debitus. Secundum autem quod ad rationem virtutis consequitur quod sit bonitas quaedam, opponitur virtuti malitia. Sed secundum id quod directe est de ratione virtutis, opponitur virtuti vitium: vitium enim uniuscuiusque rei esse videtur quod non sit disposita secundum quod convenit suae naturae. Unde Augustinus dicit, in III *de Lib. Arb.: Quod perfectioni naturae deesse perspexeris, id voca vitium.* The translation is my own. Emphasis added.

Aquinas is not inconsistent with himself; the natural end is the due end.[393] The natural end of language (or the natural end of a key part of language) is fundamental to his argument against lying.

Part Three: Objections to Aquinas's Account of the Purposes of Language

Aquinas's argument is fundamentally that lying is wrong because it violates the purposes of speech.[394] But many object to his argument. Their objections are generally of two main kinds: (a) some object to Aquinas's account of what the purpose of speech in fact is, while (b) others object to his premise that violating the purpose of speech is wrong. I will begin with the first set of objections, which concern (a) his account of what the purpose of speech in fact is.

a) Objections to Aquinas's account of the purpose of speech

These objectors accuse Aquinas of misunderstanding the teleology of language. Janet Smith, Abbé F. Dubois, Monsignor John Ryan, and Julius Dorszynski object (or would object) along these lines. Smith argues that language has other purposes beyond what Aquinas says it has:

---

[393] For other texts in Aquinas see: *De Malo*, Q2, A1 co., SCG III, 126, 127; ST I, Q63, A3, obj. 2, co.; ST I-II, Q71, A2; ST II-II, Q153, A2; also the many texts where Aquinas says virtue is the perfection of a power (ST I-II, Q55, A1, A3) imply that the natural end of a power is good, and since the good is by definition what ought to be done, the natural end of any action or power is its due end. Let me emphasize here that the second premise (the natural end is the due end) is not saying that every engagement of any action whatsoever is morally good provided it attain its proximate natural end. It is merely saying it is good qua the act in kind if it attains its natural end or is duly ordered to it. Plenty of actions are ordered to and attain their natural end, yet remain morally evil because they are contrary to higher natural ends of man, as happens in walking which may fulfill the purposes of the locomotive power, yet fail to attain the higher end of justice if it be walking in order to commit murder.

[394] Or, perhaps, a key component of speech.

The mistake that Aquinas makes (and those words do stick in my throat!) is that he analyzes the question of lying with a prelapsarian understanding of the purpose of signification, an understanding that presumes the innocence of man before the Fall....Before the Fall, there would have been no reason to engage in false signification. Before the Fall, all communication, all interaction was between innocent and trustworthy human beings. After the Fall, however, all communication is between human beings damaged by sin. Now, language must serve many other purposes besides the conveyance of the concepts on our minds. We need to correct, console, encourage, and deter one another. These actions need not involve falsehoods, but they are a use of language that differs from the fundamental purpose of communicating truth.[395]

Smith thus concludes that "after the Fall, as is the case with words of consolation and encouragement, certain falsehoods uttered in certain circumstances can be fitting and morally licit uses of language."[396]

Abbé F. Dubois objects to Aquinas, but on different grounds. He argues that "the principal end of language is not the manifestation of truth."[397] In fact, the manifestation of truth is not the only, nor the most important end of language; rather the principle end is the social good.[398] "Speech was given to man to manifest his thoughts *when it is useful to the social good.*"[399] If there are circumstances where the good of society requires that man hide the truth and equivocation or amphibology does not suffice, then man ought to hide the truth by creating discord between his speech and his thoughts.[400]

Monsignor John A. Ryan objects to Aquinas's account of the teleology of language:

While the purpose of the faculty of speech is, indeed, to communicate what is in one's mind, this may sometimes mean what one desires to

---

[395] Smith, "Fig Leaves and Falsehoods."
[396] Ibid.
[397] Abbé F. Dubois, "Une Théorie Du Mensonge Replique (1)," ed. M.L' Abbé Duflot, *La Science Catholique* 12 (december 1897 - december 1898): 169.
[398] Ibid., 169-170.
[399] Ibid., 170.
[400] Ibid., 170.

communicate, not necessarily nor always the objective truth; the fundamental relation between the faculty and its exercise is not that of speech to truth but of speech to whatever idea the speaker wishes to convey.[401]

Ryan's point is this: the purpose of speech is to communicate whatever one wishes to communicate; speech's purpose is not fundamentally the conveyance of truth to another. Since truth is not the purpose of speech, one cannot say that lying violates the purpose of speech.

Julius A. Dorszynski also rejects Aquinas's account of the purpose of language:

> Moreover, it seems to us that the essential and proper object of the faculty of speech is not to communicate ideas and judgments just as they are in the speaker's mind. This is one of the objects of speech; but it seems to us that a study of the nature of speech in all its expressions will show that speaking one's mind is not the one and only and essential object of that faculty.[402]

Dorszynski, interestingly, does not tell us what he thinks the proper object of speech is. He simply argues that "it cannot be maintained that the proper and essential object of speech is to communicate the truth as it is found in the speaker's mind" because there are too many examples where violating the adequation of the word to the mind just seems justified.[403] Falsehoods in jokes or in planning a surprise birthday party cannot possibly be wrong, so the proper object of speech cannot possibly be to communicate truth.[404]

---

[401] John A. Ryan, *The Norm of Morality: Defined and Applied to Particular Actions* (Washington, D.C.: National Catholic Welfare Conference, 1944), 42.
[402] Dorszynski, *Catholic Teaching About the Morality of Falsehood*, 73.
[403] Ibid., 74.
[404] Ibid., 74-75.

b) What is the purpose of language and did it change after the Fall?

Are these criticisms of Aquinas's account of the teleology of language accurate? We will begin first with Janet Smith's criticisms. The idea that Aquinas holds to a prelapsarian view of the purposes of language is rather curious, especially considering the fact that Aquinas seems to be glossing Aristotle on this point. In fact, in his *Quaestiones de Quodlibet,* Thomas explicitly cites Aristotle as the source of his view about the teleology of language: "written words (*verba*) or spoken words (*voces*) were invented as they are signs of understanding, *as it is said in I Periher*" (emphasis added). Aristotle wrote *I Periher*. Aristotle, who was not a Christian, had no notion of the Fall or of original sin. Yet Aristotle still concluded that the purpose of language is to convey what is on one's mind. Since Thomas is merely quoting Aristotle on this point, he cannot have a prelapsarian view of the teleology of language.

Further, even granted that the Fall occurred and that original sin entered the world, wounding human nature, it does not follow that the nature of language or its fundamental purposes have changed. As Thomas Petri, O.P. and Michael Wahl point out in their response to Smith,

> St. Thomas argues that the principles of human nature and the proper-
> ties that flow from them…were in no way destroyed by sin. They were
> not even diminished. To suggest that sin destroys our nature or even
> diminishes our nature would be to suggest that sin has fundamentally
> changed human nature; it has not. What has been diminished in human
> nature is the inclination to virtue. Thus, reason has not been dimin-
> ished, even though our virtuous use of it has. Since speech is by defini-
> tion related to reason, its function and purpose are not diminished by
> original sin either.[405]

---

[405] Petri and Wahl, "Live Action and Planned Parenthood: A New Test Case for Lying," 460. Cf. ST I-II, Q85, A1. They also argue that if human nature changed after the fall, then this has problematic views for the Incarnation, cf. ST III, Q4, A6. See also ST I, Q48, A4.

Original sin did not destroy human nature, nor did it change the faculties or properties of man. If it had changed human nature, then human nature would have ceased to be, except in an equivocal sense. A thing's nature, by definition, is unchanging. A triangle is a three-sided plane figure. When such a figure ceases to have three-sides, it ceases to be a triangle. Man's nature is rational animal. If man ceases to be an animal, then he ceases to be a man. A similar point applies to other essential aspects of human nature: if they changed by original sin, then human nature would cease to be. Likewise, if the nature of things in creation changed, they would cease to be what they are. Language as such could only be changed if the nature of man or the properties of man were changed, because language flows out of man's nature as a social animal. Man's nature and his properties, however, cannot change without he himself ceasing to be man.[406] Thus, even granting that original sin injured or diminished the good of nature, it would not change the fundamental nature or teleology of language.[407] If the inherent *telos* of language changed after the Fall, it would cease to be language.

---

[406] I am using *properties* in the Aristotelian-Thomistic sense of the term, as an attribute that follows necessarily upon the essence of the subject.

[407] A possible objection to my view would be from Genesis 3:17-19 where God curses the ground and makes it produce thorns and thistles as punishment for the first sin. An objector could argue here that just as God changed the natures of certain plants to produce thorns and thistles so too did he change the nature of language. In reply to this objection, it must be said that it is doubtful whether God really changed the natures of certain plants when he cursed the ground; other possible explanations are that he merely modified accidental attributes of plants, created new soil unconducive to certain plants, or just allowed the more noxious plants to flourish. There are fundamental philosophical objections to interpreting this verse as God changing the nature of plants. To add to or subtract from the essence of a thing is to make an entirely new nature such that the original ceases to be. If rational is taken away from the essence of man, man ceases to be, but a new animal nature is made. Likewise, if rational were added to the nature of an ox, the ox would cease to be, as there would in its place be a rational animal, namely, a man. Similarly, if God changed the nature of plants, they would not be plants or at least these particular kinds of plants, except equivocally or in appearance only. Cf. ST I, Q25, A6. Further, even if the antecedent of the objection were true, the consequent does not necessarily follow. If God changed the natures of some plants, it does not follow that he changed the natures of other things or the nature of language. There is no Scriptural basis that God changed the fundamental nature of language due to original sin.

Language certainly has a variety of uses such as conveying the truth, telling a joke, or asking a question, but none of these other uses were generated by the Fall; all of these other purposes are diverse manners of realizing the general purpose of conveying what is in the mind. Language's primary end as conveying the conceptions of the mind to another remains the primary purpose of language both before and after the Fall. If the general *telos* of conveying the conceptions of the mind were no longer the purposes of language, then language properly speaking would cease to be.

So too, neither did the nature or purpose of assertions change. Language has a general purpose of conveying the conceptions of the mind to another, which is realized in questions, requests, jokes, assertions, etc. Assertions convey something as true, which is a particular instance of the general purpose of conveying the conceptions of the mind to another. If this fundamental *telos* of assertions were to change, then assertions would cease to be assertions. Just as the Fall did not change the purpose of language as such, neither did it change the nature and fundamental purpose of asserting.

c) *Does language have further purposes?*

Smith's argument, then, does not withstand scrutiny. What of the other objections? These objections from Smith, Dubois, and Dorszynski all basically entail that language has purposes besides the conveyance of truth. Truth either is not the purpose of language or not its principal or most important end. As stated earlier, Smith argues that "language must serve many other purposes besides the conveyance of the concepts on our minds. We need to correct, console, encourage, and deter one another. These actions need not involve falsehoods, but they are a use of language that differs from the fundamental purpose of communicating truth."[408] Dubois argues that "the principal end of language is not the manifestation of truth," but rather the social good.[409] Dorszynski argues that since there is nothing wrong with telling falsehoods to deceive a

---

[408] Smith, "Fig Leaves and Falsehoods."
[409] Dubois, 169-170.

family member about an upcoming surprise party or in jokes, the conveyance of the conceptions of the mind is not the one and only purpose of speech.[410]

All of the aforementioned objections have some truth in them. The purpose of speech is not simply the conveyance of truth to another. Truth is not the primary end of language as such; rather the primary purpose is the manifestation of the conceptions of the mind to another.[411] This understanding of the nature of language is not only shared by Aristotle,[412] but also by al-Farabi,[413] Thomas Hobbes,[414] John Locke,[415] and linguists such as Paul Gaeng and Edgar Sturtevant.[416] Smith, Dubois, and Dorszynski are right to claim that there are other purposes to language besides asserting what is true. Aquinas also recognizes this, which

---

[410] Dorszynski, *Catholic Teaching About the Morality of Falsehood*, 73-75.

[411] ST I, Q107, A1: Nihil est enim aliud loqui ad alterum, quam conceptum mentis alteri manifestare.

[412] *De Interpretatione* 1.16a.

[413] "How *utterances signify the intelligible* is by imposition, convention, and legislation" (Thérèse-Anne Druart, "Al-Fârâbî: An Arabic Account of the Origin of Language and of Philosophical Vocabulary," *Proceedings of the ACPA* 84 (2011): 7, emphasis added).

[414] Hobbes, *Leviathan* (Green Dragon, St. Paul's Churchyard, 1651), Part I, Chapter 4.2.

[415] "Words, in their primary or immediate signification, stand for nothing but *the ideas in the mind of him that uses them*" (John Locke, *An Essay Concerning Human Understanding*, 2nd ed., Book III.2.2 (1690), accessed March 30, 2015, http://www.gutenberg.org/cache/epub/10616/pg10616.html). "When a man speaks to another, it is that he may be understood: and the end of speech is, that those sounds, or marks, may make known his ideas to the hearer" (*Essay*, III.2.2). I am not claiming Aquinas's account of the nature of language is identical with Locke's, but rather that there is enough of a similarity to show that Aquinas is not alone in his general views on the nature and purpose of language.

[416] Gaeng quotes Sturtevant's definition of language as "*a system of arbitrary vocal symbols by which members of a social group cooperate and interact*" (14). Later he clarifies that "the last part of Sturtevant's definition, namely, *by which members of a social group cooperate and interact,* designates the chief function of language in society, since without transfer of thought from one human mind to another there can be little or no cooperation and interaction" (Paul A. Gaeng, *Introduction to the Principles of Language* (Lanham, MD: University of America Press, 1971), 19, underline emphasis added. It is granted that his definition of language is not exactly the same as Aristotle's or Aquinas's, but the fundamental purpose of language seems to be quite similar.

is why in all of his arguments against lying, in *Super Sent.* III, D38, Q1, A3,[417] *Quodlibet* VIII, Q6, A4,[418] *Commentary on the Nicomachean Ethics* IV.7, *Lectio* 15,[419] and ST II-II, Q110, A3,[420] he consistently claims that the purpose of language is to convey what is on one's mind. Aquinas does not claim in his treatment of lying that the purpose of language is truth, rather he claims the purpose of language is for communicating with others.

Thomas knew about other purposes of language beyond the mere conveyance of truth, so much so that when differences in grammatical mood made a difference in the realm of morals Aquinas quickly points out which grammatical moods affect the morality of the act in question and which do not.[421] In his treatment of the morality of cursing (*maledicere*), for example, Aquinas is quick to distinguish between the indicative, imperative, and optative mood.[422]

Aquinas knew language has further purposes beyond the mere conveyance of the conceptions of the mind, but the mere fact that language has further purposes never detracts from its primary purpose, which is to convey what is on one's mind. In fact, these further purposes such as consoling a friend or giving a command are merely particular ends embedded into language's general purpose insofar as words of consolation or giving a command are still conveying the conceptions of the mind to another.

Conveying the conceptions of the mind is the very purpose and nature of language. If perfect mind reading were possible, there would be no need for language. We need language only because the thoughts of

---

[417] "locutio inventa sit ad exprimendam conceptionem cordis."

[418] "Written words (*verba*) or spoken words (*voces*) were invented as they are signs of understanding, as it is said in *I Periher.*"

[419] "Speech (*locutio*) was contrived for expressing the conception of the heart (*conceptionem cordis*)."

[420] "Words (*voces*) are naturally signs of understanding (*signa naturaliter intellectuum*)."

[421] Tollefsen, "Augustine, Aquinas, and the Absolute Norm Against Lying": 123. Cf. Aquinas' *Commentary on Aristotle's De Interpretatione* Book 1, lectio 7. Further, in ST II-II, Q76, A4 he distinguishes between assertion, command, and wish.

[422] ST II-II, Q76, A1. Speaking evil in the indicative mood, Aquinas says, is distinct from what he wishes to discuss in the body of the article.

another cannot be made known to us directly. This is why language was invented in the first place and why the first words were spoken.

Smith's, Dubois', and Dorszynski's objections, however, point to the need for a deeper understanding of Aquinas's arguments against lying. Aquinas claims that lying violates the teleology of speech. The purpose of speech is to manifest the conceptions of the mind to another.[423] Now, in lying one is not strictly violating this purpose of speech. For in telling a lie, one is in a manner conveying the concepts of one's mind to another, namely the interior words of the mind that one wishes to convey or the lie that is on one's mind.[424] This is why strictly speaking lying is opposed to truth and not to the manifestation of the conceptions of the mind to another.[425]

If one takes lying as being opposed merely to the conveyance of the conceptions of the mind to another, then some rather absurd conclusions follow. Saint Raymond of Pennafort, for example, mentioned that one may tell the murderer at the door that the one he is looking for is not there, if doing so does not violate one's conscience:

> If one's conscience prompts him to speak thus [that the fugitive is not here], then thus one should speak; then one is not speaking against his conscience, but is following it rather, and one shall not sin in any way.[426]

Conscience is literally to speak with knowledge. In a sense then conscience is to speak what one has on one's mind. Thus, if one says, "No Jews are here," then one is truly conveying one's thoughts, namely, the thoughts that "No Jews are here." Although one is not conveying what

---

[423] ST I, Q107, A1.

[424] As Gilson says, "In the same fashion…that there pre-exists in the mind of the artisan a certain image of the exterior object that he wishes to produce, there also exists in the thought of him who speaks a sort of interior model of the word that he wants to utter exteriorly" (*Linguistics and Philosophy: An Essay on the Philosophical Constants of Language*, 73). In lying one's exterior words are still signs of the interior word that one has fashioned (and thus of the concepts that one holds), although these interior words and concepts are not believed.

[425] ST II-II, Q110, A1.

[426] As mentioned in Dorszynski, *Catholic Teaching About the Morality of Falsehood*, 25.

one believes to be true, one is still in a sense conveying the conceptions of the mind to another.[427]

Whatever one may think about the morality of lying, the most common sense approach has it that telling the murderer at the door "No Jews are here" is in fact a lie. If one is not careful about the purpose of language, as the conveyance of the conceptions of the mind to another, then it seems as if it is simply not possible to lie. It seems, then, that if we are to understand Aquinas's account of the purpose of language, then we must first gain a deeper understanding of what Aquinas meant when he said that lying abuses language.

d) Aquinas and the disorder of lying

In the previous chapter we found that the correct definition of a lie is asserting what one does not believe to be true. We noted how assertions are fundamental to Aquinas's account of lying. The nature of assertions must be taken into account in order to understand Aquinas's argument against lying. In all the texts just mentioned where Aquinas argues lying is wrong, Aquinas describes how in the act of lying *locutio, verba, signa,* or *voces* are being abused or used unnaturally. His terminology here, however, is a bit loose. He is presuming his reader recalls his earlier more detailed discussions of the nature of a lie. So when he is speaking of *locutio, verba, signa,* or *voces* he is really using synecdoche to refer to assertions. He is not speaking about words, or language as such. Assertions are being abused and used unnaturally in every lie, not language or words as such.

e) Speaking abusively, inordinately, unnaturally

As mentioned in the earlier chapter, assertions differ from other speech acts. To assert is to put oneself behind the truth of what one says. In as-

---

[427] Interestingly, Saint Raymond held that all lies were sinful (Dorszynski, 25). Dorszynski thinks Raymond is being inconsistent here with Raymond's statements about conscience (Dorszynski, 25), but I hold that he is perhaps not. Raymond might be just using *conscience* in the sense of "speaking what is on one's mind."

serting one is claiming or presenting something as if it were true. By contrast, in asking a question, giving a command, playacting, or telling a joke, one is not making an assertion. Words by themselves are not assertions, nor is staying silent.[428]

The nature of assertions and their natural *telos* of conveying the truth to another sheds light on why every lie involves an abuse or unnatural use of assertions. In a lie, one is engaging in the act of assertion, but at the same time one does not really believe that what one asserts is true. Notice the fundamental disorder here in the very nature of the act of lying. Assertions by their very nature are ordered towards the truth. Truth is the natural end of all acts of assertion.[429] In asserting, one is engaging in an act (asserting) that has its own natural end of conveying the truth to another. But in telling a lie one is using this type of action (an assertion) for an end contrary to what it is naturally ordered towards. In other words, one is engaging in an action that has a natural end of its own, and then deliberately and at the same time frustrating that end from happening. One is engaging in an action with its own natural order to an end, and then superimposing on this action an end contrary to its natural end.[430] The *finis operis* of the action is being frustrated or acted against

---

[428] Unless, of course, the words are meant to be a sort of shorthand for an assertion, as in the words *yes* and *no*. *Yes* is simply a shorthand way of asserting, "I agree with you," or "what you just said is the case," etc.

[429] This natural end is given in part from context and social convention, and thus it is to an extent beyond the control of the speaker. For example, one cannot make an assertion not to be an assertion if one says a proposition with a straight face under oath in a court of law (unless there are good indications to the contrary such as quoting from a script in a movie).

[430] Although he was not writing directly on the topic of assertions, William Wollaston's words seem quite fitting to be quoted here: "To treat things as being what they are not is the greatest possible absurdity. It is to put bitter for sweet, darkness for light, crooked for straight, etc. It is to subvert all science, to renounce all sense of truth, and flatly to deny the existence of any thing. For nothing can be true, nothing does exist, if things are not what they are" (William Wollaston, "The Religion of Nature Delineated," 8th ed. (1759), Section IV.5, in *British Philosophy: 1600-1900, British Moralists*, ed. L.A. Selby-Bigge, M.A., vol. 2). In lying one is, in a way, treating assertions as if they were not assertions.

Similar examples would be that of a doctor who uses her power to heal so as to poison her patient. Cf. Steven J. Jensen, *Good & Evil Actions* (Washington, D.C.: CUA Press, 2010), 243-244.

by the *finis operantis* of the agent. This is why Aquinas, in ST II-II, Q110, A3, calls it an "action falling upon undue matter." False assertions are undue matter for imparting to another what one believes to be true. Every lie involves the use of an assertion, which has its own natural end, and a simultaneous frustration of this natural order to its end.[431] It is thus, as Aquinas says, an *inordinatio per abusum vocis,*[432] *inordinate agit,*[433] and *innaturale* and *indebitum.*[434] Lying is intrinsically disordered.

f) Assertions and their purpose

Strictly speaking, for Aquinas, lying is not opposed to the purpose of language as such, but rather to a particular instantiation of language, namely, assertions. Further, the fact that Aquinas recognizes that only assertions can be true or false indicates that properly speaking lying is opposed to the purpose of asserting. One cannot lie by asking a question or by making a command, so it is not possible to violate directly these other aspects of speech by lying. The purpose of assertive speech is to convey to another what you believe to be true.[435] So if one is not speaking assertively, one is not telling a lie.[436] Thus, Smith's, Dubois', and Dorszynski's objections are correct in some respects. Speech that is non-assertive does not have truth as its primary end. Further, though truth is the proximate end of assertions, it is not its only end. One may direct assertions to other remote ends so long as one does not violate its fundamental purpose. For example, one may assert words of encouragement

---

[431] Jensen seems to arrive at a similar point: "if Bruce lies to Bridget in order to deceive her, he chooses to accomplish his goal of deception through an action that is directed toward revealing the truth. The realization of this order to truth, however, is an obstacle to his goal" (*Good & Evil Actions,* 245).

[432] *Quolibets* VIII, Q6, A4.

[433] *Commentary on the Nicomachean Ethics*, Book IV.7, Lecture 15.

[434] ST II-II, Q110, A3.

[435] Cf. ST II-II, Q110, A1: Obiectum autem proprium manifestationis sive enuntiationis est verum vel falsum.

[436] By *speaking assertively,* I mean to include non-verbal assertions such as sign language or a nod of the head to indicate *yes.*

or fraternal correction without violating the purposes of speech, because one is still asserting what one believes to be true.

As for Dorszynski's argument from jokes and surprise birthday parties, it must be said that it is an error in methodology to start from moral conclusions that one wishes to justify and then change the natures of things so as to justify such conclusions. Dorszynski seems to want to justify lying or certain patterns of false speech and so he changes the purposes of language so as to accommodate his desires. This procedure is problematic. The moral good should not be changed to conform with our desires, rather our desires should conform to whatever the moral good is. Aquinas's account of the purpose of language, and of assertions, stands true against the objections. The reason why assertions exist in the first place is so that man may communicate truth to another.

As stated in the earlier chapter, lying is parasitic upon asserting's *finis operis* of truth. If assertions did not have the primary proximate end of truth, then there would be no reason for lying to exist in the first place. It is because assertions have their natural end of truth, that one is able to co-op that end for ulterior purposes, as in lying. Liars tend to be successful because people presuppose that the natural end of assertive speech is truth.

Part Four: Objections to Aquinas's Major Premise, namely, His Normative Teleology

Tollefsen objects to Aquinas's account of lying (as we have presented it) by denying that violating the purpose of speech is always wrong. In other words, Tollefsen argues that it is not always wrong to violate a natural function:

> [Aquinas's argument] looks very much like a variant of a perverted faculty argument, an argument that holds that the 'natural function' of something should not be thwarted deliberately. Such arguments are hardly compelling in their most common setting, which concerns the use of bodily organs, such as sex organs. That the natural function of an organ *is* such and such does not provide a *reason* for agents to respect that function, at least, not absent some account of the relation of the function to a good that is preserved or promoted by that function. Thus, on their own, natural function arguments are empty of motivational significance.[437]

Although I disagree with Tollefsen's example, he nevertheless has a point: not all violations of teleology are morally bad. As Aristotle says, nature sometimes results in monsters, but the monsters that result aren't necessarily morally bad. A dog may give birth to a three-legged dog. In Aristotle's terminology this three-legged dog is called a monster, as he happened due to a disorder in the act of generation. The three-legged dog is metaphysically bad as having a defect in health, but this dog certainly isn't morally bad. The defect in the teleology of the generative power in this case then certainly isn't a moral defect, although it involves a defect in natural teleology.

Further arguments can be mustered in support of Tollefsen's position that not all violations of teleology are bad.[438] The purpose of the

---

[437] Tollefsen, "Augustine, Aquinas, and the Absolute Norm Against Lying": 123. Strictly speaking Tollefsen is not objecting to what he takes to be Aquinas's position.

[438] See Michael Augros and Christopher Oleson for other examples: "St. Thomas and the Naturalistic Fallacy," 643. Augros and Oleson end up disagreeing with these objections (see p. 659-661 of their article).

teeth is for chewing food. There is nothing wrong with using them for holding a flashlight or for breaking off a piece of tape. A hammer was made for pounding nails, but there is nothing wrong with using it to defend oneself against a wild animal or to break a glass window to escape a fire. Why can one legitimately usurp the teleology of hands, teeth, and hammers, but not of speech?[439] Why does Aquinas seem to think the teleology of speech is inviolable?

A closer look at the texts may be of help. Aquinas nowhere asserts that all violations of teleology are morally bad. On the contrary, in the texts against lying, Aquinas is more precise in his wording. He says that in lying "there is a disorder through the abuse of word,"[440] that in lying one "acts disorderly and viciously,"[441] and that "it is unnatural and undue that one signify with words that which one has not in the mind."[442] In other words, the very action of lying is itself abusive, inordinate, and unnatural.[443] Aquinas's argument is about the teleology of *actions,* in this case of the *finis operis* of the act of asserting; his argument does not concern organs or artifacts abstracted from considerations of human action.

The fact that lying in itself is disordered and unnatural does not fully solve our problem. Aquinas's explanation as to why lying is disordered and unnatural, you will recall, is that it violates the purposes of assertions. This is true, but merely raises a further question: Why is vio-

---

[439] These explanations are meant only as prima facie plausible cases where it is permissible to violate teleology. Whether they, in fact, involve true violations of teleology will be discussed later.

[440] Leonine, *QuoLibet VIII, Q6, A4,* p. 75-76.

[441] Sancti Thomae de Aquino, *Opera Omnia Iussu Leonis XIII P.M. Edita, Tomus XLVII, Volumen II, Sententia Libri Ethicorum,* IV, *lectio* 15, 88, p. 252.

[442] ST II-II, Q110, A3.

[443] Further texts where Aquinas indicates the inherent disorder in every lie are as follows: ST II-II, Q110, A3, ad 4: "Ad quartum dicendum quod mendacium non solum habet rationem peccati ex damno quod infert proximo, sed *ex sua inordinatione,* ut dictum est"; *Super Sent., lib.* III, D38, Q1, A3, s.c. 2: "Praeterea, omnis inordinatio in actibus humanis, si voluntaria sit, peccatum est. Sed ubicumque est mendacium, *est aliqua inordinatio,* quia adhibetur vox ad significandum aliquid quod significabile non est. Ergo omne mendacium est peccatum"; *Super Sent., lib.* III, D38, Q1, A4, co.: "Alia vero mendacia, *quia inordinationem quamdam habent,* non tamen a dilectione Dei et proximi avertunt; peccata sunt, sed sunt venialia." Emphasis added.

lating the purposes of assertions or using assertions in an unnatural or disordered manner morally wrong? In order to arrive at greater clarity, I now turn to Aquinas's account of disorder (*inordinatio*).

a) Aquinas on inordinatio

An *inordinatio* is opposed to an *ordinatio*. Order is always in relation to some principle, and when it comes to actions it is always in relation to some end or to those things that are for an end.[444] Since *inordinatio* in human acts conveys the notion of a lack of order to an end, Aquinas at times adopts the language of *inordinatio* to describe flawed-action, which is a *peccatum* (ἁμαρτία), literally a missing the mark:

> Further, *every inordinatio in human acts, if it is voluntary, is a flawed-action.* But in every lie, there is some *inordinatio,* since it employs voice to signify something that is not signifiable. Therefore, every lie is a flawed-action.[445]
>
> -*Super Sent.* III, D38 Q1, A3 s.c. 2:

> I reply it must be said that, as has been said, for the notion of flawed-action two things concur, namely a voluntary act and its *inordinatio,* which is by a withdrawing from the law of God.[446]
>
> -ST I-II Q72, A1, co.

I reply, it must be said that in flawed-action there are two things, name-

---

[444] ST I, Q42, A3: "Dicendum quod ordo semper dicitur per comparationem ad aliquod principium."
Super Sent., lib. I, D17, Q2, A5, co.: "Inordinatio autem actus vel est circa finem, vel circa ea quae sunt ad finem"; *De Malo,* Q7, A5, ad 2: "Ad secundum dicendum, quod circa finem potest esse inordinatio dupliciter: aut quia receditur a fine, et hoc est peccatum mortale; aut quia acceptatur aliquid a fine retardans, et hoc est peccatum veniale."

[445] "Praeterea, *omnis inordinatio in actibus humanis, si voluntaria sit, peccatum est.* Sed ubicumque est *mendacium, est aliqua inordinatio,* quia adhibetur vox ad significandum aliquid quod significabile non est. Ergo omne mendacium est peccatum" [emphasis added]. The translation is my own.

[446] "Respondeo dicendum quod, sicut dictum est, *ad rationem peccati duo concurrunt,* scilicet actus voluntarius; *et inordinatio eius,* quae est per recessum a lege Dei" [emphasis added]. The translation is my own.

ly its act and its *inordinatio,* insofar as it recedes from the order of reason and the divine law.[447]

-ST I-II Q72, A8, co.

I reply, it must be said that flawed-action is a certain *actus inordinatus.*[448]

-ST I-II Q75, A1, co.

Flawed-action may be taken in the broad sense as any disordered (*inordinatus*) action and so an archer missing his mark or limping can be said to be "flawed-actions."[449] But in the realm of morals, only human acts, acts proceeding from intellect and will, can be flawed-actions. Properly speaking, flawed-action in the realm of human action is not just any lack of order to an end (otherwise, a thief would sin from failing to successfully carry out his bank heist), but rather the lack of order to a due end, which Aquinas indicates in various passages:

> It is impossible that something be which is destitute of any order. *Hence in the very act of sin [a flawed-action]*, insofar as it is a certain thing, remains some order both to the agent and to some end intended by the agent, which is the perceived good, *although it is deprived of the order to its due end.*[450]
>
> -Super Sent. II D37, Q1, A1, ad 5.

---

[447] "Respondeo dicendum quod, cum *in peccato sint duo, scilicet ipse actus, et inordinatio eius*, prout receditur ab ordine rationis et legis divinae" [emphasis added]. The translation is my own.

[448] "Respondeo. Dicendum quod *peccatum est quidam actus inordinatus*" [emphasis added]. The translation is my own. Numerous other texts in Aquinas indicate that every *inordinatio* is a sin: *Super Sent., lib.* III, D38, Q1, A4, co.; *Super Sent., lib.* 4, D1, Q1, A4, qc. 5, ad 2; *Super Sent., lib.* 4, D33, Q2, A2, qc. 2, ad 5; ST I-II, Q82, A1, ad 2; ST II-II, Q34, A4, co; *De veritate,* Q24, A7, co.; *De Malo* Q2, A2; *De Malo* Q2, A3.

[449] *Peccatum* can be understood broadly as an error in acting, whether the error be moral or non-moral.

[450] "Ad quintum dicendum, quod impossibile est aliquam rem esse quae omni ordine destituatur; *unde et in ipso actu peccati,* ut res quaedam est, remanet ordo aliquis et ad agentem et ad finem aliquem intentum ab agente, quod est aestimatum bonum; *quamvis privetur ordo ad finem debitum*" [emphasis added].

The completion of flawed-actions is not through order to an end, but more through the aversion from a due end.[451]

> -*Super Sent.* III, D33, Q2, A1, qc. 1, ad 3.

Indeed flawed-action (*peccatum*) is taken commonly insofar as it is found in natural and artificial things, from which it happens that something in acting does not attain the end on account of which it acts, which happens on account of a defect of the active principle, as the grammarian who does not write well does so from a defect of the [habit of] the art, although he intends to write well. And that nature performs-a-flawed-action in the formation of an animal occurs in the case of monsters, which happens from a defect of the active power in the semen. *But flawed-action (peccatum) insofar as properly it is said in morals has the notion of morally-flawed-action (culpae) and from which it happens that the will turns from its due end by tending to an undue end.*[452]

> -*De Malo* Q3, A1, co.

Every human act is said to be disordered when it is not proportionate to its *due end*.[453]

> -*De Malo* Q15, A1, co.

In various other texts Aquinas either says or strongly implies that flawed-action or badness in human action involves the lack of order to a due end.[454]

---

[451] "Ad tertium dicendum, quod perfectio peccatorum non est per ordinem ad finem, sed magis per aversionem a fine debito." The translation is my own.

[452] "Peccatum enim communiter dictum, secundum quod in rebus naturalibus et artificialibus invenitur, ex eo provenit quod aliquis in agendo non attingit ad finem propter quem agit; quod contingit ex defectu activi principii; sicut si grammaticus non recte scribat, contingit ex defectu artis, si tamen recte scribere intendit; et quod natura peccet in formatione animalis, sicut contingit in partibus monstruosis, contingit ex defectu activae virtutis in semine. *Peccatum vero, secundum quod proprie in moralibus dicitur, habet rationem culpae, et provenit ex eo quod voluntas deficit debito fine, per hoc quod in finem indebitum tendit*" [emphasis added].

[453] "Omnis actus humanus dicitur esse inordinatus qui non est proportionatus debito fini." The translation is my own.

[454] *Super Sent., lib.* II, D34, Q1, A2, co; *Super Sent., lib.* II, D34, Q1, A2, ad 3; *Super Sent., lib.* II, D35, Q1, A1, ad 3; *Super Sent., lib.* IV, D49, Q1, A3, qc. 4, ad 5; *Contra Gentiles, lib.* III, *cap.* 122, n. 4; ST I, Q48, A1, ad 2; ST I-II, Q18, A9, co.;

Since lying is an *inordinatio*, it is a flawed-action, and a flawed-action in the moral sense (as opposed to flawed-action broadly taken); lying involves the lack of due order to a due end. The due end in this case cannot merely be God or neighbor, because if it were then Aquinas would have condemned only lies that are directly against God and neighbor. But he condemns lies as bad (though only venially so) that do not directly injure God or neighbor, such are the officious and jocose lies, that is, the last four types of lies on Augustine's eightfold list.[455] The due end that lying violates is the natural end of asserting, which is why Aquinas condemns lying as an "abuse of word," that is, as an unnatural and undue use of words.[456] In lying the agent is employing an assertion, but contrary to its natural end of telling the truth.

ST I-II, Q19, A3, ad 2; ST I-II, Q71, A6; ST I-II, Q71, A6, ad 3; ST I-II, Q75, A1, co; ST I-II, Q75, A1, ad 1; ST I-II, Q75, A4, ad 1; ST II-II, Q45, A1, ad 1; *Compendium theologiae, lib.* I, *cap.* 116, co.; *Sententia Ethic., lib.* VI, l. 10, n. 13; *Super Rom., cap.* 2, l. 2.

[455] *Super Sent., lib.* II, D35, Q1, A5, co.: "et per hunc modum *peccatum* vel culpa, quod in actu consistit, dicitur corrumpere animam vel potentias, secundum *scilicet quod pervertit eam ab ordine rationis per quem in debitum finem dirigebatur*" [emphasis added]. *Super Sent., lib.* III, D38, Q1, A4, co.: "Alia vero mendacia, quia inordinationem quamdam habent, non tamen a dilectione Dei et proximi avertunt; peccata sunt, sed sunt venialia." *Contra Gentiles, lib.* IV, *cap.* 54, n. 8: "Sicut virtutibus homo ad beatitudinem disponitur, ita et peccatis impeditur. *Peccatum* autem virtuti contrarium, impedimentum affert beatitudini, non solum inordinationem quandam animae inducens secundum quod eam *ab ordine debiti finis abducit,* sed etiam Deum offendens, a quo beatitudinis praemium expectatur" [emphasis added]. *Super Psalmo* 50, n. 6: "Quando vero de peccatore facit justum, tunc dicitur proprie creare: Eph. 2: *ipsius creatura sumus creati in Christo Jesu in operibus bonis:* Jac. 1: *ut sitis initium aliquod creaturae Dei,* scilicet spiritualis ejus. Secundum quod *sequitur ex peccato, est inordinatio mentis, quae fit per aversionem a fine debito*" [emphasis added]. ST II-II, Q29, A3, ad 1: "Ad primum ergo dicendum quod a gratia gratum faciente nullus deficit *nisi propter peccatum, ex quo contingit quod homo sit aversus a fine debito,* in aliquo indebito finem constituens" [emphasis added]. ST II-II, Q110, A3, ad 4: "Ad quartum dicendum quod mendacium non solum habet rationem peccati ex damno quod infert proximo, sed ex sua inordinatione, ut dictum est." For Augustine's eightfold list see: ST II-II, Q110, A4; *Super Sent.* III, D38, Q1, A4.

[456] Cf. Leonine, *QuoLibet VIII, Q6, A4,* p. 75-76; ST II-II, Q110, A3.

b) Aquinas's argument

Aquinas's argument against lying can thus be put into valid form as follows:

1. Any action not ordered to its due end is a disordered action.
2. The natural end is the due end [any natural end of an action is its due end].[457]
3. Ergo, any action not ordered to its natural end is a disordered action (from 1 & 2).
4. The natural end of asserting is to tell the truth.
5. Ergo, any use of assertions not ordered to truth-telling [as is the case in telling a lie] is a disordered action (from 3, 4, & 5).

The fourth premise I have already defended in the earlier chapter of this book, but I will briefly restate the case here. The natural end is simply what assertions are for by their very nature, as the *finis operis*. If assertions were also naturally for the purpose of lying, then society would become confused as nobody would trust anybody's assertions, since they might just as well be lies as acts of truth-telling. Lying's success is parasitic upon the natural *telos* of asserting: conveying the truth. In telling a lie one is presupposing (in most cases at least) that the listener will be-

---

[457] Besides Aquinas, Augustine also holds the second premise: "If we condemn something, it is only because of some flaw that it has. But we cannot condemn a flaw in something without thereby praising the nature in which the flaw is present. For there are two possibilities. On the one hand, perhaps what you condemn is in accordance with the nature. In that case, it is no flaw, and you need to learn how to appraise things properly, but the thing you condemn needs no change at all. On the other hand, the flaw must be contrary to the nature, for every flaw, insofar as it is a flaw, is contrary to some nature. For if it does not harm the nature, it is no flaw; but if it is a flaw precisely because it harms the nature, then it is a flaw precisely because it is contrary to the nature....From this it follows that *every flaw is contrary to some nature; more specifically, every flaw is contrary to the nature of the thing in which the flaw is present*. Therefore, since nothing is condemned except a flaw, it is a flaw precisely because it is contrary to the nature of the thing in which it is present; and if a flaw is justly condemned, the nature in which it is present is thereby praised. For what displeases you in the flaw is that it spoils what pleases you in the nature" (Augustine, *On Free Choice of the Will*, trans. Thomas Williams (Indianapolis, IN: Hackett Publishing Company, 1993), 97-98; emphasis added).

176

lieve you are telling the truth. If this were not the case, one would not lie (bald-faced lies being the exception).

Further, truth-telling is what distinguishes asserting from other speech acts such as asking a question, giving a command, or telling a joke. If truth-telling were not the natural end of asserting, then there would be no way to distinguish between assertions and other types of speech acts. The fourth premise, thus, stands as true.

The first premise is *per se nota,* that is, the predicate is contained in the essence of the subject.[458] It is according to the first mode of *per se,* as discussed in the *Posterior Analytics* I.4.73a35-73b15.[459] It is true in virtue of the meaning of the terms; thus, as soon as one grasps their meaning, one sees the proposition as true.

c) Why the second premise is true

The truth of the second premise requires further examination. Some of the New Natural Law theorists object to it. As we have seen, Tollefsen argues that even granted that nature has certain ends, why should one respect such ends?[460] Why must the ends of nature be my ends?

To reply to Tollefsen's objection, one must first clarify what the second premise is and is not saying. The second premise is not using *nature* in the sense of "mother nature," "everything that animals do," "whatever is not artificial," or "the natural laws of physics." Rather it means that whatever is truly in accord with a thing's nature is what is good for that thing, whether that thing be a plant, a dog, a man, or an action with a natural end. In one sense, then, living without clothes is *natural* to human beings—in the sense of what is without artifacts—but not in the relevant sense.

The second premise does not claim that every action has a natural end. Some actions like asserting, sexual intercourse, nourishing, and

---

[458] For an excellent discussion of the four modes of *per se* in relation to the first principles of ethics I suggest Jensen, *Knowing the Natural Law*, 26-32.

[459] Aristotle, *Posterior Analytics/Topica*, trans. Hugh Tredennick and E.S. Forster, The Loeb Classical Library (Cambridge, MA: Harvard University Press, 1960), p. 42-45.

[460] Tollefsen, "Augustine, Aquinas, and the Absolute Norm Against Lying": 123.

smelling have natural ends. Others, such as using the nose, seem to have no single natural end, or easily identifiable natural end. The argument, as a whole (cf. conclusion 3 from 1 & 2), is thus not saying that any action without a natural end is disordered, but that any action that has a natural end and also lacks the order to this natural end is a disordered action.

The second premise is true because what makes something good is that it attains its natural end, and what makes something bad is that it does not. We can see this clearly in plants and animals. What makes a good corn plant is that it grows, flourishes, produces corn, does photosynthesis, etc. A bad corn plant is one that fails to produce corn, or that has stunted growth, etc. Likewise, a good eagle is one that flies, protects and feeds its young, etc. A bad eagle, a defective eagle, is one that cannot fly or that kills its young. What determines whether x is good or bad depends upon the kind of thing that it is, what the natural ends or activities of x are. What is bad for an eagle is not bad for a plant. An eagle that does not fly is a bad eagle, but a corn plant that does not do fly is not a defective corn plant. Similarly, it is good that raccoons generate more raccoons, but if a corn plant generated racoons, it would be a monstrosity of nature, a defective corn plant. Likewise, what makes humans good or bad depends upon their nature and the ends towards which they are naturally oriented.[461] Such natural ends have motivational significance, because we all want what is good for us qua human being.

What holds true about men, eagles, and corn plants, also holds true about actions. What makes an action good is that it fulfills its natural end; what makes an action bad is that it deflects from its order to its natural end. Heating is good qua act of heating if it imparts heat. An act of heating that lacks the order to imparting heat is a defective action, just as an act of cooling that lacks the order to imparting cold is a defective act of cooling. So too if an act of generating lacks the order to the generation of a new being, it is defective qua generative action. Likewise, if an act of asserting lacks the order to its end of conveying the truth to another it is a defective act of asserting and so bad.

One must be careful to distinguish, however, between an action's

---

[461] Cf. Aristotle, *Nicomachean Ethics*, Book I, Chapter 7, 1097b; Edward Feser, *Aquinas: A Beginner's Guide* (Oxford: Oneworld, 2009), 177-183; Feser, *The Last Superstition: A Refutation of the New Atheism*, 132-138.

mere failure to attain its end and an action's lack of order to its end. An act of shooting at the bull's-eye may merely fail to attain its end, as when a gust of wind deflects the arrow. This failure differs from a case of the same action lacking order to its due end, as when the archer shoots but intentionally shoots poorly. This latter case is a defective action, whereas the former is a mere failure to attain the end of hitting the bull's-eye. Similarly with assertions, one may aim to convey the (formal) truth to another, but fail, as happens when the listener misunderstands the speaker due to background noise. This mere failure differs from a case of asserting that involves the lack of order to its end, as happens in every lie—the assertor intends that the assertion lack the order to its natural end of conveying the truth to another. The lie is a defective act of asserting, whereas the listener misunderstanding is a mere failure to attain the end of asserting.

Steven Jensen explains this distinction between mere failure and defective action as follows:

> Error [an action lacking order to its end] is best understood in contrast to failure. Not every error is a failure, nor is every failure an error. Jones can aim poorly, performing an error of marksmanship, and yet by luck accomplish his goal of killing Smith, for example, if the bullet kills Smith after ricocheting off the wall. A math student might err in calculation and yet by luck land upon the correct answer. Conversely, a teacher might fail through no fault of her own—without error—because the student is ill prepared. And a doctor might fail to heal because the patient does not follow her directives.
>
> Failure, it seems is tied to the end product, for a failure is an action that does not attain its endpoint. A doctor fails, for instance, when she does not bring about health. The connection between a failure and its results, however, is clearly restricted by the end to which the action is directed. Not any and every result matters. An act of healing does not become a failure because it does not produce heat, but rather because it does not produce its endpoint of health. A failure, then, is an action that does not accomplish its endpoint, that effect toward which it is directed.
>
> Unlike a failure, an error need not be defective in its endpoint; rather, it

is defective in its starting point.[462]

So as applied to Aquinas's argument, all actions lacking order to their due end are errors or disordered actions. Actions merely failing to attain their natural end are not.

Many of the earlier examples about "the natural end is the due end," such as the corn, the eagle, and heating, do not deal with morality as such. The defects are not moral defects. Actions falling within the realm of morals, however, may be morally good or bad insofar as they are human acts, that is, actions proceeding from intellect and will, in which the defective order is intended.[463] Any action then that is a human action and that lacks its due order to its natural end, whereby this lack is intended, is a morally defective action. If the action lacks its order to its due end through no fault of the human agent, it is not a fully human act; in such a case then the agent isn't fully responsible and so moral culpability is diminished or even eliminated.

Further, what distinguishes mere natural disorders from moral disorders is that a moral disorder involves some *inordinatio* to the human good; mere natural disorders, as in a disordered act of animal eating, involve no proximate order to the human good. Truth, as the proximate end of assertions, is a human good. A disordered act of animal eating, as when a bison eats sharp rocks, involves an *inordinatio,* but only in proximate relation to its own (non-human) good. In order to take these considerations about mere natural disorders into account, however, Aquinas's argument can be slightly modified as follows:

1. Any action not ordered to its due end is a disordered action.
2. The natural end is the due end [any natural end of an action is its due end].
3. Ergo, any action not ordered to its natural end is a disordered action (from 1 & 2).
4. The natural end of asserting is to tell the truth.
5. Ergo, any use of assertions not ordered to truth-telling [as is the case in telling a lie] is a disordered action (from 3 & 4).

---

[462] Jensen, *Good & Evil Actions*, 232.
[463] Cf. ST I-II, Q1, A1.

6. Disordered *human* acts that involve the human good are morally disordered.
7. Asserting involves an order to a human good (of truth).
8. Ergo, any use of assertions not ordered to the human good (of truth) are morally disordered [as happens in every lie] (from 5, 6, & 7).[464]

What I have presented above is the argument Aquinas implicitly makes in Q110, A3 against lying.

Tollefsen's objection can easily be answered by adding the 6th and 7th premises. The human good, because it is our good, is not empty of motivational significance. Morally disordered acts all involve some sort of a human good, whether it be truth, human life, personal property, bodily health, human society, etc.

The 7th premise is true, because assertions are for truth. Truth is a distinctively human good, not a good of plants or beasts.

Whether Aquinas's argument can also show that lying is *always* bad will be discussed in the final chapter. All I wish to show in this chapter is that the argument successfully shows that lying is bad, at least in most cases. Now, we must turn to some further objections.

---

[464] That the argument is valid can be seen clearly if put into symbolic logic:
1. $(x)(y)[(Ax$ & $Dyx)$ & $\sim Oxy] > Ix$
2. $(x)(y)$ $(Nyx > Dyx)$
3. ∴ $(x)(y)[(Ax$ & $Nyx)$ & $\sim Oxy] > Ix$
4. $(Aa$ & $Nta)$
5. ∴ $[(Aa$ & $Nta)$ & $\sim Oat] > Ia$
6. (x) $[(Ix$ & $Oxh) > Mx]$
7. Oah
8. ∴ $\{[(Aa$ & $Nta)$ & $\sim Oat]$ & $Oah\} > Ma$

Key: Ax = x is an action; Dyx = y is the due end of x; Oxy = x is ordered to y; Ix = x is a disordered human action; Nyx = y is the natural end of x; Oxh = x involves a human good h; Mx = x is a morally disordered action; a = asserting; t = truth-telling; h = a human good.

d) Objection: Purported counterexamples to the second premise

Further objections to the second premise may be raised from apparent counterexamples. For example, performing an act of heating that lacks the order to heat appears to be morally acceptable. Likewise, there is no moral defect in an act of nourishment that lacks the order to nourishment due to unintentional food poisoning.

Regarding the counterexample of heating, it is technically impossible for one to engage in an act of heating and lack the order to imparting heat. If one is not imparting heat, then one is not engaging in an act of heating at all. So it is no counterexample to the premise that "the natural end is the due end." With nourishment, if one consumes food that happens to make one vomit due to food poisoning and so this results in a decrease rather than an increase in health, there is no moral defect here provided the agent consumed the defective food in ignorance. If one knowingly and willingly consumed the bad food, then one is morally responsible for the defective action and so the agent acted wrongly.

The natural end is the due end, but not any failure to attain the end or lack of order to the natural end involves moral considerations. The agent is morally culpable for the defective action only if the error is voluntary (a fully human act). Thus, an artist who through lack of skill paints poorly is not morally culpable for the defective painting insofar as his errors are not intended.

But what if the artist intentionally erred? Aquinas's third premise is "any action not ordered to its natural end is a disordered action." When erring intentionally in art, the agent is engaging in an action (of art) not ordered to its natural end (of doing art-well). Thus, it appears on Aquinas's argument that the artist acted morally wrong by engaging in a disordered action. Acts of art have natural ends, but intending not to attain them is not morally wrong. In fact, if the artist intentionally erred, we call him a better artist than the one who erred unintentionally.

Aquinas's argument, however, does not condemn such actions. When doing his own private work, what constitutes painting-well is de-

182

termined solely by the intentions of the artist. In other cases, however, the *finis operis* of the art is set by another or by society, as when the pope commissioned Michelangelo to paint the Sistine Chapel. If Michelangelo intentionally botched up his painting, he erred, and even committed a morally bad action. The commission established the *finis operis* of the art, that is, what constitutes painting-well in this case; so too in many other cases whoever sponsors the work of art determines the *finis operis* of the art, that is, what constitutes painting-well. But when an artist is merely painting his own work commissioned by nobody other than himself, the agent alone determines the *finis operis* of the art, that is, what constitutes painting-well.

Aquinas's third premise condemns only an artist who acts contrary to the end determined by the person who commissioned him. An artist, however, who intentionally errs in his own art commits no flawed-action. When the painter himself paints, and the end is set solely by himself, it is technically impossible for him intentionally to make a bad work of art qua his intention.

Other objections may be raised. The natural end of the use of the hands is for grasping things, but it is surely not the due end of the hands to use them only for grasping, as there is nothing wrong with doing handstands. Likewise, the natural end of the use of the teeth is for chewing, but it certainly does not follow that such is their due end, as there is nothing wrong with holding a flashlight between one's teeth. Similarly, the natural end of hammers is to pound nails, but it certainly does not follow that it is their due end, as there is nothing immoral about using a hammer as a weapon to ward off a wild bear.

These objections do not impinge upon the second premise. The use of the hands has the natural end of locomotion, namely, moving things. Aquinas calls them the "organ of organs" or the instrument of instruments.[465] Their end is simply for whatever a man wishes to use them.

---

[465] *Super Sent.* II, D3, Q3, A1, ad 1: "Ad primum ergo dicendum, quod anima dicitur species specierum, inquantum per intellectum agentem facit species intelligibiles actu, et recipit eas secundum intellectum possibilem, sicut ibidem sensus dicitur species sensibilium, et manus organum organorum, inquantum videlicet omnia artificialia per manus efficiuntur; unde in XIV *De animal.*, lib. IV *De part. anom.*, cap. VIII, X et XI, dicitur quod manus datae sunt homini loco cornuum, et omnium qui-

Ergo, there is nothing wrong with doing handstands.

Further, some actions have natural ends, but others do not.[466] Eating, heating, cooling, seeing, smelling, and studying all seem to have the easily identifiable natural ends respectively of bodily health, heat, cold, color, odor, and knowledge. On the other hand, the use of the hair or the teeth are such vaguely defined actions that it is difficult to see whether their use has any natural end at all. Thus, using the teeth for holding a flashlight does not violate any end of using the teeth, as there seems to be no single natural end for the general *use of the teeth* except that of locomotion in general, and chewing, biting, or communication in particular.

Assertions, by contrast, have a single natural end of conveying the truth to another. Such natural end is what is presupposed in most lies; for the success of most lies depends upon the listener assuming that the speaker is making an assertion to him. Assertions have their natural end due to the nature of human language and society.

The use of a hammer, besides being vaguely defined, is the use of an artifact, a human creation. The *telos* of the act of eating, heating, cooling, seeing, smelling, and studying is what it is independent of human invention. In other words, man does not create the ends of such actions. The ends of such actions are rather presupposed by any human agent that chooses to engage in them. With artifacts, however, it is different. Artifacts are human creations designed for a certain purpose and so it is within the power and authority of man to change their ends. Using artifacts for ends contrary to their initial purpose is in no way disordered, since human beings created such artifacts in the first place. In fact, this power over the quasi-nature of artifacts is so complete that were man to use them for ends other than their original purpose they

---

bus alia animalia juvantur" (S. Thomae Aquinatis, *Scriptum Super Libros Sententiarum Magistri Petri Lombardi Episcopi Parisiensis,* ed. R.P. Mandonnet, vol. II (Parisiis: P. Lethielleux, 1929), p. 114). ST II-II, Q187, A3: "Quia enim manus est *organum organorum,* per opus manuum omnis operatio intelligitur de qua aliquis potest licite victum lucrari."

[466] For a more complete account on what specifies actions, even acts abstracted from human agency, see Steven Jensen, "Intrinsically Evil Actions According to St. Thomas Aquinas" (PhD diss., Notre Dame, April, 1993), Chapter 2 "The Specification of Activities."

would cease to be the artifact that they are and become another one. A stick created by a man may be either a weapon or a walking staff. What it is depends upon the purpose for which it was created and/or the purpose for which it is now being used. This malleability of the purposes of artifacts does not apply to natural actions like heating, cooling, smelling, or studying. Hammers are tools designed for pounding nails, but when used to fend off an attacking wolf the hammer becomes a weapon. Assertions, however, are always assertions. Man cannot make an assertion to be other than it is anymore than he can make eating to be not eating, or heating to be cooling, or smelling to be hearing. Unlike the use of artifacts, the nature of certain actions cannot depend entirely on the upshot intended by the agent. Assertions are such a case; the agent does not determine the natural end of asserting; rather the agent must presuppose it. The agent's intentions determine whether or not one is going to make an assertion or tell a joke or ask a question, but given that he intends to assert he must presuppose the natural end of asserting.

To claim that it is wrong to assert unnaturally (namely, by telling lies) is not to say that one must always speak the truth. It is permissible to remain prudently silent at times. One need not always order oneself towards truth, nor need one always speak, nor always speak assertively.[467] Yet, if one does speak assertively, one ought never to order oneself, in the very act of asserting, to assert against the truth. Likewise, one need not eat food at exactly noon, but given that one has chosen to eat food, a certain due order is required; one should not eat food, for instance, in order to vomit it out again, etc. The very action of asserting is by its very nature ordered towards the communication of truth to another. In lying, one is engaging in an action that of its very nature is ordered towards truth, yet at the same time the agent is opposing the natural end of the action in which he is engaging. It is inherently irrational and disordered, which is why both Aristotle and Aquinas recognized lying as *"per se* perverse."[468] If one does not wish to order oneself to the natural end of an action, then do not engage in that action. Engaging in an action not ordered to its natural end is a defective action.

---

[467] Cf. ST II-II, Q109, A1, obj. 2, and ad 2; Q110, A3, ad 4.
[468] NE IV.7.5, 1127a (Irwin); Cf. ST II-II, Q110, A3, where Aquinas cites this text of Aristotle in approval.

One final clarification must be made: *ceasing to engage in an action that has a natural end is not the same as engaging in an action that has a natural end and disrupting that natural end from happening.* A man might cease to eat, which is morally different from eating in a manner not ordered towards health, as when he eats rocks. Likewise, ceasing to have sex is different from engaging in sex but disrupting the natural end of sex from occurring. If a burglar is breaking down the door, a man may legitimately stop having sex with his wife. Not engaging in an action, or ceasing to engage in it, is different from directing the action away from its natural end.

Conclusion

Despite the plethora of objections, Aquinas's argument against lying fares well:

1. Any action not ordered to its due end is a disordered action.
2. The natural end is the due end [any natural end of an action is its due end].
3. Ergo, any action not ordered to its natural end is a disordered action (from 1 & 2).
4. The natural end of asserting is to tell the truth.
5. Ergo, any use of assertions not ordered to truth-telling [as is the case in telling a lie] is a disordered action (from 3 & 4).
6. Disordered human acts that involve the human good are morally disordered.
7. Asserting involves an order to a human good (of truth).
8. Ergo, any use of assertions not ordered to the human good (of truth) are morally disordered [as happens in every lie] (from 5, 6, & 7).

This presentation of the argument, which is not explicitly in Aquinas, is implicitly the argument he does make. Whether Aquinas's argument against lying is strong enough to show that lying is always wrong is another issue to be discussed in the fifth chapter. All I wish to have shown here is that his initial account is not as implausible as some would think.

Chapter IV: Why is Homosexual Activity Wrong?

Aquinas held that homosexual activity (*sodomia*) is wrong.[469] He clearly indicated his firm opposition to such behavior throughout his philosophical career. Homosexual activity, which in Latin is called *sodomia,* refers to sexual activity between two members of the same-sex, either male with male or female with female.[470] In various texts, Aquinas indicates his disapproval of such activity:

> *Super Isaiam,* Chapter 4, verse 1:
> According as something is ordered in diverse ways to these ends, it is said to be natural or unnatural in diverse ways. Indeed that which in no way can stand with the aforementioned end [of generation] is in every

---

[469] Aquinas, of course, didn't use the phrase *homosexual activity,* but rather the Latin term *sodomia* and its variants. The Latin *sodomia* and *Sodom* or any variations thereof occur 115 times in the entire Thomistic corpus (cf. Index Thomisticus search for "sodom*"). The overwhelming majority of these occurrences, however, are from Biblical passages or commentaries. Outside of his Biblical commentaries and direct quotes from Scripture the word or its variants occurs a mere 17 times. There are also passages where Thomas obliquely refers to it as a *sin against nature.* I have taken the liberty to translate the Latin *sodomia* or its declensions as *homosexual activity.* The English word *sodomy* in some contexts means oral or anal sex, which can be committed by a male and a female, as well as between two males or two females. The phrase *homosexual activity,* however, refers to a sexual action ordered towards orgasm between two members of the same sex. Today many assume that only homosexuals engage in homosexual acts. That is not true. Heterosexuals can also engage in homosexual activity (as was the case in ancient Greece), although such cases are likely rarer than that of homosexuals. My translation of the Latin *sodomia* from hereon will be *homosexual activity* instead of *sodomy* in order to avoid confusing the reader with inaccurate connations of the English word. Further, the English word *sodomy* has a clear connection with the infamous story in Genesis; Aquinas's moral analysis wasn't fundamentally based off of that story. Although he knew of it, his philosophical argument doesn't in any manner rest upon religious premises.

[470] ST II-II, Q154, A11.

188

way unnatural, and never can be good, such as the vice of homosexual actions.[471]

Super Sent., Book IV, D14, Q2, A5, expos.:
It must be known that mortal fault is what takes away grace, which is the life of the soul, and thus every mortal fault is contrary to grace, but some are contrary to reason, such as perjury, some are even contrary to nature, such as homosexual actions.[472]

SCG III, 122:
Hence it is clear that every emission of the *semen* is contrary to the good of man, which takes place in a way whereby generation cannot follow; and if this is done on purpose, it must be a flawed-action. I mean a way in which generation cannot follow *in itself* as is the case in every emission of the *semen* without the natural union of male and female: wherefore such flawed-actions are called 'sins against nature.'[473]

Summa Theologiae II-II, Q154, A11, co.:

---

[471] "Secundum ergo quod aliquid diversimode ordinatur ad hos fines, secundum hoc diversimode dicitur naturale vel innaturale. Id enim quod nullo modo potest stare cum fine dicto est omnino innaturale et nunquam potest esse bonum, sicut vitium sodomiticum" (Sancti Thomae de Aquino, *Expositio Super Isaiam ad Litteram,* in *Opera Omnia Iussu Leonis XIII P.M. Edita,* vol. XXVIII (Roma: Editori di San Tommaso, 1974), 33). The translation is my own.

[472] "Sciendum quod culpa mortalis est quae gratiam tollit, per quam est vita animae ; et sic omnis culpa mortalis est contra gratiam. Sed *quaedam* est contra rationem, ut perjurium ; *quaedam* etiam contra naturam, ut sodomia" (S. Thomae Aquinatis, *Scriptum Super Sententiis Magistri Petri Lombardi,* vol. IV, D14, A5, *Expositio,* n.320 (Parisiis: P. Lethielleux, 1947), 633). Translation is my own.

[473] Translation, with some minor amendations, is taken from Thomas Aquinas, *Of God and His Creatures: An Annotated Translation (with Some Abridgement) of the Summa Contra Gentiles of Saint Thos. Aquinas*, trans. Joseph Ricaby, (London: Burns & Oates, 1905), Book III, chapter 122. The Latin is as follows: "Ex quo patet quod contra bonum hominis est omnis emissio seminis tali modo quod generatio sequi non possit. Et si ex proposito hoc agatur, oportet esse peccatum. Dico autem modum ex quo generatio sequi non potest *secundum se*: sicut omnis emissio semi-nis sine naturali coniunctione maris et feminae; propter quod huiusmodi peccata *contra naturam* dicuntur. Si autem per accidens generatio ex emissione seminis se-qui non possit, non propter hoc est contra naturam, nec peccatum: sicut si contingat mulierem sterilem esse" (SCG III, 122, n. 2950-2951 (Taurini, Romae: Marietti, 1961)).

There is a determinate species of lust where a special notion of deformity occurs which renders the sexual act unbecoming. This can happen in two ways: in one way, when it is repugnant to right reason, which is common to every vice of lust. In another way, when even beyond this, it is repugnant to the very natural order of the sexual act, which is fitting for the human species: which is called the vice against nature. It indeed can happen in many ways…In a third way, if it happens through sexual activity with an undue sex, as male with male or female with female, as the Apostle says in Romans 1:26-27: which is called the "vice of homosexual activity."[474]

De Malo Q15, A1:

And that every such act is disordered according to itself is apparent from the fact that every human act is disordered which is not proportionate to its due end: as eating is disordered if it be not proportioned to health of the body to which it is ordered as to an end. Now the end of the use of the genital members is the generation and education of offspring, and therefore every use of the aforementioned members which is not proportioned to the generation of offspring and their due education is according to itself disordered.[475]

---

[474] ibi est determinata luxuriae species ubi specialis ratio deformitatis occurrit quae facit indecentem actum venereum. Quod quidem potest esse dupliciter. Uno quidem modo, quia repugnat rationi rectae : quod est commune in omni vitio luxuriae. Alio modo, quia etiam, super hoc, repugnat ipsi ordini naturali venerei actus qui convenit humanae speciei : quod dicitur vitium contra naturam. Quod quidem potest pluribus modis contingere….Tertio modo, si fiat per concubitum ad non debitum sexum, puta masculi ad masculum vel feminae ad feminan, ut Apostolus dicit, ad Rom 1,26-27 : quod dicitur *sodomiticum vitium.*" Latin is from Sancti Thomae Aquinatis, *Summa Theologiae* (Matriti: Biblioteca de Autores Cristianos, 1952); hereafter referred to as the "BAC." The translation is my own. An additional clear passage in the *Summa* can be found in the very next article, namely, ST II-II, Q154, A12: "Therefore, since in the vices which are contrary to nature man transgresses that which is determined according to nature concerning the use of sexual [members], it follows that in such matter this flawed action is the most grave." The Latin is as follows: "Quia ergo in vitiis quae sunt contra naturam transgreditur homo id quod est secundum naturam determinatum circum usum venereum, inde est quod in tali materia hoc peccatum est gravissimum." Latin is from the BAC.
[475] "Et quod omnis talis actus sit inordinatus secundum se ipsum apparet ex hoc quod omnis actus humanus dicitur esse inordinatus qui non est proportionatus debito fini: sicut comestio est inordinata si non proportionetur corporis salubritati ad quam ordinatur sicut ad finem. Finis autem usus genitalium membrorum est genera-

From the above texts, it is clear that Thomas condemned sexual activity between members of the same sex as a bad action. But was he right?

Part One: Aquinas's Arguments Against Homosexual Activity

We must endeavor to assess the soundness of Aquinas's argument. We have been focusing on Aquinas, because he is the first philosopher to give a clear and robust argument against homosexual activity, and because his ethical theory still holds much sway today.

Aquinas's argument has often been interpreted as a perverted faculty argument; in other words, using a faculty contrary to its purpose is immoral. As we shall see, this interpretation isn't wholly accurate, but neither is it completely unfounded.

Anyone who searches the Thomistic corpus will find that there are only two texts where Aquinas directly argues that homosexual activity is

---

tio et educatio prolis, et ideo omnis usus predictorum membroum qui non est proportionatus generationi prolis et debite eius educationi est secundum se inordinatus. Quicumque autem actus predictorum membroum est preter commixtionem maris et femine manifestum est quod non est accomodus generationi prolis." The Latin for the *De Malo* is taken from the Leonine unless otherwise indicated: Sancti Thomae de Aquino, *Opera Omnia Iussu Leonis XIII P.M. Edita,* Tomus XXIII, *Quaestiones Disputatae de Malo,* (Romae, Paris: Commissio Leonina, 1982), p. 270. Translation is my own. An additional clear passage in the same work can be found at *De Malo* Q15, A3: "As I have said before, flawed-actions of sexual lust can be disordered in two ways: in one way regarding the desire, and such disorder does not always cause gravely flawed-action; in a second way regarding the acts themselves, which are of themselves disordered, and then there is always gravely flawed-action....And so acts of sexual lust are disordered because the acts cannot result in the begetting of offspring, and then there are sins contrary to nature, or because the acts cannot result in the proper rearing of offspring." The Latin is as follows: "Responsio. Dicendum, quod sicut supra dictum est, peccatum luxurie dupliciter habet inordinationem : uno quidem modo ex parte concupiscentie, et talis inordinatio non semper facit peccatum mortale, alio modo ex parte ipsius actus qui de se est inordinatus, et sic semper est peccatum mortale...Est autem actus luxurie inordinatus aut ex hoc quod non potest sequi ex actu generatio prolis, et sic est vitium contra naturam, aut ex eo quod non potest sequi debita educatio..." Latin is from the Leonine, p. 277. The translation with minor emendation is from Richard Regan.

a bad action: *Summa Contra Gentiles* Book III, Ch. 122, and *De Malo* Q15, A1.[476] We will begin with his earlier treatment in SCG III, 122. The question is whether fornication is a flawed-action and whether matrimony is natural. Aquinas writes:

> From the foregoing we can see the futility of the argument of certain people who say that simple fornication is not a flawed-action. For they say: Suppose there is a woman who is not married, or under the control of any man, either her father or another man. Now, if a man performs the sexual act with her, and she is willing, he does not injure her, because she favors the action and has control over her own body. Nor

---

[476] There is a text in *Super Sent.* IV, D33, Q1, A3, qc1, but the part where he seems to imply that sins against nature are evil is rather indirect. This differs from his treatment in SCG III, 122, n. 5 and DM Q15, A1 where he explicitly condemns sins against nature as evil. Below is the relevant text from the *Sentences*:
"Utrum habere concubinam sit contra legem naturae? Respondeo dicendum ad primam quaestionem, quod, sicut ex praedictis patet, illa actio dicitur esse contra legem naturae, quae non est conveniens fini debito, sive quia non ordinatur in ipsum per actionem agentis, sive quia de se est improportionata fini illi. *Finis autem quem natura ex concubitu intendit, est proles procreanda et educanda*; et ut hoc bonum quaereretur, posuit delectationem in coitu; ut Augustinus (2) dicit (lib. 1 de Nupt. et Concup., cap. 8) *Quicumque ergo concubitu utitur propter delectationem quae in ipso est, non referendo ad finem a natura intentum, contra naturam facit*; et similiter etiam nisi sit talis concubitus qui ad illum finem convenienter ordinari possit. Et quia res a fine plerumque nominantur tamquam ab optimo: sicut conjunctio matrimonii a prolis bono nomen accepit, quod per matrimonium principaliter quaeritur; ita concubinae nomen illam conjunctionem exprimit qua solus concubitus propter seipsum quaeritur; et si etiam aliquis quandoque ex tali concubitu prolem quaerat, non tamen est conveniens ad prolis bonum, in quo non solum intelligitur ipsius procreatio, per quam proles esse accipit, sed etiam educatio et instructio, per quam accipitur nutrimentum et disciplina a parentibus: in quibus tribus parentes proli tenentur, secundum Philosophum in 8 Ethicor (cap. 10 vel 12). Cum autem educatio et instructio proli a parentibus debeatur per longum tempus; exigit lex naturae ut pater et mater in longum tempus commaneant ad subveniendum communiter proli; unde et aves quae communiter pullos nutriunt, ante completam nutritionem non separantur a mutua societate quae incepit a concumbendo. Haec autem obligatio ad commanendum feminam cum marito matrimonium facit. Et ideo patet quod accedere ad mulierem non junctam sibi matrimonio, quae concubina vocatur, est contra legem naturae" (Sent. IV, D33, Q1, A3, qc1; S. Thomae Aquinatis, *Sancti Thomae Aquinatis Commentum in Quatuor Libros Sententiarum Magistri Petri Lombardi,* vol. II (Parmae: Typis Petri Fiaccadori, 1858), p. 970). Emphasis added. There is no Latin edition of this part of the *Sentences* in the Mandonnet or the Moos or the Leonine).

does he injure any other person, because she is understood to be under no other person's control. So, this does not seem to be a flawed-action. Now, to say that he injures God would not seem to be an adequate answer. For we do not offend God except by doing something contrary to our own good, as has been said. But this does not appear contrary to man's good. Hence, on this basis, no injury seems to be done to God.… Hence, we must look for a solution in our earlier considerations. We have said that God exercises care over every person on the basis of what is good for him. Now *it is good for everything to gain its end, and bad for it to be diverted from its due end. But as in the whole so also in the parts, our study should be that every part of man and every act of his may attain its due end.* Now though the semen is superfluous for the preservation of the individual, yet it is necessary to him for the propagation of the species: while other excretions, such as excrement, urine, sweat, and the like, are needful for no further purpose: hence the only good that comes to man of them is by their removal from the body. *But that is not the object in the emission of the semen, but that it is emitted for the use of generation, to which the union of the sexes is directed.* But in vain would be the generation of man unless due nurture followed, without which the offspring generated could not endure. *So therefore, the emission of the semen ought to be ordered so that both a fitting generation and education of offspring may follow.*

Hence it is clear that every emission of the semen is contrary to the good of man, which takes place in a way whereby generation cannot follow; and if this is done on purpose, it must be a flawed-action. I mean a way in which generation cannot follow in itself as is the case in every emission of the semen without the natural union of male and female: wherefore such sins are called "sins against nature." But if it is *per accidens* that generation cannot follow from the emission of the semen, the act is not against nature on that account, nor is it a flawed-action; the case of the woman being sterile would be a case in point [emphasis added].[477]

---

[477] Translation, with some minor emendations, is taken from Thomas Aquinas, *Of God and His Creatures*, trans. Joseph Ricaby, (London: Burns & Oates, 1905), Book III, Chapter 122, https://maritain.nd.edu/jmc/etext/gc3_122.htm.
The Latin is as follows: "Ex hoc autem apparet vanam esse rationem quorundam dicentium fornicationem simplicem non esse peccatum. Dicunt enim: Sit aliqua mulier a viro soluta, quae sub nullius potestate, ut patris vel alicuius alterius, existat. Si

Aquinas's argument can be reconstructed into a more rigorous logical form as follows:

1) The good of anything whatsoever is that it attains its due end, and its evil is that it diverts from its due end.
2) The due end of the emission of semen is the generation and education of offspring.
3) Thus, it is evil for the emission of semen to divert from its due end of the generation and education of offspring.

When Aquinas states, "Hence it is clear that every emission of the semen is contrary to the good of man, which takes place in a way whereby generation cannot follow; and if this is done on purpose, it must be a flawed-action," he is implying that while it is an evil for any semen qua

---

quis ad eam accedat ea volente, non facit illi iniuriam: quia sibi placet, et sui corporis habet potestatem. Alteri non facit iniuriam: quia sub nullius potestate ponitur esse. Non videtur esse peccatum. Non videtur autem esse responsio sufficiens si quis dicat quod facit iniuriam Deo. Non enim Deus a nobis offenditur nisi ex eo quod contra nostrum bonum agimus ut dictum est. Hoc autem non apparet esse contra hominis bonum. Unde ex hoc non videtur Deo aliqua iniuria fieri....Oportet igitur ex superioribus solutionem quaerere. Dictum est enim quod Deus uniuscuiusque curam habet secundum id quod est ei bonum. Est autem bonum uniuscuiusque quod finem suum consequatur: malum autem eius est quod a debito fine divertat. Sicut autem in toto, ita et in partibus hoc considerari oportet: ut scilicet unaquaeque pars hominis, et quilibet actus eius, finem debitum sortiatur. Semen autem, etsi sit superfluum quantum ad individui conservationem, est tamen necessarium quantum ad propagationem speciei. Alia vero superflua, ut egestio, urina, sudor, et similia, ad nihil necessaria sunt: unde ad bonum hominis pertinent solum quod emittantur. Non hoc autem solum quaeritur in semine, sed ut emittatur ad generationis utilitatem, ad quam coitus ordinatur. Frustra autem esset hominis generatio nisi et debita nutritio sequeretur: quia generatum non permaneret, debita nutritione subtracta. Sic igitur ordinata esse seminis debet emissio ut sequi possit et generatio conveniens, et geniti educatio. Ex quo patet contra bonum hominis est omnis emissio seminis tali modo quod generatio sequi non possit. Et si ex proposito hoc agatur, oportet esse peccatum. Dico autem modum ex quo generatio sequi non potest *secundum se*: sicut omnis emissio seminis sine naturali coniunctione maris et feminae; propter quod huiusmodi peccata *contra naturam* dicuntur. Si autem per accidens generatio ex emissione seminis sequi non possit, non propter hoc est contra naturam, nec peccatum: sicut si contingat mulierem sterilem esse" (SCG III, 122, n.2947-2948, 2950-2951 (Taurini, Romae: Marietti, 1961), p.181-182.

semen not to attain its due end (just as it is evil that any seed qua seed not generate a plant of the same kind), it is only a moral evil, that is, a flawed-human-action, if it be via *a voluntary* emission of semen. Only human acts are morally evil; mere acts of man are not.[478]

Later in the same text Aquinas raises an objection and then answers it:

> Nor yet should it be counted a slightly flawed-action for one to procure the emission of the *semen* irrespective of the due purpose of generation and rearing of issue, on the argument that it is a slightly flawed-action, or no flawed-act at all, to apply any part of one's body to another use than that to which it is naturally ordained, as if, for example, one were to walk on his hands, or do with his feet something that ought to be done with his hands. The answer is that by such inordinate applications as those mentioned the good of man is not greatly injured: but the inordinate emission of the *semen* is repugnant to the good of nature, which is the conservation of the species. Hence, after the flawed-action of murder, whereby a human nature already in actual existence is destroyed, this sort of flawed-action seems to hold the second place, whereby the generation of human nature is precluded.[479]

Notice that Aquinas does not modify the premises of his argument in reply to the objection from walking on your hands. He thinks that the ob-

---

[478] Cf. ST I-II, Q1, A1. Human acts by definition are those that proceed from intellect and will. So, the action of emitting semen while asleep isn't necessarily a morally bad action, because it isn't a human act, but an act of man. Acts of man are acts that a human being does but not as proceeding from an act of the intellect and the will.

[479] "Nec tamen oportet reputari leve peccatum esse si quis seminis emissionem procuret praeter debitum generationis et educationis finem, propter hoc quod aut leve aut nullum peccatum est si quis aliqua sui corporis parte utatur ad alium usum quam ad eum ad quem est ordinata secundum naturam, ut si quis, verbi gratia, manibus ambulet, aut pedibus aliquid operetur manibus operandum: quia per huiusmodi inordinatos usus bonum hominis non multum impeditur; inordinata vero seminis emissio repugnat bono naturae, quod est conservatio speciei. Unde post peccatum homicidii, quo natura humana iam in actu existens destruitur, huiusmodi genus peccati videtur secundum locum tenere, quo impeditur generatio humanae naturae" (Marietti, n.2955). Translation is taken from Joseph Ricaby with minor adaptions, https://maritain.nd.edu/jmc/etext/gc3_122.htm.

jection does not significantly upset his argument. More will be said on this point later.

The second place where Aquinas directly argues against homosexual activity is in his later work *De Malo* Q15, A1. There the question is raised, "Is every act of sexual lust a flawed-act?" He answers in the affirmative:

> Sexual lust is a vice contrary to temperance insofar as temperance moderates desires for things pleasurable to touch regarding sex, just as gluttony is contrary to temperance insofar as temperance moderates desires regarding things pleasurable to touch in food and drink. And so sexual lust indeed chiefly signifies a disorder by reason of excess regarding desires for sexual pleasures. And such disorder can belong either to the internal emotions alone or also in addition to external acts that are of their very selves disordered and not only because of the disordered desires from which they spring. For it belongs to disordered desire that, because of a desire for something pleasurable, one does something intrinsically disordered. For example, such is evidently the case regarding the desires for money. For one can inordinately desire to acquire or keep money that belongs to oneself, and then such acquisition or retention of money is sinful only because it springs from excessive desire, and not as such. But the disordered desire for money sometimes leads human beings also to want to acquire or keep things that belong to another, and then such acquisition or retention is disordered as such and not only because the product of disordered desire. And both of these flawed-actions belong to the vice of lack of generosity, as the Philosopher makes clear in the *Ethics*.
>
> We should say the like about sexual lust. For sexual lust indeed sometimes signifies only the disorder of internal desire, as is evidently the case regarding one who out of disordered desire has intercourse with his wife, since the very act is disordered only because it springs from disordered desire, and is not disordered as such. And sometimes the disorder of desire is also accompanied by a disorder in the very external act as such, as happens in every use of the genital organs outside the conjugal act.
>
> And every such act is evidently disordered of its very self, since we call *every human act that is not properly related to its due end a disordered act*. For example, eating is disordered if it be not properly related to

196

bodily health, for which eating is ordained as an end. And *the end of using genital members is to beget and educate offspring, and so every use of the aforementioned members that is not related to begetting and properly educating offspring is as such disordered.* And every act of the aforementioned members outside the sexual union of a man and a woman is obviously unsuitable for begetting offspring [emphasis added].[480]

---

[480] "Responsio. Dicendum, quod luxuria est quoddam uitium temperantie oppositum prout moderatur concupiscentias delectabilium tactus circa uenerea, sicut gula opponitur temperantie in quantum est moderatiua concupiscentiarum circa delectabilia tactus in cibis et potibus, unde luxuria quidem principaliter importat inordinationem quandam circa concupiscentias delectationum in uenereis secundum superhabundantiam. Huiusmodi autem inordinatio potest esse uel in solis interioribus passionibus uel etiam ulterius in ipso exteriori actu qui est inordinatus secundum se ipsum et non solum propter inordinatam concupiscentiam a qua procedit. Ad inordinatam enim concupiscentiam pertinet ut propter concupiscentiam delectabilis aliquis actum exerceat qui secundum se est inordinatus ; sicut patet circa concupiscentias pecuniarum : potest enim esse inordinata concupiscentia acquirendi uel retinendi pecunias suas sibi debitas, et tunc talis acquisitio uel retentio pecunie non est uitiosa secundum se set solum secundum quod ex immoderata concupiscentia prouenit ; quandoque uero ex inordinata concupiscentia pecuniarum prouenit quod homo etiam uelit acquirere uel retinere aliena, et tunc ipsa acceptio uel retentio secundum se inordinata est et non solum secundum quod ex inordinata concupiscentia procedit ; et utrumque pertinet ad uitium illiberalitatis, ut patet per Philosophum IV Ethicorum.

Similiter etiam dicendum est de luxuria. Quia quandoque quidem importat solam inordinationem interioris concupiscentie, sicut patet in eo qui ex immoderata concupiscentia accedit ad uxorem suam : tunc enim ipse actus non est inordinatus secundum se set solum secundum quod procedit ex inordinata concupiscentia ; quandoque uero cum inordinatione concupiscentie est etiam inordinatio ipsius actus exterioris secundum se ipsum, sicut contingit in omni usu genitalium membrorum preter [sic.] matrimonialem actum.

Et quod omnis talis actus sit inordinatus secundum se ipsum apparet ex hoc quod omnis actus humanus dicitur esse inordinatus qui non est proportionatus debito fini: sicut comestio est inordinata si non proportionetur corporis salubritati ad quam ordinatur sicut ad finem. Finis autem usus genitalium membrorum est generatio et educatio prolis, et ideo omnis usus predictorum membrorum qui non est proportionatus generationi prolis et debite eius educationi est secundum se inordinatus. Quicumque autem actus predictorum membrorum est preter commixtionem maris et femine manifestum est quod non est accomodus generationi prolis" (Sancti Thomae de Aquino, *Opera Omnia, Quaestiones Disputatae de Malo*, p.270). The translation, with minor emendations, is from Thomas Aquinas, *On Evil,* trans. Richard Regan, ed. Brian Davies (Oxford, New York: Oxford University Press, 2003), p. 421.

Aquinas's argument here can be put into valid form as follows:

1. Every human action that is not ordered to its due end is in itself a disordered action.
2. The due end of the use of the reproductive members is the generation and education of offspring.
3. Ergo, any use of the reproductive members that is not ordered to the generation and education of offspring is in itself a disordered action.

Since in homosexual activity two males or two females are using their reproductive members for ends not ordered to the generation of offspring, their action counts as a disordered action. Ergo, same-sex sexual activity is disordered and bad.

a) Why did Aquinas not repeat the hand-walking objection?

The walking-on-hands objection from SCG III, 122 is not mentioned in the more mature treatment in the *De Malo* text. Evidently, Aquinas did not think it to be a very strong objection. Aquinas held that the natural end of the hands is for whatever man wishes to use them, since they are the organ of organs.[481] Using them for handstands is not to use them unnaturally or for an undue end.

---

[481] Cf. *Super Sent.* II, D3, Q3, A1, ad 1: "Ad primum ergo dicendum, quod anima dicitur species specierum, inquantum per intellectum agentem facit species intelligibiles actu, et recipit eas secundum intellectum possibilem, sicut ibidem sensus dicitur species sensibilium, et manus organum organorum, inquantum videlicet omnia artificialia per manus efficiuntur; unde in XIV *De animal.*, lib. IV *De part. anom.*, cap. VIII, X et XI, dicitur quod manus datae sunt homini loco cornuum, et omnium quibus alia animalia juvantur" (S. Thomae Aquinatis, *Scriptum Super Libros Sententiarum Magistri Petri Lombardi Episcopi Parisiensis*, ed. R.P. Mandonnet, vol. II (Parisiis: P. Lethielleux, 1929), p.114). ST II-II, Q187, A3: "Quia enim manus est *organum organorum*, per opus manuum omnis operatio intelligitur de qua aliquis potest licite victum lucrari."

The point of the hand-walking objection has been widely misinterpreted.[482] Aquinas did not raise the objection in order to indicate that his initial argument needed modification, but to show that when it comes to sins against nature, not just any evil has been committed, but rather a grave evil. This point becomes clearer if one notices that Aquinas introduces the hand-walking objection with the words, "Nor, in fact, should it be deemed *a slightly flawed-action* for man to arrange for the emission of semen apart from the proper purpose of generating and bringing up children, *on the argument that...*" (emphasis added). Aquinas is not introducing the objection against a premise of his earlier argument; rather, the objection claims that even if the prior argument is true, it does not show that sins against nature or fornication are gravely flawed-actions. Aquinas replies by saying that sins against nature and fornication are gravely flawed-actions because they oppose the natural good of man, namely, the preservation of the species. After the good of existing human life comes the good of generating new life, and so a flawed-action against this latter order is second only to murder.[483]

Notice the parallel between SCG III, 122 and *De Malo* Q15, A2, where Aquinas also argues that such acts are gravely flawed-actions:

---

[482] John Corvino thinks Aquinas is raising it as an objection to his main argument, but that Aquinas fails to adequately answer it (*What's Wrong with Homosexuality?*, 85-86); Germain Grisez thinks that in the text Aquinas bites the bullet and admits that handstands are only slightly flawed actions (Germain G. Grisez, *Contraception and the Natural Law* (Milwaukee: Bruce Publishing Company, 1964), 29, 43, footnote 13). Though he does not mention the SCG III, 122 objection, McNeill gives a similar objection from the teleology of the hands (McNeill, *The Church and the Homosexual*, 114).

[483] Cf. SCG III, 122: "Nec tamen oportet reputari leve peccatum esse si quis seminis emissionem procuret praeter debitum generationis et educationis finem, propter hoc quod aut leve aut nullum peccatum est si quis aliqua sui corporis parte utatur ad alium usum quam ad eum ad quem est ordinata secundum naturam, ut si quis, verbi gratia, manibus ambulet, aut pedibus aliquid operetur manibus operandum: quia per huiusmodi inordinatos usus bonum hominis non multum impeditur; inordinata vero seminis emissio repugnat bono naturae, quod est conservatio speciei. Unde post peccatum homicidii, quo natura humana iam in actu existens destruitur, huiusmodi genus peccati videtur secundum locum tenere, quo impeditur generatio humane naturae (Marietti, n.2955, p.183).

But if acts of sexual lust are flawed-actions because of the very disorder of the acts, namely, because the acts are not properly related to the begetting and rearing of offspring, then I say that they are always gravely flawed-actions. For we perceive that gravely flawed-actions includes both homicide, which takes away the life of a human being, and theft, which takes away external goods ordained to sustain human life. And so Sir. 34:25 says: "The bread of the needy is the life of the poor; the person who defrauds the poor takes blood." And human semen, in which there is a potential human being, is more closely ordained for human life than any external things. And so also the Philosopher says in the *Politics* that there is something divine in human semen, namely, inasmuch as there is a potential human being. And so the disorder regarding the emission of semen concerns the proximate potentiality to human life.[484]

The above argument, which directly follows that of DM Q15, A1, parallels the treatment of SCG III, 122. The argument that such flawed-actions are gravely bad is fundamentally the same—the type of good opposed is so great that such acts must be gravely flawed-actions. In both texts Aquinas either implicitly or explicitly indicates that such flawed-actions are second only to homicide. Whether Aquinas is right on putting such actions as second only to homicide will not be treated in this book.

The hand-walking objection in SCG is not meant as an objection to Aquinas's initial argument, but to his further claim that such acts are gravely flawed-actions. In neither SCG nor in the *De Malo* does Aquinas

---

[484] Si vero sit actus luxurie peccatum propter ipsam inordinationem actus, quia scilicet actus non est proportionatus generationi et educationi prolis, tunc dico quod semper est peccatum mortale : videmus enim quod peccatum mortale est non solum homicidium, per quod vita hominis tollitur, set etiam furtum, per quod subtrahuntur exteriora bona que ad vitam hominis sustentandam ordinatur ; unde dicitur Eccli. XXXIV 'Panis egentium vita pauperis, qui defraudat illum homo sanguinis est.' Propinquius autem ordinatur ad vitam hominis semen humanum in quo est homo in potentia quam quecumque res exteriores; unde et Philosophus in sua Politica dicit in semine hominis esse quiddam divinum, in quantum scilicet est homo in potentia; et ideo inordinatio circa emissionem seminis est circa vitam hominis in potentia propinqua" (Sancti Thomae de Aquino, *Opera Omnia, Quaestiones Disputatae de Malo*, p. 274). English translation, with minor emendation, is taken from Thomas Aquinas, *On Evil*, trans. Richard Regan, ed. Brian Davies (New York: Oxford University Press, 2003), 426-427.

seem to think the hand-walking objection significantly upsets his initial argument that sins against nature are flawed-actions (even if only slightly so). If he had thought the objection upset his initial argument, then he would have modified his premises in his second treatment of the topic in the *De Malo.* But he did not.

b) An implied premise

Technically, Aquinas's argument as presented in the *De Malo* is invalid as written:

1. Every human act is said to be disordered that is not ordered to its *due end* [emphasis added].[485]
2. *The end* of the use of the reproductive members is the generation and education of offspring [emphasis added].[486]
3. Therefore, every use of the aforementioned members that is not ordered to the generation of offspring and their due education is in itself disordered.[487]

The argument equivocates between *end* in the second premise and *due end* in the first premise. If the argument is to be valid, Aquinas must mean *due end* in the second premise. A closer examination of the context of DM Q15, A1, however, indicates that by *end* Aquinas means *natural end*:

> Therefore, every voluntary emission of the semen is illicit unless it is fitting with *the end intended by nature* [emphasis added].[488]

An act of lust can be said to be contrary to nature in two ways: in one

---

[485] "Omnis actus humanus dicitur esse inordinatus qui non est proportionatus debito fini."

[486] "Finis autem usus genitalium membrorum est generatio et educatio prolis."

[487] "Ideo omnis usus predictorum membroum qui non est proportionatus generationi prolis et debite eius educationi est secundum se inordinatus."

[488] *De Malo* Q15, A1, ad 4: "Ideo omnis uoluntaria emission seminis est illicita nisi secundum conuenientiam ad finem a natura intentum" (Sancti Thomae de Aquino, *Opera Omnia, Quaestiones Disputatae de Malo,* p. 271).

way absolutely, as when it is contrary to the nature of every animal, and thus *every act of lust outside of the sexual union of male and female is said to be against nature* inasmuch as it is not ordered to generation, which happens in every kind of animal that unites with the other sex, and this is the way in which the Gloss speaks. In another way it is said to be against nature, as when it is against the proper nature of man which is to order the act of generation for due education, and thus all fornication is against nature [emphasis added].[489]

If the argument is to work, either Aquinas must mean *due end* in the second premise or he must have a way of connecting the natural end with the due end. The latter possibility seems to be the case. His argument has a suppressed premise: the natural end is the due end, or the natural end of an action is its due end. As such, the more complete (and logically rigorous) explication of his argument is as follows:

1. Any action not ordered to its due end is a disordered action.
2. The natural end is the due end [any natural end of an action is its due end].
3. Ergo, any action not ordered to its natural end is a disordered action (from 1 & 2).
4. The natural end of the use of the reproductive members is the generation and education of offspring.
5. Ergo, any use of the reproductive members not ordered to the generation and education of offspring [as in the case of homosexual activity] is a disordered action (from 3 & 4).

Although the second premise is implicit in the argument, we can find it expressed explicitly by Aquinas elsewhere:

---

[489] *De Malo* Q15, A1, ad 7: "Actus luxurie potest dici contra naturam dupliciter : uno modo absolute, quia scilicet est contra naturam omnis animalis : et sic omnis actus luxurie preter commixtionem maris et femine dicitur esse contra naturam in quantum non est proportionatus generationi, que in quolibet genere animalis fit ex commixtione utriusque sexus ; et hoc modo Glosa. Alio modo dicitur esse aliquid contra naturam quia est contra naturam propriam hominis cuius est ordinare generationis actum ad debitam educationem, et sic omnis fornication est contra naturam" (Sancti Thomae de Aquino, *Opera Omnia, Quaestiones Disputatae de Malo,* p. 272). The translation is my own.

Virtue conveys a certain disposition of anything fittingly related *according to the mode of its own nature*. And consequently it follows that virtue is a certain good in that *the good of anything is that it fittingly is related according to the mode of its nature*...the vice of each thing is that it is *not disposed according to the fittingness of its nature* [emphasis added].[490]

But on the contrary, Augustine says in Book III of *De Libero Arbitrio:* "Every vice, from the very fact that it is a vice, is contrary to nature." I reply it must be said that, as has been said, that vice is contrary to virtue. Now *the virtue of anything consists in this that it be well disposed according to the fittingness of its nature*, as has been stated above. Hence it is necessary that *in anything vice is said to be from the fact that it is a disposition contrary to that which is fitting with nature*...Hence the human virtue makes man good and renders his acts good *inasmuch as it is according to the nature of man* [emphasis added].[491]

c) A defense of the second premise

The natural end is the due end. I have already argued at length for the second premise in the earlier chapter of this book, but further evidence for its veracity is found when we reflect upon the nature of the good. A

---

[490] ST I-II, Q71, A1: "Directe quidem virtus importat dispositionem quandam alicuius convenienter se habentis secundum modum suae naturae: unde Philosophus dicit, in VII *Physic.* quod *virtus est dispositio perfecti ad optimum; dico autem perfecti, quod est dispositum secundum naturam.* Ex consequenti autem sequitur quod virtus sit bonitas quaedam: in hoc enim consistit uniuscuiusque rei bonitas, quod convenienter se habeat secundum modum suae naturae...vitium enim uniuscuiusque rei esse videtur quod non sit disposita secundum quod convenit suae naturae." The translation is my own.

[491] ST I-II, Q71, A2: "Sed contra est quod Augustinus dicit, in III *de Lib. Arb. : Omne vitium, eo ipso quod vitium est, contra naturam est.* Respondeo dicendum quod, sicut dictum est, vitium virtuti contrariatur. Virtus autem uniuscuiusque rei consistit in hoc quod sit bene disposita secundum convenientiam suae naturae, ut supra dictum est. Unde oportet quod in qualibet re vitium dicatur ex hoc quod est disposita contra id quod convenit naturae...Unde virtus humana, quae *hominem facit bonum, et opus ipsius bonum reddit,* intantum est secundum naturam hominis." The translation is my own. See also *Compendium Theologiae,* I.122.

flute-player, a mechanic, and a plant may be good, but each in different respects. What makes a flute-player good is that he plays the flute well. What makes a plant good is that it grows to appropriate size, reproduces, etc. But what makes a good flute-player is different from what makes a mechanic a good mechanic. Bob is not a bad flute-player if he cannot change a flat or does not know how to fix a carburetor, because these functions are not what are required of a flute-player qua flute-player. What makes something good depends upon the type of being it is, and what makes the type of being good is what it is for, that is, what its function is. The fulfillment of a thing's function perfects its nature and makes that thing good.

As applied to man, what makes him good qua man is that he fulfills his function——so too with regard to his powers and affiliated organs. What makes a heart a good heart is that it fulfills its end of pumping blood. What makes the liver good is that it secretes bile. The natural end is the due end and so Aquinas's second premise is true.[492]

One may object that *function* is used in a radically different way when said of animals and when said of men. Such an objection, as Philippa Foot says, is no difficulty for the second premise:

> There is the fact that a certain network of interrelated concepts such as *function* and *purpose* is found where there is evaluation of all kinds of living things, including human beings. It is possible, of course, that the meaning of words such as "function" or "purpose" should diverge when used in speaking on the one hand of characteristics and operations of plants and animals and on the other of human beings.…Moreover, if we consider the concepts involved we should be surprised to be told that there is no common meaning or shared logical structure between evaluations of botanical and zoological subjects. The common structure of evaluation seems unaffected by the radical differ-

---

[492] For a further defense of the second premise see: Aristotle, *Nicomachean Ethics,* Book I, Chapter 7, 1097b; Edward Feser, *Aquinas: A Beginner's Guide* (Oxford: Oneworld, 2009), 177-183; Feser, *The Last Superstition: A Refutation of the New Atheism,* 132-138; and Philippa Foot, *Natural Goodness* (Oxford: Oxford University Press, 2001), 15-16. Aquinas restates the second premise in SCG III, ch. 26, n. 2084 (Marietti, p. 36): "Rectus ordo rerum convenit cum ordine naturae: nam res naturales ordinantur in suum finem absque errore."

ence between the two....Yet there is no offhand reason to suppose that the word "function" has a different meaning in a sentence about the function of spreading a peacock's tail and in one that speaks of the opening of a flower in sunlight.[493]

The terms *function* and *good* can be truly predicated across various beings. Their predication, at least in some cases, is analogical, which is why not all cases of defective function imply a moral defect. Only defective functioning of human action (acts proceeding from intellect and will) involves a moral defect. A heart that misses a beat is acting defectively, but its defect is no moral defect because the defective activity is not a human action but an act of man. If, on the other hand, a man could intend for his heart to pump defectively, such an act might be a morally defective action, as it would lack the proper order to the natural (and due) end of health.

What makes humans good or bad depends upon their nature and the ends towards which they are naturally oriented.[494] Such natural ends have motivational significance, because we all want what is good for us qua human being. The natural end is the due end. Just as an act of heating is defective if it isn't ordered to imparting heat, so too an act of justice is defective if it isn't ordered to imparting what's right.

d) An additional premise

As mentioned in the earlier chapter, Tollefsen objects that such an argument entails only a natural disorder and not a moral disorder. We have already replied to his objection in that chapter; but he is correct insofar as an additional premise needs to be added to the argument. What distinguishes mere natural disorders from moral disorders is that a moral disorder involves some *inordinatio* to the human good; mere natural disorders, as in a disordered act of heating, involve no proximate order to the human good. New human life, as the proximate end of the reproductive

---

[493] Foot, *Natural Goodness*, 40-41.

[494] Cf. Aristotle, *Nicomachean Ethics,* Book I, Chapter 7, 1097b; Edward Feser, *Aquinas: A Beginner's Guide* (Oxford: Oneworld, 2009), 177-183; Feser, *The Last Superstition: A Refutation of the New Atheism*, 132-138.

members, is a human good. We must thus add an additional premise to Aquinas's argument against homosexual activity as follows:

1. Any action not ordered to its due end is a disordered action.
2. The natural end is the due end [the natural end of an action is its due end].
3. Ergo, any action not ordered to its natural end is a disordered action (from 1 & 2).
4. The natural end of the use of the reproductive members is the generation and education of offspring.
5. Ergo, any use of the reproductive members not ordered to the generation and education of offspring [as in the case of homosexual acts] is a disordered action (from 3 & 4).
6. Disordered human acts that involve the human good are morally disordered.
7. The use of the reproductive members involves an order to the human good (of new human life).
8. Ergo, any use of the reproductive members not ordered to the human good (of new human life) is morally disordered [as happens in homosexual activity] (from 5, 6, & 7).

What I have presented above is the argument Aquinas implicitly makes in SCG III, 122 and DM Q15, A1.

Tollefsen's objection can easily be answered by adding the 6th and 7th premises. The human good, because it is our good, is not empty of motivational significance. The 7th premise is true, because new human life, by definition, is a human good.

Part Two: Objections to Aquinas's Fourth Premise

Aquinas's fourth premise states that the natural end of the use of the reproductive members is the generation and education of offspring.[495] Various authors question the veracity of Aquinas's fourth premise. All these objectors either deny that the sexual members have the end that Aquinas

---

[495] "Finis autem usus genitalium membrorum est generatio et educatio prolis."

attributes to them or argue that the sexual members have other ends such that homosexual activity can be a good use of said members.

a) The objections

John Corvino, for example, argues, "Most people recognize that sex has other valuable purposes, including the expression of affection; the pursuit of mutual pleasure; and the building, replenishing, and celebrating of a special kind of intimacy."[496] John McNeill argues that Aquinas did not realize that sexual activity between two males or two females can be "an expression of genuine interpersonal love."[497] Chris Meyers argues that the human sexual organs have other purposes such as producing pleasure and expressing affection between two people in a committed romantic relationship.[498] Gareth Moore argues that the sexual organs also have a social role as a source of pleasure in bringing people together in relationships.[499] Burton Leiser asserts that "the sex organs, for one thing, seem to be particularly well adapted to give their owners and others intense sensations of pleasure...In view of the peculiar design of these organs, with their great concentration of nerve endings, it would seem that they were designed...with that very goal in mind."[500] Leiser asserts that the human sex organs may be used as an expression of love of one person to another.[501] Andrew Sullivan disagrees with Aquinas on two accounts: (a) nature has built in an excessive amount of sperm and eggs, and all of them surely cannot possibly be directed to reproduction; (b) "to treat human sexuality as entirely instrumental to the production of children surely demeans it." It reduces human beings to reproductive animals and misses the goodness of marital sex when engaged in for reasons of passion, love, commitment, or mutual support, even when pro-

---

[496] Corvino, *What's Wrong with Homosexuality?*, 86.
[497] McNeill, *The Church and the Homosexual*, 106-107.
[498] Meyers, *The Moral Defense of Homosexuality*, 120. He also asserts their purpose as an expression of love, emotional intimacy, and closeness (121).
[499] Moore, *A Question of Truth*, 223.
[500] Leiser, "Homosexuality, Morals, and the Laws of Nature," Section 4.
[501] Ibid.

creation is impossible.[502]

b) A defense of Aquinas's premise

Interestingly, none of the authors just mentioned denies that the end of the sexual organs is reproduction, perhaps, because the point is obvious.[503] What makes an organ an organ is its function—such is the teaching of modern biology.[504] The eyes of dragonflies, honeybees, owls, spiders, chameleons, and humans all look very different. But we rightly call all of them eyes because they serve the same purpose of seeing. Likewise, the structure of the ears varies widely among humans,

---

[502] Sullivan, "Unnatural Law," p. 21.

[503] Meyer's view is a bit confusing, or perhaps just inconsistent. He explicitly acknowledges that at least one of the purposes of the human sexual organs is reproduction (119), yet later denies that this is the *real* purpose of them (121). Presumably what he means is that the human sexual organs have the purpose of reproduction, but this is not *the only* reason why they exist, and it is not the primary reason why they exist. The reproductive organs exist for reproduction on his account only in the general sense in which all the organs of the body evolved for the sake of the continuance of the species. His view, however, fails to account for what makes the sexual organs distinctive from the other organs. Further, his view fails to account for the distinction between the remote purposes of the organs and proximate purposes. He is right that in evolution all organs are remotely for the sake of the preservation of the species, but mistaken to infer from this that none of them (not even the sexual members) are more proximately ordered to this end than other organs. On such an account, one might as well infer that because all organs are for the preservation of the individual that the stomach is not proximately ordered to the preservation of the individual in digesting food. Meyers also appeals to evolution to deny final causality (118), yet wants to admit that final causes exist but only on the account that an organ would not exist if it would not have promoted the achievement of the goal that it exists for (118). This argument, however, seems to sneak in the very point he is trying to deny: organs are defined by their final causes. Meyers also mistakenly thinks that modern biology has wiped out teleology, which is not true, as even modern biology explicitly mentions functions (final cause) as part of the definition of organs. Without final causality, anatomy and modern medicine become unintelligible.

[504] *Farlex Partner Medical Dictionary* (2012), s.v. "organ": "any part of the body exercising a specific function." Elaine N. Marieb and Katja Hoehn, *Human Anatomy & Physiology,* 8th ed. (San Francisco: Benjamin Cummings, 2010), 3: "An *organ* is a discrete structure composed of at least two tissue types (four is more common) that performs a specific function for the body."

rabbits, and fish, but they are still ears because their purpose is to hear. Likewise, though the penises of the Argentine lake duck, the bean weevil, the Argonaut octopus, and the human all look radically different they all remain male sexual organs insofar as their purpose is to inseminate the female in order to reproduce. This purpose remains despite the fact that the lake duck's penis is seventeen inches long and corkscrew-shaped, the bean weevil's is spiked such that it damages the female beetle's reproductive tract, and the Argonaut's temporarily detaches during mating.[505] What makes sex organs sex organs is that they are for reproduction.

Christopher Martin has an interesting thought experiment, giving further evidence that the sexual members have reproduction as their natural end:

> Broadly speaking I want to put the biology back into sexuality. Or, as I would put it, I want to put the sex back into sexuality. This works on a number of levels. First, we have to admit sex is a biological and teleological notion. Suppose we met a race of creatures – fairly clearly non-rational animals – that was very different from us: on Mars, say. And the question arises: are these creatures sexed? and if so, can we distinguish male and female? We need to think now how we would go about finding out these answers. We would not try to do it by investigating their psyches, nor even merely by just looking at (or cutting up) individuals. We would try to find out how they reproduced and what was the role of the different organs of the different individuals involved in reproduction. Thus, sex is a biological and teleological notion. Anything else which is called sexual is so called because ultimately it has some relation to this process, to these organs.[506]

---

[505] Katharine Gammon, "The Weirdest Animal Penises," LiveScience, March 09, 2011, accessed February 22, 2016, http://www.livescience.com/33105-weird-strange-animal-penises.html. For other sorts of weird examples, I refer my reader here: Colin Barras, "The Twisted World of Sexual Organs," BBC earth, September 2014, The Twisted World of Sexual Organs, accessed February 22, 2016, http://www.bbc.com/earth/bespoke/story/20140908-twisted-world-of-sexual-organs/index.html.

[506] Martin, "Are There Virtues and Vices That Belong Specifically to the Sexual Life?" Aquinas, similarly, holds that what differentiates male and female (and so too implicitly the sexual organs) is their role in reproduction: *Super Sent.* II, D20,

Martin's point is this: what makes sex sex is its natural order to procreation; what makes the sex organs sexual organs as opposed to hearing organs or seeing organs is that they are for reproduction. In short, the natural end of the use of reproductive members does seem to be, as Aquinas says, the generation and education of offspring. Reproduction is what the genital members are ordered to by nature.

c) Other purposes?

Corvino, McNeill, Meyers, and Leiser all claim there are other purposes for the sexual organs beyond that of reproduction. These other purposes are pleasure, affection, intimacy, love, and bringing people together in relationships. Let us consider each of these, beginning with pleasure, to determine in what manner each is a purpose of sexual activity.

Pleasure is an incentive for engaging in certain types of actions like eating, drinking, and sex.[507] To say eating and sex are for pleasure is to put the cart before the horse. Sexual pleasure is for the sake of sexual reproduction as gustatory pleasure is for the sake of eating. As Feser says, even a Darwinian naturalist would admit these points.[508] Aquinas makes the same point in SCG IV, Chapter 83:

> The pleasures which are in the activities mentioned [use of food and sexual union] are not the ends of those activities. It is, rather, the converse, for nature ordered the pleasure of those acts for this reason: lest the animals, in view of the labor, desist from those acts necessary to na-

---

Q1, A2, s.c. 1: Sed contra est quod dicitur Genes. 1, 27 : *Masculum et feminam creavit eos.* Sed distinctio sexuum est ordinata in animalibus ad generationem quae est per coitum. Ergo talis modus generationis ibi fuisset (S. Thomae Aquinatis, *Scriptum Super Libros Sententiarum,* vol. II, ed. R.P. Mandonnet (Parisiis: P. Lethielleux, 1929), p. 506).

ST I, Q98, A2, s.c. 1: Sed contra est quod Deus ante peccatum masculum et feminam fecit, ut dicitur *Gen.* 1 [27] et 2, [22]. Nihil autem est frustra in operibus Dei. Ergo etiam si homo non peccasset, fuisset coitus, ad quem distinctio sexuum ordinatur.

[507] Cf. Edward Feser, "In Defense of the Perverted Faculty Argument," in *Neo-Scholastic Essays* (South Bend, IN: St. Augustine's Press, 2015), 389-390.

[508] Ibid., 390.

ture, which is what would happen if they were not stimulated by pleasure. Therefore, the order is reversed and inharmonious if those operations are carried out merely for pleasure.[509]

Pleasure is not the natural purpose of any activity; rather pleasure is for the sake of natural functions.

It is possible to have disordered pleasures. A sadmasochist or someone who delights in eating coals has disordered desires. Nevertheless, the purpose of sexual pleasure as determined by nature is for reproduction. If the use of the sexual organs just had pleasure as a natural end divorced from reproduction, then eating also could have the end of pleasure divorced from any good of nourishment; ergo eating coals would be in accord with the natural purposes of eating for those who enjoy it. Pleasure in eating is for nourishment; likewise, pleasure in sexual activity is for reproduction. Pleasure is an added incentive to engage in the appropriate activity that leads to the natural goods of nourishment and new life. If sex were not pleasurable, few would engage in it, leading to the extinction of the human race. Pleasure can be said to be the purposes of the sexual organs in one way only: insofar as such pleasure is related to the good of reproduction. Ergo, contrary to the objectors, pleasure cannot be the purpose of the sexual organs apart from its natural end of generating new life.

Taking pleasure in a good act is something good, even if such resulting pleasure is not the purpose of the act as set by nature. That marital sex between a man and a woman doesn't exist for the sake of pleas-

---

[509] Translation is from *Contra Gentiles, Book Four: Salvation*, trans. Charles J. O'Neil, http://dhspriory.org/thomas/ContraGentiles4.htm#83. The Latin is as follows: "Nam delectationes quae sunt in praemissis actionibus, non sunt fines actionum, sed magis e converso; natura enim ad hoc ordinavit delectationes in istis actibus, ne animalia, propter laborem, ab istis actibus necessariis naturae desisterent: quod contingeret nisi delectatione provocarentur. Est ergo ordo praeposterus et indecens si operationes propter solas delectationes exerceantur" (Marietti, IV.83, n.4180, p.400). See also SCG III, ch. 26, n. 2084 (Marietti, p.36): "In naturalibus autem est delectatio propter operationem, et non e converso. Videmus enim quod natura illis operationibus animalium delectationem apposuit quae sunt manifeste ad fines necessarios ordinatae, sicut in usu ciborum, qui ordinatur ad conservationem individui, et in usu venereorum, qui ordinatur ad conservationem speciei: nisi enim adesset delectatio, animalia a praedictis usibus necessariis abstinerent."

ure doesn't mean it is wrong to delight in such sex. It is not wrong to seek pleasure in things provided that (i) one is not seeking the pleasure as an ultimate end, nor (ii) in bad instances of these acts, such as in consuming coal.

The objectors seemingly have two main reasons for holding that pleasure is the purpose of the reproductive members: (a) their use tends to result in pleasure; (b) many people use them for the sake of pleasure. In order to better evaluate claim (a), I will put it into premise form:

1. The use of the reproductive members tends to result in pleasure.
2. Anything that tends to result in pleasure must have pleasure as its natural end.
3. Thus, the use of the reproductive members has pleasure as its natural end.

Premise two, however, is false. Drinking water tends to result in pleasure, but the natural purpose of drinking water is hydration. Smelling also tends to result in pleasure, but its natural purpose is odor, not pleasure. If pleasure were the natural purpose of smelling, then smelling a foul odor would violate the purpose of smelling. Pleasure is a consequent good that follows from the proper end of drinking and smelling; but it does not thereby replace the proximate natural end of such actions.

If pleasure were the proximate end of the tongue, the ears, and the reproductive organs, then since organs are defined by their functions, the tongue, ears, and sex organs would all be the same. Licking someone's ears would then be an act of sex.

Claim (b) will also be easier to evaluate if put into valid form:

1. Whatever many use for the sake of pleasure must have pleasure as its natural, proximate, end.
2. Many use their reproductive organs for the sake of pleasure.
3. Thus, the reproductive organs must have pleasure as their natural, proximate, end.

The first premise is false. Many engage in smelling for pleasure, but it does not follow that pleasure is the natural, proximate end of smelling.

Smelling is for sensing odors. Pleasure tends to result from it, and many engage in it for the sake of pleasure (as when smelling roses), but if it is to be an act of smelling, it must have odor as its proximate end. If there is no odor, there is no act of smell. But there can be an act of smell without pleasure. Natural actions are defined by their ends, so what makes smelling to be smelling as opposed to eating is that it has odor as its proximate end.[510]

The authors who claim mutual affection is the end of the sexual organs give no evidence in support of their claim. Presumably, their reasons are similar to the reasons for believing the end is pleasure: (a) the use of the sexual organs results in mutual affection, or (b) many use them for the sake of mutual affection.

(A), however, rests on a faulty premise: whatever frequently results in x must have x as its proximate purpose. On such a premise it follows not only that mutual affection and STDs are the purpose of sex, but also that the purpose of pounding nails in a construction project is to make a noise, since noise almost always accompanies the pounding.

Regarding (b), a distinction must be made between the end of the work, and the end of the one working.[511] The end of the work is the end of the action as determined by nature. The end of the one working, by contrast, is what the one performing the action is intending even apart from or contrary to the ends intended by nature. In the act of heating, some may intend other actions such as cooking, burning, killing, or arson, but it does not follow that the natural end of heating itself is any of these things. The end of heating by nature is to heat, though the agent heating may add other ends on top of the natural end. The point Aquinas wishes to make, and all that is necessary for his argument, is that the natural end of the use of the sexual organs is the generation of offspring. Closer examination of the *De Malo* text under consideration indicates that Aquinas implies such a distinction between the end intended by nature and the end of the agent:

---

[510] Further, if the reproductive organs do not have reproduction, but rather pleasure as their end, then plants have no reproductive organs, as they experience no pleasure in generating a new plant. Plants are not sentient beings.

[511] Cf. *Super Sent.* II, D1, Q2, A1 and ST II-II, Q141, A6, ad 1 where Aquinas distinguishes between the *finis operis* and the *finis operantis*.

> Therefore every voluntary emission of semen is illict, unless it is fitting with the end intended by nature.[512]

> The end of the act according to its own nature is disordered, even if the agent intends a good end, which does not suffice to excuse the act, as is clear in he who steals intending to give alms.[513]

Although the agent may order the use of the sexual members to further ends such as mutual affection, this does not change their proximate natural end as determined by nature, namely, reproduction.

The case of mutual affection, however, has some basis as a secondary end, that is, one that accompanies the order to reproduction. The reproductive act is a unitive act and therefore involves a mutual order to a shared good. This mutual ordering to a shared goal fosters mutual affection. The mere act of procreating does not suffice for the perfection of the offspring. It is further required that there be a union of lives in the education and moral instruction of the child that has resulted from the act of coitus:

> It must be considered that in animals in which the female alone suffices for the education of offspring, the male and female do not remain together for any time after coitus, as is clear in dogs.

> But in whatever animals in which the female [alone] does not suffice for the education of offspring, the male and female remain together immediately after coitus however long it is necessary for the education and instruction of the offspring, as it is clear in certain birds, of which the baby hen is not able to seek food for itself immediately after being born. Since the bird does not nourish its young ones by milk, which it must do promptly, as it is prepared by nature, as occurs in quadrupeds, it is necessary that the food for the young ones be sought from another

---

[512] *De Malo* Q15, A1, ad 4: "Ideo omnis uoluntaria emissio seminis est illicita, nisi secundum conuenientiam *ad finem a natura intentum*" (Leonine, p. 271). The translation is my own.

[513] Ibid., ad 3: "Finis etiam ipsius *actus secundum suam naturam* est inordinatus, *licet ex intentione agentis* possit esse finis bonus, qui non sufficit ad excusationem actus, ut patet in eo qui furatur intendens eleemosinam dare" (Leonine, p. 271). The translation is my own.

source, and besides this, she must keep them warm by brooding over them. For this the female alone would not be sufficient. Hence, on account of divine providence there is naturally placed into the male of such animals that he remain with the female for the education of the young.

Now it is manifest that in the human species the female alone minimally suffices for the education of offspring, since the necessities of human life require many things which one alone cannot supply. Therefore, it is fitting according to human nature that man remains with his woman after coitus, and does not immediately leave her, indifferently approaching whoever, as happens among fornicators....Again, it must be considered that in the human species, offspring do not require only nourishment for the body, as with other animals, but even instruction for the soul. For other animals naturally have their own prudence whereby they can provide for their own, but man lives by reason, which it is necessary to arrive at through a long time of experience. Hence it is necessary for a son to be subject to his parents, as though they are now well-experienced, so that he may be instructed. This instruction is not bestowed at the time of birth, but after a long time, and chiefly when they have arrived at the age of discretion. For this instruction a long time is required. And even then, on account of the impetus of passion, by which the estimation of prudence is corrupted, they require not only instruction, but even restraint. And for this the woman alone does not suffice, but to a greater extent the work of the male is required in this area, in which both reason is more perfect for instruction[514] and strength more powerful for correcting. Therefore, it is necessary that in the human species no small time is needed for the advancement of the offspring, as in birds, but a great interval of life. Hence, since it is necessary for the female to remain with the male in all animals as long as the work of the father is necessary for the offspring, it is natural for man that for no small time, but for a long time that the man keeps society with a determinate woman. This society we call marriage.[515]

---

[514] I must disagree with Aquinas here about the intellectual abilities of woman.

[515] "Est enim considerandum quod in animalibus in quibus sola femina sufficit ad prolis educationem, mas et femina post coitum nullo tempore commanent, sicut patet in canibus.

Quaecumque vero animalia sunt in quibus femina non sufficit ad educationem prolis, mas et femina simul post coitum commanent quousque necessarium est ad prolis

This union of male and female then must last beyond the mere act of sexual intercourse; they must remain together as long as is needed for the children that result from the act of procreation. Mutual affection then naturally results from these shared goals of procreation and education. This mutual affection, however, is entirely secondary (as a natural purpose of coitus) upon the act or end of reproduction.[516] Coitus is only for

---

educationem et instructionem: sicut patet in quibusdam avibus, quarum pulli non statim postquam nati sunt possunt sibi cibum quaerere. Cum enim avis non nutriat lacte pullos, quod in promptu est, velut a natura praeparatum, sicut in quadrupedibus accidit, sed oportet quod cibum aliunde pullis quaerat, et praeter hoc, incubando eos foveat: non sufficeret ad hoc sola femella. Unde ex divina providentia est naturaliter inditum mari in talibus animalibus, ut commaneat femellae ad educationem fetus.

Manifestum est autem quod in specie humana femina minime sufficeret sola ad prolis educationem: cum necessitas humanae vitae multa requirat quae per unum solum parari non possunt. Est igitur conveniens secundum naturam humanam ut homo post coitum mulieri commaneat, et non statim abscedat, indifferenter ad quamcumque accedens, sicut apud fornicantes accidit....Rursus considerandum est quod in specie humana proles non indigent solum nutritione quantum ad corpus, ut in aliis animalibus; sed etiam instructione quantum ad animam. Nam alia animalia naturaliter habent suas prudentias, quibus sibi providere possunt: homo autem ratione vivit, quam per longi temporis experimentum ad prudentiam pervenire oportet; unde necesse est ut filii a parentibus, quasi iam expertis, instruantur. Nec huius instructionis sunt capaces mox geniti, sed post longum tempus, et praecipue cum ad annos discretionis perveniunt. Ad hanc etiam instructionem longum tempus requiritur. Et tunc etiam, propter impetus passionum, quibus corrumpitur aestimatio prudentiae, indigent non solum instructione, sed etiam repressione. Ad haec autem mulier sola non sufficit, sed magis in hoc requiritur opus maris, in quo est et ratio perfectior ad instruendum, et virtus potentior ad castigandum. Oportet igitur in specie humana non per parvum tempus insistere promotioni prolis, sicut in avibus, sed per magnum spatium vitae. Unde, cum necessarium sit marem feminae commanere in omnibus animalibus quousque opus patris necessarium est proli, naturale est homini quod non ad modicum tempus, sed diuturnam societatem habeat vir ad determinatam mulierem. Hanc autem societatem *matrimonium* vocamus" (S. Thomae Aquinatis, *Liber de Veritate Catholicae Fidei contra errores Infidelium seu Summa Contra Gentiles* (Taurini, Romae: Marietti, 1961), Ch. 122, n. 2952-2954, p. 182-183). The translation is my own.

[516] In a sense it can be said that the purpose of the sexual organs is for mutual affection insofar as this mutual affection is ordered to the upbringing of the offspring. Ironically, Chris Meyers at the very point where he wishes to disagree with Aquinas's point gives adequate evidence that the upbringing of offspring is indeed the purposes of human mutual affection resulting from sexual activity: "When a human

the sake of mutual affection insofar as this mutual affection is needed in order to educate any offspring that results. Mutual affection alone cannot be the purpose of sexual intercourse as the *finis operis* of the act. It is a part of the *finis operis* only as connected with the proximate end of procreation.

Mutual affection can and should be the goal of a married couple as the *finis operantis* of their act of sexual intercourse. Such mutual affection is even possible in a same-sex couple who commits an act of sexual activity together, but it in no way follows that mutual affection is the proximate end of sexual activity between two people as the *finis operis*. That mutual affection generally follows from sexual activity hardly makes it the end of the act as the *finis operis* anymore than that a loud noise happens from jackhammering is the purpose of jackhammering.

Further, for the sake of argument let us grant that the end of the sexual organs by nature is the generation and education of offspring, and also pleasure, mutual affection, the building up of a relationship, intimacy, and love. Aquinas's argument would still stand against homosexual activity:

1. Any human action not ordered to its due end is a disordered action.
2. The due end of the use of the reproductive members is the generation and education of offspring, and pleasure, mutual affection, in-

---

has an orgasm, the body releases hormones such as oxytocin and vasopressin. These substances act as neurotransmitters in the brain. There they give rise to feelings of emotional closeness, foster trust, and facilitate pair-bonding. Humans are not the only animals that get a release of oxytocin and vasopressin upon orgasm. Some other mammals do. Those animals, like wolves and dogs, whose bodies release these substances upon orgasm tend to be monogamous. Animals that don't get a rush of oxytocin and vasopressin upon orgasm, such as cats, tend to be more promiscuous and do not form couples.

Pair-bonding is crucial for humans because human babies are so helpless. A female cat can easily raise her kittens without help. They require only eight to ten weeks before they are ready to take care of themselves. But a lone cavewoman would have great difficulty raising her human baby, who takes over a year just to learn to walk. Proto-humans with sex organs that release neuro-transmitters that facilitate pair-bonding will have children who are more likely to be raised by two parents and thus more likely to survive to adulthood" (Meyers, *The Moral Defense of Homosexuality*, 120-121). Human affection or pair-bonding is by nature ordered towards the upbringing of offspring.

timacy, love, etc.

3. Ergo, any use of the reproductive organs apart from the generation and education of offspring, pleasure, mutual affection, etc. is disordered.

Notice that the conclusion would be that any action not ordered towards *any* of these ends would be declared wrong on Aquinas's argument. So it would not suffice that just because one of those ends is fulfilled that it is a morally good action. If there be a lack of order towards *even one* of the ends such as the generation of offspring, then the action itself is disordered. Homosexual activity would still be wrong though it may fulfill the other ends of intimacy and affection, etc. All the objectors acknowledge the sexual members have reproduction as a natural end, even if they emphasize other ends. In doing so, they have already granted enough for Aquinas's conclusion to follow.

Interestingly, on the objectors' account (with the added first premise), any use of the sexual members not ordered towards pleasure would be a disordered action. On such an account, it follows that an old couple that gets no pleasure out of sexual intercourse (or a woman who gets no pleasure, even if her husband does) would be engaging in a disordered action.

Aquinas does indicate that the sexual organs have a secondary purpose beyond procreation:

> The end of the use of the reproductive members is the generation *and education of offspring*. Therefore, every use of the aforementioned members which is not proportionate to the generation of offspring and their due education is disordered in itself.[517]

---

[517] "Finis autem usus genitalium membrorum est generatio et educatio prolis, et ideo omnis usus predictorum membrorum qui non est proportionatus generationi prolis et debite eius educationi est secundum se inordinatus." (Sancti Thomae de Aquino, *Opera Omnia, Quaestiones Disputatae de Malo*, p. 270). The translation is my own; emphasis added.
Aquinas also mentions that the principal end of marriage is the good of offspring, but its secondary end is the mutual care of the spouses for each other by sharing in domestic responsibilities (ST Supplement, Q41, A1, co.; also Q65, A1, co.). The context, however, is about the ends of marriage and not about the ends of the gener-

This secondary purpose, however, is only intelligible in light of the primary purpose of the use of the reproductive members. Education of offspring presupposes that such offspring have first been brought into existence by procreation.

What makes the sexual organs distinctively sexual, without which there would be no sexual organs, is the purpose of reproduction; that intimacy and love also result from their use does not do away with this fact of nature. Neither mutual affection, nor intimacy, nor love, are the primary purposes of the sexual organs; they are not what make the sexual organs sex organs. Mutual affection, intimacy, and love can also result from the action of the hands giving flowers, of the lips kissing, or of the tongue sharing intimate thoughts, feelings, and desires. If the primary purpose of an organ is simply some remote end such as love, then the sexual organs are actually the same as the hands, the lips, and the tongue. What differentiates one organ from another, however, is its proximate end.[518] Consequently, these objections to Aquinas fail.

---

ative power per se. Marriage may have a secondary end of mutual care of the spouses for each other which may be obtained in all sorts of ways apart from sexual intercourse. Same-sex couples of course may share in this end of mutual care, but their union cannot constitute marriage, because their union is missing one of the essential features of marriage, namely, the order to procreation through each other. This order still holds in the case of infertile male-female marriages, because they can still engage in sexual intercourse; whereas same-sex couples properly speaking cannot. Sex is defined by its natural order to procreation just as heating is by its order to heat.

[518] I do not mean to deny here that there are secondary, remote ends, of the sexual organs that are determined by nature, such as the union of the spouses in mutual affection.

d) The excess sperm objection

Andrew Sullivan's objection also fails. Sullivan argues that since an excessive number of sperm are wasted and many eggs go unfertilized, nature must have non-procreative purposes built-in for them.[519] This wastage, however, is beside the point. Take the example of many plant seeds or a shotgun.[520] A good-sized puffball can produce 8 trillion spores.[521] Many, or even most, of these seeds die; nevertheless, the purpose of these seeds is for a new plant to germinate. Likewise, a shotgun propels many smaller pellets, only some of which hit the bird, rabbit, etc. All the BBs are for the purpose of hitting the animal, even if most miss it. Likewise, that most sperm or eggs die does not mean that they are not ordered towards the end of new human life. If sperm and egg are not for reproduction because many of them die, then plant seeds are not meant for new plants, nor were the pellets meant to hit the animal. Nature has her purposes, even if these purposes do not actually obtain in all cases. She has accommodated for the fact that many cases fail to attain their end by drastically increasing the number of seeds to increase the overall

---

[519] Sullivan, "Unnatural Law." Presumably, Sullivan's point is that since the average male ejaculation contains close to 100 million sperm ("Sperm: How Long Sperm Live, Sperm Count, and More," WebMD, accessed March 02, 2016, http://www.webmd.com/infertility-and-reproduction/guide/sperm-and-semen-faq), and the average male produces over 525 billion sperm over his lifetime (Eric R. Olson, "Why Are 250 Million Sperm Cells Released During Sex?," LiveScience, January 24, 2013, accessed March 02, 2016, http://www.livescience.com/32437-why-are-250 million-sperm-cells-released-during-sex.html), the purposes of the sperm cannot possibly be for procreation. If they were, then why are so many of them wasted?

[520] A single female corpse lily flower may produce up to four million seeds: W.P. Armstrong, "Botanical Record-Breakers (Part 2 of 2)," Botanical Record-Breakers (Part 2 of 2), January 26, 2014, accessed February 22, 2016, http://waynesword.palomar.edu/ww0601.htm. Likewise, a single four-inch wide mushroom can produce 16 billion spores (Bayard Webster, "Mushroom Spores Suspected As Culprit in Allergic Reactions That Baffled," The New York Times, April 20, 1982, accessed March 02, 2016, http://www.nytimes.com/1982/04/20/science/mushroom-spores-suspected-as-culprit-in-allergic-reactions-that-baffled.html).

[521] Eldon D. Enger, Frederick C. Ross, and David B. Bailey, *Concepts in Biology*, 12th ed. (New York, NY: McGraw-Hill, 2007), 458.

probability of success.

e) If animals do it, then isn't homosexual activity the natural end of the sexual organs?

Many animals engage in homosexual activity.[522] In many, homosexual activity is so common that its occurrence does not appear to be due to defect.[523] Why such homosexual activity occurs is still largely unknown in many cases and currently the topic of much ongoing research.[524] As Volker Sommer and Paul Vasey attest, homosexual activity occurs "broadly, albeit, unevenly distributed across the animal kingdom (see also Dagg, 1984; Sommer, 1990; Vasey 1995). Indeed, with a select number of species homosexual activity is widespread and occurs at levels that approach or sometimes even surpass heterosexual activity."[525] If animals use their organs for homosexual actions, then is not homosexual activity the natural end of the organ?

---

[522] This fact is well attested to in the literature. Cf. Bruce Bagemihl, *Biological Exuberance: Animal Homosexuality and Natural Diversity* (New York: St. Martin's Press, 1999). Bagemihl's book references a host of articles about same-sex sexual behavior in animals. See also Nathan W. Bailey and Marlene Zuk, "Same-sex Sexual Behavior and Evolution," Trends in Ecology and Evolution 30, no. 10 (2009). Bailey and Zuk alone reference 76 different articles. Also see Volker Sommer and Paul L. Vasey, *Homosexual Behaviour in Animals: An Evolutionary Perspective* (Cambridge: Cambridge University Press, 2010); Aldo Poiani, *Animal Homosexuality: A Biosocial Perspective* (New York: Cambridge University Press, 2010).

[523] In American Bison homosexual mounting occurs more frequently than heterosexual mounting (Bagemihl, *Biological Exuberance: Animal Homosexuality and Natural Diversity*, 415); "roughly 45 percent of sexual interactions [in Asiatic elephants] involve same-sex participants" (Ibid., 429); in Guinan Cock-of-the-Rock male-male mountings are nearly half of all copulations (Ibid., 568); 46% of sexual activity in female Langur monkeys is homosexual (Sommer and Vasey, *Homosexual Behaviour in Animals*, 261); "male calves of musk ox (*Ovibus moschatus*) mounted other males as often as females" (Sommer and Vasey, 132); and in bottlenose dolphins about 50% of all male sexual activity is with other males (Bailey and Zuk, "Same-sex Sexual Behavior and Evolution," 5).

[524] There are many different possible explanations currently being debated, but no single one applies across all species; they may be closer to an explanation regarding certain species.

[525] Sommer and Vasey, *Homosexual Behaviour in Animals: An Evolutionary Perspective*, 5.

The conclusion does not follow. Mere statistical frequency of the occurrence of x in relation to y is not a good argument that x is the function of y. Statistically speaking, all mosquitoes eventually die, but it hardly follows that their purpose is death. Likwise, most plant seeds (at least in many species) do not germinate, but it hardly follows that they were not meant to germinate. Conversely, all humans have the Vitamin C gene, whose purpose is to make Vitamin C. But statistically speaking, in 100% of all humans it is broken and it never produces Vitamin C.[526] If mere statistical occurrence determined function, scientists would never have posited its purpose for making Vitamin C. Likewise, merely because homosexual activity frequently occurs in animals does not show that it is the proximate natural end of the sexual members.

Further, many animals use their teeth to eat their young. Male chimps are known to kill baby chimps when they like a female.[527] Tarantulas rip out their hair to throw it at their enemies.[528] Many crocodiles consume rocks.[529] After mating, the female praying mantis regularly bites off the head of the male.[530] Horned lizards shoot blood out of their eyes.[531] What is the natural end for certain or many animals is not the natural end for all animals, let alone for human beings.

If all animals or most individuals of most species had an organ for the most part used for homosexual activity, then such might be the natu-

---

[526] Nathan H. Lents, "Why Humans Must Eat Vitamin C," *The Human Evolution Blog* (blog), September 13, 2014, accessed November 21, 2016, https://thehumanevolutionblog.com/2014/09/13/why-humans-must-eat-vitamin-c/.

[527] "Adult Chimpanzee Kills Baby Chimp in Front of Shocked Los Angeles Zoo Visitors," CBS News, June 27, 2012, accessed September 16, 2016, http://www.cbsnews.com/news/adult-chimpanzee-kills-baby-chimp-in-front-of-shocked-los-angeles-zoo-visitors/.

[528] Jessie Szalay, "Tarantula Facts," LiveScience, December 23, 2014, accessed September 16, 2016, http://www.livescience.com/39963-tarantula.html.

[529] Matt Wedel, "Gastroliths," Gastroliths, May 2007, accessed September 16, 2016, http://www.ucmp.berkeley.edu/taxa/verts/archosaurs/gastroliths.php.

[530] National Geographic, "World's Weirdest: Deadly Praying Mantis Love," World's Weirdest: Deadly Praying Mantis Love, accessed September 16, 2016, http://video.nationalgeographic.com/video/weirdest-praying-mantis.

[531] "Blood Shooting Eyes," Nat Geo WILD, accessed September 14, 2016, http://channel.nationalgeographic.com/wild/worlds-weirdest/videos/blood-shooting-eyes/.

222

ral end.[532] But such is hardly the case. While many animal species do engage in homosexual activity, it is unknown in how many species of animals this occurs. There are over 7 million species of animals on earth; most lack any systematic scientific study on homosexual activity. In many species, such as domestic and wild cats,[533] mule deer,[534] Moose,[535] Caribou,[536] Vicuñas llamas,[537] spotted hyenas,[538] Oystercatcher and Golden Plovers,[539] and Silver and Herring Gulls,[540] homosexual activity occurs only occasionally. As Volker and Vasey say, "[Bruce Bagemihl's book] compilation made it clear, however, that the evidence for homosexual behavior in animals is overwhelmingly sketchy and anecdotal."[541]

Further, many cases where animals engage in homosexual activity have been found to be either aberrations or have a *per accidens* order to the good of procreation.[542] As biologists Marlene Zuk and Nathan Bailey state, "in the dung fly *Hydromyza livens,* for example, males have been hypothesized to mount other males to deny them the opportunity to mate, thereby increasing the likelihood that the mounting male obtains more mating opportunities,"[543] and in other species "same-sex encounters might provide younger animals with practice for…behaviors associated with reproduction, so as to improve their reproductive success when a heterosexual partner becomes available later on."[544] Perhaps then ho-

---

[532] Insofar as statistical frequency seems to have some epistemological connection with determining function.

[533] Sommer and Vasey, *Homosexual Behaviour in Animals,* 181.

[534] Bagemihl, *Biological Exuberance,* 380.

[535] Ibid., 388.

[536] Ibid.

[537] Ibid., 426.

[538] Ibid., 447.

[539] Ibid., 541.

[540] Ibid., 554.

[541] Sommer and Vasey, *Homosexual Behaviour in Animals,* 7.

[542] Bailey and Zuk, "Same-sex Sexual Behavior and Evolution," 2, 4. Out of the 11 major explanations given by biologists for homosexual behavior in animals (in terms of its function), 5 of them involve a *per accidens* order towards procreation: acquisition of alloparental care, mate attraction, inhibition of competitor's reproduction, practice for heterosexual activities, and kin selection (Sommer and Vasey, *Homosexual Behaviour in Animals,* 27-31).

[543] Bailey and Zuk, "Same-sex Sexual Behavior and Evolution," 4.

[544] Bailey and Zuk, 5.

mosexual acts have persisted in some animals as an unintended result of nature due to the resulting evolutionary advantage, much like how sickle cell anemia has persisted in humans due to its evolutionary advantage of protecting against malaria. Defects and evolutionary advantage aren't necessarily incompatible. A defect may still be a defect, and yet give certain members of a species an evolutionary advantage.

In some cases what appears to be homosexual sexual activity is not. Marine flatworms penis-fence, but closer examination reveals their action is not homosexual. Each flatworm possesses both male and female reproductive organs and each wants to be the male that impregnates the other. They penis-fence to be the first to impregnate the other, all the while trying to avoid impregnation themselves.[545]

While there are many weird animal behaviors, such as homosexual activity, it remains universally true that the natural end of the reproductive members across *all* animal species is reproduction. If that were not their natural end, they would cease to be the reproductive members. If they ceased to be the reproductive members, then their use in homosexual activity would cease to be sexual and so the act in question would no longer be homo*sexual* activity but the activity of some other organs touching each other. Aquinas's fourth premise stands true: the natural end of the generative members is the generation (and education) of offspring, which is why we call them the *generative* or *reproductive* members.

Part Three: Objections to Aquinas's Second Premise

The second premise states, "The natural end is the due end." Germain Grisez, Burton Leiser, John Corvino, Chris Meyers, John McNeill, Gareth Moore, Paul Weithmam, and Andrew Sullivan all object to it or to what they think this premise is saying. Although in many cases these authors aren't directly attacking Aquinas, what they have said sheds much light upon the argument Aquinas has in truth given. Since their

---

[545] Gammon, "The Weirdest Animal Penises."

objections are so numerous, I will categorize similar objections together and answer them accordingly.

a) Is using an artifact contrary to its purpose wrong?

Burton Leiser argues that although a hammer was designed for pounding nails, there is nothing wrong with using it to crack open nuts.[546] He is right, but the objection does not apply to Aquinas's argument. Artifacts, that is, man-made material objects, are created by man and given their natures or quasi-natures by their human creators, which Aquinas implies in various texts:

> Just as artifacts are compared to human art, so too all natural things are compared to the divine art.[547]

> All creatures are compared to God as artifacts to the artificer.[548]

As God gives natural things their nature,[549] so too man bestows "natures" upon human artifacts.[550] Since man is the artificer of his artifacts and the giver of their forms, he can justifiably take that form away or give it a new one.[551] Further, what makes a human artifact the type of artifact it is, is what it is used for.[552] If one uses a piece of metal to

---

[546] Leiser, "Homosexuality and the 'Unnaturalness Argument" [sic.], Section 4. Ronald E. Long gives a similar objection about using screwdrivers for opening paint cans: "Of Argument and Aesthetic Distaste, A Response to J. Budziszewski," *Philosophia Christi* 7, no. 1 (2005): 56.

[547] ST I-II, Q13, A2, ad 3: "Sicut autem comparantur artificialia ad artem humanam, ita comparantur omnia naturalia ad artem divinam."

[548] SCG III, 100, n. 2761, "Omnes creaturae comparantur ad Deum sicut artificiata ad artificem" (Latin is from the Marietti, p. 153; cf. also SCG II, 24, n. 5).

[549] SCG III, 100, n. 5.

[550] The difference, of course, is that God gives *esse ex nihilo,* whereas man cannot, but rather must make out of pre-existing things.

[551] Aquinas seems to imply this possibility in SCG III, 100, n. 2761: "Non est autem contra rationem artificii si artifex aliter aliquid operetur in suo artificio, etiam postquam ei primam formam dedit" (Latin is from the Marietti, p. 153).

[552] Cf. Anna Marmodoro and Ben Page, "Aquinas on Forms, Substances and Artifacts," *Vivarium* 54, no. 1 (2016): 14: "The artificial form, for example the shape of a table, does not determine the nature of the body, what it is to be wood, but only its

pound nails it becomes a hammer, but if one uses it to crack nuts it becomes a nutcracker. There is no natural end of an artifact apart from what is given to it by man. The case of artifacts counts as no objection to "the natural end is the due end," because the end and "nature" of the artifact changes according to its use. The second premise still stands.

b) Preventing a natural function?

Many have interpreted Aquinas as saying that any use of a faculty contrary to its purpose is immoral. In other words, Aquinas is giving a variant of what has more recently been called the perverted faculty argument. Based on this assumption about what Aquinas is saying, various authors have objected to Aquinas's account. Germain Grisez and Paul Weithmam, for example, object to the perverted faculty argument along similar lines.[553] If preventing a natural function from happening is immoral, then the use of earplugs, blindfolds, and antiperspirants is immoral. So too would holding one's breath, shaving one's head, or having a hysterectomy be immoral.[554]

But these counterexamples miss the point of Aquinas's argument. Engaging in an action not ordered towards its natural end is not the same as preventing a natural process from happening. In using earplugs one is not engaging the action of hearing and then also failing to order this act

use or function." The following texts in Aquinas indicate that the end determines the nature of an artifact: Q. d. de anima, Q13, ad 5: "Unde potentie non distinguuntur penes habitus, set penes obiecta; sicut nec artificialia penes accidentia, sed penes fines" (Sancti Thomae de Aquino, *Quaestiones Disputatae de Anima,* in *Opera Omnia Iussu Leonis XIII P.M. Edita Cura et Studio Fratrum Praedicatorum,* vol. XXIV, 1, ed B.C. Bazán (Roma: Commissio Leonina, 1996), p.120). *De Veritate* Q4, A1, co.; S. Thomae Aquinatis, *In Octo Libros Phyiscorum Aristotelis Expositio,* ed. P.M. Maggiòlo (Taurini, Romae: Marietti, 1965), Book II, Lectio 4, n. 173, p. 88.

[553] Weithmam, "Natural Law, Morality, and Sexual Complementarity," 236: "[Defenders of the perverted faculty argument] are faced with the task of drawing a principled distinction between reproductive organs, whose frustration the principle forbids, and other organs whose operation it is permissible to impede." Many thanks to Feser for pointing out these texts in Grisez and Weithmam; cf. Feser, "In Defense of the Perverted Faculty Argument," 405-406.

[554] For a treatment of some of these counterexamples see: Hsiao, "A Defense of the Perverted Faculty Argument against Homosexual Sex": 756.

of hearing to its natural end. Rather, in using earplugs one is simply preventing the activity of hearing from occurring. Likewise, in holding one's breath one is not engaging in the action of breathing *and also* failing to order breathing to its natural end. One is simply not breathing. Likewise, in shaving one's head, one is not engaging in the action of growing hair *and also* failing to order growing hair to its natural end. The natural end of an action is its due end, but this does not mean that the act in question must always be performed.

Aquinas's argument against homosexual activity is not saying that someone must engage in sex; he is merely saying that *if* you are to engage in sexual activity then your action must be ordered to such and such ends. Preventing the act of sexual intercourse from happening need not be immoral. Maybe the wife has a migraine headache or is just tired and doesn't want to have sex. There is nothing wrong with her going to bed early and writing a note for her husband who is still at work: "Sorry, not tonight honey. I'm just exhausted from a long day at work." Preventing sexual activity from occurring is not morally wrong on Aquinas's argument. Rather, what is wrong, is that one engages in sexual activity that lacks any per se order to procreation.

Likewise, though the removal of a diseased uterus prevents its natural function from happening, this is not engaging in an action not ordered to its natural end. All parts of the body are ordered to the good of the whole in some manner or other, and as such may be cut off for the sake of the good of the whole.[555] In removing a diseased organ one is not engaging the power of that organ for an unnatural end; rather one is not engaging the power of that organ at all.

None of the counterexamples affect Aquinas's second premise that "the natural end is the due end," nor do they affect the first premise that "every human action that is not proportionate to its due end is in itself a disordered action." These objections are beside the point. As Steven Jen-

---

[555] ST II-II, Q65, A1. The sexual organs are, of course, ordered to the good of the species, and not the individual. Nevertheless, they contribute to the good of the individual in that they are part of the integrity of the whole, and also in some respects contribute to the proper functioning of the individual qua the secretion of hormones, etc.; also the individual shares in the good of the species by way of these organs.

sen says, "Not every instance of inhibiting some natural function…counts as a voluntary error."[556]

c) Using an organ not for its purpose?

Another set of objections to Aquinas's premise that "the natural end is
the due end" claim that there is nothing wrong with using an organ contrary to its purpose. Grisez, Meyers, Corvino, Moore, McNeill, and Sullivan raise this objection.

Sullivan argues that though the eye is for seeing, using it to wink
is not immoral, and that though the mouth is for eating, using it to smile
is not immoral.[557] Similarly, it could be argued that though the purpose
of the tongue is for tasting, using it to lick envelopes is not immoral.

Timothy Hsiao gives a good response to these and other counterexamples: "It is not inherently wrong to enhance or to impose another
purpose of our own on top of a faculty's natural function, so long as it is
consistent with its function being achieved. A person who uses his eyes
to flirt is still seeing, and a person who uses his tongue to lick stamps is
still tasting."[558] Thus, using the tongue to lick a stamp or the eyelids to
wink is not using them for an end they are not ordered to by nature, as
the tongue is still tasting and the eyelids are still doing their natural function of blinking.

Grisez, Corvino, McNeill, Meyers, and Moore could put forth further objections. In using the hands to walk, one is performing a human
action that uses the hands for the sake of an end that is not ordered to
grasping.[559] On the second premise, then, such an action appears to be
undue. The same seems to apply with the case of playing the guitar with
the feet, kicking soccer balls, pedaling a bike, tap dancing, and crushing

---

[556] Jensen, *Good & Evil Actions*, 245.

[557] Sullivan, "Unnatural Law."

[558] Hsiao, "A Defense of the Perverted Faculty Argument against Homosexual
Sex": 756.

[559] This objection is mentioned by John Corvino (*What's Wrong with Homosexuality?*, 85-86) and Grisez, *Contraception and the Natural Law*, 29. McNeill also mentions the hands but gives the example of using them to wield a pen or a brush instead (McNeill, *The Church and the Homosexual*, 114).

cockroaches under the heel.[560] Grisez also mentions the example of lactation when excess milk is pumped out of the breasts and thrown away.[561]

Regarding, the hands, Aquinas in both the *Summa* and his *Commentary on the Sentences* calls the hands the "organ of organs."[562] In ST I, Q91, A3, ad 2, he says,

> But in place of [horns and claws, toughness of hide, and feathers] man has reason and the hands, by which he can furnish for himself weapons and clothing and other necessities of life in an infinite number of ways. Hence the hand, as it is said in *De Anima* III, is called the organ of organs. And this was even more fitting with the rational nature, which is of infinite conceptions so that it had a faculty given to it for an infinite number of instruments.[563]

This teaching hearkens back to the words of Aristotle in *The Parts of Animals* IV.10:

---

[560] Cf. Meyers, *The Moral Defense of Homosexuality*, 122-123.

[561] Grisez, *Contraception and the Natural Law*, 29-30.

[562] *Super Sent.* II, D3, Q3, A1, ad 1: "Ad primum ergo dicendum, quod anima dicitur species specierum, inquantum per intellectum agentem facit species intelligibiles actu, et recipit eas secundum intellectum possibilem, sicut ibidem sensus dicitur species sensibilium, et manus organum organorum, inquantum videlicet omnia artificialia per manus efficiuntur; unde in XIV *De animal.*, lib. IV *De part. anom.*, cap. VIII, X et XI, dicitur quod manus datae sunt homini loco cornuum, et omnium quibus alia animalia juvantur" (S. Thomae Aquinatis, *Scriptum Super Libros Sententiarum Magistri Petri Lombardi Episcopi Parisiensis,* ed. R.P. Mandonnet, vol. II (Parisiis: P. Lethielleux, 1929), 114). See also: ST II-II, Q187, A3: "Quia enim manus est *organum organorum*, per opus manuum omnis operatio intelligitur de qua aliquis potest licite victum lucrari."

[563] ST I, Q91, A3, ad 2: "Ad secundum dicendum quod cornua et ungulae, quae sunt quorundam animalium arma, et spissitudo corii, et multitudo pilorum aut plumarum, quae sunt tegumenta animalium, attestantur, abundantiae terrestris elementi; quae repugnat aequalitati et teneritudini complexionis humanae. Et ideo haec homini non competebant. Sed loco horum habet rationem et manus, quibus potest parare sibi arma et tegumenta et alia vitae necessaria, infinitis modis. Unde et manus, in III *de Anima,* dicitur *organum organorum.* Et hoc etiam magis competebat rationali naturae, quae est infinitarum conceptionum, ut haberet facultatem infinita instrumenta sibi parandi." The translation is my own.

> The hand is not to be looked on as one organ but as many; for it is, as it were, an instrument for further instruments. This instrument, therefore,—the hand—of all instruments the most variously serviceable, has been given by nature to man, the animal of all animals the most capable of acquiring the most varied handicrafts.[564]

Aquinas cites this work of Aristotle multiple times.[565]

Given Aristotle's and Aquinas's account of the purposes of the hands the counterexample of walking on one's hands fails. The hands are meant to be used for whatever man wills to use them. They are the instrument of instruments. In using them to walk, to punch an assailant, to grasp a brush, or to make a sign, one is not using them contrary to their natural purpose.

Further, humans in late infancy use their hands for walking——as babies crawl, a fact acknowledged by Aristotle in the *Parts of Animals*.[566] Such use of the hands by babies provides further evidence that the use of the hands is naturally ordered to many things beyond grasping. Their natural end is any sort of movement good for the creature or others.

A similar analysis can be made regarding the feet. Since Aristotle in *The Parts of Animals* cites examples of animals that use their feet for swimming or defense, Aquinas probably knew about these other uses of the feet.[567] The end of the feet as determined by nature is for moving things.[568] Since in playing the guitar with the feet, in kicking a soccer

---

[564] Aristotle, *On the Parts of Animals*, trans. William Ogle, Bk. IV, Part 10, accessed February 23, 2016, http://classics.mit.edu/Aristotle/parts_animals.4.iv.html.

[565] *Super Sent.* II, D15, Q1, A2, ad 5; ST I-II, Q45, A3 co; ST I-II, Q66, A5, ad 3; ST II-II, Q180, A7, ad 3; *In De generatione*, I, pr. 2.

[566] *On the Parts of Animals* IV, 10:
http://classics.mit.edu/Aristotle/parts_animals.4.iv.html

[567] *On the Parts of Animals* IV, 9; IV, 5:
http://classics.mit.edu/Aristotle/parts_animals.4.iv.html. In fact, Aquinas explicitly mentions the example of the coot bird, or *Porphyrio*, and its use of the feet to swim and walk in ST I-II Q102, A6, ad 1.

[568] I do not know what precisely distinguishes the feet from the hands given that the functions of both overlap so much. It seems to be that the feet are better ordered towards walking and the hands for grasping, but nevertheless both seem to be able to do any of the functions that the other can do (at least in humans and monkeys). In other creatures the distinction seems clearer in that the feet do not grasp and there

ball, or in tap dancing one is still using the feet for their natural end of locomotion, it follows there is no violation of their natural teleology. These counterexamples do not affect Aquinas's second premise that "the natural end is the due end."

The same goes for Grisez's example of lactation. Lactation is by definition the act of suckling milk, but in pumping out the milk by hand there is no act of suckling.[569] Further, the purpose of the milk is to feed the infant. If the milk is excessive or the infant has died the milk is no longer needed for such purposes.

Other counterexamples remain. McNeill argues that though the tongue, teeth, and lips are by nature for eating, there is nothing wrong with using them for speech or song.[570] Likewise, in using the teeth to hold carpentry nails one is performing a human action that engages the teeth for the sake of an end that is not ordered towards chewing.[571] So we have at least one case where the natural end (of the use of the teeth) is not the due end (since there is nothing immoral about using the teeth to hold things).

In reply, it must be said that Aquinas knew of other uses of the teeth besides the mastication of food, since in the *Parts of Animals,* often cited by Aquinas, Aristotle mentions teeth being used as weapons in various creatures.[572] There is no one single natural end for "the use of the teeth" besides some sort of motion as ordered to the good of the creature

---

are no hands. However, in all creatures that have hands they seem to be able to do anything that the feet can. So, on an evolutionary account perhaps the hands are just more evolved feet. Snakes, which are less evolved than the higher animals, also use their spines, scales, and muscles to move. The point here is that it is unclear whether there is any single natural end for the feet that is clearly distinguished from the natural end of the hands.

I do not mean to deny that the human hands are particularly well-suited for grasping things (and better suited than are the hands of many of the apes). But it does not follow from the fact that the hands are well-suited for grasping things that such is their only or even primary purpose. They are well-suited for all sorts of other actions as well.

[569] Cf. OED, s.v. "lactation;" the very etymology of the word indicates that it is an act of sucking milk, as it is from the Latin *lactatio,* from *lactare* (to suckle) and *lac* (milk) (cf. the OED entry).

[570] McNeill, *The Church and the Homosexual,* 114.

[571] Cf. Moore, *A Question of Truth,* 223.

[572] *Parts of Animals* IV, 5 and 8.

or society. To say that the natural end is the due end (as stated in the second premise) is not to say that every action has a natural end, or that every action that has a natural end has only one natural end. "The use of the teeth" is so vague as it may include things like biting, chewing, speaking, grasping, or cutting (whether that be food, an enemy, or masking tape makes no significant difference).[573] As evidence that the teeth have other natural ends besides merely chewing, one can observe that many animals such as leopards and alligators naturally use them for holding things. Hippos have huge canines, but do not use them at all for eating, but only for fighting against rivals or predators.[574] Walruses use their big teeth for climbing out of the water onto the ice.[575] Gelada Baboons also have enormous canines, but do not use them for eating.[576] Animals also use their teeth as weapons, for carrying their young (as in leopards), or for communicating. The use of the teeth has no single natural end except perhaps some sort of motion as ordered towards the good of the animal or the species. Perhaps the teeth have a primary end of chewing food, but they certainly have other natural uses such as for fighting, carrying things, climbing, communicating, etc.

Certainly, the teeth themselves, as understood as *the-instrument-for-chewing-food* have the natural end of chewing food, but that is only because we have assumed the purpose of the teeth within the very definition of the teeth. But when the teeth are used for holding a flashlight or other things, they are no being used qua teeth, but qua instrument-for-

---

[573] None of these other purposes are meant to deny that the teeth for the most part are used for the reduction of food. That the teeth are mostly used for one end does not mean there are not other natural ends specific to the species in which they are found; cf. Aristotle, *On the Parts of Animals,* Book III. The teeth themselves that cannot chew are said to be bad teeth, but so too are teeth that do not allow one to speak or chew gum.

[574] S.K. Eltringham, *The Hippos* (London: T & AD Poyser, 2002), 14.

[575] Alina Bradford, "Walrus Facts," LiveScience, November 21, 2014, accessed August 20, 2016, http://www.livescience.com/27442-walrus-facts.html.

[576] Gregory Warner, "What A Chatty Monkey May Tell Us About Learning To Talk," NPR, September 13, 2013, Vocal Grooming, accessed August 20, 2016, http://www.npr.org/2013/09/13/216440443/what-a-chatty-monkey-may-tell-us-about-learning-to-talk; BBCEarth, "Fearsome Teeth of the Gelada Baboon - Deadly 60 - Ethiopia - Series 3 - BBC," Youtube, March 07, 2014, accessed August 20, 2016, https://www.youtube.com/watch?v=CsO_hGQVwiQ.

232

holding. In homosexual activity, by contrast, the reproductive power is engaged. Recall that homosexual activity by definition is sexual acts between two persons of the same sex. Since the activity in question is *sexual* and sexual is defined in relation to the reproductive members, homosexual activity necessarily engages the reproductive power. So it's not merely an engagement of some instrument-for-moving. Likewise, in making an assertion, there isn't merely some instrument-for-making-sounds that is engaged, but an action ordered by its nature to truth. Aquinas's argument is about actions, not mere organs abstracted from their use.

d) The meaning of organs and powers

All of these counterexamples are ultimately undercut by Aquinas's robust philosophical account of human nature. Given normal physical development, every human being is born with certain natural fundamental abilities in virtue of the kind of being that he is.[577] Men naturally are born with the ability to see, the ability to hear, and the ability to understand universal concepts such as "five" or "triangle." These natural fundamental abilites Aquinas and Aristotle called powers. Every action that man does qua living thing is reducible to these powers, which can be categorized into five general kinds: (1) vegetative powers – nutrition, growth, and reproduction, (2) sensitive powers – the five exterior senses (sight, hearing, smell, taste, touch) and the inner sense powers (common sense, memory, imagination, and the cogitative), (3) intellectual power – intellect, (4) desiring powers – irascible, concupiscible, and will, and (5)

---

[577] According to Aquinas some of these powers are the quasi-forms of material organs (cf. Sancti Thomae de Aquino, *Sentencia Libri de Anima,* in *Opera Omnia Iussu Leonis XIII P.M. Edita,* vol. XLV (Romae, 1984), lecture/chapter 24, 424a24.88-89, p. 170): "potencia enim est quasi forma organi"). So if the organ/s in which they reside have been totally destroyed, the corresponding power in question ceases to be (cf. *In IV Sent.* D44, Q3, A3, qc. 1). Accordingly, anyone born without eyes properly speaking doesn't fully have the power to see in the relevant sense. It might be said that they have the ability to see given that they are human and given the proper matter, but that isn't the relevant sense of potency as used by Aquinas in the *power* to see.

motive power – the ability to move things in place.[578] This schema has much explanatory power; any human act (or act of man insofar as he is a living thing) whatsoever can be explained by the action of one or a combination of these powers. These powers are *fundamental* because all other natural abilites are reducible to them, but the powers are not reducible to one another.[579] The organs of the human body are the instruments of these powers. As Aquinas says, the organs are for the sake of the powers and not vice-versa.[580] Some organs are the seat of a power and only one power is able to use them. For example, the cogitative power resides in a portion of the brain and only it is able to use that portion of the brain.[581] Other organs are instruments of many powers; they can be used by more than one power either simultaneously or at different times. Sight resides in the eye, but the organ of the eye can be used by the motive power simultaneous with the act of seeing. The reproductive power for males resides in the penis and so this organ can be used for sex, but the penis is also a part of the nutritive power and can be used for urinating (although not simultaneously with the action of sex).

Unlike powers, organs properly speaking are instruments. The word *organ* is from the Latin *organum,* which is merely a transliteration of the Greek ὀργάνων. An ὀργάνων is literally just an instrument.[582] Aquinas uses the Latin *organum* in the sense of instrument in his *Commentary on the De Anima* Bk. II, Chapter 1, lectio 2, n. 237, where he cites Aristotle in calling an axe an *organum.*[583] This is because an organ,

---

[578] ST I, Q78, A1.

[579] There remains an ordering among the powers, as some are higher than others, but none are reducible to others in the way in which the ability to drink and eat are reducible to the nutritive and locomotive powers.

[580] ST I, Q78, A3: Sed nihil istorum conveniens est. Non enim potentiae sunt propter organa, sed organa propter potentias: unde non propter hoc sunt diversae potentiae, quia sunt diversa organa; sed ideo natura instituit diversitatem in organis, ut congruerent diversitati potentiarum.

[581] Or at least such could be the case.

[582] I am indebted to Brandon K. White for helpful discussion regarding this point and others in this section.

[583] *Organum* in this text from Aquinas is merely a transliteration of Aristotle's Greek word ὀργάνων.
Aquinas also uses *organum* synonymously with *instrument* in the following text: *Super Sent.* III, D37, Q1, A3, ad 2: Ad secundum dicendum, quod *artificialia* non

like an axe, is simply an instrument. The organs of the body are instruments of the soul and more precisely instruments of the powers.[584] Instruments qua instruments properly speaking have no natural end. The end of an instrument is whatever it is used for.[585] Its use determines the type of instrument it is. Thus, when a pole is used to beat off an attacker it becomes a weapon, and when used to dig a hole it becomes a hole-digger. Likewise, the end of the hands is to hold things when we use them to hold things, and when we use them to punch an assailant they are for self-defense. When the teeth are used to chew they become a chewing-instrument, but when used to hold nails they become a holding-instrument. Some organs have a primary use, namely, for that which they are used for most of the time; from this primary usage we impose the name and the meaning of the organ. Included in the very notion of *teeth* is the organ-for-chewing-food. It is from this primary use (most frequent) that they are given their name; since this focal meaning holds in most cases we extend the same name to the same physical member even in cases where it ceases to be the organ-for-chewing-food and becomes the organ-for-holding-things.

The end of an instrument is malleable according to the use of the instrument. By contrast, the ends of powers are not malleable according to their use, because their ends are fixed by nature, since powers follow as proper accidents from the nature of man.[586] If their end changed, they would cease to be the type of power in question. Instruments, by contrast, have no natural end, no single end fixed by nature, unless the organ is identical with and able to be used by only one power.

---

reducuntur in naturalia ita quod natura sit eorum primum et principale principium, sed inquantum ars utitur naturalibus organis ad complementum artificii (*Scriptum Super Sententiis Magistri Petri Lombardi,* ed. R.P. Maria Fabianus Moos, vol. III (Parisiis: P. Lethielleux, 1933), p.1245).

[584] Adhuc. Cum membra corporis sint quaedam animae instrumenta, cuiuslibet membri finis est usus eius: sicut et cuiuslibet alterius instrumenti (SCG III, 126, Marietti, n. 2988, p.187). Technically Aquinas does not use the word *organum* here, but what he says here about *membrum* accords perfectly with the other texts when he speaks about *organum.* As such I take it there is no significant difference between what he says here about *membrum* and *organum* in this context.

[585] Ibid.

[586] ST I, Q77, A1, ad 5.

Since organs are instruments of a power, they have natural ends insofar as they are used by a power.[587] What power is using the instrument determines what the natural end is. When the penis is used to ejaculate, the reproductive power is engaged, which has the natural end of reproduction. But when the penis is used to urinate, the nutritive power is engaged, with the natural end of bodily health. When the teeth are used to hold a flashlight only the motive power is engaged, which has the natural end of motion and rest. The use of the teeth for holding nails is no more unnatural than the motive power using instruments for motion and rest.

This account may seem to contradict the teachings of modern biology. Typically, anatomy books define organs according to their function.[588] What makes a heart a heart is that it is for pumping blood. What makes the eye an eye is that it is for seeing. Just because we can use organs for other ends does not seem to mean we can automatically give them new natures or new ends. The nature of the heart is what it is from birth; we cannot give it a purpose other than pumping blood without it thereby ceasing to be a heart.

In reply, it must be said that Aquinas's powers strengthen rather than contradict modern biology.[589] Only after repeated observation do the biologists decide upon the end and thus label the organ in question as the beak or jaws. Some cases are more confusing, because the same body part may have multiple ends. In leopards there is a hard, white structure used for eating and so the name of teeth is imposed. Biologists, however, have discovered other uses for the same physical organ, such as for carrying cubs by the neck, and so the name imposed normally would be something to indicate the instrument-for-carrying-cubs. But

---

[587] "Omnis pars diffinitur per suam operationem et per virtutem qua operator" (Sancti Thomae de Aquino (*Sententia Libri Politicorum*, in *Opera Omnia Iussu Leonis XIII P.M. Edita*, vol. XLVIII (Romae, 1971), Ch. 1/b, 171-172, p. 79).

[588] *Farlex Partner Medical Dictionary* (2012), s.v. "organ": "any part of the body exercising a specific function." Elaine N. Marieb and Katja Hoehn, *Human Anatomy & Physiology*, 8th ed. (San Francisco: Benjamin Cummings, 2010), 3: "An *organ* is a discrete structure composed of at least two tissue types (four is more common) that performs a specific function for the body."

[589] I am not claiming Aquinas was right on all biological facts, as he was clearly mistaken on some.

the name *teeth* have been kept because that same physical part is usually used as the instrument-for-eating. Linguistic convention determined that it is easier to use one name rather than two for the same physical body part.

Further, since the use of the teeth for eating is shared in common with other animals, the name *teeth* generally indicates the-instrument-for-eating. Only in some species are teeth used as the-instrument-for-carrying-cubs. When an organ has a general purpose shared across all species it can still have other purposes peculiar to certain species.[590] Some organs have dual purposes. The penis, for example, is for both reproduction and urination. Aquinas would explain that when used in reproduction (or any sexual act), the penis is used qua generative power, but when used in urination, it is used qua nutritive power. The same name, however, has been retained for the same physical body part for ease of linguistic communication.

Any time the reproductive organs are used in a sexual manner the generative power is engaged. Since homosexual activity makes use of the generative power and the generative power has its natural end of generation, the use of the reproductive organs in homosexual activity is unnatural. The natural end of the generative power is generation and so its natural use is generative type acts. Homosexual activity, thus, is contrary to nature insofar as it is contrary to the generative use of the generative power.

All the counterexamples against Aquinas's second premise fail. The natural end is the due end. Just as the action of a plant that is not ordered to its natural end contains some defect, so too does the action of a

---

[590] Aristotle, *On the Parts of Animals,* trans. William Ogle, Bk. III, Part 1, accessed March 8, 2017, http://classics.mit.edu/Aristotle/parts_animals.3.iii.html: "The teeth have one invariable office, namely the reduction of food; but *besides this general function they have other special ones*, and these differ in different groups. Thus in some animals the teeth serve as weapons… In man, however, the number and the character even of these sharp teeth have been mainly determined by the requirements of speech" (emphasis added). In some species the teeth have a dual proximate function, namely, the reduction of food and their use as weapons. Aristotle does not mean by *general* function what is the more proximate end, but merely the function that is shared in common across all animal species. In some species, thus, they serve as an-instrument-for-carrying-cubs.

person using his generative power in ways not ordered to the natural end of generation; furthermore, such defect is a moral defect if done intentionally.

Part Four: Further Considerations

I will now examine various questions that have been raised not against any of the premises of Aquinas's argument but against the conclusion. Clearly, however, if the premises are true and the argument is valid, then the conclusion follows even if one wishes the conclusion were false.

a) Does this make sex mechanical?

Sullivan thinks Aquinas's account is demeaning to human sexuality in reducing it to an entirely instrumental means for procreation: "A marital sexual act, engaged in for reasons of passion, love, commitment, or mutual comfort is not rendered meaningless or immoral if it doesn't happen to produce another human being at the end of it."[591]

Sullivan's objection, however, misses the distinction made earlier between the end of the worker and the end of the work. There is nothing wrong on Aquinas's account with engaging in sex for other good purposes such as love or intimacy so long as one is engaging in sexual intercourse that is naturally ordered towards the good of new human life.[592] There is nothing mechanical or boring about this. Plenty of married couples live by the truth of Aquinas's position and enjoy sex.

Further, Aquinas's argument says nothing about a human being necessarily having to be produced in every act of sexual intercourse in order for the sex to be morally good. Aquinas indicates only that every act of the sexual members must be ordered to their natural end of procreation. That sex fails in attaining its natural end due to an unintentional defect such as sterility is not morally bad, because only human actions,

---

[591] Sullivan, "Unnatural Law," p. 21.

[592] I invite my reader to consider the following passages in Aquinas: DM Q15, A1, ad 4, *Super Sent.* II, D1, Q2, A1, ST II-II, Q141, A6, ad 1, and ST I-II, Q1, A6, ad 3.

proceeding from intellect and will, count as moral actions.[593] A defect due to old age does not render the action bad because such a defect is not intended.

Sullivan is also equivocating on the term *end*. By *end* Aquinas means the goal or purpose of that towards which something (whether in nature or human agency) is directed. Sullivan, by contrast, is using *end* as the mere stopping point where something ends up. On his account, the *end* of an acorn is the lake into which it fell, which is certainly not what Aquinas meant by the term.

b) *What about infertile couples?*

John Corvino,[594] Adriano Oliva,[595] and Chris Meyers[596] have implied that Aquinas's account shows that infertile couples who have sex are acting wrongfully.[597] But Aquinas forestalls their very objection in *De*

---

[593] Cf. ST I-II, Q1, A1; Q18, A8.

[594] Corvino, *What's Wrong with Homosexuality?*, 90-93; technically Corvino's criticisms here are against the NNL view, but seemingly they would apply to Aquinas as well.

[595] Oliva, *Amours,* 102-104.

[596] Meyers, *The Moral Defense of Homosexuality,* 124-125; the context is his criticism of the NNL reply to the sterile-couple objection, but Meyers would likely raise a similar objection to Aquinas: "It is no more biologically possible for an infertile heterosexual couple to reproduce sexually than it is for a same-sex couple to reproduce sexually" (125). Meyers' objection fails to distinguish between different senses of possibility and potency. On his account a blind man cannot see anymore than a plant cannot see. But there is a significant difference between the sense in which a blind man cannot see and a plant cannot see. A blind man is the kind of organism that has the potentiality to see given his nature; a disease has robbed him of his eyesight. A plant is not the kind of organism that has the potency to see by nature; it is due to its nature and not some defect that it cannot see. Likewise, the sex of an infertile opposite-sex couple is the kind of action that has the potency to result in offspring given the kind of action that it is, namely sex; a disease or defect has just robbed the action of the ability to procreate. The buggery of an opposite-sex couple, by contrast, is the kind of action that of its nature cannot result in offspring; it is not due to some defect or disease that the action does not result in procreation. Lack of potency *per se* is not the same as a lack of potency *per accidens.*

[597] Erik Anderson has put forth the infertility objection to the NNL account, but he would likely raise a similar criticism of Aquinas: see Erik Anderson, "A Defense of the 'Sterility Objection' to the New Natural Lawyers' Argument Against Same-Sex

Malo Q15, A2, ad 14:

> An act is said to be contrary to nature in the genus of lust from which
> generation cannot follow according to the act common to the species;
> not that from which it cannot follow according to any particular acci-
> dent, as happens in old age or infirmity.[598]

Likewise, in the earlier text of SCG III, Ch. 122, n. 2951 he says something similar:

> Now I say the way from which generation cannot follow *secundum se*:
> as happens in every emission of semen outside of the natural union of
> male and female, on account of which sins of this kind are said to be
> against nature. Now if *per accidens* generation cannot follow from the
> emission of semen, it is not contrary to nature, nor a sin; as in the case

---

Marriage," *Ethical Theory and Moral Practice* 16, no. 4 (2013): 759-775. Patrick
Tully overall does a good job refuting Anderson's arguments: see Patrick Tully,
"Arbitrariness, Irrationality, and the Sterility Objection: A Reply to Anderson," *Ethical Theory and Moral Practice* 18, no. 1 (2015): 135-144. I cannot agree with Tully's examples of practicing-fishing, because practicing-fishing is not an actual case
of fishing anymore than an engaged couple practicing their marriage vows is an actual case of exchanging vows.

[598] Sancti Thomae de Aquino, *Opera Omnia Iussu Leonis XIII P.M. Edita,* Tomus
XXIII, *Quaestiones Disputatae de Malo,* 276: "dicitur actus ille esse contra naturam
in genere luxurie, ex quo non potest sequi generatio secundum communem speciem
actus; non autem ille ex quo non potest sequi propter aliquod particulare accidens,
sicut est senectus vel infirmitas." The translation is my own. For a similar discussion see G.E.M Anscombe, "You Can have Sex without Children: Christianity and
the New Offer," in *Ethics, Religion and Politics, Collected Philosophical Papers,*
vol. III (Minneapolis: University of Minnesota Press, 1981), 85: "In order to be a
intrinsically generative *sort* of act, an act need not *itself* be actually generative; any
more than an acorn needs to produce an actual oak tree in order to be an acorn. (In
fact most acorns never produce oaks, and most copulations produce no offspring.)
When we characterize something as an acorn we are looking to a wider context than
can be seen in the acorn itself. Acorns come from oaks, and oaks come from acorns;
an acorn is thus *as such generative* (of an oak), whether or not it does generate an
oak; this is still true if it is planted in infertile ground or left on a shelf so that it
cannot develop into an oak tree....And it is in this sense that copulation is intrinsically generative – though there are very many copulations which in fact do not generate."

of a woman who happens to be sterile.[599]

Aquinas is using technical terminology in his use of the term *per accidens*. By *accidental* he does not merely mean what might happen unintentionally, but the accidents of the action as opposed to those things that make up the substance of the act (and so give it its species). The accidents of an action for Aquinas are the circumstances of an action, which do not give species.[600] The substance of an action is composed of the essential parts of the action, namely, the object and the proximate end.[601] Just as with natural substances, the accidents can change with the substance remaining the same, so with actions, the accidents can change with the action remaining the same. An action of eating remains an action of eating though it happens at noon or at 5pm, with red or green food. Likewise, sex is still sex even if the circumstances surrounding the act change. Sex during the infertile period of the woman's cycle remains sex, because the infertile time is a circumstance of the action of sex.

If the substance of the action changes, then the kind of action in question must also change, and so either there is a new kind of action or no action at all. Since actions are defined by their ends, if the proximate natural end of an action changes, then the type of action in question ceases to be.[602] Take the example of heating: what makes heating to be an act of heating is its natural order to imparting heat. If this order to the

---

[599] S. Thomae Aquinatis, *Liber de Veritate Catholicae Fidei contra errores Infidelium seu Summa Contra Gentiles* (Taurini, Romae: Marietti, 1961), SCG III, 122, n.2951, p.182: "Dico autem modum ex quo generatio sequi non potest *secundum se*: sicut omnis emissio seminis sine naturali coniunctione maris et feminae; propter quod huiusmodi peccata *contra naturam* dicuntur. Si autem per accidens generatio ex emissione seminis sequi non possit, non propter hoc est contra naturam, nec peccatum: sicut si contingat mulierem sterilem esse." The translation is my own.

[600] ST I-II, Q7, A1; ST I-II, Q7, A3; cf. also *De Malo* Q2, A4, ad 5.

[601] That the object is an essential part: see *De Malo* Q2, A6, ad 2: "Ad secundum dicendum quod sicut actus in communi recipit speciem ab obiecto, ita actus moralis recipit speciem ab obiecto morali" (Leonine, p.48); ST I-II, Q18, A2. That the proximate end is an essential part: see DM Q2, A6, ad 9: "Ad nonum dicendum quod actus moralis non habet speciem a fine remoto set a fine proximo qui est obiectum" (Leonine, p.49); ST I-II, Q18, A6, co. and ad 1.

[602] For a fuller discussion of this point and what specifies actions see Jensen, "Intrinsically Evil Actions According to St. Thomas Aquinas," Chapter 2; Pilsner, *The Specification of Human Actions in St Thomas Aquinas*, 47-60.

end of heat ceases to be, then the act of heating ceases to be. Likewise, since killing is defined by an order towards death, when this order ceases there ceases to be an act of killing.

What makes sex to be an act of sexual intercourse? It cannot be merely the touching together of body parts, or the inserting of one into another; the insertion of a man's finger up his wife's nostril, for instance, is not an act of sexual intercourse. It cannot be the touching of the sexual organs to each other, as then a man who merely touched the outside of his wife's vagina with his penis would be having sex. Ends define acts, so what makes sex to be sex must be the kind of end that it is ordered towards by nature, even apart from the intentions of the agent. The end of sexual intercourse is reproduction——this is what distinguishes it from other actions.

But which actions have an order to reproduction and which do not? Playing golf, it seems, does not. Coitus between a heterosexual fertile couple that results in a child, it seems, does. But what of coitus between an infertile couple? And what of homosexual activity? These latter two cases are less clear. I will suggest that the order to an end can have four different levels. First, the order might be entirely absent, as the order to reproduction is absent from the act of playing golf. Second, the order might be present in the power (or virtually); this level will apply to the act of homosexual activity. Third, the order might be present in the act, as in the act of coitus between an infertile couple. Finally, the order might be present in the result, which is the case for the act of coitus that does result in a child.

The same fourfold division might be applied to assertions as well. In what way is the order toward conveying the truth present in an action? It is entirely absent from an act of sneezing or walking. It is present in the power (virtually) in an act of lying. It is present in the act (but not the result) in a true assertion that is misunderstood by the listener. Finally, it is present in the result in a true assertion that is correctly understood by the listener.

The levels build one upon the other. In order for an action to have an order to the end, it must first have the order in the power, and for an action to have the actual attainment of the end, it must first have an order in the action to the end. Of course, some action might accidentally produce the result, but it would not be ordered to it. Someone might yawn from sheer exhaustion, and this action might result in his companion recognizing that he is tired. The yawn, then, results in the effect of conveying the truth. Nevertheless, the yawn is not ordered to this end, for it does not have the order either in power or in action.

i) Successful actions versus failed actions

Some levels, such as the first, are clear enough, but the others need further explanation. The difference between an order being present in result (fourth level) and in action (third level) is the difference between a successful action and a failed action. Both acts remain the same kind of action, although they differ as success does from failure. As Patrick Tully says,

> Consider a pack of wolves hunting elk in Yellowstone Park. These wolves engage in a corporate effort——pack hunting——and are sometimes successful, but often not. Yet even if a particular hunt is not successful, it seems correct, if not inelegant to say that the pack engaged in an act "of a hunting kind."…Imagine that one day the pack was exposed to a toxin that left their muscles so weak and their senses so diminished that their hunts from that point on had no chance of success. In these circumstances, were the doomed wolves to engage in the same set of corporate behaviors that they engaged in when healthy, albeit in a much diminished way, would it be unreasonable to claim that they still engaged in acts "of a hunting kind"…? Surely not…. Similar examples are rather easy to imagine: fisherman fishing in a lake that, unbeknownst to him, has no fish, or a miner digging for gold in an area that has none.[603]

Hunting still remains an act of hunting even if an unsucessful act of hunting. Digging for gold remains digging for gold even if unsuccessful. Fishing remains fishing even if unsuccessful. Likewise, sexual intercourse remains an act of sexual intercourse even if it fails to attain its end of procreation. Each of these acts still retains its natural order to its

---

[603] Tully, "Arbitrariness, Irrationality, and the Sterility Objection: A Reply to Anderson," 140.

end, thereby still being an act of its kind, albeit one that fails to attain its end. The difference is merely between a successful act of its kind and a failed act of its kind.

Mere failure to attain the end can result from a variety of causes. Aquinas distinguishes mere failures into two general kinds: (a) those that fail due to a defect in the agent, and (b) those that fail due to a defect from an extrinsic impediment (i.e. due to defective matter or another outside agent):

> But that something is said to be impossible according to some power can be taken in two ways. *In one way on account of a defect of the very power from itself,* since evidently it cannot extend to that effect, as when the agent naturally cannot change some matter. *In another way on account of something extrinsic,* as when the power of anything is impeded or held bound. Thus something is said to be impossible in three ways. In one way on account of a defect of the active power, either in changing the matter, or in any other way; in another way on account of something resisting or impeding. In a third way on account of that which is said to be impossible cannot be the terminus of an action [emphasis added].[604]

The failure in the agent may be in regards to either (i) the principal or (ii) the instrumental efficient agent:

> For evidence of which it must be known that evil is caused in one way in action and in another way in its effect. *Indeed, in action, evil is caused by a defect of any of the principles of action, either the princi-*

---

[604] *De Potentia,* Q1, A3: "Impossibile vero quod dicitur secundum aliquam potentiam potest attendi dupliciter. *Uno modo propter defectum ipsius potentiae ex se ipsa,* quia videlicet ad illum effectum non potest se extendere, utpote quando non potest agens naturale transmutare aliquam materiam. *Alio modo ab extrinseco, utpote cum potentia alicuius impeditur vel ligatur.* Sic ergo aliquid dicitur impossibile fieri tribus modis. Uno modo propter defectum activae potentiae, sive in transmutando materiam, sive in quocumque alio; alio modo propter aliquod resistens vel impediens; tertio modo propter hoc quod id quod dicitur impossibile fieri, non potest esse terminus actionis" (St. Thomae Aquinatis, *De Potentia,* in *Quaestiones Disputatae,* volumen II (Taurini, Romae: Marietti, 1965), p. 14). The translation is my own. For other similar texts in Aquinas see: ST I, Q49, A1 and *De Veritate,* Q24, A7.

pal agent, or the instrument, just as a defect in the motion of an animal can happen either on account of the weakness of the motive power as in children, or on account of only an ineptitude of the instrument, as in limping [emphasis added].[605]

Regarding heating, the agent may fail to heat due to a defect in the agent (lack of power in the intensity of the heat) or in the instrument of the agent, or due to an extrinsic cause (a snowfall). Regarding hunting the agent may fail due to a defect in the wolves themselves (the agent) or their dull teeth (the instrument), or due to bad weather (an extrinsic agent cause) or the impermeable skin of the prey (a "defect" in the matter). Likewise, regarding sexual intercourse it may fail to attain its end due to a defect in the principal agent generating (a man with a weak generative power), or in the instrument (i.e. a defective semen), or due to a killer who breaks into the home during the time of coitus (an extrinsic cause) or the infertility of the woman (a defect in the matter).[606] In all three of the aforementioned cases and their corresponding defects, the actions still remain the kind of actions they are (viz. heating, hunting, or sexual intercourse), although they fail to attain their end. Since these acts retain an actual order to their respective ends, they remain the same act even when they are unsuccessful in reaching their ends.

ii) Actual order versus mere virtual order

Successful and failed acts of hunting differ fundamentally from acts of the first level. If you take away all order to the end, then the act ceases to be an act of the same kind (or it ceases to be an action at all). If you take

---

[605] ST I, Q49, A1: "Ad cuius evidentiam, sciendum est quod aliter causatur malum in actione, et aliter in effectu. *In actione quidem causatur malum propter defectum alicuius principiorum actionis, vel principalis agentis, vel instrumentalis*: sicut defectus in motu animalis potest contingere vel propter debilitatem virtutis motivae, ut in pueris; vel propter solam ineptitudinem instrumenti, ut in claudis." The translation is my own.

[606] Chemical contraception would also fall into the case of an interfering instrument; it is an extrinsic cause in the sense in which it is an extrinsic order imposed upon the natural order of sexual intercourse; such is not to deny that the same man who is the agent of the action of sex may also be the one who is the cause of this extrinsic order. A condom, by contrast, is improper matter rather than an interfering extrinsic cause.

away any order to capturing prey, then the action ceases to be an act of hunting, as happens when wolves give up the hunt and run away from a charging moose. Remove the order to procreation and the act ceases to be one of sexual intercourse; such is why urinating or walking are not acts of sexual intercourse. Urinating and walking involve no order at all to procreation. Acts of the first level then differ fundamentally from acts of the third and fourth level. Running away (first level) is fundamentally different from a failed act of hunting (third level) and even more fundamentally different from a successful act of hunting (fourth level).

To have an order in action, the person performing the action need not himself consciously desire the end. The act of the fertile couple has the order to reproduction in the action, even if the couple themselves do not want to have a child. Similarly, the act of the infertile couple has this order, even though the action may be a failure and even though the couple does not desire the end of reproduction. The action does not necessarily receive its order from the conscious desire of the agent. Sometimes it receives the order from another agent.

Suppose Werner Heisenberg has a research project and he directs Albert Einstein and Niels Bohr to solve a certain mathematical equation. The act of solving the equation is directed to the end of the research project by Heisenberg, even if Einstein and Bohr do not desire the end of the overall research project (but merely the continuation of their friendly relationship with Heisenberg). Indeed, Einstein and Bohr might believe (perhaps correctly) that Heisenberg's project is doomed to failure. Nevertheless, their act of solving the equation is ordered (by Heisenberg and not by themselves) to the end of the research project. Similarly, a couple may know that they are infertile; nevertheless, their act of coitus is ordered to the end of reproduction, even though they themselves do not consciously order it (since they believe it is impossible). The act is ordered not by the couple themselves but by another agency, namely, by the power of reproduction.

If it is the power of reproduction that provides the order, then it seems as if this action is ordered to the end in power but not in action. In order to understand how the action has the order in the act and not merely in the power, we must now turn our attention to this last distinction: what is the difference between an action having an order to an end in the power (or virtually) and having an order to an end in the action? In other words, what is the distinction between the second and third levels?

As noted above, the order in the action presupposes the order in the power. Before Einstein's action can be ordered to the end of Heisenberg's research project, Heisenberg himself must so order it. Heisenberg's order, however, is not sufficient to make Einstein's action have the order in the action. Heisenberg plays the role of the power, so his order provides the order in the power. Something more is needed for the order to be present in the action. Einstein does not have to consciously order his action to the overall end of the project as seen by Heisenberg, but he does at least have to follow Heisenberg's direction. If Einstein deliberately distorts the solution to the equation (perhaps because he believes Heisenberg's project is misguided), then his action has the order to the end in the power (which it receives from Heisenberg) but it does not have the order to the end in the action. This order requires that he do what Heisenberg directs him to do.

Similarly, an act of engaging the power of reproduction, is directed to the end of reproduction by the power. In order for this order to be present in the action, something more is needed. The person using the power of reproduction need not consciously desire the end of reproduction, but he must do what the power directs him to do.[607] A heterosexual couple that has intercourse – even an infertile couple – does what the power directs them to do if they consummate the act with the man depositing his sperm in the woman's vaginal tract. If he deposits his sperm in her anus, then he does not faithfully do that to which the power directs him. In the latter case, the action has the order to the end in the power, that is, virtually, but not in the action.

---

[607] In other words, during the act of sexual intercourse the man need not always be thinking, nor even beforehand have explicitly thought, "I am doing this for the sake of children." He may licitly engage in the act of sex with his wife for all sorts of other reasons, such as to show her his love, so long as the act remains essentially ordered to procreation.
Cf. ST I-II, Q1, A6, ad 3: "non oportet ut semper aliquis cogitet de ultimo fine, quandocumque aliquid appetit vel operatur: sed virtus primae intentionis, quae est respectu ultimi finis, manet in quolibet appetitu cuiuscumque rei, etiam si de ultimo fine actu non cogitetur. Sicut non oportet quod qui vadit per viam, in quolibet passu cogitet de fine."

For any given species of action there are thus: (1) completely unrelated actions (or lack of action), (2) errors, (3) failures, and (4) successful actions. Truthful assertions that impart truth to another successfully are cases of (4). Asserting truthfully when the listener misunderstands you is a case of (3). Asserting a lie is a case of (2). Breathing and smelling are cases of (1) in relation to asserting.

Successful actions (4) and failures (3) retain an actual order to the end. Both successful and unsuccessful acts of asserting still retain an actual order to the end of conveying the truth to another. Lies (2), by contrast, lack this actual order, because the agent deliberately orders himself against the end intended by nature. Yet lies (2) differ from level 1 insofar as lies retain a type of virtual order to the end.[608] Since every lie is an assertion, a lie is the type of act that could attain its end, or even that has this end as a goal to strive to, given that it is an assertion (but not insofar as it is a lie). Other actions (level 1), such as sleeping, lack even this virtual order to conveying the truth.

iii) Back to Aquinas's argument

Aquinas's argument concluded that "any use of the reproductive members not ordered to the generation and education of offspring is a disordered action." Aquinas does not elucidate explicitly what level of *order* he means in the *De Malo* text. He does, however, imply that the action of an opposite-sex couple is *per se* ordered to the end of procreation, even if *per accidens* it is permanently impeded from attaining its end.[609] By contrast, sexual activity between two men or two women is essentially infertile; it is *in se* (and not *per accidens*) unable to attain its end. Aquinas then is only speaking in terms of the order shared in common by levels 3 (failed actions) and 4 (successful actions of the same kind) when he implies that coitus between a man and woman (whether fertile or infertile) is *per se* ordered to procreation. His argument in the *De Malo* text then is meant to show that actions of level 2 (errors) are moral

---

[608] By virtual order I mean the order of the power itself.
[609] *De Malo,* Q15, A2, ad 14; SCG III, 122.

errors when pertaining to the intentional use of the generative power. If these implicit qualifications are made explicit, Aquinas's argument is as follows:

1. Any human action not *in se* [actually] ordered to its due end is a disordered action.[610]
2. The natural end is the due end [any natural end of an action is its due end].
3. Ergo, any human action not *in se* [actually] ordered to its natural end is a disordered action (from 1 & 2).
4. The natural end of the use of the reproductive members is the generation and education of offspring.
5. Ergo, any use of the reproductive members not ordered *in se* [actually] to the generation and education of offspring [as in the case of homosexual activity] is a disordered action (from 3 & 4).
6. Disordered human acts that involve the human good are morally disordered.
7. The use of the reproductive members involve an order to a human good (of new human life).
8. Ergo, any use of the reproductive members not ordered *in se* to the human good (of new human life) are morally disordered [as happens in homosexual activity] (from 5, 6, & 7).

Since homosexual activity is both an act of the generative power and *in se* not ordered to the end of generation, it follows based on the conclusion (5) that it is a disordered action, and disordered morally because it is a human act.[611] In the infertile sexual intercourse of opposite-sex couples there is both a use of the generative power and a use that is *in se* (though *per accidens* not) ordered to the end of generation. Aquinas's

---

[610] If a human action is disordered because it is *per accidens* not ordered to its due end, then an unsuccessful action is a morally disordered action; but such is hardly the case. An unsuccessful act of giving alms to the poor is morally good even if one gets robbed in the process.

[611] Homosexual activity is not "a generative act" or "an act of the generative kind," but rather "an act of the generative power," because it makes use of the sexual members in a sexual manner (as opposed to using the penis in a nonsexual way, as for pushing a rock).

argument condemns homosexual activity, not sexual intercourse between opposite-sex infertile couples.

iv) Does it make a difference if the couple knows they are infertile? Corvino has objected that it makes a difference whether one is ignorant of the impossibility of attaining the end.[612] A fisherman, unless he is deranged, would never fish in a lake if he knew for certain it had no fish. Likewise, if the wolf knew his prey was too strong to kill, he would not hunt (unless there is a defect in the wolf). How can humans rationally *and knowingly* engage in sex during infertile times of the woman's cycle?

The objection conflates two distinct questions: (a) does Aquinas's argument condemn sex during knowingly infertile times of the woman's cycle?; and (b) is it rational ever to engage in an action that one knows can never attain its natural end? We have already discussed (a) extensively and shown it makes no difference for Aquinas whether an opposite-sex couple engages in sexual intercourse during infertile times.

---

[612] Corvino discusses the analogy of Sherif Girgis, Robert George, and Ryan Anderson about Einstein and Bohr who can coordinate intellectually toward a real good even if they fail to attain their desired end, just as infertile couples can reproductively unite even if they cannot procreate. Corvino objects, "The problem with this explanation is that there's a big difference between a goal which 'does not' occur even though people are 'honestly seeking' it, and a goal which *cannot* occur, and which thus cannot be honestly sought by anyone aware of its impossibility. NNL theorists regularly blur this difference. The heterosexual couple who know themselves to be permanently infertile cannot seek conception in their sexual acts. They are akin to a pair of scientists who mull over a problem which they know to be insolvable. There may be value in such mulling—a flexing of the mental muscles, perhaps—but that value has nothing to do with a solution, because the solution is known to be impossible. Similarly, there may be value in the sterile heterosexual couple's coitus, but that value has nothing to do with reproduction..." (*What's Wrong with Homosexuality?*, 91). Corvino is conflating the distinction between the *finis operis* and the *finis operantis*. His objection is on the mark in that the Einstein-Bohr case is not exactly parallel to the infertile couple: indeed, it would be nonsense for Einstein and Bohr to engage in their mutual research if they knew their end was unattainable (even if *per accidens* due to permanent lack of access to libraries, etc.) and they had no further reasons for engaging in such fruitless research. Likewise, an infertile opposite-sex couple cannot intend (*finis operantis*) to conceive, but they can intend an action ordered to conception (*finis operis*), namely, sexual intercourse where the sperm is deposited in the vagina.

Question (b) requires further elaboration.

In one respect, the answer to (b) is quite easy. Few people would condemn a couple using natural family planning (NFP). In NFP the couple engages in sex even when they know procreation cannot result due to the timing of the woman's cycle. The action does not lack the order to the due end; true, it cannot attain the end, but still it is *in se* ordered to the end insofar as it retains an actual order. The couple cannot possibly be engaging in the act in order to procreate (as they know it is impossible), but they have good secondary reasons for engaging in sex, such as the strengthening of the marriage bond, expressing love, etc.

In another respect answering (b) is difficult because there are few parallel cases. It is senseless to engage in most, if not all, other bodily functions if one knows it is impossible for their natural end to be obtained. There are, however, parallel examples not involving a bodily function: under threat of death to yourself and your family, you are required to do research on time travel technology. You know that in principle time travel is impossible; but you wish to save your family. One can rationally engage in this act of research even though one knows its end, as set by the evil villain threatening you, of successfully making a time machine is impossible. Just as there are good reasons to engage in an act of time travel research that one knows cannot attain its end, so too there may be good reasons to engage in an act of sexual intercourse while knowing that its end of new human life cannot obtain. Although the end of the act itself (*finis operis*) cannot be attained, there are other good reasons qua *finis operantis* to engage in sexual intercourse. Among these other reasons are expressions of love, mutual intimacy, or the deepening of the marriage bond.

Regarding (b) there is also another parallel case: a judge gives due process of law to a black man in court, though he knows the jury is stacked with racist KKK members. The purpose of due process is justice, but the judge knows justice cannot be attained. No matter what he does he cannot save the black man, yet he must run the court and allow the corrupt jury to deliberate and pass sentence. The judge is rationally engaging in an act (due process) knowing that its due end (justice) cannot possibly be attained.[613] So too a couple practicing NFP during an infertile time is engaging in an act (sexual intercourse) knowing that its due end (procreation) cannot be attained. The judge is engaging in an act act *per se* ordered to justice (as justice is the whole reason why due process was established), even though *per accidens* he knows it cannot be attained. His act significantly differs from an act *per se* ordered to injustice. So too the NFP couple is engaging in an act *per se* ordered to procreation even though they know *per accidens* its end cannot be attained. The couple's action significantly differs from an act of homosexual activity, which *per se* cannot generate. It is possible to rationally engage in certain actions even when one knows the *finis operis* cannot be attained.[614] Though Aquinas did not know about NFP, his argument does

---

[613] I am indebted to Brandon K. White for the above example.

[614] Another possible parallel case to the NFP couple is as follows: a general has four majors under him, namely, major one, major two, major three, and major four. He orders major one to capture point one, major two to capture point two, and so on. If each major captures the point assigned to him, the general will win the battle; although if any major fails the battle will be lost. The general wants not only to win the battle but also to improve the morale of his troops. He orders each major to capture each point not just for victory, but also for improving morale.

Major one knows that major two plans to disobey, not fulfilling the command given to him. Major one knows then that victory will not follow (since victory depends upon all of the majors capturing their assigned points). Since major one knows the attainment of victory is impossible, he cannot and does not capture point one with the intent of victory. Nevertheless, he still intends to capture point one for the sake of improving the morale of his troops.

Capturing point one is not ordered to victory given the *finis operantis* of major one. Nevertheless, it is ordered to victory in this sense: capturing point one is exactly what this part of the army needs to do in order to attain victory. In short, it orders this part to victory, even if the whole army ends up not being ordered to victory on account of the defect in major two.

On the other hand, if major one chooses to attack another point, with the hope of improving the morale of the troops, then he disobeys the general. His action is not ordered to victory even in the sense described above.

By capturing point one, major one fulfills himself as a part; for he is a part of the general's army. By choosing to capture another point, major one might get some kind of fulfillment or other, but it would not be a fulfillment of a part of the army; it would cut the major off from the general and from the army.

The analogy here then with the NFP couple is as follows: the general is nature; major one is the infertile couple who knowingly and rationally acts for their end even if the end cannot be attained; capturing point one is the depositing of the sperm in

not condemn it.[615]

c) Are homosexual acts really contrary to the good of new life?

Robert George objects to the perverted faculty argument along the following lines:

> It is not clear, for example, that acting against the orientation of a biological power is necessarily wrong, nor is it clear that sodomitical and other non-marital acts are really *contrary* to that direction.[616]

George seems to be indicating that the notion of contrariety is unclear when homosexual activity is said to be contrary to generation. He is correct to point out this ambiguity. "Contrary to x" could mean: (a) directly harming x, (b) not actually ordered towards x, or (c) some other sense of contrary to x.

Sense (a) of contrary is problematic. Many evils are contrary to a good in that they directly harm the good they are contrary to: murder is contrary to innocent human life, maiming to bodily organs, and arson to personal property. Homosexual activity, however, does not directly harm the generative organs (at least not in all cases), nor does it directly harm new life, because such life does not exist yet.

---

the vagina; defeating the enemy (or victory) is reproducing; improving the morale of the troops is the realization of the secondary ends of sexual intercourse for which the infertile couple acts; the other majors are various other activities that must be accomplished for reproduction to occur between a man and a woman, viz. the non-voluntary activities of ovulation, sperm production, etc.; major two not fulfilling his role is analogous to some aspect of nature that is defective, leading to infertility. It is still rational for major one to act for the sake of capturing point one, even if he knows victory cannot be obtained. This analogy is from Steven J. Jensen; many thanks to him for this parallel case.

[615] There maybe other reasons why NFP is wrong in some cases; e.g. if used to avoid pregnancy by an unmarried man and woman, or if the couple is using it out of excessive desire for hoarding possessions instead of being generous and having children.

[616] George, *In Defense of Natural Law*, 181.

Sense (b) of contrary is also problematic. Celibacy and merely sitting around are also not actually ordered to generation. Yet Aquinas does not mean to condemn them. Is there perhaps a third sense of contrary that we are missing?

The notion of contrary need not involve direct harming of a good to be opposed to it. Contraries are opposites under the same genus.[617] Under the genus of the use of the reproductive members the opposites are generative and ungenerative uses. They are opposed as natural use to unnatural use (not according to the natural end of the reproductive members). Homosexual activity is said to be contrary to the generation of new life, not as if it directly harms new offspring or potential human beings, but in that it is opposed to the generative or natural use of the generative power. Such a notion of contrarierty is what Aquinas meant when he called homosexual acts *contra naturam*.[618] Homosexual activity is contrary to generation just as lying is contrary to asserting truly. The following chart may make this point clearer:

---

[617] Cf. Aristotle, *Categories* 6.6a15-20.

[618] Cf. *De Malo* Q15, A1, ad 7: "omnis actus luxurie preter commixtionem maris et femine dicitur esse contra naturam in quantum non est proportionatus generationi" (Sancti Thomae de Aquino, *Opera Omnia Iussu Leonis XIII, Quaestiones Disputatae de Malo*, p.272). *Commentary on Romans* 1:26-27: "Alio modo dicitur esse aliquid contra naturam hominis ratione generis, quod est animal. Manifestum est autem quod, secundum naturae intentionem, commixtio sexuum in animalibus ordinatur ad actum generationis, unde omnis commixtionis modus, ex quo generatio sequi non potest, est contra naturam hominis inquantum est animal. Et secundum hoc dicitur in Glossa 'naturalis usus est ut vir et mulier in uno concubitu coeant, contra naturam vero ut masculus masculum polluat et mulier mulierem.' Et eadem ratio est de omni actu coitus ex quo generatio sequi non potest" (S. Thomae Aquinatis, *Super Epistolas S. Pauli Lectura, Super Rom.* Cap. 1, Lectio 8, n.149, ed. P. Raphaelis Cai, O.P., VIII Revisa ed., vol. I (Taurini, Romae: Marietti, 1953), p. 28).

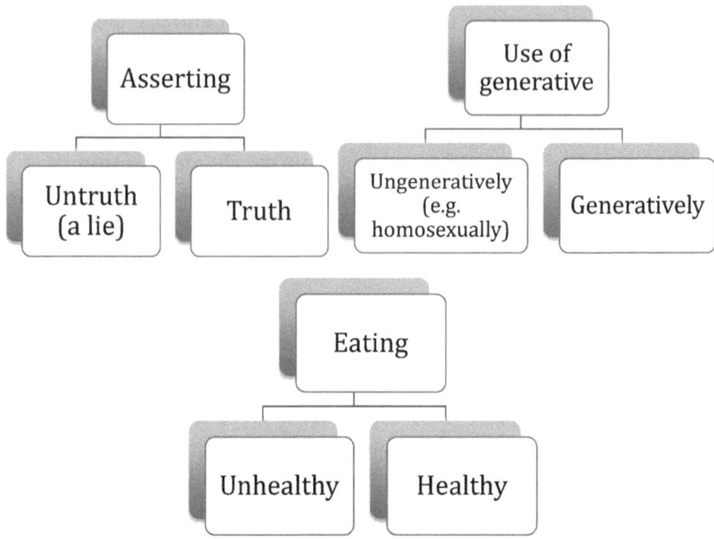

Not asserting (by silence) is opposed to truth, but it is not under the same genus of action as telling a lie. So it is not opposed to truth in the same way as a lie is. Likewise, celibacy is opposed to generation, but not in the same way as homosexual activity is. Homosexual activity and celibacy do not fall under the same genus of action. Homosexual activity is contrary to male-female sexual intercourse insofar as the ungenerative use of the sexual members is contrary to their generative use.

Perhaps, due to such confusions over the notion of contrary, in neither the SCG nor the DM argument does Aquinas use the premise "homosexual activity is contrary to nature" or "homosexual activity is contrary to the purposes of reproduction." Rather, his argument is much more nuanced, but clearer:

1. Any human action not [actually] ordered to its due end is a disordered action.
2. The natural end is the due end [any natural end of an action is its due end].
3. Ergo, any human action not [actually] ordered to its natural end is a disordered action (from 1 & 2).
4. The natural end of the use of the reproductive members is the gen-

eration and education of offspring.

5. Ergo, any use of the reproductive members not [actually] ordered to the generation and education of offspring [as in the case of homosexual activity] is a disordered action (from 3 & 4).

Since the argument in the *De Malo* of Aquinas nowhere uses the premise "homosexual activity is contrary to a biological orientation," George's worries do not affect the argument.

d) Isn't celibacy contrary to procreation?

The notion of contrariety leads into Corvino's objection: "failure to pursue a good…is not equivalent to undermining or attacking that good….As the utilitarian philosopher Jeremy Bentham sharply observed over 200 years ago, if gays should be burned at the stake for failure to procreate, then 'monks ought to be roasted alive by a slow fire.'"[619] Celibacy is opposed to the good of new life in that celibates do not engage in sex and do not act for this good, but rather explicitly renounce it. If homosexual activity is contrary to the natural end of the generative members, then celibacy would seem to be as well.

Corvino is missing the point of Aquinas's argument.[620] Not using the generative power is not the same as using the generative power for ungenerative ends. Refraining from an action involving the sexual members is distinct from engaging a power (such as the generative power) for unnatural ends. Just as not asserting is distinct from a disordered act of asserting (viz. telling a lie), so too is not having sex distinct from using the sexual members improperly. Thus, Aquinas's argument remains unaffected by the objection.

---

[619] Corvino, *What's Wrong with Homosexuality?*, 86.

[620] In all fairness to Corvino he is discussing the SCG III, 122 example of walking on the hands and Aquinas's reply. Corvino does not seem to be aware of Aquinas's later argument in the *De Malo.*

e) Only a natural disorder?

A final objection remains: Aquinas's conclusion shows only that there is a natural disorder, but not a moral disorder. An archer's arrow that misses its mark fails to attain its due end and so the action is disordered, but not morally so. Germain Grisez states the objection well:

> Another way to explain the major is by arguing that just as the end of man determines the rightness and wrongness of his action on the whole, so the end of each of his faculties determines its right and wrong use. The trouble with this argument is that it proves the wrongness of contraception only from the point of view of the sexual faculty considered in isolation. No doubt, contraception is evil for the reproductive capacity, but this faculty is not a supposit with absolute rights of its own.[621]

Likewise, any defect inherent in homosexual activity would seem to be only a natural disorder, that is, bad only for the reproductive power but not for the whole human being.

In reply to the objection, it must be said that a mechanic becomes bad qua mechanic when he intentionally botches up the car.[622] A grammarian becomes bad qua grammarian when he intentionally commits a

---

[621] Grisez, *Contraception and the Natural Law*, 28.

[622] It is true that one who intentionally errs in matters of skill is better than the one who does so involuntarily, but such is because the former already possesses the skill in question whereas the latter does not. But the one who errs intentionally is acting not out of his habit of skill; he is doing an act that tends to corrupt his skill, which would likely corrupt it if repeated enough. The baker who continually intentionally bakes bad cakes tends to become a bad baker just as one who tends to bake good cakes becomes a better baker. Cf. Aristotle, *Nicomachean Ethics* II.1 1103b: "Further, the sources and means that develop each virtue also ruin it, just as they do in a craft. For playing the harp makes both good and bad harpists, and it is analogous in the case of builders and all the rest; for building well makes good builders, and building badly makes bad ones. Otherwise no teacher would be needed, but everyone would be born a good or bad craftsman" (trans. Terence Irwin, 2nd ed. (Indianapolis/Cambridge: Hackett Publishing Company, Inc., 1999), p.19). See also Aquinas's commentary on the passage: Sancti Thomae de Aquino, *Sententia Libri Ethicorum,* Book II, lectio 1, 1103b6, n.145-159, in *Opera Omnia Iussu Leonis XIII P.M. Edita,* vol. XLVII.1 (Romae, 1969), p.78.

solecism. These are not necessarily moral evils, but evils of skill.[623] Moral evil is the evil of a human being insofar as he is human, so a human becomes morally evil when he intentionally opposes the good to which he is ordered by his human nature.[624] Since the generative power is a part of human nature, as a property flowing from the essence of the soul, any unnatural use of it is contrary to human nature, just as any unnatural use of the intellect (viz. for error) is contrary to human nature.[625] The unnatural use of any fundamental human power is a moral evil insofar as the powers are constitutive parts of human nature.[626] Consequently, Aquinas says, "any emission of the semen in such a way that generation cannot follow is *contrary to the good of man*."[627] Acting contrary to human nature makes one bad qua man, just as a dog that acts contrary to its nature is bad qua dog. In homosexual activity one becomes bad qua human being because one is using a power of human nature unnaturally. Homosexual activity is a moral disorder, not merely a natural one.[628] Since homosexual activity is voluntary as falling within one's power to will it or not, it is morally bad.

---

[623] I do not mean that these are errors proceeding from the habit of grammar, etc., but only that such acts corrupt the habit, although they do not proceed from the habit (cf. ST I-II, Q57, A3, ad 1).

[624] Cf. *Super Sent.* III, D33, Q2, A2, qc 1: "Et quia prudens dicitur bene consiliativus simpliciter, oportet quod consilietur de his quae sunt ordinata ad *bonum hominis* simpliciter. *Hoc autem consistit in animae perfectione, cujus ultima perfectio est debita operatio potentiarum animae*" (Mandonnet, p.1053; emphasis added). See also Jensen, *Knowing the Natural Law*, Chapter 5: Nature.

[625] The ability to make assertions, while not strictly a power of the soul is unique to humans (as material beings) and flows from the combined action of several powers, chiefly the intellect.

[626] Engaging the nutritive power for an end contrary to bodily health is thus morally evil.

[627] SCG III, Ch. 122, n. 5: "Ex quo patet *contra bonum hominis* est omnis emissio seminis talis modo quod generatio sequi non potest" (Leonine, vol. 14, p. 378; emphasis added). The translation is my own.

[628] For more on the distinction between moral disorders and other disorders see ST I-II, Q21, A1-A2.

Part Five: Alternate Versions of the Perverted Faculty Argument

There is no single perverted faculty argument, but multiple perverted faculty arguments. Aquinas's version has been confused with other more contemporary versions. Many of these other arguments (as understood by their authors) either fail or the authors' replies to various objections have been inadequate; in this section I will address both why they are not Aquinas's argument and why they fail.

J. Budziszewski and Timothy Hsiao argue as follows:

1. Using a bodily organ contrary to its purpose is immoral.
2. In homosexual activity one is using the reproductive organs contrary to their purpose.
3. Ergo, homosexual activity is immoral.[629]

This argument is not precisely the same as that of Aquinas. Aquinas has the premise "every human action that is not ordered to its due end is a disordered action."[630] He does not have the premise "using any organ contrary to its purpose is immoral." Further if organs are instruments, then it is not possible to use an organ contrary to its purpose. Instruments are defined by their use; whatever you use an instrument for is its purpose.

Second, Aquinas does not share the second premise with Budziszewski or Hsiao (BH). Their second premise is "in homosexual activity one is using the reproductive organs *contrary* to their purpose," but Aquinas's second premise is "the due end of the use of the genital

---

[629] Cf. J. Budziszewski, "What the Point Isn't, A Response to Marvin M. Ellison": 16-17. In this article it may not be clear that Budziszewski holds the major premise I have attributed to him, but in a personal email correspondence Budziszewski has indicated he does hold to this premise: violating the teleology of an organ is immoral (email message to author, May 17, 2013). Hsiao, "A Defense of the Perverted Faculty Argument against Homosexual Sex": 754: "We may thus state the argument as follows: It is always immoral to misuse a bodily faculty, for in doing so we reject the human good."

[630] DM Q15, A1: "Omnis actus humanus dicitur esse inordinatus qui non est proportionatus debito fini."

members is the generation and education of offspring." Further, Aquinas's argument doesn't rely upon some unclear notion of *contrary*.

Third, Aquinas's major premise is self-evident or *per se nota:* any human action not ordered to its due end is a disordered action. The argument of BH, by contrast, has a major premise that is far from *per se nota*: "using any organ contrary to its purpose is immoral."

These differences between Aquinas's argument and that of Budziszewski and Hsiao are significant insofar as Budziszewski and Hsiao's argument cannot handle certain objections, whereas Aquinas's can.

For the sake of argument let us grant that it is possible to use an organ contrary to its purpose. In that case, BH's major premise seems to condemn using the teeth to hold a flashlight. The purpose of the teeth is to chew food, not to hold a flashlight.[631]

Hsiao replies to various counterexamples by claiming that using an organ contrary to its purpose is not the same as preventing a natural function from being engaged.[632] There is nothing wrong with using the tongue to lick an envelope, because in so licking one is still tasting. As Hsiao says, "It is not inherently wrong to enhance or impose another purpose of our own on top of a faculty's natural function, so long as it is consistent with its function being achieved."[633]

Hsiao's reply, however, doesn't stand if he holds the teeth have the sole purpose of chewing. A better option would be to argue that powers can be used contrary to their purpose, but organs (as mere physical parts of the body) cannot be understood or made intelligible apart from the powers that actualize them. The first premise of BH's argument is unintelligible insofar as organs (as abstracted from any underlying power that is engaged) are mere instruments.

Feser gives a different, although similar argument to Hsiao's:

---

[631] On their account, as BH do not appeal to the distinctions I make about "the use of the teeth."

[632] Hsiao, "A Defense of the Perverted Faculty Argument against Homosexual Sex," 756.

[633] Ibid.

1. "Where some faculty *F* is natural to a rational agent *A* and by nature exists for the sake of some end *E* (and exists precisely *so that* A might pursue *E*), then it is metaphysically impossible for it to be good for *A* to use *F* in a manner contrary to *E*.[634]
2. But our sexual faculties exist by nature for the sake of procreative and unitive ends, and exist in us precisely so that we might pursue these ends.
3. So it is metaphysically impossible for it to be good for us to use those faculties in a manner contrary to their procreative and unitive ends.
4. But…homosexual acts, and acts of bestiality involve the use of our sexual faculties in a manner that is contrary to their procreative and/or unitive ends.
5. So it is metaphysically impossible for it to be good for us to engage in…homosexual acts, or acts of bestiality."[635]

Feser's argument holds provided that *contrary* is understood in the sense in which we have earlier explained in this chapter, and provided that by *faculty* Feser doesn't mean a mere physical organ abstracted from an understanding of the power being engaged when the organ is put to use.

Feser, however, doesn't seem to appeal to the sense of *contrary* I have elucidated, nor does he elucidate much on the notion of organs versus faculties or powers. Instead he distinguishes between using an organ contrary to its purpose and using an organ for something other than its purpose. In chewing gum, Feser claims one is not acting contrary to the natural end of our digestive faculties, but using them for something *other than* their natural end.[636]

The problem with this distinction is that it fails to show that the counterexamples in question are morally okay and that same-sex sexual

---

[634] In an earlier work Feser phrased this key premise differently: "Natural law theory does not condemn using a natural capacity or organ *other than* for its natural function, but only using it in a manner *contrary* to its natural function, frustrating its natural end" (Feser, *The Last Superstition: A Refutation of the New Atheism*, 148).

[635] "In Defense of the Perverted Faculty Argument," in *Neo-Scholastic Essays*, 403-404.

[636] Feser, "In Defense of the Perverted Faculty Argument," 406.

activity is also morally wrong. According to Feser's distinction—between *contrary use* and *other than use*—in using the teeth to hold a flashlight one is not using the teeth contrary to their purpose but for something other than their purpose. But the same could easily be said about an act of homosexual activity. One is not using the reproductive organs contrary to their purpose in an act of homosexual activity but for something other than their purpose. The use of the reproductive organs in homosexual activity is no more contrary to their purpose than is the use of the teeth in holding a flashlight opposed to their use in chewing.[637]

Furthermore, Feser's distinction between *contrary use* and *other than use* is ad hoc. He seems to have no principled basis for distinguishing between when a use is *other than* or *contrary to.* Is using the toes to wiggle using them for something other than their purpose or contrary to their purpose? If the former, then why is a couple that uses contraception not merely using their sexual organs for something other than their purpose of procreation? The couple is not necessarily damaging their sexual organs. Likewise, in homosexual activity two males are not attacking the good of procreation; they are just unable to pursue that good. On Feser's account, there seems to be no principled basis for saying homosexual activity is a contrary use, while wiggling the toes is not a contrary use.

Perhaps Feser could provide a more robust account of the meaning of *contrary*, or of the connection between organs and powers, but he does not. Feser relies upon an unclear account of *contrary use* and *other than use*, which is either ad hoc or cannot grant him the conclusion he desires. If Feser's argument is read, however, according to the sense of contrary we have given and according to a more robust account of powers and organs, then his argument is sound, but its first premise is less clearly true than Aquinas's. Aquinas's first premise is self-evident, that is, true in virtue of the meaning of the terms. Feser's is not. On Feser's argument there is a natural use, a contrary use, and *an other than use* for the sexual faculties. So too for the teeth there should be a natural use, a contrary use, and *an other than use*. Perhaps, this *other*

---

[637] Provided that the sexual members are not damaged in such use, which is at least possible in some if not many cases (e.g. intercrural sexual activity between two men).

than use is merely something like engaging a different power for the same physical member, as when the penis is used to urinate a different power is being engaged than when it is being used for generation. The natural use of the teeth then would be for chewing food, and their other than use would be when we use them to push a pen across a table. But what would their contrary use be? It seems no such contrary use exists in the case of the teeth, except perhaps a use contrary to the good of the animal possessing them. The three-part distinction then between natural, contrary, and *other than use* isn't necessary. *Other than use* is a tertium quid that ought to be discarded; Aquinas's argument needs only the distinction between *natural use* and *unnatural use*. The *natural use* is rooted in the power; insofar as organs are instruments of a power, their natural end changes according to the power that uses them. Any *other than use* that isn't a contrary use is really a natural use if a power is being engaged for its natural end. It is important not to multiply distinctions beyond necessity.

The perverted faculty argument stands against homosexual activity, but only if properly interpreted in light of the thought of Thomas Aquinas.

Conclusion

Despite the great number of objections raised by John Corvino, John McNeill, Chris Meyers, Gareth Moore, Burton Leiser, Andrew Sullivan, Germain Grisez, and Paul Weithmam, Aquinas's argument still stands:

1. Any human action not per se ordered to its due end is a disordered action.
2. The natural end is the due end [the natural end of an action is its due end].
3. Ergo, any human action not per se ordered to its natural end is a disordered action (from 1 & 2).
4. The natural end of the use of the reproductive members is the generation and education of offspring.
5. Ergo, any use of the reproductive members not per se ordered to the generation and education of offspring [as in the case of same-

sex sexual activity] is a disordered action (from 3 & 4).

6. Disordered human acts that involve the human good are morally disordered.
7. The use of the reproductive members involve an order to a human good (of new human life).
8. Ergo, any use of the reproductive members not per se ordered to the human good (of new human life) are morally disordered [as happens in homosexual activity] (from 5, 6, & 7).

Many homosexuals struggle with their inclinations, which many have developed through no fault of their own. Insofar as these desires are unintentional and occur prior to any act of the will, moral responsibility is mitigated.[638] Homosexuals are persons with souls who deserve our love and respect. Hatred or disparaging language against them is morally wrong. But it is not love to call what is bad good or what is good bad. Persons with homosexual desires are meant for more than merely homosexual acts; such desires and acts do not define them as persons. They are meant to give of themselves in a unique way to society through their sacrifice, to witness that true happiness is found in pursuing what is truly good. Encouraging them to pursue homosexual activity fails to love them adequately, because it encourages them to pursue what is truly bad.

---

[638] Cf. ST I-II, Q24, A3, ad 1.

Chapter V: But Always Wrong?

Even if it is granted that lying, homosexual activity, and bestiality are bad actions, does it follow that they are bad in all circumstances? It is bad to fail to return a borrowed item, but there are exceptions to the rule as when the person has gone insane or has turned against his country. Lying and homosexual acts, however, are always bad actions, or so says Aquinas.[639] There are no exceptions to the rule, even when human lives

---

[639] Cf. ST II-II, Q110, A3, especially obj. 4 and ad 4. Aquinas repeats eight times that "omne mendacium est peccatum" –see: *Super Sent.* III, D38, Q1, pr.; A3, s.c. 1; s.c. 2; A3, s.c. 3; A3, *responsio*; Q1, A4, s.c. 2; ST II-II, Q70, A4, *responsio;* II-II, Q110, A3, *responsio.* He says "omne mendacium peccatum est" in two places: *Super Sent.* III, D38, Q1, A3, s.c. 2; ST II-II, Q124, A5, ad 2. In other places he says things like "mendacium omne sit peccatum" (*Super Sent.* III, D38, Q1, pr.) "omne mendacium sit peccatum" (*Super Sent.* IV, D21, Q2, A3, *s.c.* 1; ST II-II, Q111, A1, *responsio*), "mendacium semper est peccatum" (*Quodlibet* VIII, Q6, A4, *responsio*), "mendacium nullum sine peccato est" (*Super de Trinitate II,* Q3, A3, co. 1). In *De Malo* Q15, A1, obj. 5 and ad 5 Thomas opposes a commentator's view that one may commit adultery in order to kill a tyrant. In condemning the commentator's point Thomas says, "On behalf of no utility ought one commit adultery *just as neither ought one tell a lie on account of any usefulness,* as Augustine says in the book *Against Lying*" (emphasis added; Ad quintum dicendum quod ille Commentator in hoc non est sustinendus : pro nulla enim utilitate debet aliquis adulterium committere sicut nec mendacium dicere debet aliquis propter utilitatem aliquam, ut Augustinus dicit in libro Contra mendacium [Sancti Thomae de Aquino, *Quaestiones Disputatae de Malo,* in *Opera Omnia Iussu Leonis XIII P.M. Edita,* vol. XXIII [Roma. Commissio Leonina, 1982], p. 271]). If Aquinas ever indeed held that a lie was justified in some cases, he had plenty of opportunities to say so, but he never did. In multiple contexts where the objection is raised that lying is not a flawed action or that not every lie is a flawed action (e.g. *Super Sent.* III, D38, Q1, A3, obj. 1, obj. 2, obj. 3, obj. 4, obj. 6, obj. 7; ST II-II, Q110, A3, obj. 1 obj. 2, obj. 3, obj. 6; *Quodlibet* VIII, Q6, A4, obj. 2) Aquinas never backs down on his statement that every lie is a sin. If Aquinas really had held that the officious lie is not a lie in some cases, then he would have said so. On the contrary, he says explicitly that the officious lie is a flawed action in all cases: "nullum mendacium officiosum sum est sine peccato" (*Super Psalmo 5,* n. 3). He says also in *Super Sent.* III, D38, Q1, A4, s.c. 3 that "Ergo mendacium officiosum est peccatum veniale" and in response to obj. 4 about officious lies in II-II, Q110, A3, he allows for no exceptions: "Et ideo non est licitum mendacium dicere ad hoc quod aliquis alium a quocumque periculo liberet." See also ST II-II, Q69, A1-2. According to Aquinas lying is always wrong and

ought never to be done in any circumstances. Aquinas clearly holds that homosexual is always wrong in his *Commentary on Isaiah* Ch. 4, lecture 1: "That which in no way can stand with the aforementioned end is in every way unnatural, and *never can be good*, such as the vice of sodomy." The Latin context is as follows: "Sed ex hoc videtur quod sit licitum habere plures uxores, quia Dominus numquam consolatur per illicitum. Preterea, omne peccatum est innaturale ; sed habere unum virum plures uxores est naturale, quia unus potest fecundare plures. — Ad quod dicendum, quod, sicut dicit Philosophus, coniunctio maris et femine in hominibus non est tantum propter generationem, sicut in brutis, sed etiam ad commodum vite : unde et maris et femine sunt diverse operationes, in quibus auxiliantur sibi invicem. Secundum ergo quod aliquid diversimode ordinatur ad hos fines, secundum hoc diversimode dicitur naturale vel innaturale. *Id enim quod nullo modo potest stare cum fine dicto est omnino innaturale et numquam potest esse bonum, sicut vitium sodomiticum,* et sicut hoc quod una mulier habeat plures viros, quia una non fecundatur a pluribus et, quantum ad vitam civilem, quia una non regitur a pluribus, sed e converso. Aliquid autem potest se habere ad dictum finem indifferenter quantum in se est ; et hoc potest determinari diversis temporibus diversimode, secundum diversos casus, per legislatorem : et erit iustum positivum, sicut de gradibus consanguinitatis. Aliquid autem est per quod aliquis potest consequi finem, tamen est impeditivum finis ut in pluribus : et hoc quantum est de se innaturale, sed potest esse licitum secundum dispensationem legislatoris attendentis speciales casus. Et huiusmodi est quod unus habeat plures : potest enim unus plures regere secundum vitam civilem, et unus plures fecundare ; sed tamen aliquod impedimentum prestat generationi, cum oporteat semen viri esse digestum, et hoc non potest fieri in frequenter coeuntibus, propter quod frequenter tales steriles sunt. Et adhuc magis impedit communem vitam, quia perfecta amicitia qualis est inter virum et uxorem, propter quam etiam homo patrem et matrem derelinquit, Genes. II, non potest esse ad multas" (emphasis added; Sancti Thomae de Aquino, *Expositio Super Isaiam ad Litteram*, in *Opera Omnia Iussu Leonis XIII P.M. Edita,* vol. XXVIII (Roma, 1974), Ch. IV, lecture 1.28-68, p. 33). The translation is my own. Also, in ST II-II, Q154, A12, ad 1, he clearly holds that same-sex sexual activity is intrinsically evil: "In sins contrary to nature, whereby the very order of nature is violated, an injury is done to God, the Author of nature. Hence Augustine says (Confess. iii, 8): 'Those foul offenses that are against nature should be *everywhere and at all times detested and punished, such as were those of the people of Sodom,* which should all nations commit, they should all stand guilty of the same crime'" (emphasis added; "Et ideo in peccatis contra naturam, in quibus ipse ordo naturae violatur, fit iniuria ipsi Deo, Ordinatori naturae. Unde Augustinus dicit, III *Confess. : Flagitia quae sunt contra naturam, ubique ac semper detestanda atqua punienda sunt, qualia Sodomitarum fuerunt: quae si omnes gentes facerent, eodem criminis reatu.*" The English translation is from *The Summa Theologica of St. Thomas Aquinas,* trans. The Fathers of the English Dominican Province (1920), http://www.newadvent.org/summa/3154.htm#article11). Further, in DM Q15, A1 Aquinas refers to homosexual activity as *secundum se inordinatus,* which is practi-

might perish. But why? What is Aquinas's justification? Aquinas does not explicitly say; nevertheless, we can gather what he would say from various texts. In this chapter, I will first explain Aquinas's implicit account as to why lying and homosexual activity are always wrong; I will then reply to various objections against Aquinas's position.

Part One: A Positive Account

Let us begin with the distinction between the order to an intrinsic good and the mere production of an intrinsic good.[640] An intrinsic good may happen to be produced in all sorts of ways, apart from any per se order to that good. A judge may flout the law and condemn an innocent man to death, yet justice ends up being served because the man is actually guilty of the crime, although all the evidence indicated he was innocent. Justice, in its mere production was served, but the order to justice was not. Similarly, a tyrant may merely produce more offspring by raping another man's wife; in doing so he has produced the good end of new human life, but he has not properly ordered himself to it.

In matters of skill, the mere production of the end is more important than the order to the end. Whether a clogged sink is emptied by Drano, by a snake, or by physically removing the piping matters little, except insofar as the end is attained or most efficiently attained. The mere production of the end trumps the order to the end. With the virtues, such as prudence, justice, fortitude, temperance, and truthfulness, however, the inverse is the case: the order to the end is more important than its mere production. As Aquinas says in *De Malo* Q2, A1, co.: "From which it is clear that it more pertains to the notion of flawed-action to disregard the rule of action than even to fail to attain the end of the action."[641] Mere production of the end is strictly speaking not as important as the proper order to the end.

---

cally the same language he uses to describe lying as always wrong in ST II-II, Q110, A3, ad 4 (*mendacium...ex sua inordinatione*).

[640] By *intrinsic good* I mean a *bonum honestum* as opposed to a *bonum mere utile.*

[641] Sancti Thomae de Aquino, *Quaestiones Disputatae de Malo,* in *Opera Omnia Iussu Leonis XIII P.M. Edita,* vol. XXIII (Roma: Commissio Leonina, 1982), p. 29: "Ex quo patet quod magis est de ratione peccati preterire regulam actionis quam

That the judge's action happens to result in justice makes neither him nor his action to be just. For a community of agents to order themselves to a shared end of justice, what matters is not merely that justice happens to result but that each member of the community orders himself towards justice and not away from it. Ordering oneself away from justice makes one less just and corrupts the corresponding habit in question or impedes its development. Unlike the case of the unclogged sink, the very order our actions take in matters of justice are more crucial than the mere production of a just result. The ordering of oneself towards justice is intrinsic to the very possession of or exercise of justice. He who does not so order himself does not possess the habit in question or is not participating in a true act of justice. In the case of the clogged sink, by contrast, there is no such essential link between its mere unclogging and the order to its unclogging. The unclogging of a sink need not be intended; it can happen by accident as when a man pours Drano down the sink thinking it is concrete. But the very exercise of the habit of justice cannot happen by accident; by definition it must be intended. The order to the end is intrinsic to its production and so more important than its mere production alone when it comes to the virtues.

When figuring out how to clear the drain we begin with the end in mind and then reason to a means apt for clearing it. On account of our knowledge we can make more or less accurate predictions about what will or will not clear the drain. In other matters, however, such as those involving human agents, we often divide up the work and figure out only what must be done for us to complete our part. A teacher, for instance, considers what is apt to lead students to learn. He realizes that in order to bring his students to learn, he must do his part in preparing his lesson plan and orally presenting the material. A student may be obstinate and unwilling to learn or to listen, but the teacher is still required to do his part. At this point, note that the teacher is ordered to the student's learning, even if the student fails to do his part. Likewise, note that the judge is ordered to justice even if others fail to do their part. As Aquinas says,

---

etiam deficere ab actionis fine. Hoc est ergo per se de ratione peccati, sive in natura sive in arte sive in moribus, quod opponitur regule actionis."

if in the stomach is put something indigestible such as iron or a stone, a defect of digestion occurs without an error of nature; similarly, *if the doctor according to his art makes a concoction and the sick person is not healed,* either because he has an incurable disease or because the sick person acts against his health, *the doctor still does not err although the end was not attained.*[642]

The importance of doing our part and thereby ordering ourselves to the good, even if not produced, can be recognized in friendship. Among true friends, the relationship is more important than any external material goods that may enhance it. Certainly the gift of a new book is a certain physical good, but the act of giving and receiving the book is greater. A true friend, in valuing the good of the other above any mere material goods, values the friendship and the act of giving more than the mere book. A friend is attached to the good of another. Similarly, a judge is attached to the good of society and a teacher to the good of his students. Just as the attachment of friendship is realized through the order of one friend's actions to the other, so too the attachment of a judge to justice is realized through just actions, and the attachment of a teacher to his students is realized through his order to them. The attachment is realized through the order of actions, not through the mere result of the actions. The order itself is more important than the mere result. Thus, a teacher who properly orders himself to teaching but fails due to the obstinacy of his students is morally better than a teacher who happens to be successful in teaching even though he orders himself poorly in teaching.

All of these cases involve a part whole relationship in which the individual attaches himself to the whole through his actions; the individual orders himself to the good of the whole by doing his part. The proper order is more important than the mere end result because the order itself is more constitutive of the good of the whole.

---

[642] *De Malo,* Q2, A1, co.: "In natura quidem sicut si in stomacho ponatur aliquid non digestibile ut ferrum vel lapis, defectus digestionis absque peccato nature contingit; similiter si medicus secundum artem det potionem et infirmus non sanetur, vel quia habet morbum incurabilem vel quia aliquid contra suam sanationem agit, medicus quidem non peccat licet finem non consequatur" (Sancti Thomae de Aquino, *Quaestiones Disputatae de Malo*, p. 29).

In the case of the human good, then, the order itself is more constitutive of the good of the whole than the mere production of individual goods. The good of the whole, that is, the good for human society, is a good of nature. Unlike red pandas, platypuses, and leopards, which spend most of their lives alone[643], human beings are by nature social animals. In order for society to be realized, however, we must co-order ourselves to a common or shared good. Among these shared goods is the good of reproduction. We all desire, or ought to desire, the continuation of our race. As mortal beings, we are limited in time, and know that by ourselves we cannot attain the human good unto perpetuity. We must will that others take our place and, if necessary, reproduce in order that the species may continue to be. We must do our part in properly ordering ourselves to the good of the species. We need not at every moment, nor in every action, order ourselves to the good of the species, but we must never order ourselves against it.

Since the good of the species is a type of shared or common good, it involves a part-whole relationship. The parts ought to be ordered to the good of the whole. As a part of society, and as participating in human nature, we ought to do our part to order ourselves to the whole of society. Just as a teacher must do his part in presenting the material to his students, so we must do our part in ordering ourselves to the good of the species.

In a part-whole relationship we do our part of ordering ourselves to the good of the whole by following the direction provided by the whole. Just as we reason back to Drano to clear the plug, so we start with the whole and reason back to the role the parts must play. Given the goal, for example, of safe driving we must drive on the right side of the street in the United States. Given justice as a good we need the role of the judge. Similarly, when the whole is the natural whole of the species, nature designates roles as fitting for the end. Just as the public authority

---

[643] "Red Panda," National Geographic, accessed September 26, 2017, http://www.nationalgeographic.com/animals/mammals/r/red-panda/; "Platypus Videos, News and Facts," BBC Nature, accessed November 17, 2017, http://www.bbc.co.uk/nature/life/Platypus; "Leopard," National Geographic, accessed September 26, 2017, http://www.nationalgeographic.com/animals/mammals/l/leopard/.

representing the whole of society designates that the individual must drive on the right side of the road, or that those convicted on public evidence must be condemned, so too nature plays the role of an authority in directing the parts to their end. Given the end of the continuation of the species, nature designates the role of the sexes in copulating between male and female. This good of the continuation of the species then involves the good of reproduction, which involves the voluntary act of sexual intercourse. In particular, a male individual shares in the good of the species by doing his part in depositing his semen into the vaginal tract of a woman. By contrast, a male who deposits his semen onto another man's groin is not doing his part, and orders himself away from the end of nature. By opposing the natural end of the generative power, the individual cuts himself off from the good he shares with others in nature. In short, he no longer participates in the shared good, even if he performs the homosexual act in company with others. Thieves may participate in the same crime and so be in company with one another, but they nevertheless cut themselves off from the shared good of justice by the very act of thieving. Two men engaging in sexual acts upon each other perform the act together, but nevertheless cut themselves off from the shared good of the continuation of the species by their very act of homosexual activity.

A man may deposit his semen into his wife's vagina, but what happens beyond that point is largely beyond his control (it is not his part to play). Nevertheless, the individual must play his part and never turn away from the good of the whole. To turn away from his part is to reject the good of nature as shared. It is not mere biological functioning, then, that is at stake. Rather, it is a union of human beings in nature. It is a union towards the true human good.

Often in human affairs, when some whole directs the movements of the parts, it does so with a little leeway, allowing the individual to determine the order for himself in emergency situations. For the goal of safe driving, for instance, the whole of society (or its delegate) has determined that the part must play the role of driving on the right side of the street (in the United States and most of the world). In general, then, if we wish to maintain our order to the good of safe driving, we must drive on the right side of the street. We recognize, however, that the law allows for exceptions in emergency situations.

This leeway is excluded from the order that nature gives. Nature does not allow the individual to judge for himself that a little bit of homosexual activity might be a good thing in an emergency situation. Nature directs according to types (such as male and female) and does not allow for exceptions. As Aquinas says in *De Malo* Q15, A2:

[Objection 12:] The sexual union of a man and a woman is ordained for the begetting and rearing of offspring. But fornication can sometimes fittingly result in begetting and rearing offspring. Therefore, not every fornication is a gravely flawed-action.

[Reply to objection 12:] The reproductive act is ordained for the good of the species, which is the common good. And law can ordain the common good, but private good is subject to the ordination of each person....And law considers what is wont to happen generally, not what can happen in a particular case. And so although the aim of nature regarding the begetting and rearing of offspring can be provided for in particular cases of fornication, the acts as such are still disordered and gravely flawed-acts.[644]

---

[644] "Preterea. Commixtio maris et femine ordinata est ad actum generationis et educationis prolis. Set quandoque ex fornicario concubitu potest sequi convenienter generatio et educatio prolis. Ergo non omnis fornicarius concubitus est peccatum mortale."
"Ad duodecimem dicendum quod actus generationis ordinatur ad bonum speciei, quod est bonum commune ; bonum autem commune est ordinabile lege set bonum privatum subiacet ordinationi uniuscuiusque : et ideo quamvis in actu nutritive virtutis qui ordinatur ad conservationem individui unusquisque possit sibi determinare cibum convenientem sibi, tamen determinare qualis debeat esse generationis actus non pertinent ad unumquemque set ad legislatorem cuius est ordinare de procreatione filiorum, ut etiam Philosophus dicit in II Politicorum. Lex autem non considerat quid in aliquo casu accidere possit set quid communiter esse consueuit ; et ideo licet in aliquo casu possit saluari intentio nature in actu fornicario quantum ad generationem prolis et educationem, nichilominus actus est secundum se inordinatus et peccatum mortale" (*Quaestiones Disputatae de Malo*, p. 273, 276). Translation, with minor emendation, is from Thomas Aquinas, *On Evil*, trans. Richard Regan (New York: Oxford Univesity Press, 2003), p. 425, 428-429.

The law of nature determines that the sexual union of male and female in a permanent commitment of marriage is the only way in which the individual may order himself to the generation and education of offspring. Similarly, nature determines that the only way in which generation may be attained is by the sexual union of male and female. The union of two males or two females will not suffice. A same-sex couple cannot, in homosexual activity, order themselves towards the shared good of generation. Instead, in willing homosexual activity, they order their generative parts to ungenerative ends. In willing an ungenerative end their action is opposed to the good of generation, that is, the good of the species. That their action does not physically hurt any existing or future member of the species is beside the point. The mere disorder in their action is what counts. The order against the end of nature is worse than any mere production that happens to result in its benefit. If an act of sexual activity between two men were to save five lives, it would still be bad, for it would cut the part away from its order to the whole. Indeed, this action would be worse than an act of sexual intercourse between a man and woman that accidentally results in death.

Nature dictates that the end of the generative power is for generation. Under no circumstances whatsoever can this end be changed. By contrast, what counts as justice can change depending upon whether you are dealing with a madman, a traitor, or a good neighbor.

Similarly, nature dictates that assertions have truth as their natural end. Under no circumstances whatsoever can this be changed.[645] To order oneself against the truth by lying is to turn against the shared good of truth. Liars are untruthful. In their very act of lying, they undermine the order of assertions to truth. Whether their act happens to result in much good, such as the saving of lives, is beside the point. The mere disorder in their action is what counts. The order against the end of nature is worse than any mere production that happens to result in its benefit. That

---

[645] It is true that what counts as an assertion is largely designated by human convention, but that doesn't mitigate the point that assertions have an order towards truth that isn't dictated by mere convention, but by nature. In other words, what the societal-contextual clues are that can change a sentence into an assertion are dictated by convention, but given that one is performing an assertion its end is dictated by nature.

five lives are saved by one lie is worse than a truthful assertion that accidentally results in death.

A further argument

To order oneself against the shared good, the end of nature, then is worse than any mere negative result. The shared good of man contains truth as well as the good of the species. Nature has dictated that certain acts or powers are the only means whereby one may per se order oneself to these shared goods. Using these means contrary to their purpose, whether by using assertions untruthfully or the generative power ungeneratively, is to oppose the shared good, the good of nature, and thus the good of man. As Aquinas says,

> Any privation of the good of anything constitutes the notion of evil, but flawed-action properly consists in an act which is done on account of some end not having due order to that end. Now the due order to the end is measured by some rule. *Indeed the rule in those which act according to nature is the natural power, which inclines to such an end. Therefore, when an act proceeds from a natural power, according to a natural inclination, into the end, then the rectitude of the act is preserved*, since the mean does not go beyond the extremes, namely, the act from the order of the active principle unto the end. *Now when any act recedes from such rectitude, then it becomes a flawed-action.*[646]

While this argument will suffice for our purposes, an even stronger argument may be had. In creating man, God gave him the generative power. In giving him the generative power he also gave him the natural end

---

[646] ST I-II, Q21, A1 (emphasis added to the translation): "Quaelibet enim privatio boni in quocumque constituit rationem mali: sed peccatum proprie consistit in actu qui agitur propter finem aliquem, cum non habet debitum ordinem ad finem illum. Debitus autem ordo ad finem secundum aliquam regulam mensuratur. Quae quidem regula in his quae secundum naturam agunt, est ipsa virtus naturae, quae inclinat in talem finem. Quando ergo actus procedit a virtute naturali secundum naturalem inclinationem in finem, tunc servatur rectitudo in actu: quia medium non exit ab extremis, scilicet actus ab ordine activi principii ad finem. Quando autem a rectitudine tali actus aliquis recedit, tunc incidit ratio peccati."

of the generative power, namely, the generation of human offspring. To create a generative power that is not meant for generation is an impossibility, a contradiction in terms. No more could God make a generative power that has no order to generate than could he make a square circle. Some men are sterile and cannot generate, but this inability is due to defect. Given the proper physical conditions and human development each individual human being could generate new human life. Except in mythology, clay doesn't generate new human life. Only the generative power of man does.

Since God created natures and natures are defined by their ends, anyone who acts contrary to nature is acting contrary to God:

> Just as the order of right reason is from man, so too the order of nature is from God himself. And therefore in sins contrary to nature, in which the very order of nature is violated, an injury is done to God himself, the Ordainer of nature.[647]

To act contrary to nature and the natural ends of things is to act against God. God, as the author of nature, wills that natural things act for their natural ends. To act against the natural end of the generative power is to act contrary to God.

A similar account applies to lying. Assertions are given their nature not by the human race, but by God. We have determined by convention that certain uses of words qualify as assertions, but we do not determine the nature of assertions as such. The first man did not magically decide, nor could he have decided, that assertions would have the natural *telos* of truth; rather, the first man in engaging in assertive acts presupposed the natural end of asserting as truth. This presupposition of the natural end of assertion indicates that it was not his prerogative, nor any man's prerogative, to determine what makes an assertion to be an assertion.[648] Certainly a man can choose whether to engage in an assertive

---

[647] ST II-II, Q154, A12, ad 1: "Ad primum ergo dicendum quod, sicut ordo rationis rectae est ab homine, ita ordo naturae est ab ipso Deo. Et ideo in peccatis contra naturam, in quibus ipse ordo naturae violatur, fit iniuria ipsi Deo, Ordinatori naturae."

[648] An individual human being may determine whether an individual assertion is ordered to truth insofar as it is up to him whether he decides to speak truly or tell a

act, or choose to abuse an assertive act by lying, but no man can change the end of assertions anymore than he can make language to be a rock. In creating the universe, and in creating assertions, God gave them their nature and in giving them their nature he gave them their end of conveying the truth to another.

Thus, to act against the natural end of asserting is either to act contrary to or beside the order established by God.[649] Every lie is, in a sense, contrary to God, just as every sin is. Since acting contrary to God is always and everywhere wrong, lying and same-sex sexual activity are always wrong.

Part Two: A Negative Account – The Strongest Objections Fail

Numeous objections can still be raised against Aquinas's position. These remaining objections do not so much object to any of the premises of Aquinas's argument, but rather to his conclusion. In this next section, then, we will address the strongest objections to Aquinas's position. These objections can be categorized into seven kinds as follows: (1) intuitionist objections, (2) consequentialist objections, (3) objections from the common good, (4) objections from an analogy with violence, (5) objections from the principle of totality, (6) objections that it's an impossible standard, (7) objections from moral culpability, and (8) objections from an analogy with eating. Let us address each set of objections in turn.

---

lie. But nobody has the authority to determine what the nature of assertions are as such. The definition of an assertion and its natural *telos* are determined by nature, not by the individual.

Human society in general also does not determine the definition or nature of what an assertion is. It is true that societal convention has the prerogative to determine whether this particular sign can be baptized as an assertive speech act, but doing so presupposes the very nature of assertions.

[649] I add the words "or beside the order established by God" in order to indicate the reality of lies that are only slight, non-seriously, flawed actions. Some lies are only bad in a small way.

a) Intuitionism

Peter Kreeft argues from moral intuitions to justify lying. Moral intuitons are intuitions that x is morally good or morally wrong. Anyone with any sense knows that you ought to tell a lie if it will save human lives:

> But in this short piece I want to appeal to something that I think is prior in importance, in clarity, and in time [to logic], namely our immediate, intuitive moral experience....If you don't know that [you should lie to the Nazis], you're morally stupid....If anyone is more certain of his philosophical principles than he is that this deception [to the Nazis] is good, I say he is not functioning as a human being but as a computer, an angel, a Gnostic, or a Kantian. He is a Laputan, like Swift's absent-minded professors who live on an island in the sky in Gulliver's Travels, and who make eye contact with abstractions but not with human beings.[650]

Kreeft's intuitionist account also finds support in Henry Sidgwick, who appeals to moral intuitions to justify lying in difficult circumstances.[651] According to Kreeft's argument, Aristotle, Augustine, Aquinas, practically every major medieval theologian, and Immanuel Kant are morally stupid, for all held that lying is always morally bad.[652]

Moral intuitionism fails to account for the fact that moral intuitions can be wrong or corrupted, as happens in the case of vice, bad arguments, or ignorance.[653] Some people's intuitions are much better than others, either on account of their virtue or on account of the keenness of their intellect. Certainly, both the virtue and intellect of Augustine, Aquinas, Duns Scotus, and many other medieval theologians are likely

---

[650] Peter Kreeft, "Why Live Action Did Right."

[651] H. Sidgwick, "The Classification of Duties—Veracity," quoted in Sissela Bok, *Lying* (New York: Pantheon Books, 1978), 273: "Again where deception is designed to benefit the person deceived, Common Sense seems to concede it may sometimes be right."

[652] Tollefsen and Pruss, "The Case Against False Assertions": "Moreover, as the teaching on lying is shared by Saint Augustine, Saint Gregory the Great, Saint Thomas Aquinas and almost every other significant medieval theologian...the demand for such assent [to their teaching] is quite strong."

[653] Cf. ST I-II, Q94, A6.

to have been high even by contemporary standards.[654] Many virtuous and brilliant men, presumably better than us, held the absolutist view.

The second big problem with moral intuitionism is that it makes moral disagreement unresolvable. Any disagreement on a moral issue is simply due to differing moral intuitions. If moral intuitions alone are always sufficient standards for us to know that an action is morally good or morally evil, then what about a case where Bob and Mark have contradictory moral intuitions? If Bob wished to convince Mark that he (Mark) is right, appealing to his own intuitions won't do much good. If Bob, however, could appeal to a standard beyond his mere intuitions, then that would be to admit that mere intuitions alone aren't sufficient for determining moral goodness or badness.

The aforementioned problems not only hold against those who appeal to moral intuitionism in favor of lying, but also against those who appeal to moral intuitionism in favor of same-sex sexual activity. Peter Kreeft's argument for lying could easily be used to justify same-sex sexual activity; many of the young today, as well as practicing homosexuals, just intuit it as morally good.

b) Consequentialism

The second set of objections to Aquinas's absolutist position on lying and sins against nature are consequentialist in nature. If a tyrant has hold over your entire family and says he will kill you and your family unless you commit an act of homosexual activity, what should you do? According to the consequentialist, just as you are required to eat excrement to save lives, so too are you required to engage in same-sex sexual activity to save your family. If the act leads to better consequences, it ought to be done. A similar argument could be made with regard to lying: if one is told to tell a jocose lie or be burned at the stake, surely the lesser evil is

---

[654] Cf. Tollefsen and Pruss, "The Case Against False Assertions."
Cf. Dorszynski, *Catholic Teaching About the Morality of Falsehood*, 22-27. Dorzynski's magisterial dissertation on the topic cites Gregory the Great, Saint Gregory VII, Hugh of Saint Victor, Pope Alexander III, Saint Raymond of Pennafort, and Duns Scotus.

to tell the jocose lie.[655] One always ought to act so as to maximize the good. So in cases where a greater good is at stake one ought to tell a lie or sin against nature.

Problems with Consequentialism

Consequentialism itself is susceptible to a host of objections, some of which we have already mentioned in the introduction of this book. Many of these, however, relied upon moral intuitions, which I noted aren't always reliable. Intuitions might be a good place to start, but they alone aren't sufficient guides to morality. We must see whether there are more principled objections to consequentialism than the ones given earlier.

Consequentialism is self-refuting

Among the stronger objections to consequentialism is that it is self-refuting. Brad Hooker states the objection well:

> If we had just the one rule 'Maximize the good,' sooner or later awareness of this would become widespread. And becoming aware of this would undermine people's ability to rely confidently on others to behave in agreed upon ways. Trust would break down. In short, terrible consequences would result from the public expectation that this rule would prescribe killing, stealing, and so on when such acts would maximize the good.[656]

According to consequentialism there are no intrinsic evils (except the violation of the rule "maximize the good"), no goods that one cannot possibly violate; all goods are merely instrumental to the end of promoting the greatest good for the greatest number. What this means practically is that if a society adopts the consequentialist ethic one will value things like life, faithfulness, honesty, and chastity less than an absolutist who holds that murder, breaking your marriage vows, lying, and same-sex sexual activity are intrinsically bad. In short, if a society believed and acted upon consequentialist moral theory, there would be very bad consequences for that society as a whole. Compared with a society that

---

[655] Cf. Kreeft, "Why Live Action Did Right."
[656] As quoted in Driver, *Consequentialism,* 88-89.

held to the absolutist moral position on intrinsically evil actions, the consequentialist society is likely to be morally worse. Men will always be tempted to go further than what the moral law allows; there will always be cases of men tempted to commit adultery, of politicians tempted to cover up the heinous acts of their colleagues with lies, and of lawyers tempted by greed to withhold evidence that would exonerate the other party. In an absolutist society there is greater reason not to engage in adultery, lying, or injustice. Such acts are always wrong regardless of consequences. But in a consequentialist society such persons need not even regard such cases as genuine cases of temptation at all. No such moral law exists informing them that such acts ought not to be done. Instead they are left with a consequentialist calculus, which the individual will always be tempted to bend according to their desires. Human nature has it that we tend to go with the easiest route. Consequentialism will make it easier to justify cases of murder, lying, marital breakup, and injustice, etc. Any consequentialist society, then, will likely have more of these common evils than one that believes somethings ought never to be done. Due to this objection some consequentialists have claimed that although their moral theory is true, the general populace ought not to act upon it, but only the elite few.

Besides the self-refuting objection, we have already mentioned the problem with consequentialism's account of the good. It's incoherent. Neither of these objections rely upon moral intuitions. Consequentialist moral theory is just a false moral theory.

c) Objections from the Common Good

The third set of objections stem from the common good. Aquinas justifies the maiming of heinous criminals,[657] the seizure of property,[658] and even capital punishment[659] on account of the common good. If what is normally not licit can become so on account of the common good, then why can't an act of lying or homosexual activity become morally good if

---

[657] ST II-II, Q65, A1, co.
[658] ST II-II Q66, A8, ad 3.
[659] ST II-II, Q64, A2, co.

the common good demands it? To answer that question, we must investigate the content of the common good. What is the common good?

i) What is the Common Good?

The consequentialist assumes an aggregate account of the common good. The common good merely consists in the sum total of physical shelter, income, opportunity, freedom, etc. that each individual within society has. The relation between the individual and the good of the whole is like that of one pebble in relation to the whole heap. One pebble's goodness only adds to the good of the whole by quantitative addition. As Charles De Koninck says, "the individual person is ordered and subjected to society....We are left with a mere aggregate of individuals."[660] The common good is merely an aggregate of individuals added up to form a whole. This view risks becoming totalitarian. What if the sum total of goods for the community increases by sacrificing merely one of its parts? What difference is the loss of one insignificant pebble if the remaining million are better off?

Aquinas does not hold such an aggregate account of the common good. An explication of his account and its non-consequentialist nature can be found in an examination of his absolutist position on murder. Intentionally killing the innocent is always wrong for Aquinas, because "the life of the just is preserving and promoting of the common good, since they are a more principal part of the multitude."[661] In other words, the innocent are principal parts of the common good. Principal parts, for Aquinas, are are those parts to which the other parts are ordained.[662]

---

[660] "The Primacy of the Common Good against the Personalists," in *The Writings of Charles De Koninck,* 325. See also the section of the same work on "Personalism and Totalitarianism," 105-108.

[661] ST II-II, Q64, A6: "Vita autem iustorum est conservative et promotiva boni communis : quia ipsi sunt principalior pars multitudinis. *Et ideo nullo modo licet occidere innocentem.*" Latin is from the BAC with emphasis added; the translation is my own.

[662] As evidence that such is the meaning of principal parts I cite ST I, Q22, A1 where Aquinas calls *providentia* the *principalis pars* of prudence "to which the other parts are ordained, namely *memoria* of things past, and *intelligentia* of present things." Further in ST III, Q66, A7, ad 3 Aquinas calls the head the principal part of the body. This text then strengthens my interpretation of "principal part" as the part towards which the secondary parts are ordained; for the body is willing to lose cir-

Secondary parts are ordained to the good of the principal parts.[663] Thus, since the soul is the principal part of man, the good of the body is ordained to the good of the soul, as a secondary to a principal part. Likewise, since the rational part is the principal part of the soul, the vegetative and sensitive parts are ordained to the good of the rational part. The secondary parts may be harmed for the sake of the principal parts, because the secondary parts are for the sake of the principal parts and using something for its purpose is not wrong. It is licit then to cut off a diseased limb for the sake of the rest of the body or lose one's bodily integrity for the sake of the good of the soul and its virtue, because the body is ordained to the soul as a secondary part to a principal part.[664] It is not licit, however, to sacrifice one's head for the sake of saving the hands, nor is it licit to sacrifice the good of virtue for the sake of preserving the body, because that would be to ordain a principal part to a secondary part.

Similarly, since the innocent are principal parts of the community the secondary parts of the community are ordered to their good. It is licit to sacrifice these secondary parts (provided certain conditions are met) for the sake of the primary, but it is never licit to sacrifice the primary for the sake of the secondary. The innocent are the principal parts of the multitude.[665] They are the chief part of the common good, as soldiers are the chief part of an army. Other parts of the army such as the black-

---

culation to the other parts before it loses it in the head, such is because the other parts of the body are ordained to the good of the head as the head being the house of the brain is more proximately and chiefly ordered to man's good of reason. In *De Potentia* Q3, A9, ad 1 Aquinas indicates that the soul is the principal part of man. Since the body is for the sake of the soul and may be sacrificed for its sake, this text also indicates what we would expect if a principal part is that towards which the others are ordained. Further evidence for my interpretation of *principal part* can be found in *De Virtutibus* Q5, A1, ad 11 where Aquinas says the principal part of man is the *pars rationalis, In Catena in Mc.* cap. 7, 1. 2 where he says the principal part of the soul is the mind, in his *Commentary on the Metaphysics* VII, *lectio* 10, n. 1489 where he calls the head and heart principal parts of the body, in *Super Iob,* Ch. 7, 1. 7 where he indicates that the soul is the principal part of man and the body is the secondary part.

[663] Cf. Jensen, *Good & Evil Actions,* 152-154.
[664] Cf. ST II-II, A65, A1.
[665] Cf. ST II-II, Q64, A6.

smiths, the cook, and the groomers are ordered to the good of the soldiers, because it is in the soldiers that the army attains its chief end of victory.[666] As Jensen says, "Only the soldiers are the subject of the good of fighting well. Those who prepare the armor or care for the horses are not the subject of the good but in some manner produce this good. If the whole army is to fight well, then the soldiers must actually possess this good."[667] Like the soldiers the innocent are the principal or chief parts of the common good. As the soldiers are the subject of fighting well and are the ones who primarily attain and are chiefly ordered to the end of victory, so too the innocent are the subject of the common good and are the ones who primarily attain and are chiefly ordered to the shared common goal of the community, which is called the common good.

Intentionally killing the innocent then is to act against the greater good and against the true common good. As Jensen says,

> The human community consists not merely in an aggregate of individuals; it consists in individuals properly ordered and united with one another. One essential order is that they be united in sharing the good. This union is directly opposed when we use others. By using others we cut them off from sharing our good. We subordinate them to the good, so that they are no longer parts that partake in the good. The chief parts of the multitude, then, should never be violated. They should never be treated as means, subject to the good, for then they are viewed not as chief parts. Precisely because the chief parts share in the good, they are protected from being used. To harm and use a chief part for the sake of the whole is a kind of oxymoron. If we harm a chief part, then our action cannot possibly be for the good of the whole. The good of the whole is precisely sharing the good between those chief parts. To harm, then, is not to share the good but to attack it….the common good protects the innocent, for the common good is nothing other than sharing the good with these innocents.[668]

---

[666] Cf. Jensen, *Good & Evil Actions,* 152-154.

[667] Ibid., 154.

[668] Jensen, *Good & Evil Actions,* 158. There is no significant difference between Jensen's use of the phrase *chief parts* and my use of the phrase *principal part.* They both indicate the same thing and are merely different translations of the phrase *principalis pars* as found in ST II-II, Q64, A6.

The guilty, however, are not chief parts of the common good. In ordering themselves against the common good, they cut themselves off from it and reject it.[669] As such, the guilty cease to be chief parts of the common good. They no longer are the part that is ordered to or attains the shared good, because they have ordered themselves against it. They remain as part of the community but only as a sort of secondary part. If this secondary part is ordered grievously against the good of the whole, then the good of the whole may require it to be put down or destroyed.[670]

Public authority, who has been entrusted with the care of the whole, can put down or destroy a secondary part for the sake of the chief part. But they must never oppose the primary parts, for to oppose them is to oppose the good of the whole. Further, to oppose the order to the primary parts, especially an order dictated by the whole towards the primary parts, is to oppose the good of the whole. This opposition need not be one of actual physical harm; all that is necessary is the harm of offense.[671] A man who acts against God does not physically harm God, but still commits the harm of offense by disdaining his commands.[672] So too a man may oppose the common good merely by opposing the order to it without thereby actually physically harming it.

Nature has dictated that assertions are ordered to the shared good of truth. The final cause of assertions is that men may convey what they believe to one another. This natural end of assertions follows upon the definition of an assertion, just as generation follows upon the definition of the generative power. Assertions are ordered to the good of the primary parts, namely, the lives of the just. Without assertions a community would literally perish. But the community itself, namely, the just themselves as primarily making up the community, is a community in virtue of their order to a shared goal. This shared goal is the common good, which according to Aquinas is the life of virtue. As he says in Book I, Chapter 14 of *De Regno*:

---

[669] Cf. Jensen, 169.
[670] Cf. ST II-II, Q64, A2.
[671] Cf. Jensen, *Good & Evil Actions*, 162.
[672] Cf. Jensen, 162-163.

Now the same judgment is to be formed about the end of society as a whole as about the end of one man. If, therefore, the ultimate end of man were some good that existed in himself, then the ultimate end of the multitude to be governed would likewise be for the multitude to acquire such good, and persevere in its possession.

If such an ultimate end either of an individual man or a multitude were a corporeal one, namely, life and health of body, to govern would then be a physician's charge. If that ultimate end were an abundance of wealth, then knowledge of economics would have the last word in the community's government. If the good of the knowledge of truth were of such a kind that the multitude might attain to it, the king would have to be a teacher. *It is, however, clear that the end of a multitude gathered together is to live virtuously.* For men form a group for the purpose of living well together, a thing which the individual man living alone could not attain, and good life is virtuous life. *Therefore, virtuous life is the end for which men gather together* [emphasis added].[673]

And in his commentary on Aristotle's *Politics* Book I, lecture 1, n. 31, Aquinas makes a similar point:

Thirdly, [Aristotle] shows *to what the city is ordered.* It is originally made for the sake of living, namely, that men might find sufficiently that from which they might be able to live; but from its existence it

---

[673] "Idem autem oportet esse iudicium de fine totius multitudinis, et unius. Si igitur finis hominis esset bonum quodcumque in ipso existens, et regendae multitudinis finis ultimus esset similiter ut tale bonum multitudo acquireret, et in eo permaneret; et si quidem talis ultimus sive unius hominis, sive multitudinis finis esset corporalis, vita et sanitas corporis, medici esset officium. Si autem ultimus finis esset divitiarum affluentia, oeconomus rex quidam multitudinis esset. Si vero bonum cognoscendae veritatis tale quid esset, ad quod posset multitudo pertingere, rex haberet doctoris officium. Videtur autem finis esse multitudinis congregatae vivere secundum virtutem. Ad hoc enim homines congregantur, ut simul bene vivant, quod consequi non posset unusquisque singulariter vivens; bona autem vita est secundum virtutem; virtuosa igitur vita est congregationis humanae finis" (Divi Thomae Aquinatis Doctoris Angelici, *De Regimine Principum ad Regem Cypri,* in *Politica Divi Thomae Aquinatis Opuscula Duo,* 2nd rev. ed. (Marietti, 1971), Book I, Ch. XIV, p.17). The translation is from *De regno ad regem Cypri,* trans. Gerald B. Phelan and Th. Eschmann (Toronto: PIMS, 1949), http://dhspriory.org/thomas/DeRegno.htm#15. The chapter numbering is different in the translation than in the Marietti.

comes about that men not only live but that they live well, in so far as *by the laws of the city the life of men is ordered to the virtues* [emphasis added].[674]

The innocent then are chief parts of the common good, because they are that wherein the shared good chiefly resides and they are that which primarily are ordered to and attain the shared good. The innocent then are an intrinsic part of the common good. But they are ordained to an extrinsic end, namely, the life of virtue.[675] So to oppose the life of virtue is to oppose the common good. Opposing the good of virtue is a greater evil than opposing the mere lives of the innocent, because the innocent exist for the sake of virtue.

Included among the extrinsic ends of the community is truth. For any community to be truly good it must be properly ordered to the truth. Since the moral virtues are subordinate to the intellectual virtues, and the active life to the contemplative, speculative truth lies high in the hierarchy of shared goods.[676]

Assertions by their very nature are ordered to the truth, not just the formal truth, but even material truth. In other words, the author of nature instituted assertions so that men may converse with one another regarding what they believe, lest society literally perish. But the point of conveying to others what you believe is so that men may attain to the full knowledge of the truth, that is, truth taken not merely as what you believe to be so, but what, in fact, in reality actually is true. To use asser-

---

[674] "Tertio ostendit ad quid est civitas ordinate. Est enim primitus facta gratia vivendi, ut scilicet homines sufficienter invenirent unde vivere possent ; set ex eius esse provenit, quod homines non solum vivant, set quod bene vivant in quantum per leges civitatis ordinatur vita hominum ad virtutem" (Sancti Thomae de Aquino, *Sententia Libri Politicorum,* in *Opera Omnia Iussu Leonis XIII P.M. Edita,* vol. XLVIII (Romae: 1971), Book I, Ch. 1/b, lines 26-32, p. 77-78). Translation is from Ernest L. Fortin and Peter D. O'Neill, http://dhspriory.org/thomas/Politics.htm.

[675] An intrinsic common good is the good as it exists within the community, whereas an extrinsic common good is the good for the sake of which the community exists, as existing separately from the community. For more on the distinction between intrinsic and extrinsic common goods see Froelich, "The Equivocal Status of Bonum Commune," 50-51 and the citations there from *In XII Meta.,* lect. 12, n. 2627, and n. 2630, *In I Sent.,* D44, Q1, A2, *QD de caritate,* Q.un, A4, ad 2, and ST I, Q103, A2, ad 3.

[676] Cf. ST II-II, Q152, A2; SCG III, Ch. 25, no. 9.

tions then contrary to their natural end is not merely to oppose formal truth, but also to oppose the order to attaining knowledge of things as they, in fact, are. A culture that tells frequent lies then not merely leads to a lack of trustful communication, but also a lack of truth regarding the nature of reality. Such is why those caught in a web of lies have difficulty telling fact from fiction. Communist lies distort people's perceptions of reality.

The end of the community then is truth. Since assertions are ordained by nature to truth, to abuse them by using them contrary to truth is to oppose that end. To oppose truth is to oppose the true shared good, namely, the common good. One may not then use them contrary to that purpose anymore than one may use chief parts of the common good by treating them as if they weren't chief parts. To intentionally kill the innocent is to attack the common good and to tell a lie is to oppose the end for which the community exists. Both are an attack upon the common good. Aquinas's account of the common good then prohibits certain acts as always wrong. The modern consequentialist account by contrast prescribes that any act whatsoever may be necessary for the common good. This prescription follows from its aggregate account of the common good.

ii) Problems with the consequentialist account of the common good
The problems with the aggregate account of the common good need not go any farther than numerous well-developed criticisms of utilitarian moral theory, which we have mentioned before. The aggregate view also tends towards totalitarianism. Anything, however horrific, may be done to any member of the community if the good of the state requires it. This view of the common good has a bad historical track record in its instantiation in the fascist and communist regimes of the 20th century.[677] The individual, even the innocent, may be killed for the good of the multitude. Murder, theft, adultery, wife-murder, lying, bestiality, homosexual acts, rape, wholesale slavery, and scapegoating of an entire ethnic group

---

[677] For more on a critique of the totalitarian view of the common good see Jacques Maritain, *The Person and the Common Good,* trans. John J. Fitzgerald (New York: Charles Scribner's Sons, 1947), Chapter 5, https://www3.nd.edu/~maritain/jmc/etext/CG05.HTM.

may all be necessary on account of the common good, the good of the state. Lying and homosexual activity could be justified on the totalitarian conception of the common good, but so too can just about anything.[678] The common good isn't a mere aggregate of parts, but an ordered whole.

d) Objections from an Analogy with Violence[679]

Many reject Aquinas's absolutist position on lying based upon an analogy with violence. If violence is generally evil, but allowable in exceptional cases, cannot the same be said about lying? Various scholars have rejected the absolutist position on lying based upon an analogy with violence.[680] They hold that in difficult situations one ought to tell a lie. Sidgwick, for example, argues: "if we may even kill in defence of our-

---

[678] That Aquinas does not maintain such a view should be evident from the fact that he says that murder, theft, lying, homosexual activity, etc. can never be done (cf. ST II-II, Q64, A6; Q66, A6 and A7; Q110, A3, ad 4; Q154, A12, ad 1). There are some actions the common good can never justify. The person is related to the community as part to whole, but his dignity is not so totally subsumed into the whole that the whole can inflict whatever it likes upon the part for the good of the whole.

[679] Much of this section is developed from my earlier article: John Skalko, "Why Did Aquinas Hold Killing is Sometimes Just, But Never Lying?" *Proceedings of the American Catholic Philosophical Association* 90, (2016): 227-241. What has been repeated from that article here has been used with permission.

[680] "Thomas Aquinas said that even torture is sometimes justified; in emergency situations like that; if torture, then *a fortiori* lying" (Kreeft, "Why Live Action Did Right").

Though she does not directly attack Aquinas' position in this regard, Sissela Bok rejects the absolute position on lying and argues for this rejection by means of an analogy with violence. This argument is repeatedly used throughout her book: *Lying*, 41, 45-46, 109, 115, 126, 130, 144, 213.

In the appendix Bok also quotes a lengthy passage from Sidgwick who also argues from an analogy with violence (273). Other authors who argue similarly are as follows: Decosimo, "JUST LIES: Finding Augustine's Ethics of Public Lying in His Treatments of Lying and Killing"; Alasdair MacIntyre, "Truthfulness, Lies, and Moral Philosophers," 351-352, 356. MacIntyre does not explicitly cite Aquinas in his rejection of the absolutist position that all lies are wrong. Nevertheless, his reasoning logically entails a rejection of Aquinas: "In this type of case [of a Dutch housewife hiding Jews from a Nazi official] the normally illegitimate power exercised by the successful liar becomes legitimate" (356).

selves and others, it seems strange if we may not lie, if lying will defend us better against a palpable invasion of our rights."[681]

Those who reject the absolutist position on lying based upon an analogy with violence can be divided into two groups: (a) those who hold that lying is sometimes permissible,[682] and (b) those who hold that lying ceases to be lying in certain difficult situations, especially situations wherein violence normally would be allowable.[683] Dubois, repre-

---

[681] Bok, *Lying*, 273.

[682] Kreeft, Bok, Sidgwick, Decosimo, and MacIntyre hold this view.

[683] Cf. Abbé F. Dubois, "Une Théorie Du Mensonge Replique (1)," 168: "It must be added: *the violation of a right*, which constitutes the *formal* element of a lie and morally *specifies* it. Thus, the saying of a falsity with the intention to deceive is the material element of a lie, analogous to the material act of killing, indifferent like it, that is to say good or evil according to the circumstances and determining the moral conditions of the act, that is, like in the act of killing, the violation of a right, of the right to life in the first case, of the right to the truth in the second" (translation from the French is my own).
Vermeersch holds a similar view: "Indeed, just as an unjust aggression of another brings it about that an action, which otherwise would be homicide is not homicide as an action, but the defense of self, so also the unjust aggression can be the cause why words, which, if offered outside of aggression would become lies, now also they might be a defense of a secret and are chosen and intended only as such. Nor is it required that the aggressor be aware of his unjust aggression. For one is able to repel by force also one who is materially unjust" (As quoted in Dorszynski, 60).
Dorszynski argues similarly: "We realize that deceptive speech *ordinarily* harms mutual trust in society; but we maintain that there are times when it may be used without injury to mutual trust. One of the times it does not endanger that trust is when it is employed to protect a lawful secret from unjust aggression. We believe that in a conflict of the rights of the speaker and hearer we could aptly apply the usual rules involved in cases of unjust aggression of life and property" (88).
Smith in "Fig Leaves and Falsehoods" argues, "Aquinas' rigorism about uttering falsehoods is certainly cogent, but hard to reconcile with some of his other positions. Aquinas (and the Church) approve of killing someone for the sake of protecting innocent life as well as commandeering or destroying the property of another to protect other goods. Thus the question: Why shouldn't Aquinas (and the Church) permit false signification uttered in order to protect innocent life and other important goods?"
Smith, "Why Tollefsen and Pruss Are Wrong about Lying": "Indeed, one could kill the Nazi or forcibly take his weapons from him to prevent him from killing Jews. Why is false signification morally impermissible in the same circumstances? The work that needs to be done now is to study why Aquinas thought it moral to kill in self-defense and to take what belongs to others when in dire need. What justifies those actions? Would that justification extend to false signification?"

290

sentative of the second group of authors, succinctly sums up their position as follows:

> The saying of a falsity with the intention to deceive is the material element of a lie, analogous to the material act of killing, indifferent like it, that is to say good or evil according to the circumstances and determining the moral conditions of the act, that is, like in the act of killing, the violation of a right, of the right to life in the first case, of the right to the truth in the second.[684]

Effectively, in situations where human lives are at stake, what normally counts as a lie ceases to be so. Despite their differences, both groups of authors reject Aquinas's absolutist position based upon an analogy with violence.

In that respect, they have a point. Aquinas allows for killing in self-defense, killing in capital punishment, and killing in a just war.[685] If Aquinas holds that killing is generally evil, but allows for broad exceptions to it in certain contexts, cannot the same be said about lying? The purpose of this section is to show that the analogy between killing and lying fails to hold up under scrutiny. Aquinas's justifications for killing in certain contexts cannot be used to justify lying. In order to argue for that point, I will proceed as follows: first, I will explicate Aquinas's account of killing; second, I will briefly recount Aquinas's account of lying; finally, I will conclude by showing that killing and lying are not analogous. Though killing is not always wrong, lying always is.

i) Killing in Aquinas

I will begin with an explication of Aquinas's account of killing. Aquinas allows for the killing of plants and animals because they are ordered towards our good. Plants are ordered towards the good of animals, and both plants and animals are ordered towards the good of man. Since it is not illicit to use things for their purpose, it is not illicit to kill plants or animals for man's good.[686] Thus, it is good for man to kill plants or ani-

---

[684] Dubois, "Une Théorie Du Mensonge Replique (1)," 168.
[685] ST II-II, Q64, A7; ST II-II, Q64, A2; SCG III, 146, n. 4-5; ST II-II, Q40, A1.
[686] ST II-II, Q64, A1.

mals for food or for his own use. Life itself is not so absolute a good that it can never rightly be taken away.

Capital Punishment

Does Aquinas allow for killing human beings? That depends upon whether they are guilty or innocent. Grievous evildoers may be licitly killed provided certain conditions are met, but the innocent may never be intentionally killed.

In *Summa Theologiae* (ST) II-II, Q64, A2, co. Aquinas argues that "if any man is dangerous to the community and corruptive of it on account of some sin, then it is praiseworthy and profitable to kill him in order that the common good be preserved."[687] Aquinas reasons for his conclusion as follows:

> It is licit to kill brute animals inasmuch as they are naturally ordered to the use of man, as the imperfect are ordered to the perfect. Now every part is naturally ordered to the whole as the imperfect to the perfect. Therefore, every part naturally is for the sake of the whole. On account of this, we see that if the cutting off of a member is expedient to the health of the whole human body, as when it is rotten and corruptive of the others, it is praiseworthy and profitable to be cutoff. Now any singular person is compared to the community as a part to a whole. Therefore, if any man is dangerous to the community and corruptive of it on account of some flawed-action, then it is praiseworthy and profitable to kill him in order that the common good be preserved.[688]

---

[687] "Et ideo si aliquis homo sit periculosus communitati et corruptivus ipsius propter aliquod peccatum, laudabiliter et salubriter occiditur, ut bonum commune conservetur." Latin is from the BAC; the translation is my own.

[688] "Respondeo dicendum quod, sicut dictum est (a.1), licitum est occidere animalia bruta inquantum ordinantur naturaliter ad hominum usum, sicut imperfectum ordinatur ad perfectum. Omnis autem pars ordinatur ad totum ut imperfectum ad perfectum. Et ideo omnis pars naturaliter est propter totum. Et propter hoc videmus quod si saluti totius corporis humani expediat praecisio alicuius membri, puta cum est putridum et corruptivum aliorum, laudabiliter et salubriter abscinditur. Quaelibet autem persona singularis comparatur ad totam communitatem sicut pars ad totum. Et ideo si aliquis homo sit periculosus communitati et corruptivus ipsius propter aliquod peccatum, laudabiliter et salubriter occiditur, ut bonum commune conservetur: *modicum* enim *fermentum totam massam corrumpit,* ut dicitur I ad Cor. 5,6." Latin is from the BAC; the translation is my own.

Now, in the very next article, ST II-II, Q64, A3, Aquinas adds the qualifier that only those in public authority may kill in the case of capital punishment.[689] Aquinas reasons that only those who have been entrusted with the care of the whole may sacrifice a part for the sake of the good of the whole. The care of the common good has not been entrusted to private individuals as such. It has been entrusted, rather, to those in public authority. Thus, only those in public authority may kill a grievous malefactor for the sake of the common good.

In ST II-II, Q64, A4, Aquinas then argues that clerics may not kill another human being. In the reply to the third objection, Aquinas argues that if the cleric happens to hold public office, he cannot himself carry out the capital punishment but may delegate others to do so in virtue of his authority.

Just War

Aquinas's justifications for killing in self-defense and killing in a just war are dependent upon his justifications for killing in the case of capital punishment. In ST II-II, Q40, A1, co., Aquinas argues that a war may be just provided that three conditions are met: proper authority, just cause, and rightful intention. Proper authority means that not just anyone can declare or wage war; only those in public authority have the right to wage war. Because the care of the common good is entrusted to those in public authority, it belongs to those in public authority to gather together the private individuals as needed in wartime. Further, "just as [those in public authority] licitly defend it [the republic] by means of the sword against internal disturbances, as they punish malefactors...so too by means of the sword in war it pertains to them to safeguard the republic from exterior enemies."[690] One must note that Aquinas is very adamant here about the fact that only public authority has the proper authority to wage war. The private individual *qua* private individual cannot wage a

---

[689] ST II-II, Q64, A3.

[690] "Et sicut licite defendunt eam materiali gladio contra interiores quidem perturbatores, dum malefactores puniunt...ita etiam gladio bellico ad eos pertinent rempublicam tueri ab exterioribus hostibus." Latin is from the BAC; the translation is my own.

just war. His rationale for this claim ultimately must be traced back to the rationale he used – in ST II-II, Q64, A3 – about why only those in public authority can execute criminals for capital offenses: the public authority alone has been entrusted with the care of the common good. Ergo, only the public authority may put a part in harm's way for the good of the whole.

Aquinas's second criterion for a just war is that "it requires a just cause, namely, that those whom one is fighting against deserve to be fought against on account of some fault (*culpam*)."[691] Aquinas's reasoning here echoes back to his reasoning in ST II-II, Q64, A2, about the case of capital punishment.[692] Capital punishment may be done only if the person is *periculosus* and *corruptivus* of the community. This implies that the person is guilty of some *culpa*. Although the terminology is different in ST II-II, Q40, A1, and ST II-II, Q64, A2, the rationale is the same: in order for killing to be legitimate the person to be killed must be guilty of some grievous fault. In a just war, the enemy is guilty and so are all of his soldiers. In capital punishment the criminal is guilty. Aquinas's allowance for killing in war is heavily dependent upon his account as to why killing in capital punishment is allowable.

The third criterion for a just war is that it must be waged with a rightful intention. It must be done for the sake of some good and not out of mere bloodlust or cruelty. The need for a right intention permeates Aquinas's teaching on punishment and his ethics in general.[693] Any ac-

---

[691] "Secundo, requiritur causa iusta : ut scilicet illi qui impugnantur propter aliquam culpam impugnationem mereantur." Latin is from the BAC; the translation is my own.

[692] That this text occurs chronologically after Q40 is no difficulty. In Q40 Aquinas is merely sketching his account of just war theory; evidently, he saved his full account as to why killing the guilty is licit until Q64. Logically, even if not chronologically, the justification for intentional killing in just war in Q40 is dependent upon Q64.

[693] ST II-II, Q108, A1; ST II-II, Q64, A6; ST I, Q19, A9; ST I-II, Q19, A10, ad 2; ST I-II, Q87, A3, ad 3. For an excellent analysis of this point see Lawrence Dewan, "Thomas Aquinas, Gerard Bradley, and the Death Penalty: Some Observations," *Gregorianum* 82, no. 1 (2001): 161-164. "*No one* (whether a public official or a private person) is *ever* allowed to 'intend the death of this person', in the way that involves pleasure in that person's suffering, or hate of that person as possessed of human nature" (Dewan, 162).

tion may be rendered evil on account of an evil end intended.[694] Thus, for Aquinas the intention must be good in any type of killing.

Self Defense

I will now proceed from Aquinas's account of just war to his account of self-defense. Like Aquinas's account of just war, Aquinas's account of self-defense in large part is parasitic upon his account of capital punishment. In ST II-II, Q64, A7, Aquinas argues that it is licit to kill another in self-defense, but only those in public authority may intend to kill their attacker. The private individual may perform an action from which the death of the aggressor *sometimes* follows, but he may never intend to kill his attacker.[695] As support for his contention that only those in public authority may intend to kill another for the sake of the common good, Aquinas explicitly cites the earlier article, Q64, A3, where he had previously argued that in capital punishment only the public authority may intend to kill.[696] Only public authority may intend to kill an attacker in self-defense because only public authority has been entrusted with the care of the whole such that only they may kill a part for the sake of the good of the whole.

ST II-II, Q64, A7, has been the subject of much disputed interpretation.[697] The New Natural Lawyers hold that Aquinas would allow for

---

[694] ST I-II, Q18, A4, co. and ad 3.

[695] ST II-II, Q64, A7, ad 4: "Ad quartum dicendum quod actus fornicationis vel adulterii non ordinatur ad conservationem propriae vitae ex necessitate, sicut actus ex quo *quandoque* sequitur homicidium" (emphasis added). This implies that Aquinas would allow for the swinging of one's sword so as to deflect the opponent's blows or so as to strike the opponent's sword out of his hand. From such an action *sometimes* the death of the aggressor follows if accidentally the aggressor steps into the way of the sword and suffers a fatal blow. Decapitating the attacker, however, is not an action from which the death of the attacker merely *sometimes* follows. It follows rather in all cases.
Aquinas is very clear that the private individual may never intend to kill the attacker: "Illicitum est quod homo intendat occidere hominem ut seipsum defendat, nisi ei qui habet publicam auctoritatem."

[696] "Sed quia occidere hominem non licet nisi publica auctoritate propter bonum commune, ut ex supradictis (a.3) patet."

[697] I am only mentioning two prominent interpretations here, but there are others. Cf. Steven A. Long, "A Brief Disquisition Regarding the Nature of the Object of the Moral Act according to St. Thomas Aquinas," *The Thomist* 67 (2003): 71. It is

the private individual (even one who is an expert swordsman and has full control of his sword at all times) to stab the assailant in the heart so long as he does not intend death.[698] Steven Jensen, on the other hand, holds that not only is it illicit for the private individual to stab the assailant in the heart intentionally, but that it is also illicit for him intentionally to harm the attacker in any way.[699] For Jensen, the only type of killing that Aquinas allows for the private individual in Q64, A7 is that which is incidental. All he may do is deflect the blows or scare off the attacker or swing his sword so as to knock the blade out of his attacker's hand. Whereas the New Natural Law account holds that it is possible, as an expert swordsman, to push your sword knowingly through the assailant's heart without intending harm, Jensen and various other authors hold that such an account of intention is either false or unintelligible.[700] Jensen's account, it seems, is the better interpretation of Aquinas.

On either interpretation, however, Aquinas's argument that the private individual may kill in self-defense cannot be used to support lying in self-defense. Lying includes intention in its very definition. An unintentional lie is a contradiction in terms. So even if it were possible for the private individual to stab the assailant in the heart without the in-

---

there that Long quotes from Francisco de Vitoria as holding the same position. For two other interpretations see: Joannis a S. Thoma, *Cursus Theologicus in Summam Theologicam D. Thomae, Tomus Septimus In Secundam Secundae, Q64, Disputatio XI De Homicidio, A4, XV*, ed. Ludovicus Vives, (Parisiis, 1886), 495; Gregory M. Reichberg, "Aquinas on Defensive Killing: A Case of Double Effect?," *Thomist: A Speculative Quarterly Review* 69, no. 3 (2005): 341-370.

[698] Finnis, *Aquinas: Moral, Legal, and Political Theory*, 287.

[699] Steven J. Jensen, "The Trouble with Secunda Secundae 64, 7: Self-Defense," *Modern Schoolman: A Quarterly Journal of Philosophy* 83, no. 2 (2006): 152-153. Jensen cites ST II-II, Q65, A1, Q64, A3, ad 3, and Q41, A1 in support of his position.

[700] Cf. Nicanor Pier Giorgio Austriaco, "On Reshaping Skulls and Unintelligible Intentions," *Nova et Vetera*, English Edition 3, no. 1 (2005): 81-100; Jean Porter, "'Direct' and 'indirect' in Grisez's moral theory," *Theological Studies* 57, no. 4 (1996): 620: "The relationship between the agent's intention and the causal structure of the act did play a crucial role in traditional moral theology, because it provided an objective basis for assessing the intention of the agent. Without some such basis, the agent's intention could be described in terms of whatever could be said to be the agent's purpose or motive in acting. In that case, it would be difficult to see how the doctrine of double effect would rule anything out..."

tent to kill, in no way could one argue that the private individual may tell a lie to a public enemy without intending to lie.

In sum, Aquinas's entire account of justifiable killing is fundamentally dependent upon his understanding of public authority and the common good. Aquinas's justification of intentional killing in self-defense, intentional killing in a just war, and intentional killing in capital punishment, all hinge upon the fact that only those in public authority have been entrusted with the care of the common good as such.

This care of the common good by public authority is significant for answering the objection to Aquinas's account of lying from the analogy with violence. Aquinas's rationale for killing could be used to justify lying only if the lies were done by one in public authority for the sake of the common good and upon an enemy or a guilty party. Can this justification for killing by public authority be used to show that Aquinas's account of the intrinsic wrongness of lying is incoherent? Before we answer that question, we must restate Aquinas's account of the intrinsic wrongness of lying.

ii) Aquinas on Lying Redux

Throughout his philosophical career Aquinas insisted that every lie is a flawed-action. In all four major texts where Aquinas argues that lying is a flawed-action his argument is fundamentally the same.[701] Lying is wrong because it violates the purposes of assertions. Assertions are different from other speech acts. They are, by their very nature, ordered towards truth as their proximate end. An assertion, by definition, is to present something as if it were true to another. As Christopher Tollefsen puts it, in an assertion one is communicating to another that one believes *that P* is true.[702]

Nature directs us toward the end, towards the good of our nature. As a social animal our end is not a solitary good, but a shared good, that is, a common good. Nature directs us to the good of the whole. One aspect of that shared good is truth. Nature has given us assertions to direct

---

[701] Cf. *Commentary on the Sentences,* Book III, D38, Q1, A3; *Quodlibet* VIII, Q6, A4; *Commentary on the Nicomachean Ethics,* Book IV.7, *Lectio* 15, n. 837; ST II-II, Q110, A3 and Q111, A1.
[702] Cf. Tollefsen, *Lying and Christian Ethics*, 20.

us toward that shared end. Assertions are of their very nature ordered towards truth as their final cause. To abuse the order of assertions then is to abuse the very order of nature in her direction to our shared goal. The liar thus in the very act of lying cuts himself off from the order to this shared good by acting directly against it.

Just as a judge must play his part in ordering himself in accordance with the law to justice, so too a speaker must play his part in ordering his assertions to truth, which are directed by the law of nature. Just as what follows beyond the judge's just judgment according to the law, such as a riot on the street, need not detract from his order to justice, so too what follows beyond the speaker ordering his assertions to truth may be beyond his role. A judge may excuse himself from the bench, and a person may choose to opt out of asserting by remaining silent, but given that the judge is judging he must order himself to justice; so too given that a person is asserting he must order himself to truth.

iii) Is There an Analogy between Killing and Lying?

Now that we have discussed Aquinas's account of killing and his account of lying, we may proceed to see whether his account of killing can be used against his account of lying. Janet Smith seems to think so: how can Aquinas consistently hold that you can kill the Nazi, but not lie to him?[703] In this section, I argue directly that Aquinas was not inconsistent.

Killing is permissible in two ways: *either* as a punishment by proper authority (which includes just war) *or* as outside intention within double effect reasoning. If such acts of killing are permissible, then could not lying be in similar cases?

Let us take the first horn of the dilemma. If the same rationale to support killing is to be applied to lying, then only those in proper authority may tell a lie as punishment upon a guilty party for the sake of the common good. Presumably then only public authorities may tell a lie to the Nazi at the door, and even then they may lie *only insofar as lying is an act of punishment for the Nazi.* But in the case of the Nazi at the door,

---

[703] Smith, "Why Tollefsen and Pruss Are Wrong about Lying."

most people aren't intending to punish the Nazi, but rather are just doing whatever seems necessary to save the Jews they are hiding.

Further, punishment involves acting upon some guilty party. In capital punishment or a just war the guilty party or enemy soldier is the *materia circa quam* of the action. By contrast, in lying the *materia cira quam* of the action is the assertion you are making.[704]

There is a third problem with applying Aquinas's rationale about capital punishment to the case of lying. In capital punishment one is killing or permanently destroying a corrupt part for the good of the whole. But what part of what whole is permanently destroyed by lying? Two possibilities suggest themselves: (a) the words are destroyed, or (b) the Nazi is harmed or destroyed. But neither possibility seems plausible. For lying involves words or assertions. Words or assertions can be understood in two senses: (i) as words or assertions as such, that is, taken universally, or (ii) words or assertions insofar as we mean this particular word or this particular assertion uttered by this particular person to the Nazi at the door. Assertions in sense (i) cannot be destroyed, unless perhaps the whole human race ceased to exist. Assertions in sense (ii) cease to exist immediately after they are spoken, so how then can you destroy what has ceased to be? In telling a lie it is unclear how one could be intending to destroy an assertion in order to save the Jews. Further, language is the larger whole of which words or assertions are a part. So if Aquinas's reasoning about capital punishment were applied to the case of lying, this would mean that public authorities would be intending to destroy assertions for the sake of language. This, however, hardly makes sense. Ultimately, the parts and the wholes in the case of assertions and capital punishment are simply not analogous.

One possibility remains then: in telling a lie to the Nazi at the door the liar is intending to destroy or harm the Nazi for the sake of the whole (the common good). But in what way then is the Nazi harmed? In the aforementioned scenario, the Nazi is certainly not destroyed by the lie. He is certainly harmed by false information insofar as his intellect re-

---

[704] Cf. ST II-II, Q110, A3, co. where Aquinas calls the act of lying "actus cadens super indebitam materiam" indicating that lying is putting a form (of falsehood) into the matter of assertions. As mentioned earlier, in this text Aquinas is using *voces* as synecdoche for *assertions*.

ceives what is false, but that occurs unbeknownst to him and such false information need not physically harm him. Is he morally harmed? It would seem not; for he is not incited to do evil by the lie. In telling the lie you are not causing the Nazi to do evil, but presumably (in the ideal situation) causing him to desist from evil by having him not kill the Jews you are hiding. The Nazi then is not harmed nor destroyed by telling a lie in any relevant sense. Neither are assertions or words in any relevant sense harmed or destroyed. Aquinas's rationale for destroying a part for the good of the whole, then, hardly applies to the Nazi-at-the-door scenario.

So much then for the first horn of the dilemma; let us look at the second horn: can the double effect reasoning used to justify certain types of killing also justify similar types of lying?[705] It is possible for the private individual to perform an action that foreseeably may cause death without intending the death that follows. Double effect reasoning entails that one intends the good effect (viz. of saving one's own life), but not the bad effect (viz. of death or the killing that results in the death of the assailant). For this rationale to apply to lying to the Nazi at the door, one would have to intend the saving of one's own life (or of the Jews), but not the bad effect of lying. This scenario, however, hardly makes sense. Lying by definition includes intention. It is not possible to perform an act of lying without intending to lie. This is why animals cannot strictly speaking tell lies, nor can the insane. This is also why a slip of the tongue, or a drunken man who blurts out something accidentally, is not lying even if what is spoken is what the agent knows to be untrue. Double effect reasoning, then, cannot be used to justify lying. Thus, neither killing as used in legitimate punishment nor killing in cases of double effect can be used to justify lying. Killing and lying are not analogous.

Double effect reasoning, however, can justify certain types of mental reservation or equivocal speech. I may intend to say what I believe to be true, even if I foreknow that my listener will misunderstand me, provided that I have proportionate reason for my listener to misunderstand me. For example, I may tell the Nazi at the door, "There are no bloody Jews here!" intending to signify that there literally are no Jews

---

[705] For more on this point see Tollefsen, *Lying and Christian Ethics*, 150-151.

who are bleeding in my house. The Nazi will likely take *bloody* to signify the derogatory meaning of the word. I may still say and intend to say *bloody Jews* in the literal sense of the term, even if I foreknow that the Nazi will likely take it in the derogatory sense. Equivocal speech is justified provided I have good reasons for engaging in it.

Similarly, a mental reservation can be justified provided I have a good reason for uttering one. A mental reservation is the uttering of a sentence in which much of it is spoken, but part of it is silently implied or reserved in the mind of the speaker. "I am leaving" implies "I am leaving [now]" or "I am leaving [soon]" depending upon the context and intention of the speaker. We use mental reservations often in order to be more efficient in our use of words (although sometimes it is also due to carelessness). Since these presumably are not morally wrong, neither is it morally wrong to use a mental reservation to the Nazi at the door. "There are no Jews here" can mean "There are no Jews at my house [but they are hiding in the backyard cellar]." Similarly, in asserting "I am not harboring any Jews" one can justifiably mentally reserve "at the moment" (because I was harboring them until five minutes ago when they ran off my property).

The analogy between killing and lying suffers from yet another problem: lying is disordered in the very nature of its action, whereas killing is not. In lying one is engaging in an action that is naturally ordered to an end, while deliberately frustrating that end from happening. One is engaging in an assertion that is naturally ordered to truth, while deliberately acting against that truth. In killing, even in unjustified types of killing, there is no such fundamental frustration of teleology. Murder is wrong, but it does not involve the frustration of the natural *telos* of an action in which one is engaging. As Edward Feser says, "[lying] is in this respect like contraception, or deliberately vomiting up a meal so one can gorge oneself indefinitely. [The] argument is thus a species of what is known as a 'perverted faculty' argument. Murder and stealing do not involve the perversion of a faculty; they are immoral for other, more complex reasons."[706]

---

[706] Edward Feser, "Smith, Tollefsen, and Pruss on Lying": "The problem with Smith's argument is that the cases of murder, stealing, and lying are simply not parallel in the way she supposes, certainly not from the point of view of the classical

One final point can be made. The argument for lying based upon an analogy with violence proves too much. If lying may be done for the sake of the common good when lives are in danger, then cannot the same rationale apply to other actions as well? Could not adultery, murder, or homosexual actions be justified in similar situations?[707] Imagine a blackmail situation: a gang breaks into a bank and recognizes you as their old lost enemy. They insist that they will murder everyone else in the bank and leave the gun in your cold dead hands unless you kill one of the innocent bank tellers. If you can lie for the sake of the common good, then why can you not murder? This Augustinian challenge has yet to be answered by advocates of the noble lie.

---

approach to natural law theory represented by Aquinas. For Aquinas and the classical natural law tradition that informed the thinking of the Scholastic manualists, deliberately telling a falsehood is *intrinsically* immoral, whether or not the listener has a right to know the truth, because it involves acting contrary to the natural end of our communicative faculties. It is in this respect like contraception, or deliberately vomiting up a meal so that one can gorge oneself indefinitely. Their argument is thus a species of what is known as a 'perverted faculty' argument. Murder and stealing do not involve the perversion of a faculty; they are immoral for other, more complex reasons. Hence the analogy Smith needs in order to make her case does not hold."

[707] Cf. Augustine, *De Mendacio* n. 11: "But if anyone thinks that a lie must be told to one person for the sake of another, so that the latter may live longer…there is no crime to which he may not be forced by the same reason" (Augustine, *Lying,* trans. Mary Sarah Muldowney, in *The Fathers of the Church: A New Translation*, vol. 16, ed. Roy J. Deferrari (Washington, D.C., The Catholic University of America Press, 1952), p. 70). Augustine, *Contra Mendacium,* n. 38: "what is he saying who opposes me in pleading and defending the case for lying if he is not saying the truth? But, if he is to be heard because he is telling the truth, how can he in telling the truth want to make me a liar? How can lying claim truth as its advocate? Or does truth conquer for her adversary so as to be conquered by herself? Who can abide this absurdity? Therefore, let us not in any way hold that they who declare that sometimes we ought to lie are truthful in declaring so, lest—and this is most absurd and foolish to believe!—the truth teaches us to be liars. How is it that, while no one learns from chastity that he ought to commit adultery or from piety that he ought to harm his neighbor, we should learn from truth that we ought to lie?" (Augustine, *Against Lying,* trans. Harold B. Jaffee, in *The Fathers of the Church: A New Translation*, vol. 16, ed. Roy J. Deferrari (Washington, D.C., The Catholic University of America Press, 1952), p. 174-175). See also *Contra Mendacium*, n. 1, n. 18-22, and n. 40 (Ibid., p. 126, 143-151, 179 (the selection from n. 40 here is n. 41 in the newadvent.org translation).

iv) *Violence and Same-Sex Sexual Activity*

Most of the previous section dealt with lying. What about homosexual activity? If you can kill someone for the sake of punishment, then why can't you forcibly engage in homosexual activity with him for the sake of punishment?

Recall in the previous section that only those in public authority may intend to kill (or harm a part) for the sake of the common good. What this means is that if the same rationale were to apply to homosexual activity, then only those in public authority could engage in such homosexual acts or command another to engage in them for the sake of the common good. A private individual would not have the authority to commit the act of same-sex sexual activity, even if it meant saving lives.

Can Aquinas's rationale for capital punishment be used to justify forcibly engaging in homosexual activity with another as punishment? Note that for Aquinas's rationale to apply (1) only those in public authority could engage in such an action, (2) only those grievously guilty could be homosexually acted upon by them, and (3) even then they could be homosexually acted upon only for the sake of the common good. Conditions (1) and (2) presumably could easily be satisfied; the question is whether condition (3) could be.

Punishment is meant to restore the order of justice. It is putting a part that has risen against the good of the whole back into its proper place or reestablishing it in a proper order to the good of the whole.[708] Certain aspects of the common good, however, are set not by the community but by nature. As Aquinas says, there is a natural common good.[709] This common good (insofar as it involves the end of the generative faculty) is set by nature as an end towards which the community ought to strive, lest the community die out. The generative power is by its very nature ordered to this shared end of generation. If it were not, it would cease to be the generative power. A person in public authority then has no authority over the due end of the generative power insofar as its due end is simply generation; its due end is set by nature, not by the

---

[708] Cf. Jensen, *Good & Evil Actions,* 167-169.
[709] Cf. ST I-II, Q94, A3, ad 1.

community. No human law can change the nature of the generative power.

Any public authority, then, who used his generative power upon a criminal in an act of same-sex sexual activity would be using his generative power for ungenerative purposes. In doing so, he would be using it contrary to nature, going against the role given to human beings by nature. The end of generation, however, is an aspect of the common good. Thus, any use of the generative power contrary to generation is against the common good. The public authority, then, who forcibly engaged in same-sex sexual activity with a criminal would be acting contrary to the common good, regardless of his praiseworthy remote motives.

e) Objections from the Principle of Totality

An objection similar to the capital punishment objection may be raised: if we may legitimately cut off a diseased limb for the sake of the good of the whole body, can we not also tell a lie or commit an act of same-sex sexual activity for the sake of the good of the preservation of one's own life?[710] Aquinas raises this very objection in ST II-II, Q110, A3, obj. 4:

> The lesser evil is to be chosen so that one avoid the greater evil, as for example the medical practitioner amputates the member lest the entire body be corrupted. But it is a lesser harm that someone give rise to a false opinion in the mind of someone than that someone kill or be killed. Therefore, a man can licitly lie so as to preserve one [person] from homicide and preserve another [person] from death.[711]

To further strengthen the objection, one could note that according to the principle of totality the parts of the body are for the good of the whole, so one may amputate a diseased member for the good of the whole body. Likewise, the ability to speak or assert is part of man, and so if necessary

---

[710] Cf. ST II-II, Q65, A1.

[711] "Praeterea, minus malum est eligendum ut vitetur maius malum: sicut medicus praecidit membrum ne corrumpatur totum corpus. Sed minus nocumentum est quod aliquis generet falsam opinionem in animo alicuius quam quod aliquis occidat vel occidatur. Ergo licite potest homo mentiri ut unum praeservet ab homicidio, et alium praeservet a morte."

304

one may sacrifice the natural *telos* of assertions for the good of the whole. Similarly, the powers of the soul are for the good of man, so why couldn't one commit an act of same-sex sexual activity for the good of the whole?

Aquinas disagrees with the objection. He answers it by noting that one may never do evil for the sake of good:

> A lie not only has the notion of flawed-action from the loss which it infers upon another, but also from its own disorder, as has been said. Now, it is not licit to use any illicit thing in a disordered way to prevent the injuries and defects of others: just as it is not licit to steal in order to give alms (except perhaps in case of necessity, in which all things are in common). And therefore it is not licit to tell a lie in order to save anyone from any danger whatsoever. Nevertheless, it is licit to hide the truth prudently under some dissimulation, as Augustine says in *contra Mendacium*.[712]

A lie is disordered of its very nature; a lie remains disordered no matter when, where, or why it is told (even for saving one's own life). The unnatural use of assertions (as using them contrary to their natural proximate end of truth) is inherent in every lie, even those told to save one's own life.

Aquinas's reply, however, does not seem fully to suffice. According to the principle of totality, amputating an organ is normally morally wrong. But if the good of the whole body requires it, it ceases to be wrong to amputate. Similarly, even if normally lying and homosexual acts are morally wrong, they might cease to be wrong if the good of the whole person requires it.

---

[712] ST II-II, Q110, A3, ad 4: "Ad quartum dicendum quod mendacium non solum habet rationem peccati ex damno quod infert proximo, sed ex sua inordinatione, ut dictum est. Non licet autem aliqua illicita inordinatione uti ad impediendum nocumenta et defectus aliorum: sicut non licet furari ad hoc quod homo eleemosynam faciat (nisi forte in casu necessitatis, in quo omnia sunt communia). Et ideo non est licitum mendacium dicere ad hoc quod aliquis alium a quocumque periculo liberet. Licet tamen veritatem occultare prudenter sub aliqua dissimulatione: ut Augustinus dicit, *contra Mendacium*."

In reply, it must be said that the parts and wholes are not analogous. Assertions are not part of one's body or one's health, or even one's soul. Assertions are parts of language. So even if it were possible to sacrifice assertions for the good of the whole, it would not be the body for which they could be sacrificed, but rather for the good of language. Second, in cutting off a diseased member one is actually destroying that member. In telling a lie, however, one is not destroying assertions, but rather abusing them contrary to their purpose. If one truly destroyed assertions in telling a lie, then one would not be lying at all, for asserting is essential to every lie.

Presumably then, the analogy could be recast in terms of the *telos* of the whole person. The power of language is part of the whole person, so its *telos* can be abandoned for the *telos* of the whole person.

But such a recasting will not do. The *telos* of the whole person comes from nature and it is nature that gives assertions their order to truth. This order cannot change without assertions ceasing to be.

Much of what was said concerning lying and the principle of totality can be said of homosexual activity. An act of homosexual activity remains disordered as the unnatural use of the generative power, even if done to save one's own life. Same-sex sexual activity in its very *ratio* involves the ungenerative use of the generative power, which is contrary to the natural end of the generative power as the generation and education of offspring. Nature dictates that the natural end of the generative power is for generation and so to oppose that end is to oppose the good of nature, and thus to oppose one's own good. It is this mere disorder in the action itself that counts, apart from any good consequences that happen to result. As stated earlier, in moral matters the order to the end trumps the mere production of the end. Morality is not a matter of technical skill.

Same-sex sexual activity is in principle wrong not because the generative organs are damaged or even permanently destroyed (not every case of homosexual activity necessarily damages the physical organs). Rather, homosexual activity is wrong in principle, because the generative power is being misused; it is being used for an end contrary to its natural purpose. It is used for ungenerative ends, contrary to its natural end of generation. This ungenerative use holds even in the case of blackmail to save one's own life. If the analogy with the diseased limb were to hold, one would actually have to destroy the generative power for the good of the whole. But such an action would not be same-sex sexual activity, but rather something like castration. The same rationale applies to the case of bestiality to save one's own life.

Again, as was the case with assertions, neither the individual nor public authority has authority over the nature of the generative power as such. The generative power is by its very nature for generation. This end is the very reason for the institution and creation of the generative power. Nature dictates the natural proximate end of the generative power; man does not and cannot. In certain cases, public authorities may dictate in what circumstances the generative power may be used. They may limit matrimony, excluding those of close consanguinity or the insane, but public authority has no say over whether the generative power is for generation; it rather must presuppose that end of nature.

If the public authority cannot change the natural end of the generative power, then neither can the individual. The end of the generative power is generation. So in using the generative power for homosexual purposes one is using that part contrary to its purpose, and so the rationale for cutting off a part for the good of the whole does not apply to the case at hand. You may use a part for its purpose: thus, if needed, you may cut off a part for the good of the whole; but the ungenerative use of the generative is always the use of a part contrary to its purpose. The principle of totality then cannot justify homosexual actions to save one's own life. Perhaps, it can justify cutting off the generative organs for the good of the whole body, but that would not be to engage the generative power.

f) But an Impossible Standard?

Various authors, such as Janet Smith, have objected that Aquinas's position is so stringent it would rule out many common socially accepted instances of lying, such as certain police work, sting operations, spying, etc.[713] Morally right action cannot be something impossible to attain, but Aquinas's standard seems to be. Thus, Aquinas must be mistaken.

In reply to Smith, it must be said that the absolutist position is not strictly speaking impossible. It may require much sacrifice, and possibly even rule out certain modes of undercover work, but it is certainly conceivable that a society could forgo such undercover lies for the sake of truth. Furthermore, the absolutist position is not as seemingly impossible as one would think. Many good consequences would follow from adopting an absolutist position in police work, hostage negotiations, and spying.

Regarding police operations, the vast majority of law enforcement activities would still be permissible, such as patrolling the neighborhoods, arresting suspects, interrogation, etc. None of these activities need involve lying, let alone deception. As for undercover or sting operations, it depends on how they are done. An undercover agent who buys illegal drugs from a dealer on the street is not lying. Wearing civilian clothing or driving an unmarked police car is not lying because no assertion is being made. If wearing civilian clothing were an assertion, then everyone who gets dressed in the morning would be intending to assert to the world that they are civilians.

Sting operations or interrogation techniques that involve lying, however, would be ruled out. This position may seem harsh to some, but if police officers had a general policy of not lying, public respect for the honesty of the profession would greatly improve. Further, any suspect who goes into interrogation knowing he is likely to be lied to is less likely to be cooperative or helpful in giving out any key information. If the police are untrustworthy in interrogation, then the suspect cannot be certain they will be trustworthy in plea bargaining.

---

[713] Cf. Smith, "Why Tollefsen and Pruss Are Wrong about Lying"; Kreeft, "Why Live Action Did Right"; Arkes, "When Speaking Falsely is Right."

Furthermore, the entrapment defense exists only because of sting operations. If a person normally would not have committed a crime were it not for the instigation of the police, is it really right to prosecute? Sting operations that involve an undercover agent who helps plan a bank heist involve the agent in formal cooperation in evil. The agent helps plan the heist only so that the suspect will be caught in the act of committing a robbery. To attain this end the undercover cop must intend that the suspect actually intend to go through with the robbery.[714] Intending that another do evil is itself evil. Ergo, such sting operations involve formal cooperation in evil. As Tollefsen says, "some of what does certainly involve lying [in police work] is such as to seem dubious to those who are not moral absolutists about lying, such as lying to entrap criminals, or planting evidence and then lying about it. A police profession purged of lying would be obviously improved in many ways and not necessarily greatly disadvantaged."[715]

In hostage negotiations, much of the literature indicates that successful negotiators do not lie to the hostage-taker.[716] Since hostage situa-

---

[714] It does not matter whether the suspect actually carries through the robbery or not; merely intending to carry it through or planning to do so is itself a moral evil even if the suspect is never able to carry out the heist successfully. Cf. ST I-II, Q20, A4.

[715] Tollefsen, *Lying and Christian Ethics*, 185. The point about formal cooperation in evil is my own and not Tollefsen's.

[716] Laurence Miller, *Practical Police Psychology: Stress Management and Crisis Intervention for Law Enforcement* (Springfield, IL: Charles C. Thomas, 2006), 151: "constructive manipulation and truthfulness are perfectly compatible. This goes beyond the standard protocol of not lying to HTs [hostage-takers] out of fear of compromising future credibility, but also involves a certain honesty of purpose....After a well-negotiated hostage crisis resolution, it is not uncommon for a HT to relate that the main reason they decided to end the crisis peacefully was because they really felt the negotiator's sincere concern for *everybody's* safety. That's something that's hard to fake, especially over hours and hours of prolonged negotiation."
See also Thomas Strentz, *Psychological Aspects of Crisis Negotiation*, 2nd ed. (Boca Raton, FL: Taylor & Francis Group, 2012), 30; Joseph Betz, "Moral Considerations Concerning the Police Response to Hostage Takers," in *Ethics, Public Policy and Criminal Justice*, ed. Frederick Elliston (Oelgeschlager, Gunn & Hain, 1982), 120: "The negotiator must not lie, but still must lead the hostage taker to the state in which he or she estimates small concessions as large ones." Michael J. McMains and Wayman C. Mullins advocate against lying to hostage takers with antisocial personality disorders: *Crisis Negotiations: Managing Critical Incidents and Hos-

tions tend to be highly publicized, any lies the authorities tell will likely be remembered by any future hostage-takers; future hostage-takers, being less likely to trust anything the negotiator says, will be less likely to surrender or even make small concessions.[717] Some of the terrorist groups that take hostages "remember and sometimes act out of revenge in later hostage-taking incidents for the tricks used on their comrades in earlier incidents."[718] As Adam Dolnik and Keith Fitzgerald say,

> deceiving the hostage takers is a short-sighted approach that is likely to have negative consequences for future incidents. Firstly, the wide media coverage barricade situations receive can make bluffing costly in the long run, as public familiarity with deceptive police tactics will make establishing credibility in future hostage negotiations much more challenging. Secondly, the proliferation of advanced communication technologies makes the terrorists' independent verification of official versions of events much easier, thus increasing the likelihood that any deceptive tactics will be detected, even during the incident. And finally, lying to hostage takers will only reinforce the terrorists' perception of the evil and untrustworthy nature of their adversary, leading not only to the escalation of tactics but also increased recruitment opportunities through propaganda. As we have seen in Nord-Ost and Beslan in particular, one of the most important moments of escalation came with media censorship and apparently deliberate release of inaccurate information about the number of hostages and the denial of the existence of terrorist demands. It follows that given the "new terrorists" increased ability to detect deception and effectively disseminate their own version of events, ensuring the accuracy of official statements and media reporting will be essential to the credibility of the government—a critical component of any successful negotiation efforts.[719]

---

tage Situations in Law Enforcement and Corrections, 5th ed. (New York: Routledge, 2015), 294.

[717] Cf. Betz, "Moral Considerations Concerning the Police Response to Hostage Takers," 122; Francis V. Burke, "Lying During Crisis Negotiations: A Costly Means to Expedient Resolution," *Criminal Justice Ethics* 14, no. 1 (1995); Adam Dolnik and Keith M. Fitzgerald, *Negotiating Hostage Crises with the New Terrorists* (Westport, CT: Praeger Security International, 2008), 159.

[718] Betz, 123.

[719] Dolnik and Fitzgerald, *Negotiating Hostage Crises with the New Terrorists*, 159.

Dolnik and Fitzgerald's conclusion that you should not lie to the hostage-taker comes from extensive research into a multitude of hostage situations. We will present one such case here in particular: on September 1st, 2004, Chechan terrorists took over 1,200 people hostage at School No. 1 in Beslan, Russia.[720] Prior to the incident the Russians had already established themselves as an untrustworthy adversary who lied to hostage takers.[721] Throughout the Beslan crisis the Russian government repeatedly lied through the media about the number of hostages (saying there were only 354 hostages when the reality was about 1,200)[722] in order to downplay the magnitude of the crisis. The Russians also falsely claimed that the children in the school were not in danger of dying from dehydration or thirst (when, in truth, many were).[723] The hostage-takers discovered these lies from the media reports, which inflamed their anger all the more.[724] The Russians then stormed the building, during which one of the terrorists screamed into his cell phone: "What have you done, you want to storm? Do you not know how many children there are? *You lied to us.* You bear responsibility for everything."[725] To which the negotiator replied, "But there's no assault!"[726] To which the terrorist retorted, "That's it. We're blowing up."[727] Over 330 people were killed, including 186 children, and over 700 wounded.[728] A later report by the European Court of Human Rights found Russian authorities had "serious failings" in responding to the crisis and ordered them to pay about 3 million euros to the victims' families. Russia later agreed to the damages.[729]

The absolutist rule against lying, if instituted earlier by hostage negotiators, could have saved many lives. Due to such horrific past scenarios, and the need for building a trustful rapport between the negotia-

---

[720] Ibid., 109.

[721] See, for example, the earlier Kizlyar crisis: Dolnik and Fitzgerald, 49-50.

[722] Ibid., 113.

[723] Ibid., 116.

[724] Ibid.

[725] Dolnik and Fitzgerald, 118; emphasis added.

[726] Ibid.

[727] Ibid.

[728] "Beslan School Siege Fast Facts," *CNN,* August 26, 2018, https://www.cnn.com/2013/09/09/world/europe/beslan-school-siege-fast-facts/index.html.

[729] Ibid.

tor and the hostage-taker, the current standard operating procedure for hostage negotiators is Aquinas's position: do not lie.

Intelligence operations could largely continue under the absolutist position. Most intelligence information can be gathered from open sources or methods that need not involve lying, such as foreign newspapers, diplomatic correspondence, monitoring social media networks, code-breaking, hacking, satellite imagery, local informants, or merely covert agent monitoring of local neighborhoods.[730] While the absolutist position would not allow for double agents or covert agents who assume false identities or passports, not all covert operations need cease. A covert agent or local informer who merely passes off regular tips about terrorist neighbors to the authorities need not be a liar.[731] Going overseas to sell a product, albeit unsuccessfully, need not constitute lying even if the salesman has further clandestine intentions. He can still try to sell the product and truthfully tell people he intends to do so, even if the spy agency, rather than his company, pays most of his salary.

Many covert CIA operations have so blackened the reputation of the United States abroad in previous years (particularly during the 1970s) that Roger Hilsman, former Assistant Secretary of State for Intelligence and Research, who served in the OSS [Office of Strategic Services, the predecessor to the CIA] during the 1940s, called for the abolishment of the agency's covert operations:

---

[730] "Most of the information referred to as 'intelligence' is obtained from open sources, but some of it is derived from secret intelligence; that is actionable intelligence obtained by covert means;" "in today's information age, the meticulous examination of open sources of information can illuminate a threat and provide much, if not all, the information required" (Angela Gendron, "Just War, Just Intelligence: An Ethical Framework for Foreign Espionage," *International Journal of Intelligence and CounterIntelligence* 18, no. 3 (2005): 398). "The vast majority of intelligence information on which U.S. policy depends comes from analyzing the open sources of foreign publications and broadcasts, routine diplomatic reporting, and the activities of newspaper reporters, and only a tiny fraction comes from espionage or covert action" (Roger Hilsman, "Does the CIA Still Have a Role?," *Foreign Affairs*, September/October 1995, 112-113). Six out of the seven principal techniques that MI5 uses for gathering intelligence do not generally involve lying: United Kingdom, MI5 - The Security Service, *Gathering Intelligence,* accessed January 2, 2017, https://www.mi5.gov.uk/gathering-intelligence.

[731] Cf. June Kelly, prod., *The Role of the Covert Agent*, BBC Radio, December 29, 2013, accessed January 2, 2017, http://www.bbc.co.uk/programmes/p01p31cw.

> Covert political action has been overused as an instrument of foreign policy and the reputation of the United States has suffered….the cumulative effect of several hundred blots has been to blacken it entirely, thus corroding one of America's major political assets—a belief abroad in American intentions and integrity. Covert political action is not only something the United States can do without in the post-Cold War world, it is something the United States could have done without during the Cold War as well.
> If the United States gets out of the business of espionage and covert political action…. the dollar savings would be substantial, the gain in political terms greater still.[732]

Hilsman is not alone. John Stockwell, former CIA agent in Congo, Vietnam, and Angola holds that the long-term damage of covert ops to the American reputation has not been worth the relatively little payoffs.[733] Even the very founder of the CIA Harry S. Truman, in a 1963 *Washington Post* article, questioned the need for the agency's covert operations:

> I never had any thought that when I set up the CIA that it would be injected into peacetime cloak and dagger operations. Some of the complications and embarrassment I think we have experienced are in part attributable to the fact that this quiet intelligence arm of the President has been so removed from its intended role that it is being interpreted as a symbol of sinister and mysterious foreign intrigue—and a subject for cold war enemy propaganda….I, therefore, would like to see the CIA be restored to its original assignment as the intelligence arm of the President, and that whatever else it can properly perform in that special field—and that its operational duties be terminated or properly used elsewhere. We have grown up as a nation, respected for our free institutions and for our ability to maintain a free and open society. There is

---

[732] Hilsman, "Does the CIA Still Have a Role?," 112. Of the $14.7 billion CIA budget, covert action costs $2.6 billion (Wilson Andrews and Todd Lindeman, "The 'Black Budget' How Intelligence Agencies Spend $52 Billion," *The Washington Post*, August 29, 2013, accessed January 2, 2017, http://www.washingtonpost.com/wp-srv/special/national/black-budget/).

[733] John Stockwell, "The Case against the C.I.A.," *Issue: A Journal of Opinion* 9, no. 1/2 (Spring - Summer 1979): 21-23.

something about the way the CIA has been functioning that is casting a shadow over our historic position and I feel that we need to correct it.[734]

If secret intelligence agencies and their operatives really stand for the truth, then what good is it if they win by telling lies? Truman's words, in some respects, echo that of Augustine in *Contra Mendacium.* Consentius had written Augustine asking whether it be advisable to expose a secret heretical sect called the Priscillianists by a covert sting operation. What could be wrong with pretending to be a Priscillianist in order to expose them and bring them to knowledge of the truth? Augustine wrote *Contra Mendacium* in reply, arguing that, among other reasons, covert operations easily lend themselves to the agent doing worse things than merely lying: the spy begins by pretending he is a Priscillianist, but as he infiltrates deeper and deeper into the organization this lie leads to more lies. The spy lyingly praises Priscillian (despite the many errors he espoused), then going even further lyingly praises the book called *The Pound,* which contains many blasphemies.[735] Augustine's point is that if you need to prove that you are one with the enemy by lying to them, then you may need to commit further evils to maintain your cover. If lying is necessary in covert operations, then why not blasphemies, adultery, theft, or even murder?[736]

An intelligence agency that refuses to sponsor operations of lying and falsehood better serves its ultimate purpose of truth.[737] Certainly in some instances, the absolutist position will require sacrifices, but in general leading a moral life demands sacrifices.

---

[734] Harry S. Truman, "Limit CIA Role To Intelligence," *The Washington Post*, December 22, 1963, A11.

[735] Augustine, *Against Lying,* trans. Harold B. Jaffee, Chapter 3, n. 5, p. 131-132.

[736] Cf. Ibid., Chapter 7, n. 17-18, p. 142-143.

[737] For more on lying for a good cause see Tollefsen, *Lying and Christian Ethics,* 173-197.

g) If You Don't Lie, Are You Morally Responsible for the Deaths that Follow?

John Cassian argues that if a person does not lie in cases of necessity, but instead speaks the truth, he becomes responsible for the death that follows.[738] Cassian is partially right, but offers a false dichotomy. If one tells the truth to the Nazi at the door, one is in part responsible for the death of the Jews that follows. But telling the truth or lying are not the only two options. One could also utter a mental reservation, equivocate, stay silent, make a distraction, run away, or punch the Nazi. Say, however, that none of these other options are likely to be successful. A very bright Nazi, skilled at picking out equivocal speech, is at the door. If only lying will save the Jews, is one morally responsible for their deaths if one refuses to lie?

An affirmative answer implies a faulty premise: an individual is morally responsible for any evil that he could have prevented but did not prevent. On such a premise, if he could have prevented a murder by committing adultery, he is morally responsible for the murder. On such an argument it also follows that the martyrs are murderers of themselves.[739] If they had renounced their faith, they would have prevented another from committing murder.

In fact, a person is not morally responsible for these other actions. They are not his actions, but the acts of others.[740] Someone is not morally responsible for an evil if the only way to prevent it is to do evil. Each person is required to do his part by ordering himself towards the due end, just as a judge must order himself towards justice. It may incidentally follow that others will die from mob riots when the verdict is read, but that is beyond the role of the judge. So too what follows from the proper order may be beyond an individual's role as an assertor of

---

[738] John Cassian, *Conferences* 17.19, trans. C.S. Gibson, in *Nicene and Post-Nicene Fathers*, ed. Philip Schaff and Henry Wace, vol. 11, Second Series (Buffalo, NY: Christian Literature Publishing, 1894), accessed January 7, 2017, http://www.newadvent.org/fathers/350817.htm.
[739] Cf. Augustine, *Lying* [*De Mendacio*], trans. Sister Mary Sarah Muldowney, Ch. 9, n. 13, p. 72.
[740] Ibid., n. 14, p. 74.

truth. As Aquinas says,

> He who does not remove something from which homicide follows, if he ought to remove it, will in a way incur the sin of voluntary homicide.…[but] he who devotes himself to the work of something licit, [and] taking due caution, from which homicide follows, does not incur the guilt of homicide.[741]

Note that Aquinas implies that an individual is guilty of homicide only if there was something he could have and *should* have done to prevent it.[742] But doing evil is in no way something a person ought ever to do. Consequently, if a person can prevent homicide only by doing evil, he is not guilty of the homicide that follows from his refraining to act. Cassian's argument, or any like it, cannot justify lying.

h) Is Eating Dessert Disordered?

A final class of objections are raised from an analogy with eating or the nutritive power. Jeremy Bentham states the objection as follows:

> The portion of food which constitutes what is called dinner, whatever demand a man has for nutrition and sustenance is, as above, in the case of ordinary health, if pecuniary circumstances admitt, considerably more than satisfied. Yet afterward, another portion constituting what is called *desert* may be partaken of without scruple or need of apology or danger of incurring reproach. Yet no more does any part of this desert contribute to nutrition—to the preservation of the individual, than any portion of sexual appetite employed in an utterly unprolific shape does

---

[741] ST II-II, Q64, A8, co.: "ille qui non removet ea ex quibus sequitur homicidium, si debeat removere, erit quodammodo homicidium voluntarium.…si aliquis det operam rei licitae, debitam diligentiam adhibens, et ex hoc homicidium sequatur, non incurrit homicidii reatum."

[742] Cf. ST I-II, Q6, A3, co.: "Respondeo dicendum quod voluntarium dicitur quod est a voluntate. Ab aliquo autem dicitur esse aliquid dupliciter. Uno modo, directe: quod scilicet procedit ab aliquo inquantum est agens, sicut calefactio a calore. Alio modo, indirecte, ex hoc ipso quod non agit: sicut submersio navis dicitur esse a gubernatore, inquantum desistit a gubernando. Sed sciendum quod non semper id quod sequitur ad defectum actionis, reducitur sicut in causam in agens, ex eo quod non agit: *sed solum tunc cum potest et debet agere*." Emphasis added.

to propagation—to the preservation and perhaps increase of the species.[743]

Just as not every act of eating must be ordered to the preservation of the individual or to bodily health, not every act of the sexual faculties must be ordered to the generation of offspring.

Bentham's objection does not hold against the argument we have given in this book. Any action not ordered to its natural end is a disordered action. The natural end of eating is the preservation of the individual in existence and due quantity. Eating dessert, however, is ordered to and does attain that end. Nourishment includes all foods, both nutritious and less nutritious.[744] Dessert remains food and so its consumption can be ordered towards the preservation of the individual. Eating dessert sometimes may be wrong, as in the case of gluttony or excessive quantity, but it is not wrong due to the perversion of a faculty.

Aquinas's discussion of the ethics of using the nutritive power generally deals with the more common cases of eating, namely, the consumption of food and drink. Man's proper function is to live in accord with reason. Every human act must be in accordance with reason. To subordinate reason to the lower powers or desires, then, is to invert the

---

[743] Jeremy Bentham, *Sextus,* in *Of Sexual Irregularities, and Other Writings on Sexual Morality*, 60-61. The original old English spelling from Bentham is retained.

[744] Chewing sugarless gum then does not fall under Aquinas's argument. The due end of the act of chewing is the reforming or remolding of something by the teeth, which can be done for all sorts of reasons such as preparation for swallowing, exercise of the jawbone and muscles surrounding it, etc. In chewing sugarless gum the engagement of the nutritive faculty isn't necessarily intended. Someone could just as easily intend to chew off a piece of a rubberband to break it in half without any intent to engage the nutritive faculty. The nutritive faculty is non-voluntary in its proper act and so cannot be commanded. But the act of chewing must be commanded. So, the act of chewing isn't properly an act of the nutritive, but rather is an act of the locomotive power. Further, even if the nutritive is engaged it would still be acting for its proper end insofar as even sugarless chewing gum technically has some nutritional value, albeit minimal (such as a few grams of carbohydrates; cf. Elizabeth Wolfenden, "Nutrition Information on Extra Sugar Free Gum," LIVESTRONG.COM, October 03, 2017, accessed December 11, 2017, https://www.livestrong.com/article/154394-ingredients-in-wrigleys-extra-gum/). Generally, it is not considered healthy to swallow the gum base, although the body will merely pass it through.

proper order. Our lower non-rational desires must serve and be subordinated to reason. The desires for food, drink, and sex, then, need to be properly ruled by reason, lest they rule us. Man must be the master of his desires for food; the desires for food must not be the master of man. Desires for food and drink that are beyond the rule of reason are inordinate desires. These inordinate desires for food Aquinas groups under the vice of gluttony, which is defined as excessive desire for pleasures of food and drink.[745] Thus, those who out of excessive desire consume excessive quantities of food have gluttonous desires.[746] But gluttony doesn't merely pertain to excessive quantity. One can have inordinate desires for food that also result in seeking out the most expensive foods, those most daintily prepared, etc.[747] The consumption of dessert need not be an act of gluttony; it only becomes gluttonous when one consumes dessert out of excessive desire for pleasures of the palate. Not every case of consuming dessert need involve excessive desire. Perhaps, it is a holiday; perhaps no other foods are readily available to eat; perhaps, I need to eat dessert out of social etiquette for my host. Many such reasons are perfectly legitimate reasons to eat dessert *ceteris paribus*.

---

[745] Cf. ST II-II, Q148, A1, co: "gula non nominat quemlibet appetitum edendi et bibendi, sed inordinatum;" A2, co: "vitium gulae proprie consistit in concupiscentia inordinata." Aquinas's definition of gluttony in Q148 regards *excess* as pertaining only to the desire and not the act itself.
[746] ST I, Q148, A4, co.
[747] Ibid.

Conclusion

In conclusion, Aquinas's account has withstood a multitude of objections. I have endeavored to bring up not just any objections, but rather the strongest possible objections to Aquinas. If all such objections fail, as seems to be the case here, then it is reasonable to conclude Aquinas must be right on these issues, regardless of what our desires might be.

Those closest to us, even our very friends, may protest. But true love adheres to what remains true. Aristotle himself faced a similar situation in refuting the Platonic theory of forms. Those who held the Platonic theory were his friends; yet he could not in truth agree with them: "Though we love both the truth and our friends, reverence is due to the truth first."[748]

Aquinas's perverted faculty argument has been widely misinterpreted by many on both sides of the debate. This confusion has led to a multitude of superfluous objections. Here I have endeavored to take Aquinas at his word: any action not ordered to its due end is a disordered action. The natural end of an action is its due end. Since the natural end of the act of using the generative power is for generation, any use of it not ordered to generation is disordered in itself. Since the natural end of the act of asserting is truth, any act of asserting not ordered to truth is itself disordered. This disorder is a moral disorder if it is a human action, because truth and generation are parts of the human good. Disordered actions lacking any due order to the human good are morally defective acts. Thus, both sexual activity between two persons of the same-sex and lying are morally wrong. They are always wrong because they both entail a rejection of the shared good, that is, the common good. Homosexual acts always entail a rejection of the shared good of new life. Lying always entails a rejection of the shared good of truth. Any good society ought to desire to continue itself in existence. Homsexual activity rejects this order by warping the only means to that end away from that end. Any good society ought to desire truth. Lying rejects that order by warping the only means to that end away from that end.

---

[748] Aristotle, *Nicomachean Ethics* I.6 1096a16, trans. Irwin, p. 5.

Many actions are morally evil, but not all are *intrinsece malum.* Lying never admits of exceptions because assertions as assertions are always for truth. To twist assertions away from their end is to go beyond or contrary to the order set by God who created assertions and their natural order to truth. Similarly, homosexual activity admits of no exceptions because the generative power is always for generation. To twist the generative power away from its end is contrary to the very will of God who created the generative power and its natural order to generation. Any action not ordered to its natural end is always a disordered action, because God is the very author of nature; he is the author of every act's natural order to its end. Thus, to pervert an act away from its natural end is to act beside or contrary to the order intended by God. True happiness cannot be found apart from this ordering of our actions to their due ends. We must follow our nature; if we are to use our natural powers, we must use them for their natural ends. There cannot be good in warping our powers away from their ends anymore than an oak can be good in using its nutritive power to wither, wilt, and waste away. The nutritive power is for nutrition, using it for unnutritive purposes is evil; so too using the generative power for ungenerative acts cannot be morally good.

From these considerations we must be careful not to conclude that homosexual activity and lying are morally equivalent. Some actions are always wrong regardless of consequences, but not all acts that are always wrong are gravely wrong. Murder is always wrong, but lying is definitely not equivalent to murder. Lying is always wrong, but in itself it is only a slight evil. Every lie in itself is only against the particular truth from which it deviates. Homosexual activity, however, is much worse in its moral badness. Every act of same-sex sexual activity is against the order to new human life. Since the order to new human life is a much greater good than a particular truth, homosexual acts are morally speaking much worse than a mere act of lying. The moral species of lying then is wrong, but only minimally so, whereas the moral species of homosexual activity is wrong and seriously wrong.

Any moral species, however, can be aggravated by adding further bad remote intentions or circumstances. Lying then for the sake of murder is worse than mere lying for its own sake. Likewise, lying in order to save money is much less bad than lying to injure another. Likewise, engaging in same-sex sexual conduct when you have been pressured into it is much less bad than engaging in the action in public in order to encourage others to engage in similar practices. All of these further intentions can aggravate or lessen the badness of the human action. Some cases of lying then, such as lies told in order to kill another, are worse in kind than a mere act of homosexual conduct. Lying in its moral species (abstracted from further considerations about circumstances and remote intentions) is much less wrong than the moral species of homosexual conduct (abstracted from further considerations about circumstances and remote intentions).

If we wish to find true happiness, that is, happiness as more than a feeling, we must seek what is truly good. Sometimes our passions and desires prevent us from seeing what is truly good. Sometimes we wish it were otherwise and try to conform reality to our desires instead of conforming our own desires to reality. Sometimes we have been misinformed through no fault of own. Still we must seek the truth inasmuch as it is reasonably possible. In morals, the stakes stand high. Indeed, it is not merely important that we know what the true moral good is, it is all important. Morality isn't about following arbitrary rules, but about ordering ourselves to what is truly good, because true happiness can only consist in what is truly good. If we wish to attain the end, we must be careful to order ourselves to it and not hinder its attainment in ourselves or others. The experience of many practicing homosexuals, even in countries where homosexuality is widely accepted, indicates that true happiness cannot be found in these lower things. The higher prevalence of disorders in them is a sign that something has gone wrong. Many today explain these disorders away in terms of societal oppression, but we have seen that societal oppression cannot account for all of the phenomena. We have proposed here that the better, honest explanation is that it should be no surprise if disordered actions themselves tend to produce disordered psychological states. In the West, we have defrauded and horribly persecuted gays. To this day, the cultural elites continue to defraud them by selling them a counterfeit of the truth. We must love the truth by calling what is good good and what is evil evil. Gays are good, but homosexual activity, like lying, is morally evil.

Homosexual actions are not the only moral evil, nor the most grievous. We do not call here for their criminalization, but in no way ought people be encouraged to participate in intrinsically evil actions, just as nobody ought to be encouraged to tell a lie.

Many advocates of homosexual activity have been far from honest in their work. In fact, many if not most in the gay movement think that lying is sometimes morally acceptable for the sake of their cause. In this country it had often been said that gays just want to marry like the rest of us. Once marriage has been redefined to include same-sex unions nothing more will happen. There will be no implications for religious liberty or free speech.[749] After the announcement of *Obergefell v. Hodges,* however, those in the gay movement revealed their true colors. Two days after the announcement, *Time Magazine* published an article arguing the state ought to start taxing religious institutions.[750]

---

[749] Emily Bazelon, "Will Churches Be Forced To Conduct Gay Weddings?" *Slate,* December 12, 2012, accessed March 27, 2018, http://www.slate.com/business/2018/03/trumps-global-trade-war-is-morphing-into-a-showdown-with-china-for-now.html: "It's just wrong to spook voters about gay rights by arguing that gay people are coming for their churches. It's not gonna happen."

[750] Mark Oppenheimer, "Now's the Time To End Tax Exemptions for Religious Institutions," *Time*, June 28, 2015, accessed March 27, 2018, http://time.com/3939143/nows-the-time-to-end-tax-exemptions-for-religious-institutions/.

See also Robert P. George, "Marriage, Religious Liberty, and the 'Grand Bargain,'" Public Discourse, July 19, 2012, accessed March 27, 2018, http://www.thepublicdiscourse.com/2012/07/5884/: "It was only yesterday, was it not, that we were being assured that the redefinition of marriage to include same-sex partnerships would have no impact on persons and institutions that hold to the traditional view of marriage as a conjugal union?... No one, they assured us, would require Catholic or other foster care and adoption services to place children in same-sex headed households. No one, they said, would require religiously affiliated schools and social-service agencies to treat same-sex partners as spouses, or impose penalties or disabilities on those that dissent. No one would be fired from his or her job (or suffer employment discrimination) for voicing support for conjugal marriage or criticizing same-sex sexual conduct and relationships. And no one was proposing to recognize polyamorous relationships or normalize 'open marriages,' nor would redefinition undermine the norms of sexual exclusivity and monogamy in theory or practice."

Unlike my opponents, I believe that every lie is morally bad. Under no circumstances is lying morally licit. We must adhere to the truth in all cases; we must never lie. Many within the gay movements, however, say that you can. But if your very ideology teaches that lying is sometimes licit, then how can I believe that what you preach is true?[751]

As lovers of truth then let us stand with Aquinas: lying and homosexual activity are always bad. But such actions are not the only actions that are always wrong. As Aristotle says,

> Now not every action admits of the mean. For the names of some automatically include baseness—for instance, spite, shamelessness, envy [among feelings], and adultery, theft, murder, among actions....Hence in doing these things we can never be correct, but must invariably be in error. We cannot do them well or not well—by committing adultery, for instance, with the right woman at the right time in the right way. On the contrary, it is true without qualification that to do any of them is to be in error.[752]

I hold that a similar account holds for both lying and homosexual activity. We must never do them. "Presumably there are some things we cannot be compelled to do. Rather than do them we should suffer the most terrible consequences and accept death."[753] Intrinsically evil actions ought never to be done. Let us reject evil and turn towards the good. Let us be lovers of truth and new life.

---

[751] Cf. Augustine, *Against Lying,* trans. Harold B. Jaffee, n. 4, n. 7.

[752] Aristotle, *Nicomachean Ethics* II.6 1107a, trans. Terence Irwin, p. 25.

[753] Ibid., III.1 1110a25-27, trans. Irwin, p. 31.

Bibliography

Works of Aquinas:

Aquinas, Thomas. *Commentary on the Nicomachean Ethics.* Translated by C.I. Litzinger, O.P. Chicago: Henry Regnery Company, 1964. http://dhspriory.org/thomas/Ethics.htm.

————. *Expositio Libri Peryermeneias.* Translated by Jean T. Oesterle. Milwaukee: Marquette University Press, 1962. Accessed June 1, 2015. http://dhspriory.org/thomas/PeriHermeneias.htm#1.

————. *Liber de Veritate Catholicae Fidei contra errores Infidelium seu Summa Contra Gentiles,* Vol. III. Taurini, Romae: Marietti, 1961.

————. *Of God and His Creatures,* Book III. Translated by Joseph Ricaby. London: Burns & Oates, 1905. https://maritain.nd.edu/jmc/etext/gc3_122.htm.

————. *On Evil.* Translated by Richard Regan. Edited by Brian Davies. New York: Oxford University Press, 2003.

————. *Summa Theologica.* Translated by Fathers of the English Dominican Province. 2nd and Revised edition. 1920. http://www.newadvent.org/summa/.

Aquinatis, Sancti Thomas. *Quaestiones de Quolibet.* In *Opera Omnia Iussu Leonis XIII P.M. Edita, Tomus* XXV, *Volumen* 1. Roma: Commissio Leonina, 1996.

————. *Summa Theologiae.* Matriti: Biblioteca de Autores Cristianos, 1952.

Aquinatis, S. Thomae. *De Potentia.* In *Quaestiones Disputatae.* Volumen II. Taurini, Romae: Marietti, 1965.

─────. *In Octo Libros Phyiscorum Aristotelis Expositio.* Edited by P.M. Maggiòlo. Taurini, Romae: Marietti, 1965.

─────. *In Quattuor Libros Sententiarum.* In *Opera Omnia.* Edited by Roberto Busa. Vol. I. fromman-holzboog, 1980.

─────. *Liber de Veritate Catholicae Fidei contra errores Infidelium seu Summa Contra Gentiles.* Taurini, Romae: Marietti, 1961.

─────. *Quaestiones Disputatae.* Vol. II. Taurini, Romae: Marietti, 1965.

─────. *Sancti Thomae Aquinatis Commentum in Quatuor Libros Sententiarum Magistri Petri Lombardi.* Vol. II. Parmae: Typis Petri Fiaccadori, 1858.

─────. *Scriptum Super Libros Sententiarum Magistri Petri Lombardi Episcopi Parisiensis.* Vol. II. Edited by R.P. Mandonnet. Parisiis: P. Lethielleux, 1929.

─────. *Scriptum Super Sententiis Magistri Petri Lombardi.* Vol. III. Edited by R.P. Maria Fabianus Moos, O.P. Parisiis: P. Lethielleux, 1933.

─────. *Scriptum Super Sententiis Magistri Petri Lombardi.* Vol. IV. Parisiis: P. Lethielleux, 1947.

─────. *Super Epistolas S. Pauli Lectura, Super Rom.* Edited by P. Raphaelis Cai, O.P., VIII Revisa ed., vol. I. Taurini, Romae: Marietti, 1953.

─────. *Super Evangelium S. Ioannis Lectura.* Edited by P. Raphaelis Cai. Taurini, Romae: Marietti, 1952.

Sancti Thomae de Aquino. *Compendium Theologiae*. In *Opera Omnia Iussu Leonis XIII P.M. Edita*. Vol. XLII. Roma, 1979.

―――――. *Expositio Libri Peryermenias, Editio altera retractata*. In *Opera Omnia Iussu Leonis XIII P.M. Edita, Tomus I* 1*. Roma: Commissio Leonina, 1989.

―――――. *Expositio Super Isaiam ad Litteram,* in *Opera Omnia Iussu Leonis XIII P.M. Edita*. Vol. XXVIII. Roma: Editori di San Tommaso, 1974.

―――――. *Quaestiones de Quolibet*. In *Opera Omnia Iussu Leonis XIII P.M. Edita*. Vol. XXV, volumen 1. Roma: Commissio Leonina, 1996.

―――――. *Quaestiones Disputatae de Anima*. In *Opera Omnia Iussu Leonis XIII P.M. Edita Cura et Studio Fratrum Praedicatorum*. Vol. XXIV, 1, ed B.C. Bazán. Roma: Commissio Leonina, 1996.

―――――. *Quaestiones Disputatae de Malo*. In *Opera Omnia Iussu Leonis XIII P.M. Edita,* vol. XXIII. Roma: Commissio Leonina, 1982.

―――――. *Sentencia Libri de Anima*. In *Opera Omnia Iussu Leonis XIII P.M. Edita,* vol. XLV. Romae, 1984.

―――――. *Sententia Libri Ethicorum*. In *Opera Omnia Iussu Leonis XIII P.M. Edita*. Vol. XLVII.1. Romae, 1969.

―――――. *Sententia Libri Ethicorum*. In *Opera Omnia Iussu Leonis XIII P.M. Edita,* Vol. XLVII.2. Romae: Sanctae Sabinae, 1969.

―――――. *Sententia Libri Politicorum*. In *Opera Omnia Iussu Leonis XIII P.M. Edita*. Vol. XLVIII. Romae, 1971.

—————. *Sententiae Primi Libri Ethicorum.* In *Opera Omnia Iussu Leonis XIII P.M. Edita,* vol. XLVII, volume I. Romae, 1969.

—————. *Sententiae Tertii Libri Ethicorum.* In *Opera Omnia Iussu Leonis XIII P.M. Edita,* Tomus XLVII, Volumen I. Roma, 1969.

—————. *Summa Theologiae.* Rome: Editiones Paulinae, 1962.

Other Works:

ΑΘΗΝΓΟΡΟΥ ΑΘΗΝΑΙΟΥ ΦΙΛΟΣΟΦΟΥ ΧΡΙΣΤΙΑΝΟΥ (Athenagorae Atheniensis Philosophi Christiani), *ΠΡΕΣΒΕΙΑ ΠΕΡΙ ΧΡΙΣΤΙΑΝΩΝ (Legatio pro Christianis)*, Latin translated by Gesnero. In *Patrologiae Graecae,* vol. 6. Edited by J.P. Migne (In via dicta *d'amboise,* prope portam lutetiae parisiorum vulgo *d'enfer* nominatam seu petit-montrouge, 1856).

Abaelardus, Petrus. *Expositio in Hexameron.* CC CM, 15 (M. Romig, D. Luscombe, 2004). In *Library of Latin Texts – Series A, Brepolis.*

Abelard, Peter. *Carmen Ad Astralabium.* Groningen, 1987.

—————. *Carmen ad Astralabium.* Translated by Juanita Feros Ruys. In *The Repentant Abelard: Family, Gender, and Ethics in Peter Abelard's Carmen ad Astralabium and Planctus.* New York: Palgrave MacMillan, 2014.

Adler, Jonathan E. "Lying, Deceiving, or Falsely Implicating." *The Journal of Philosophy* 94, no. 9 (September 01, 1997): 435-52.

Adorno, Theodor W. *Minima Moralia: Reflexionen aus dem beschädigten Leben.* Frankfurt: Suhrkamp, 1951.

"Adult Chimpanzee Kills Baby Chimp in Front of Shocked Los Angeles Zoo Visitors." CBS News. June 27, 2012. Accessed September 16,

2016. http://www.cbsnews.com/news/adult-chimpanzee-kills-baby-chimp-in-front-of-shocked-los-angeles-zoo-visitors/.

D. Alberti Magni. *Commentarii in IV Sententiarum*, vol. 29. Edited by Borgnet. Parisiis apud Ludovicum Vives, Bibliopolam Editorem, 1894.

D. Alberti Magni, Ratisbonensis Episcopi, Ordinis Praedicatorum. *Ennarationes in Secundam Partem Lucae (X-XXIV)*. In *Opera Omnia*, vol. 23. Edited by Borgnet. Parisiis apud Ludovicum Vives, Biblipolam Editorem, 1895.

D. Alberti Magni. *Summae Theologiae, Secunda Pars*. Parisiis: Ludovicum Vives, Bibliopolam Editorem, 1895.

Sancti Doctoris Ecclesiae Alberti Magni Ordinis Fratrum Praedictorum Episcopi. *Quaestio de Luxuria*. In *Opera Omnia*, vol. XXV, part II, *Quaestiones*. Monasterii Westfalorum in Aedibus Aschendorff, 1993.

Al-Ghazali. "*Kasr al Shahwatayn* (Curbing the Two Appetites)." In *Ihya"Ulum al-Din (Revivification of the Sciences of Religion)*. Translated by Caesar E. Farah. Minneapolis: Bibliotheca Islamica, 1992. http://www.ghazali.org/works/abstin.htm. Accessed December 30, 2017.

Allsopp, Michael E., and John J. O'Keefe, eds. *Veritatis Splendor: American Responses*. Kansas City, MO: Sheed & Ward, 1995.

Anderson, Erik A. "A Defense of the 'Sterility Objection' to the New Natural Lawyers' Argument Against Same-Sex Marriage." *Ethical Theory and Moral Practice* 16, no. 4 (2013): 759-75.

Andrews, Wilson, and Todd Lindeman. "The 'Black Budget' How Intelligence Agencies Spend $52 Billion." *The Washington Post*, August 29, 2013. Accessed January 2, 2017.

http://www.washingtonpost.com/wp-srv/special/national/black-budget/.

Anscombe, G.E.M. "Contraception and Chastity," 1972. Accessed February 03, 2016. http://www.orthodoxytoday.org/articles/ AnscombeChastity.php.

———. "You Can have Sex without Children: Christianity and the New Offer." In *Ethics, Religion and Politics, Collected Philosophical Papers.* Vol. III. Minneapolis: University of Minnesota Press, 1981.

Arico, Adam J., and Don Fallis. "Lies, Damned Lies, and Statistics: An Empirical Investigation of the Concept of Lying." *Philosophical Psychology* 26, no. 6 (2013): 790-816.

Aristotle. *De Interpretatione.* Translated by E.M. Edghill. In *The Basic Works Of Aristotle*, edited by Richard McKeon, 40-61. New York: Modern Library, 2001.

———. *Nicomachean Ethics.* In *Aristotle's Ethica Nicomachea.* Edited by J. Bywater. Oxford: Clarendon Press, 1894. http://www.perseus.tufts.edu/hopper/text?doc=Perseus% 3Atext%3A1999.01.0053%3Abekker+page%3D1094a%3Abekker +line%3D1.

———. *Nicomachean Ethics.* Translated by Terence Irwin. 2nd ed. Indianapolis/Cambridge: Hackett Publishing Company, 1999.

———. *On the Parts of Animals.* Translated by William Ogle. Vol. IV. Accessed February 23, 2016. http://classics.mit.edu/Aristotle/parts_animals.4.iv.html.

———. *Posterior Analytics/Topica.* Translated by Hugh Tredennick and E.S. Forster. The Loeb Classical Library. Cambridge, MA: Harvard University Press, 1960.

Arkes, Hadley. "When Speaking Falsely Is Right." *Public Discourse.* February 19, 2011. Accessed November 17, 2014. http://www.thepublicdiscourse.com/2011/02/2631/.

Armstrong, W.P. "Botanical Record-Breakers (Part 2 of 2)." Botanical Record-Breakers (Part 2 of 2). January 26, 2014. Accessed February 22, 2016. http://waynesword.palomar.edu/ww0601.htm.

Athenagoras of Athens. "A Plea for Christians." Translated by B.P. Pratten. Edited by Kevin Knight. In *Ante-Nicene Fathers*, vol. 2. Edited by Alexander Roberts, James Donaldson, and A. Cleveland Coxe. Buffalo: Christian Literature Publishing, 1885. Accessed December 29, 2017. http://www.newadvent.org/fathers/0205.htm.

Augros, Michael, and Christopher Oleson. "St. Thomas and the Naturalistic Fallacy." *The National Catholic Bioethics Quarterly* 13, no. 4 (winter 2013): 637-61.

Augustine. *Against Lying.* Translated by Harold B. Jaffee. In *The Fathers of the Church: A New Translation*, vol. 16, edited by Roy J. Deferrari. Washington, D.C., The Catholic University of America Press, 1952.

———. *The City of God.* Translated by Marcus Dods. In *Nicene and Post-Nicene Fathers, First Series,* vol. 2. Edited by Philip Schaff. Buffalo, NY: Christian Publishing Co., 1887. Revised and edited by Kevin Knight. http://www.newadvent.org/fathers/120116.htm.

———. *Confessions.* Translated by Henry Chadwick. Oxford, New York: Oxford University Press, 1992.

———. *Lying.* Translated by Mary Sarah Muldowney. In *The Fathers of the Church: A New Translation*, vol. 16, edited by Roy J. Deferrari. Washington, D.C., The Catholic University of America Press, 1952.

————. *On Free Choice of the Will*. Translated by Thomas Williams. Indianapolis, IN: Hackett Publishing Company, 1993.

————. *To Consentius, Against Lying.* Translated by H. Browne. In *Nicene and Post-Nicene Fathers, First Series,* vol. 3. Edited by Philip Schaff. Buffalo, NY: Christian Literature Publishing Co., 1887. Revised and edited by Kevin Knight, http://www.newadvent.org/fathers/1313.htm.

Augustine Hipponensis. *Confessionum libri tredecim,* III.8.1-7, CC SL, 27 (L. Verheijen, 1981), *Notitia Clavis Patrum Latinorum*, 251, in *Library of Latin Texts – Series A, Brepolis.* http://clt.brepolis.net/LLTA/pages/TextSearch.aspx?key=PAUG_0 251_.

————. *Contra mendacium,* s. 5 p.C, CPL 0304, CSEL, 41 (J. Zycha, 1900), p. 469-528, in *Library of Latin Texts –Series A, Brepolis.* http://clt.brepolis.net/LLTA/pages/TextSearch.aspx?key=PAUG_0 304_.

————. *De Ciuitate Dei,* CC SL, 47; 48 (B. Dombart / A. Kalb, 1955), in *Library of Latin Texts – Series A, Brepolis.* http://clt.brepolis.net/LLTA/pages/TextSearch.aspx?key=PAUG_0 313_.

Austriaco, Nicanor Pier Giorgio. "On Reshaping Skulls and Unintelligible Intentions." *Nova et Vetera.* English Edition 3, no. 1 (2005): 81-100.

Averrois Cordubensis. *In Moralia Nicomachia Expositione.* In *Tertium Volumen Aristotelis Stagiritae Libri Moralem totam Philosophiam complectentes cum Averrois Cordubensis in Moralia Nicomachia Expositione, Et in Platonis Libros de Republica Paraphrasi.* Venetiis Apud Iunctas, 1562.

Averroes ((Ibn Rushd) of Cordoba. *Long Commentary on the De Anima of Aristotle.* Translated by Richard C. Taylor. New Haven & London: Yale University Press, 2009.

Avicenna. *The Metaphysics of the Healing.* Translated by Michael E. Marmura. Provo, Utah: Brigham Young University Press, 2005.

Ayer, A.J., C.H. Rolph, and Anthony Grey. "Debate on Homosexuality." *Sunday Times* (London), December 12, 1965.

Bacon, Roger. *The Opus Major of Roger Bacon,* vol. II. Translated by Robert Belle Burke. Philadelphia: University of Pennsylvania Press, 1928.

————. *Rogeri Baconis Moralis Philosophia.* Edited by Ferdinand Delorme and Eugenio Massa. Turici, 1953.

Bacon, Sir Francis. *The New Atlantis.* Edited by Michael and William Fishburne. 1627. http://www.gutenberg.org/files/2434/2434-h/2434-h.htm. Accessed December 30, 2017.

Bagemihl, Bruce. *Biological Exuberance: Animal Homosexuality and Natural Diversity.* New York: St. Martin's Press, 1999.

Bailey, Nathan W., and Marlene Zuk. "Same-sex Sexual Behavior and Evolution." *Trends in Ecology and Evolution* 30, no. 10 (2009).

Barras, Colin. "The Twisted World of Sexual Organs." BBC earth. September 2014. The Twisted World of Sexual Organs. Accessed February 22, 2016. http://www.bbc.com/earth/bespoke/story/20140908-twisted-world-of-sexual-organs/index.html.

BBCEarth. "Fearsome Teeth of the Gelada Baboon - Deadly 60 - Ethiopia - Series 3 - BBC." Youtube. March 07, 2014. Accessed August 20, 2016. https://www.youtube.com/watch?v=CsO_hGQVwiQ.

Beauvoir, Simone De. *The Second Sex*. Translated by H.M. Parshley. New York: Alfred A. Knopf, 1957.

Bentham, Jeremy. *Offences Against One's Self: Paederasty*. MS. May 5, 2002. Accessed November 13, 2015. http://www.columbia.edu/cu/lweb/eresources/exhibitions/sw25/bentham/index.html.

———. *Of Sexual Irregularities, and Other Writings on Sexual Morality*. Edited by Philip Schofield, Catherine Pease-Watkin, and Michael Quinn. Oxford, UK: Clarendon Press, 2014.

Betz, Joseph. "Moral Considerations Concerning the Police Response to Hostage Takers." In *Ethics, Public Policy and Criminal Justice*, edited by Frederick Elliston, 110-32. Oelgeschlager, Gunn & Hain, 1982.

"Blood Shooting Eyes." Nat Geo WILD. Accessed September 14, 2016. http://channel.nationalgeographic.com/wild/worlds-weirdest/videos/blood-shooting-eyes/.

Bok, Sissela. *Lying*. New York: Pantheon Books, 1978.

De Cou, Christopher R. and Shannon M. Lynch. "Sexual Orientation, Gender, and Attempted Suicide Among Adolescent Psychiatric Inpatients." *Psychological Services* 15, no. 3 (2018): 363-369.

Doctoris Seraphici S. Bonaventurae S.R.E. Episcopi Cardinalis. *Commentarius In Evangelium S. Lucae*. In *Opera Omnia*, vol. VII. Edited by Collegii A S. Bonaventura. Ad Claras Aquas (Quaracchi) Prope Florentiam, Ex Typographia Collegii S. Bonaventurae, 1895.

St. Bonaventure. *St. Bonaventure's Commentary on the Gospel of Luke Chapters 17-24.* Translated by Robert J. Karris, O.F.M., Th.D. Saint Bonaventure, NY: Franciscan Institute Publications, 2004.

Boyle, J. "The Absolute Prohibition of Lying and the Origins of the Casuistry of Mental Reservation: Augustinian Arguments and Thomistic Developments." *The American Journal of Jurisprudence* 44, no. 1 (1999): 43-65.

Bradford, Alina. "Walrus Facts." LiveScience. November 21, 2014. Accessed August 20, 2016. http://www.livescience.com/27442-walrus-facts.html.

Bruno, Giordano. *The Expulsion of the Triumphant Beast.* Translated & edited by Arthur D. Imerti. New Brunswick, NJ: Rutgers University Press, 1964.

Budziszewski, J. "The Illusion of Gay Marriage." *Philosophia Christi* 7, no. 1 (2005): 45-52.

————. "What the Point Isn't, A Response to Marvin M. Ellison." *Philosophia Christi* 7, no. 1 (2005): 15-17.

Burke, Edmund. *The Correspondence of Edmund Burke,* vol. IV. Edited by John A. Woods. Cambridge/Chicago: Cambridge University Press/The University of Chicago Press, 1963.

————. *Sketch of the Negro Code.* In *Library of Economics and Liberty.* http://www.econlib.org/library/LFBooks/Burke/brkSWv4c7.html.

Burke, Francis V. "Lying During Crisis Negotiations: A Costly Means to Expedient Resolution." *Criminal Justice Ethics* 14, no. 1 (1995): 49-62.

Burlaeus, Gualterus. *Expositio Gualteri Burlei super decem Libros Eth-icorum Aristotelis*. Venetiis: Arte Simonis de Luere, 1500. http://hdl.handle.net/2027/uc1.31158010821410.

Carson, Thomas L. "The Definition of Lying*." *Nous* 40, no. 2 (2006): 284-306.

———. "Liar Liar." *International Journal of Applied Philosophy* 22, no. 2 (2008): 189-210.

———. "Lying, Deception, and Related Concepts." In *The Philosophy of Deception*, by Clancy W. Martin. Oxford: Oxford University Press, 2009.

———. "Second Thoughts about Bluffing." *Business Ethics Quarterly* 3, no. 4 (1993): 317.

Cassian, John. "Conferences 17.19." Translated by C.S. Gibson. In *Nicene and Post-Nicene Fathers*, edited by Philip Schaff and Henry Wace. Vol. 11. Second Series. Buffalo, NY: Christian Literature Publishing, 1894. Accessed January 7, 2017. http://www.newadvent.org/fathers/350817.htm.

Catechism of the Catholic Church. Rome: Ubi Et Orbi Communications, 1994.

Chisholm, Roderick M., and Thomas D. Feehan. "The Intent to Deceive." *The Journal of Philosophy* 74, no. 3 (March 01, 1977): 143-59.

Cicero, M. Tullius. *Against Catiline*. Edited by Albert Clark and Albert Curtis Clark. Scriptorum Classicorum Bibliotheca Oxoniensis, 1908. http://www.perseus.tufts.edu/hopper/text?doc=Perseus% 3Atext%3A1999.02.0010%3Atext%3DCatil.%3Aspeech%3D1%3 Achapter%3D1.

————. *Against Verres.* Edited by Albert Clark and William Peterson. Scriptorum Classicorum Bibliotheca Oxoniensis, 1917. http://www.perseus.tufts.edu/hopper/text?doc=Perseus%3Atext%3 A1999.02.0012%3Atext%3DVer.

————. *De Haruspicum Responsis.* In *Cicero: The Speeches with an English Translation.* Cambridge/London: Harvard University Press, William Heinemann Ltd., 1961.

————. *Librorum de Re Publica Sex* 4.4. Edited by C.F.W. Mueller. Leipzig: Teubner, 1889. http://www.perseus.tufts.edu/hopper/text? doc=Perseus%3Atext%3A2007.01.0031%3Abook%3D1%3Asecti on%3D1.

Clay, Rebecca. "Suicide and Intimate Partner Violence." *Monitor on Psychology* 45, no. 10 (2014), accessed January 5, 2018: http://www.apa.org/monitor/2014/11/suicide-violence.aspx.

Comte, Auguste. *Physique sociale (Cours De Philosophia Positive, Leçons 46 à 60).* Vol. II. Edited by Jean-Paul Enthoven. Paris: Hermann, 1975.

Corvino, John. "Why Shouldn't Tommy and Jim Have Sex?" In *Same Sex: Debating the Ethics, Science, and Culture of Homosexuality,* edited by John Corvino, 2-16. Lanham, MD: Rowman & Littlefield, 1997.

————. *What's Wrong with Homosexuality?* New York: Oxford University Press, 2013.

Curran, Charles E. "Absolute Norms and Medical Ethics." In *Absolutes in Moral Theology?*, 108-53. Washington, D.C.: Corpus Books, 1968.

————. "Veritatis Splendor: A Revisionist Perspective." In *Veritatis Splendor: American Responses*, edited by Michael E. Allsopp and John J. O'Keefe, 224-43. Kansas City, MO: Sheed & Ward, 1995.

————. *Absolutes in Moral Theology?* Washington: Corpus Books, 1968.

Dalrymple, Alexander. *Thoughts of an Old Man, of Independent Mind, Though Dependent Fortune, on the Present High Price of Corn.* London: Bunney and Gold, Shoe-lane, 1800.

Davidson, Donald. "Deception and Division." In *The Multiple Self*, edited by Jon Elster, 79-92. Cambridge: Cambridge University Press, 1987.

De Koninck, Charles. "The Primacy of the Common Good against the Personalists." In *The Writings of Charles De Koninck Volume 2*, edited by Ralph McInerny, translated by Ralph McInerny, 63-108. Vol. 2. Notre Dame, IN: University of Notre Dame Press, 2009.

de Sade, Marquis. *La Philosophie dans le boudoir,* vol. I. London: 1795. https://fr.wikisource.org/wiki/La_Philosophie_dans_le_boudoir/Tome_I/Troisième_Dialogue.

————. *Philosophy in the Boudoir.* Translated by Joachim Neugroschel. New York: Penguin, 2006.

Decosimo, David. "JUST LIES: Finding Augustine's Ethics of Public Lying in His Treatments of Lying and Killing." *Journal of Religious Ethics* 38, no. 4 (2010): 661-97.

Desire of the Everlasting Hills. https://everlastinghills.org/movie/.

Dewan, Lawrence. "St. Thomas, Lying and Venial Sin." *Thomist: A Speculative Quarterly Review* 61, no. 2 (April 1, 1997): 279-99.

————. "Thomas Aquinas, Gerard Bradley, and the Death Penalty: Some Observations." *Gregorianum* 82, no. 1 (2001): 149-65.

Dio Chrysostom. *Orationes.* Edited by J. de Arnim. Berlin: Weidmann, 1893. http://www.perseus.tufts.edu/hopper/text?doc=Perseus%3Atext%3A2008.01.0567%3Aspeech%3D1%3Asection%3D1.

Dolnik, Adam, and Keith M. Fitzgerald. *Negotiating Hostage Crises with the New Terrorists.* Westport, CT: Praeger Security International, 2008.

Dorszynski, Julius A. *Catholic Teaching About the Morality of Falsehood.* PhD diss., The Catholic University of America, 1948. Washington, D.C.: Catholic University of America Press, 1948.

Doyle, John P. *Collected Studies on Francisco Suarez, S.J.* Leuven University Press, 2011.

Driver, Julia. *Consequentialism.* New York: Routledge, 2012.

Druart, Thérèse-Anne. "Al-Fârâbî: An Arabic Account of the Origin of Language and of Philosophical Vocabulary." *Proceedings of the ACPA* 84 (2011): 1-17.

Dubois, Abbé F. "Une Théorie Du Mensonge Replique (1)." Edited by M.L' Abbé Duflot. *La Science Catholique* 12 (december 1897 - december 1898): 165-73.

Eckhart, Meister. *Liber parabolarum Genesis, Capitulum Undevicesimum.* In *Die Deutschen und lateinischen Werke,* vol. 1. Stuttgart-Berlin: Verlag von W. Kohlhammer, Juli 1938.

The Editors of Encyclopædia Britannica. "Bion of Borysthenes." *Encyclopaedia Britannica.* Accessed August 21, 2015. http://www.britannica.com/biography/Bion-of-Borysthenes.

Eltringham, S.K. *The Hippos*. London: T & AD Poyser, 2002.

Enger, Eldon D., Frederick C. Ross, and David B. Bailey. *Concepts in Biology*. 12th ed. New York, NY: McGraw-Hill, 2007.

The Etablissements de Saint Louis: Thirteententh-Century Law Texts from Tours, Orléans, and Paris. Translated by F.R.P. Akehurst. University of Pennsylvania Press, 1996.

Fallis, Don. "Davidson Was Almost Right about Lying." *Australasian Journal of Philosophy* 91, no. 2 (2013): 337-53.

———. "Lying and Deception." *Philosophers' Imprint* 10, no. 11 (November 1, 2010): 1-21.

———. "What Is Lying?" *Journal of Philosophy* 106, no. 1 (January 1, 2009): 29-56.

Fergusson, D.M., J. Horwood, and A. Beautrais. "Is Sexual Orientation Related to Mental Health Problems and Suicidality in Young People?" *Archives of General Psychiatry* 56, no. 10 (1999): 876-880.

Feser, Edward. *Aquinas: A Beginner's Guide*. Oxford: Oneworld, 2009.

———. "In Defense of the Perverted Faculty Argument." In *Neo-Scholastic Essays*. South Bend, IN. St. Augustine's Press, 2015.

———. *Neo-Scholastic Essays*. South Bend, IN: St. Augustine's Press, 2015.

———. "Smith, Tollefsen, and Pruss on Lying." *Edwardfeser.blogspot.com* (blog), January 5, 2012. Accessed December 27, 2017. http://edwardfeser.blogspot.com/2012/01/ smith-tollefsen-and-pruss-on-lying.html.

—————. *The Last Superstition: A Refutation of the New Atheism.* South Bend, IN: St. Augustine's Press, 2008.

—————. "What Counts as a Lie?" *Edwardfeser.blogspot.com*, November 15, 2010. Accessed January 29, 2015. http://edwardfeser.blogspot.com/2010/11/what-counts-as-lie.html.

Fichte, Johann Gottlieb. *Grundlage des Naturrechts nach Principien der Wissenschaftslehre, 1796.* In *sämmtliche Werke,* vol. III. Berlin: Verlag von Veit und Comp., 1845.

—————. *The Science of Ethics as Based on the Science of Knowledge.* Translated by A.E. Kroeger. Edited by W.T. Harris. London: Kegan Paul, Trench, Trübner & Co., Ltd., 1897.

—————. *The Science of Rights.* Translated by A.E. Kroeger. Philadelphia: J.B. Lippincott & Co., 1869.

—————. *System der Sittenlehre nach den Principien der Wissenschaftslehre, 1798,* in *sämmtliche Werke,* vol. IV. Berlin: Verlag von Veit und Comp., 1845.

Finnis, John. *Aquinas: Moral, Political, and Legal Theory.* New York: Oxford University Press, 1998.

—————. "Law, Morality, and 'Sexual Orientation.'" *Notre Dame Law Review* 69, no. 5 (1994): 1049-076.

—————. "Law, Morality, and 'Sexual Orientation.'" In *Same Sex: Debating the Ethics, Science, and Culture of Homosexuality,* edited by John Corvino, 31-43. Lanham-New York-London: Rowman and Littlefield, 1997.

Foot, Philippa. *Natural Goodness.* Oxford: Oxford University Press, 2001.

Foucault, Michel. "Friendship as a Way of Life." In *Ethics: Subjectivity and Truth.* Edited by Paul Rabinow. New York: The New Press, 1997.

———. *The History of Sexuality.* Vol. I. Translated by Robert Hurley. New York: Vintage Books, 1978.

Francisco de Vitoria. *Primera Relección De Los Indios, De los títulos ilegítimos de conquista,* in *Relecciones Teológicas,* vol. II. Edited by Luis G. Getino. Madrid: Imprenta La Rafa, 1934.

———. *Relectio de temperantia, Quarta Conclusio.* In *Obras de Francisco de Vitoria.* Madrid: Biblioteca de Autores Cristianos, 1960.

Franciscus de Victoria. *De Indis et de Iure Belli Relectiones Being Parts of Relectiones Theologicae XII.* Translated by John Pawley Bate, ed. Ernest Nys. Oceana Publications, http://www.constitution.org/victoria/victoria_4.htm. Accessed December 30, 2017.

Frankfurt, Harry G. *On Bullshit.* Princeton, NJ: Princeton University Press, 2005.

Gaeng, Paul A. *Introduction to the Principles of Language.* Lanham, MD: University of America Press, 1971.

Gallup. "Gay and Lesbian Rights." https://news.gallup.com/poll/1651/gay-lesbian-rights.aspx, accessed November 16, 2018.

Gammon, Katharine. "The Weirdest Animal Penises." LiveScience. March 09, 2011. Accessed February 22, 2016. http://www.livescience.com/33105-weird-strange-animal-penises.html.

Gascoigne, John. *Science in the Service of Empire: Joseph Banks, the British State and the Uses of Science in the Age of Revolution.* Cambridge, UK: Cambridge University Press, 1998.

Geach, Peter. "Good and Evil." *Analysis* 17, no. 2 (December 1956): 33-42.

————. *The Virtues: The Stanton Lectures 1973-4.* Cambridge: Cambridge University Press, 1977.

Gellner, Sarah. "[Letter to the Editor] Memories of Ernest Gellner." *London Review of Books*, August 25, 2011, Vol. 33, No. 16. Accessed February 2, 2016. http://www.lrb.co.uk/v33/n16/letters.

Gendron, Angela. "Just War, Just Intelligence: An Ethical Framework for Foreign Espionage." *International Journal of Intelligence and CounterIntelligence* 18, no. 3 (2005): 398-434.

Gennuso, Mary. "What's in a Lie? Rousseau's 'Reveries' and Ribbon Incident." *International Studies In Philosophy* 38, no. 1 (January 1, 2006): 46-62.

George, Robert P. *In Defense of Natural Law.* Oxford: Clarendon Press, 1999.

George, Robert P., and Gerard V. Bradley. "Marriage and the Liberal Imagination." *The Georgetown Law Journal* 84: 301-20.

Gilson, Etienne. *Linguistics and Philosophy: An Essay on the Philosophical Constants of Language.* Notre Dame, IN: University of Notre Dame Press, 1988.

Green, Kelley E. and Brian A. Feinstein, "Substance Use in Lesbian,

Gay, and Bisexual Populations: An Update on Empirical Research and Implications for Treatment." *Psychology of Addictive Behaviors* 26, no. 2 (2012): 265-278.

Greenwood, Gregory L., M. Relf, B. Huang, L. Pollack. J. Canchola, and J. Catania. "Battering Victimization among a Probability-based Sample of Men Who Have Sex with Men." *American Journal of Public Health* 92, no. 12 (December 2002): 1964-1969.

Grice, Paul. *Studies in the Way of Words.* Cambridge, MA: Harvard University Press, 1989.

Grisez, Germain G. *Contraception and the Natural Law.* Milwaukee: Bruce Publishing Company, 1964.

Grotius, Hugo. *On the Law of War and Peace.* Translated by A.C. Campbell. London, 1814. Accessed November 7, 2014. http://www.constitution.org/gro/djbp.htm.

Guevin, Benedict. "When a Lie Is Not a Lie: The Importance of Ethical Context." *Thomist: A Speculative Quarterly Review* 66, no. 2 (April 1, 2002): 267-74.

Herrell, R., J. Goldberg, W. True, V. Ramakrishnan, M. Lyons, S. Eisen, and M. Tsuang. "Sexual Orientation and Suicidality." *Archives of General Psychiatry* 56, no. 10 (1999): 867-874.

Hilsman, Roger. "Does the CIA Still Have a Role?" *Foreign Affairs*, September/October 1995, 104-16.

Hobbes, Thomas. *The Elements of Law, Human Nature and De Corpore Politico.* Edited by Gaskin. Oxford/New York: Oxford University Press, 2008.

———. *Leviathan.* Edited by Noel Malcolm, vol. 2, The English and Latin Texts. Oxford: Clarendon Press, 2012.

————. *Leviathan*. Green Dragon, St. Paul's Churchyard, 1651. Accessed June 4, 2015. http://www.gutenberg.org/files/3207/ 3207-h/3207-h.htm#link2H_4_0019.

Horkheimer, Max, and Theodor W. Adorno. *Dialectic of Enlightenment: Philosophical Fragments.* Translated by Edmund Jephcott. Edited by Gunzelin Schmid Noerr. Stanford, CA: Stanford University Press, 2002.

————. *Dialektik der Aufklärung: Philosophische Fragmente.* Surkamp: 1981.

Hsiao, Timothy. "A Defense of the Perverted Faculty Argument against Homosexual Sex." *The Heythrop Journal* 56, no. 5 (September 2015): 751-58.

Hubbard, Thomas K., ed. *Homosexuality in Greece and Rome: A Sourcebook of Basic Documents.* Berkeley, Los Angeles, London: University of California Press, 2003.

Hughes, John R. "A General Review of Recent Reports on Homosexuality and Lesbianism." *Sexuality and Disability* 24, no. 4 (December 2006): 195-205.

Hume, David. *An Enquiry Concerning the Principles of Morals, A Critical Edition.* Edited by Tom L. Beauchamp. Oxford: Clarendon Press/Oxford University Press, 2010.

James, William. *The Principles of Psychology.* Vol. II. New York: Henry Holt and Company, 1913.

Jardine, Lisa, and Alan Stewart. *Hostage to Fortune: The Troubled Life of Francis Bacon.* New York: Hill and Wang, 1999.

Jensen, Steven J. *Good & Evil Actions*. Washington, D.C.: CUA Press, 2010.

————. "Intrinsically Evil Actions According to St. Thomas Aquinas." PhD diss., Notre Dame, April, 1993.

————. *Knowing the Natural Law: From Precepts and Inclinations to Deriving Oughts*. Washington, D.C,: Catholic University of America Press, 2015.

————. "The Trouble with Secunda Secundae 64, 7: Self-Defense." *Modern Schoolman: A Quarterly Journal of Philosophy* 83, no. 2 (2006): 143-162.

Joannis a S. Thoma. *Cursus Theologicus in Summam Theologicam D. Thomae, Tomus Septimus*. Edited by Ludovicus Vives. Parisiis, 1886.

Jordan, Mark D. *The Invention of Sodomy in Christian Theology*. Chicago: University of Chicago Press, 1997.

Kaczor, Christopher. "Can It Be Morally Permissible to Assert a Falsehood in Service of a Good Cause?" *American Catholic Philosophical Quarterly* 86, no. 1 (2012): 97-109.

Kant, Immanuel *Die Metaphysik der Sitten*. In *Kant's Werke,* Band VI. Berlin: Königlich Preukishen Akademie der Wissenschaften, Druck und Verlag von Georg Reimer, 1907.

————. *Lectures on Ethics*. Edited by Peter Heath and J.B. Schneewind. Translated by Peter Heath. Cambridge: Cambridge University Press, 1997.

————. *The Metaphysics of Morals*. Translated by Mary Gregor. Cambridge, New York, Melbourne: Cambridge University Press, 1996.

Kelly, June, prod. *The Role of the Covert Agent*. BBC Radio. December 29, 2013. Accessed January 02, 2017. http://www.bbc.co.uk/programmes/p01p31cw.

Kemp, Kenneth W., and Thomas Sullivan. "Speaking Falsely and Telling Lies." *Proceedings of the American Catholic Philosophical Association* 67 (February 1, 1993): 151-70.

Kers, Susanne. *Empirical Analysis I: L(G)BT Communities Handling Domestic Violence in Women-to-women Relationships*. Report. June 2010. Accessed March 17, 2016. http://www.lars-europe.eu/en/material/1rst_national_report_nl.pdf.

Kreeft, Peter. "Why Live Action Did Right and Why We All Should Know That." Catholic Education Resource Center. Accessed December 6, 2018. https://www.catholiceducation.org/en/religion-and-philosophy/apologetics/why-live-action-did-right-and-why-we-all-should-know-that.html.

Lackey, Jennifer. "Lies and Deception: An Unhappy Divorce." *Analysis* 73, no. 2 (2013): 236-248.

Lee, Patrick. *Abortion & Unborn Human Life*. 2nd ed. Washington, D.C.: Catholic University of America Press, 2010.

Leibniz. *Consilium Aegyptiacum*. In *Leibnitii De Expeditione Aegyptiaca Ludovico XIV Franciae Regi Proponenda Scripta Quae Supersunt Omnia Adjecta Praefatione Historico-Critica*. Edited by Onno Klopp. Hanoverae, 1864.

Leiser, Burton M. "Homosexuality and the 'Unnaturalness Argument.'" Leiser. Accessed February 1, 2019. http://faculty.cbu.ca/sstewart/sexlove/leiser.htm.

————. "Homosexuality, Morals, and the Laws of Nature." Accessed February 1, 2019. https://faculty.mc3.edu/barmstro/leiser.html.

Lenferna, Georges A. "Natural Law Ethics, Homosexuality and Morality." 2010. MS, Presented at the Postgraduate Philosophical Association Conference. Accessed September 18, 2014. https://washington.academia.edu/AlexLenferna/Papers.

Lents, Nathan H. "Why Humans Must Eat Vitamin C." *The Human Evolution Blog* (blog), September 13, 2014. Accessed November 21, 2016. https://thehumanevolutionblog.com/2014/09/13/why-humans-must-eat-vitamin-c/.

"Leopard." National Geographic. Accessed September 26, 2017. http://www.nationalgeographic.com/animals/mammals/l/leopard/.

Levin, Michael. "Why Homosexuality Is Abnormal." *Monist* 67, no. 2 (April 1984): 251-83.

Liddell, Henry George, and Robert Scott, comps. *A Greek-English Lexicon*.

Locke, John. *An Essay Concerning Human Understanding*. 2nd ed. Vol. III. 1690. Accessed March 30, 2015. http://www.gutenberg.org/cache/epub/10616/pg10616.html.

————. *Two Treatises of Government: In the Former, The False Principles and Foundation of Sir Robert Filmer, and His Followers are Detected and Overthrown. The Latter is an Essay concerning the True Original, Extent, and End of Civil-Government*. In *Two Treatises of Government*. Edited by Peter Laslett. New York: Cambridge University Press, 2013.

Long, Ronald E. "Of Argument and Aesthetic Distaste, A Response to J. Budziszewski." *Philosophia Christi* 7, no. 1 (2005): 53-58.

Long, Steven A. "A Brief Disquisition Regarding the Nature of the Object of the Moral Act according to St. Thomas Aquinas." *The Thomist* 67 (2003): 45-71.

MacIntyre, Alasdair. "Truthfulness, Lies, and Moral Philosophers." In *The Tanner Lectures on Human Values*. Edited by Grethe B. Peterson. Vol. 16. Salt Lake City: University of Utah Press, 1995.

Mahon, James Edwin. "The Definition of Lying and Deception." *Stanford Encyclopedia of Philosophy.* June 30, 2015. Accessed July 11, 2015. http://plato.stanford.edu/entries/lying-definition/.

————. "Two Definitions of Lying." *International Journal of Applied Philosophy* 22, no. 2 (2008): 211-30.

Maimonides, Moses. *Mishneh Torah, Sefer Kedushah, Issurei Biah.* Translated by Eliyahu Touger. Moznaim Publications. http://www.chabad.org/library/article_cdo/aid/960647/jewish/Issurei-Biah-Chapter-One.htm. Accessed December 30, 2017.

Mainwaring, Doug. "Hearts, Parts, and Minds: The Truth Comes Out." *Public Discourse.* March 09, 2015. Accessed January 5, 2018. http://www.thepublicdiscourse.com/2015/03/14510/.

Marieb, Elaine N., and Katja Hoehn. *Human Anatomy & Physiology.* 8th ed. San Francisco: Benjamin Cummings, 2010.

Marmodoro, Anna, and Ben Page. "Aquinas on Forms, Substances and Artifacts." *Vivarium* 54, no. 1 (2016): 1-21.

Martin, C.F.J. "Are There Virtues and Vices That Belong Specifically to the Sexual Life?" *Acta Philosophica* IV, no. 2 (1995): 205-21.

————. *Thomas Aquinas: God and Explanations.* Edinburgh: Edinburgh University Press, 1997.

Martin, Clancy W. *The Philosophy of Deception*. Oxford: Oxford University Press, 2009.

McCloskey, H. J. "An Examination of Restricted Utilitarianism." *The Philosophical Review* 66, no. 4 (October 1957): 466-85.

McMains, Michael J., and Wayman C. Mullins. *Crisis Negotiations: Managing Critical Incidents and Hostage Situations in Law Enforcement and Corrections*. 5th ed. New York: Routledge, 2015.

McNeill, John J., S.J. *The Church and the Homosexual*. New York: Pocket Books, 1976.

Meyers, Chris. *The Moral Defense of Homosexuality: Why Every Argument Against Gay Rights Fails*. Lanham, Boulder, New York, London: Rowman & Littlefield, 2015.

Miller, Laurence. *Practical Police Psychology: Stress Management and Crisis Intervention for Law Enforcement*. Springfield, IL: Charles C. Thomas, 2006.

Montesquieu. *De l'Esprit des lois,* vol. I. Rue des Saints-Pères, Paris: Éditions Garnier Frères 6, 1961.

————. *The Spirit of the Laws*. Translated and edited by Anne M. Cohler, Basia Carolyn Miller, and Harold Samuel Stone. Cambridge: Cambridge University Press, 1989.

Moore, Gareth. *A Question of Truth: Christianity and Homosexuality*. London: Continuum, 2003.

Musonius Rufus. *C. Musonii Rufi Reliquiae*. Edited by O. Hense. Lipsiae: In Aedibus B.G. Teubneri, 1905.

————. *Musonius Rufus: The Roman Socrates. Lectures and Fragments.* Translated by Cora E. Lutz. Yale University Press, 1947. https://sites.google.com/site/thestoiclife/ the_teachers/musonius-rufus.

Müller, Gregor, OSB. *Die Wahrhaftigkeitspflicht Und Die Problematik Der Lüge.* Freiburg, Basel, Wien: Herder, 1962.

Nagel, Thomas. "Sexual Perversion." In *The Philosophy of Sex: Contemporary Readings*, by Nicholas Power, Alan Soble, and Raja Halwani, 31-44. Lanham: Rowman & Littlefield, 2012.

National Geographic. "World's Weirdest: Deadly Praying Mantis Love." World's Weirdest: Deadly Praying Mantis Love. Accessed September 16, 2016. http://video.nationalgeographic.com/video/ weirdest-praying-mantis.

Nicholas of Cusa. *Sermo V.* In *Cusanus Portal.* http://www.cusanus-portal.de/content/werke.php?id=Sermo_V_29. Accessed December 30, 2017.

Norton, Rictor, ed. "Burke Proposes Abolition of the Pillory, 1780." *Homosexuality in Eighteenth-Century England: A Sourcebook*, 23 February 2007, updated 25 November 2014. Accessed January 6, 2018. http://rictornorton.co.uk/eighteen/1780burk.htm.

Nozick, Robert. *Anarchy, State, and Utopia.* Basic Books, 1974.

Oliva, Adriano. *Amours: L'Église, Les Divorcés Remariés, Les Couples Homosexuels.* Paris: Les Éditions Du Cerf, 2015.

Olsen, Glenn W. "St. Anselm and Homosexuality." *Anselm Studies, Proceedings of the Fifth International Saint Anselm Conference: St. Anselm and St. Augustine-Episcopi Ad Saecula* II (1988): 93-141.

Olson, Eric R. "Why Are 250 Million Sperm Cells Released During Sex?" LiveScience. January 24, 2013. Accessed March 02, 2016. http://www.livescience.com/32437-why-are-250-million-sperm-cells-released-during-sex.html.

Padilla, Heberto. *Self-Portrait of the Other: A Memoir.* Translated by Alexander Coleman. New York: Farrar, Straus, and Giroux, Inc., 1990.

Perry, Michael J. "The Morality of Homosexual Conduct: A Response to John Finnis." *Notre Dame Journal of Law, Ethics & Public Policy* 9, no. 1 (1995): 41-74.

Petri, Thomas, O.P., and Michael Wahl. "Live Action and Planned Parenthood: A New Test Case for Lying." *Nova Et Vetera*, English Edition, 10, no. 2 (2012): 437-62.

Pilsner, Joseph. *The Specification of Human Actions in St Thomas Aquinas.* Oxford: Oxford University Press, 2006.

Plato. *Laws.* In *Platonis Opera.* Edited by John Burnet. Oxford University Press, 1903. http://www.perseus.tufts.edu/hopper/text?doc=Perseus%3Atext%3A1999.01.0165%3Abook%3D1%3Asection%3D624a.

—————. *Laws*, vol. I. Translated by R.G. Bury, Litt. D. London: William Heinemann; New York: G.P. Putnam's Sons, 1961.

—————. *The Laws of Plato.* Translated by Thomas L. Pangle. New York: Basic Books, Inc., Publishers, 1980.

—————. *Phaedrus.* In *Platonis Opera.* Edited by John Burnet. Oxford University Press, 1903. http://www.perseus.tufts.edu/hopper/text?doc=Perseus%3Atext%3A1999.01.0173%3Atext%3DPhaedrus.

————. *Phaedrus.* Translated by Robin Waterfield. New York: Oxford University Press Inc., 2002.

"Platypus Videos, News and Facts." BBC Nature. Accessed September 26, 2017. http://www.bbc.co.uk/nature/life/Platypus.

Poiani, Aldo. *Animal Homosexuality: A Biosocial Perspective.* New York: Cambridge University Press, 2010.

Porphyry. *Porphyry On the Life of Plotinus and the Order of His Books.* Translated by A.H. Armstrong. Cambridge, MA: Harvard University Press; London: William Heinemann Ltd., 1966.

Porter, Jean. "'Direct' and 'Indirect' in Grisez's Moral Theory." *Theological Studies* 57, no. 4 (1996): 611-32.

Poteat, Tonia. "Top Ten Things Lesbians Should Discuss with their Health Care Providers." *Gay and Lesbian Medical Association,* May 2012. Accessed January 5, 2018. http://www.glma.org/ index.cfm?fuseaction=Page.viewPage&pageID=691.

Pruss, Alexander R. "Lies and Dishonest Endorsements." *Proceedings of the American Catholic Philosophical Association* 84 (January 1, 2010): 213-22.

————. "Lying and Speaking Your Interlocutor's Language." *Thomist: A Speculative Quarterly Review* 63 (July 1, 1999): 439-53.

————. *One Body: An Essay in Christian Sexual Ethics.* Notre Dame: University of Notre Dame Press, 2013.

"Red Panda." National Geographic. Accessed September 26, 2017. http://www.nationalgeographic.com/animals/mammals/r/red-panda/.

Regnerus, Mark. "Scientists Have Unwittingly Revealed that the

Obergefell Decision Did Nothing to Diminish Sexual Minority Distress." *Public Discourse.* June 9, 2018, https://www.thepublicdiscourse.com/2018/06/21866/.

Reichberg, Gregory M. "Aquinas on Defensive Killing: A Case of Double Effect?" *Thomist: A Speculative Quarterly Review* 69, no. 3 (2005): 341-370.

Reuter, Tyson R., Michael E. Newcomb, and Sarah W. Whitton. "Intimate Partner Violence Victimization in LBGT Young Adults: Demographic Differences and Associations With Health Behaviors." *Psychology of Violence,* 7, no. 1 (2017): 101-109.

Robinson, Hilary, ed. *Feminist-Art-Theory: An Anthology 1968-2014.* 2nd ed. West Sussex, UK: Wiley Blackwell, 2015.

Rockcastle, S. Austen. "St. Thomas Aquinas On The Nature And Morality Of Lying." PhD diss., University of St. Thomas - Houston, 1993.

Rogers, Ben. *A.J. Ayer: A Life.* New York: Grove Press, 1999.

Rorty, Richard. *An Ethics for Today: Finding Common Ground between Philosophy and Religion.* New York and Chichester, West Sussex: Columbia University Press, 2011.

————. "Religion in the Public Square: A Reconsideration." *Journal of Religious Ethics* 31 no. 1 (Spring 2003): 141-149.

Russell, Bertrand. Letter 255, To Ottoline Morrell, 8 March 1915. In *The Selected Letters of Bertrand Russell, The Public Years, 1914-1970.* Edited by Nicholas Griffin. London and New York: Routledge, 2002.

Ryan, John A. *The Norm of Morality: Defined and Applied to Particular Actions.* Washington, D.C.: National Catholic Welfare Conference, 1944.

Sandfort, T.G. "Same-Sex Behavior and Psychiatric Disorders, Findings from the Netherlands Mental Health Survey and Incidence Study." *Archives of General Psychiatry* 58, 1(2001): 85-91.

Sandfort, T.G., F. Bakker, F. Schellevis, and I. Vanwesenbeeck. "Sexual Orientation and Mental and Physical Health Status: Findings from a Dutch Population Survey." *American Public Health Association* 96, no. 6 (June 2006): 1119-1125.

Sandfort, T.G., R. de Graaf, and R.V. Bijl. "Same-Sex Sexuality and Quality of Life: Findings from the Netherlands Mental Health Survey and Incidence Study." *Archives of Sexual Behavior* 32, no. 1 (2003): 15-22.

Santayana, George. "Americanism." In *The Idler and His Works and Other Essays.* Edited by Daniel Cory. New York: George Braziller, Inc., 1957.

————. *Reason in Art.* In *The Life of Reason.* Vol. IV. New York: Dover Publications, 1982. Accessed January 5, 2018. https://www.gutenberg.org/files/15000/15000-h/vol4.html.

Sartre, Jean-Paul. *Being and Nothingness: An Essay on Phenomological Ontology.* Translated by Hazel E. Barnes. New York: Philosophical Library, 1956.

Schleiermacher, Friedrich Daniel Ernst. *Ethik (1812/13).* Edited by Hans-Joachim Birkner. Hamburg: Felix Meiner Verlag, 1981.

Schleiermacher, Friedrich. *Schleiermacher: Lectures on Philosophical Ethics.* Translated by Louise Adey Huish. Edited by Robert B. Louden. Cambridge, U.K.: Cambridge University Press, 2002.

Schopenhauer, Arthur. *Die Welt als Wille und Vorstellung, Dritte, verbesserte und beträchtlich vermehrte Auflage, Zweiter Band.* Leipzig: Brodhaus, 1859.

———. *The World as Will and Representation.* 3rd ed. Vol. II. Indian Hills, CO: Falcon's Wing Press, 1958.

Seneca. *Naturales Quaestiones.* In *Seneca in Ten Volumes,* vol. VII, *Naturales Quaestiones,* vol. I. Cambridge: Harvard University Press; London: William Heinemann Ltd, 1971.

Singer, Peter. "Heavy Petting." *Utilitarian.net (originally Published in Nerve Magazine),* 2001. Accessed November 22, 2014. http://www.utilitarian.net/singer/by/2001----.htm.

———. "Homosexuality Is Not Immoral." Project Syndicate. 2006. Accessed December 6, 2018. http://www.utilitarian.net/singer/by/200610--.htm.

Skalko, John. "Catholics and Hugo Grotius' Definition of Lying: A Critique." *Proceedings of the American Catholic Philosophical Association* 89 (2015): 159-179.

———. "Homosexuality and Bad Arguments." *Public Discourse.* August 5, 2016, http://www.thepublicdiscourse.com/2016/08/16808/.

———. "Why Did Aquinas Hold Killing is Sometimes Just, But Never Lying?" *Proceedings of the American Catholic Philosophical Association* 90 (2016): 227-241.

———. "Why the Revised Grotian Definition of Lying Still Fails: A Reply to Vincelette," *Bogoslovni vestnik* 78, no. 1 (2018): 67-77.

Skegg, K., S. Nada-Raja, N. Dickson, C. Paul, and S. Williams. "Sexual Orientation and Self-harm in Men and Women." *American Journal of Psychiatry* 160, no. 3 (2003): 541-546.

"Slavery." Augnet. Accessed December 27, 2017. http://www.augnet.org/en/works-of-augustine/his-impact/2437-slavery/.

Smith, Janet E. "Fig Leaves and Falsehoods, Pace Thomas Aquinas, Sometimes We Need to Deceive." *First Things*, June 2011. Accessed October 7, 2014. http://www.firstthings.com/article/2011/06/fig-leaves-and-falsehoods.

————. "Thomas Aquinas On Homosexuality." In *Homosexuality and American Public Life*, by Christopher Wolfe, 129-40. Dallas: Spence Publishing Company, 1999.

————. "Why Tollefsen and Pruss Are Wrong about Lying." *First Things*, December 15, 2011. Accessed October 7, 2014. http://www.firstthings.com/web-exclusives/2011/12/why-tollefsen-and-pruss-are-wrong-about-lying.

Sommer, Volker, and Paul L. Vasey. *Homosexual Behaviour in Animals: An Evolutionary Perspective*. Cambridge: Cambridge University Press, 2010.

Sorensen, Roy. "Bald-Faced Lies! Lying Without The Intent To Deceive." *Pacific Philosophical Quarterly* 88, no. 2 (2007): 251-64.

Spampanato, Vincenzo, ed. *Vita di Giordano Bruno: con documenti editi e inediti,* vol. 2, *Documenti veneti, XII.* Messina: G. Principato, 1921.

"Sperm: How Long Sperm Live, Sperm Count, and More." WebMD. Accessed March 02, 2016. http://www.webmd.com/infertility-and-reproduction/guide/sperm-and-semen-faq.

Stenson, Nancy. *Basic Irish: A Grammar and Workbook.* New York: Routledge, 2008.

Stockwell, John. "The Case against the C.I.A." *Issue: A Journal of Opinion* 9, no. 1/2 (Spring 1979): 21-23.

Stokke, Andreas. "Lying and Asserting." *Journal of Philosophy* 110, no. 1 (2013): 33-60.

Strentz, Thomas. *Psychological Aspects of Crisis Negotiation.* 2nd ed. Boca Raton, FL: Taylor & Francis Group, 2012.

Stults, Christopher B., Shabnam Javdani, Chloe A. Greenbaum, Staci C. Barton, Farzana Kapadia, and Perry N. Halkitis. "Intimate Partner Violence Perpetration and Victimization Among YMSM: The P18 Cohort Study." *Psychology of Sexual Orientation and Gender Diversity* 2, no. 2 (2015); 152-158.

Suarez, R.P. Francisci. *Tractatus de Gratia Dei, Lib. XI De Perpetuitate Gratiae, Vel Amissione, Caput III.* In *Opera Omnia,* vol. 9. Parisiis: Ludovicum Vivès, 1858.

Sullivan, Andrew. "Unnatural Law." *The New Republic*, March 24, 2003.

Szalay, Jessie. "Tarantula Facts." LiveScience. December 23, 2014. Accessed September 16, 2016. http://www.livescience.com/ 39963-tarantula.html.

The Third Way. April 27th, 2014; Los Angeles: Blackstone Films. *http://www.blackstonefilms.co/thethirdway/.*

Thompson, E. P. *Customs in Common: Studies in Traditional Popular Culture.* New York: New Press, 1993.

Tollefsen, Christopher. "Augustine, Aquinas, and the Absolute Norm Against Lying." *American Catholic Philosophical Quarterly* 86, no. 1 (2012): 111-34.

————. *Lying and Christian Ethics*. New York, NY: Cambridge University Press, 2014.

————. "Lying: The Integrity Approach." *The American Journal of Jurisprudence* 52, no. 1 (2007): 273-91.

————. "The New Natural Law Theory." *Lyceum* X, no. 1.

Tollefsen, Christopher, and Alexander Pruss. "The Case Against False Assertions." *First Things*, September 22, 2011. Accessed October 7, 2014. http://www.firstthings.com/web-exclusives/2011/09/the-case-against-false-assertions.

Torrell, Jean-Pierre, O.P. *Saint Thomas Aquinas*. Translated by Robert Royal. Vol. I. Washington, D.C.: Catholic University of America Press, 1996.

Truman, Harry S. "Limit CIA Role To Intelligence." *The Washington Post*, December 22, 1963. Accessed January 2, 2017. https://archive.org/stream/LimitCIARoleToIntelligenceByHarrySTruman/Limit%20CIA%20Role%20To%20Intelligence%20by%20Harry%20S%20Truman_djvu.txt.

Tully, Patrick A. "Arbitrariness, Irrationality, and the Sterility Objection: A Reply to Anderson." *Ethical Theory and Moral Practice* 18, no. 1 (2015): 135-44.

Turell, Susan C. "A Descriptive Analysis of Same-Sex Relationship Violence for a Diverse Sample." *Journal of Family Violence* 13, no. 3 (2000): 281-293.

United Kingdom. MI5 - The Security Service. *Gathering Intelligence*. Accessed January 2, 2017. https://www.mi5.gov.uk/gathering-intelligence.

Voltaire. *Dictionnaire philosophique*, s.v. "Amour Nommé Socratique." Garnier Press, 1967.

———. *Philosophical Dictionary*. Translated Peter Gay, s.v. "*Amour Nommé Socratique/So-Called Socratic Love*." New York: Harcourt, Brace & World, Inc., 1962.

———. *Prix de la Justice et de L'humanité. A Géneve*: 1778.

Walton, Douglas. *Appeal to Expert Opinion: Arguments from Authority*. University Park, PA: The Pennsylvania State University Press, 1997.

Warner, Gregory. "What A Chatty Monkey May Tell Us About Learning To Talk." NPR, September 13, 2013, Vocal Grooming, accessed December 29, 2017. http://www.npr.org/2013/09/13/216440443/what-a-chatty-monkey-may-tell-us-about-learning-to-talk.

Webster, Bayard. "Mushroom Spores Suspected As Culprit in Allergic Reactions That Baffled." The New York Times. April 20, 1982. Accessed March 02, 2016. http://www.nytimes.com/1982/04/20/science/mushroom-spores-suspected-as-culprit-in-allergic-reactions-that-baffled.html.

Wedel, Matt. "Gastroliths." Gastroliths. May 2007. Accessed September 16, 2016. http://www.ucmp.berkeley.edu/taxa/verts/archosaurs/gastroliths.php.

Weithmam, Paul J. "Natural Law, Morality, and Sexual Complementarity." In *Sex, Preference, and Family: Essays on Law and Nature*.

Edited by David M. Estlund and Martha C. Nussbaum. New York: Oxford University Press, 1997.

Wolfenden, Elizabeth. "Nutrition Information on Extra Sugar Free Gum." LIVESTRONG.COM. October 03, 2017. Accessed December 11, 2017. https://www.livestrong.com/article/154394-ingredients-in-wrigleys-extra-gum/.

Wollaston, William. "The Religion of Nature Delineated." 8th ed. 1759. In *British Philosophy: 1600-1900, British Moralists*, edited by L.A. Selby-Bigge, M.A. Vol. 2.

World Health Organization. *Understanding and Addressing Violence against Women,* Publication no. WHO/RHR/12.36, 2012, accessed January 5, 2018, http://apps.who.int/iris/bitstream/10665/77432/1/WHO_RHR_12.36_eng.pdf.

Zagzebski, Linda. *Epistemic Authority: A Theory of Trust, Authority, and Autonomy in Belief.* New York: Oxford University Press, 2012.

Index